T3-BOH-848

DISCARDED

jQuery Recipes

B.M. Harwani

Apress®

jQuery Recipes

Copyright © 2010 by B.M. Harwani

All rights reserved. No part of this work may be reproduced or transmitted in any form or by any means, electronic or mechanical, including photocopying, recording, or by any information storage or retrieval system, without the prior written permission of the copyright owner and the publisher.

ISBN-13 (pbk): 978-1-4302-2709-0

ISBN-13 (electronic): 978-1-4302-2710-6

Printed and bound in the United States of America 9 8 7 6 5 4 3 2 1

Trademarked names may appear in this book. Rather than use a trademark symbol with every occurrence of a trademarked name, we use the names only in an editorial fashion and to the benefit of the trademark owner, with no intention of infringement of the trademark.

President and Publisher: Paul Manning
Lead Editor: Steve Anglin
Developmental Editor: Matthew Moodie
Technical Reviewer: Massimo Nardone
Editorial Board: Clay Andres, Steve Anglin, Mark Beckner, Ewan Buckingham, Gary Cornell, Jonathan Gennick, Jonathan Hassell, Michelle Lowman, Matthew Moodie, Duncan Parkes, Jeffrey Pepper, Frank Pohlmann, Douglas Pundick, Ben Renow-Clarke, Dominic Shakeshaft, Matt Wade, Tom Welsh
Coordinating Editor: Kelly Moritz
Copy Editor: Candace English
Production Support: Patrick Cunningham
Indexer:
Artist: April Milne
Cover Designer: Anna Ishchenko

Distributed to the book trade worldwide by Springer-Verlag New York, Inc., 233 Spring Street, 6th Floor, New York, NY 10013. Phone 1-800-SPRINGER, fax 201-348-4505, e-mail orders-ny@springer-sbm.com, or visit http://www.springeronline.com.

For information on translations, please e-mail info@apress.com, or visit http://www.apress.com.

Apress and friends of ED books may be purchased in bulk for academic, corporate, or promotional use. eBook versions and licenses are also available for most titles. For more information, reference our Special Bulk Sales–eBook Licensing web page at http://www.apress.com/info/bulksales.

The information in this book is distributed on an "as is" basis, without warranty. Although every precaution has been taken in the preparation of this work, neither the author(s) nor Apress shall have any liability to any person or entity with respect to any loss or damage caused or alleged to be caused directly or indirectly by the information contained in this work.

To my mother Mrs. Nita Harwani. My mother is next to God for me. Whatever I am today is just because of the Moral values taught by her

To Dennis Ritchie and Ken Thompson - the creators of UNIX. I appreciate Ken Thompson's work with B programming language and have been fond of programming in Ritchie's invention: 'C' programming language since I was doing Engineering. I am a great admirer of the security features of Unix and used to love making shell scripts on UNIX operating sytem during my study days. Their achievments are the inspiration for the millions of programmers around the world.

Contents at a Glance

Contents

About the Author

■**B.M. Harwani** is managing director of Computer Education Centre - Microchip Computer Education (MCE), based in Ajmer, India. He graduated with a BE in computer engineering from the University of Pune, and also has a 'C' Level (master's diploma in computer technology) from DOEACC, Government Of India.

Involved in the teaching field for over 15 years, he has developed the art of explaining even the most complicated topics in a manner that everybody can easily understand. He has written several successful books, including *Programming & Problem Solving through 'C'* (BPB, 2004), *Learn Tally in Just Three Weeks* (Pragya, 2005), *Data Structures and Algorithms through C* (CBC, 2006), *Master Unix Shell Programming* (CBC, 2006), *Business Systems* (CBC, 2006), *Practical Java Project* (Shroff, 2007), *Practical Web Services* (Shroff, 2007), *Java for Professionals* (Shroff, 2008), *C++ for Beginners* (Shroff, 2009), *Practical ASP.NET 3.5 Projects* (Shroff, 2009), *Java Server Faces - A Practical Approach for Beginners* (PHI Learning, 2009), *Practical JSF Project using NetBeans* (PHI Learning, 2009), *Foundation Joomla* (friendsof ED, 2009), and *Practical EJB Project* (Shroff, 2009). He also writes articles on a variety of computer subjects which can be seen on a number of websites. To find more visit http://bmharwani.com.

About the Technical Reviewer

■**Massimo Nardone** was born under the Vesuvius and holds a Master Science Degree in Computing Science from the University of Salerno, Italy. He currently works as a Senior IT Security and Infrastructure Architect and Finnish Invention Development Team Leader (FIDTL) for IBM Finland. He is an IT lead Architect with main security responsibilities regarding IT Infrastructure, Security Auditing and Assessment, PKI/WPKI, Secure tunneling, LDAP Security, and SmartCard Security.

With more then 15 years of work experience in Mobile, Security and WWW technology areas for both national and international projects, Nardone has been working as a Project Manager, Software Engineer, Research Engineer, Chief Security Architect and Software Specialist. He also worked as Visiting lecturer and supervisor for exercises at the Networking Laboratory of the Helsinki University of Technology (TKK) for the course of "Security of Communication Protocols". Nardone is very familiar with Security Communication Protocols testing tools and methodologies, and has been developing Internet and mobile applications in many programming languages, with many evolving.

Massimo Nardone works as Technical Reviewer in many different IT areas, including security, www-technology, and database. He researched, designed, and implemented security methodologies for Standard BS7799, PKI and WPKI, Security Java (JAAS, JSSE, JCE, etc), BEA Web logic Security, J2EE Security, LDAP Security, SSO, Apache Security, MS SQL Server Security, XML Security, and SmartCard Security. Nardone currently holds four International Patents (PKI, SIP, SAML and Proxy areas)

Acknowledgments

I owe a debt of gratitude to Steve Anglin, Asst Editorial Director for his initial acceptance of my book, and for giving me an opportunity to create this work. I am highly grateful to the whole team at Apress for their constant cooperation and contribution to the creation this book.

My gratitude goes out to Matthew Moodie who, as a Development Editor, offered a significant amount of feedback that helped to improve the chapters. He played a vital role in improving the structure and quality of the information.

I must thank Massimo Nardone, the technical reviewer, for his excellent detailed reviewing of the work and the many helpful comments and suggestions he made.

Special thanks to Candace English, the copy editor, for her first class structural and language editing. I appreciate her efforts in enhancing the contents of the book and giving it a polished look.

Big and ongoing thanks to Kelly Moritz, Coordinating Editor, for doing a great job, and for her sincere efforts with the whole team to get the book published on time.

A great big thank you to the editorial and production staff and the entire team at Apress who worked tirelessely to produce this book. Really, I enjoyed working with each of you.

I am also thankful to my family – my small world: Anu (my wife) and my two little darlings: Chirag and Naman for allowing me to work on the book, even during the time that I was supposed to spend with them.

I should not forget to thank my dear students, who have been good teachers for me. They allow me to understand the basic probelms they face in a subject, and enable me to directly address those problem topics. The endless interesting queries of my students helped me in writing this book with a practical and focused approach.

Introduction

What the book is about

jQuery a rich bundle of JavaScript libraries that helps users apply dynamic functionality to web pages with great ease. jQuery provides several powerful features, including the ability to access a part of a web page, modify the content on fly, add animation, apply AJAX, and more.

This book uses a problem-solution approach to understanding the wide features provided by this open source project. Beginning by using selectors to apply effects to paragraphs and lists, we learn how to set the layouts of a web page. After that, we cover techniques involved in event handling, followed by performing validations to different form elements. Applying visual effects, navigations, AJAX and many more facets of jQuery are also explained in the form of recipes. The coding used in all the recipes is completely explained with screen shots at each step. If you know a bit of HTML, CSS and jQuery, then this is the book for you, as it is covers most of the problems a person faces while working with jQuery.

Who the book is for

This book is suitable for web developers, professionals, trainers, students and professionals who are looking for quick solutions to the problems that are usually encountered while applying features to web pages.

What you will learn from this book

- Applying effects to Paragraphs and Lists
- Setting Layouts
- Event Handling
- Form Validation
- Page Navigations
- Visual Effects
- Dealing with Tables
- AJAX
- Using Plug ins

■ ■ ■

jQuery Basics

In this chapter, we will be dealing with the basics of jQuery, from installing it to working with DOM nodes. These fundamental recipes will help refresh your memory or fill in any gaps in your knowledge. We will be covering the following recipes in this chapter:

- Installing jQuery
- Selecting nodes in the DOM
- Delaying the execution of JavaScript
- Applying CSS to elements
- Selecting a non-standard series of HTML elements
- Counting the number of nodes in the DOM and displaying their text
- Obtaining the HTML of an element
- Changing the content of a DOM node
- Creating a DOM node on the fly
- Assigning the same class name to different HTML elements and applying styles to them

---

■ **Note** CSS will be covered in more depth in Chapter 10. We will be covering CSS techniques that can complement your jQuery code. Because CSS is a basic jQuery skill, we'll also include some basic CSS recipes.

1-1. Installing jQuery

Problem

You want to install jQuery so you can use it in your application and follow the recipes in this book.

Solution

jQuery comes as a single `.js` (JavaScript) file and it is very easy to download and install jQuery in any web application. Download the latest version of jQuery from its official site: `http://jquery.com/`. This book uses version `jquery-1.3.2`. Copy the downloaded file to the folder where you are going to write jQuery programs.

The statement to load the jQuery library is written in the **head** tag of the HTML file and the statement is as follows:

```
<script src="jquery-1[1].3.2.js" type="text/javascript"></script>
```

In almost all the recipes, we will be adding the following three lines in HTML files (in the **head** tag):

```
<link rel="stylesheet" href="style.css" type="text/css" />
<script src="jquery-1[1].3.2.js" type="text/javascript"></script>
<script src="d1.js" type="text/javascript"></script>
```

How It Works

The first line is used to link the external style sheet file `style.css` (or any name you wish to call it) to the HTML file. The second line is to load the jQuery library and the third line is to specify the JavaScript file name (`d1.js` here, but it can be any name) that contains the jQuery code from the recipes in this book.

1-2. Selecting Nodes in the DOM

Problem

You want to use jQuery to access elements in the Document Object Model (DOM) in order to manipulate them.

Solution

jQuery makes use of CSS and XPath selectors to access elements in the DOM. When a selector is applied to access elements in the DOM, the elements are retrieved in the form of jQuery objects. For using any selector, whether CSS or XPath, to access elements in the DOM, we make use of the `$()` function.

A typical JavaScript file to select a paragraph using jQuery code appears as follows:

```
//d1.js
$(document).ready(function() {
  $('p').addClass('highlight');
});
```

How It Works

The $() function is used for selecting a part of the document. It accepts any CSS selector expression and zero or more DOM nodes. It returns all the matched elements, which allows us to manipulate them to change their appearance.

Here are some examples:

- $('p')—Accesses all the paragraph elements in the HTML file

- $('div')—Accesses all the div elements in the HTML file

- $('#A')—Accesses all the HTML elements with id=A

- $('.b')—Accesses all the HTML elements with class=b

So, in our recipe we select all the paragraph elements and call the addClass() method on them. This will apply the CSS class highlight to all the paragraphs in the document.

1-3. Delaying the Execution of JavaScript

Problem

A JavaScript file referenced in the head section of the HTML file is executed as soon as the browser finds the script line, but there are no HTML elements to which the styles can be applied (because the JavaScript file is referenced in the head section, and HTML elements are present in the body section and won't be loaded yet). So, we need to delay the execution of the JavaScript code until the DOM is loaded.

Solution

The method used to inform us when the DOM is ready is $(document).ready(). This method executes the function call (written as its argument) when the DOM is loaded and ready:

```
$(document).ready(function() {
  $('p').addClass('highlight');
});
```

How It Works

We use the function keyword (without the function name) and define the body of the function to use when the DOM has loaded. The function body is used as an argument to the method for the simple reason that we want the function to be executed immediately, but once only. We don't want it to be reused again. In other words, $(document).ready() registers a ready event for the document.

The $('p') in the preceding solution is a selector that accesses the paragraph elements of the HTML file, and to those elements the addClass() method will apply the specified CSS class.

1-4. Applying CSS to Elements

Problem

You want to apply a CSS class to certain elements on your page.

Solution

The `addClass()` method is used for applying a CSS class to the selected part of the page. It contains the name of the class to be applied as a parameter. By defining style rules for CSS classes in a separate stylesheet, we can use this method very easily. The style rule written for different CSS classes in the stylesheet may be as follows:

```
.highlight {
  font-style: italic;
  background-color: #0f0;
}
```

Here's how to apply the CSS class:

```
$('div').addClass('highlight');
$('body').addClass('highlight');
```

How It Works

In the first line of jQuery code, `$('div')` selects all the `div` elements of the HTML file and applies the style rules in `highlight` class to them. In the second line, the `$('body')` selector accesses the `body` element of the HTML file and then the CSS class `highlight` is applied to it.

1-5. Selecting a Non-Standard Series of HTML Elements

Problem

You want to select unconventional HTML elements, such as HTML elements that may contain a given piece of text, elements in a particular place in a sequence, or odd- or even-numbered elements in the HTML file.

Solution

To select unconventional HTML elements, we need to use custom selectors. Custom selectors help us to select groups of HTML elements, such as HTML elements that contain a given piece of text or that are in a particular place in the document (for example, the third paragraph). Custom selectors also help in selecting odd- or even-numbered elements in an HTML file.

Here's how to select all the elements that contain the text Life:

```
$('span:contains(Life)').addClass('highlight');
```

In the following example, we will apply styles to even- and odd-numbered div elements and the paragraph of a given sequence number of the HTML file:

```
$('div:odd').addClass('highlight');
$('div:even').addClass('boundary');
$('p:eq(1)').addClass('linkstyle');
```

How It Works

Our first example selects span elements that contain the word Life and applies the CSS class highlight to them. Then in our next example :odd and :even are jQuery custom selectors that help in choosing the desired element. The numbering in JavaScript begins with 0, which is even, 1 which is odd, and so on. The example statement here selects the odd div elements (numbered 1,3,...) and applies the CSS class highlight to them:

```
$('div:odd').addClass('highlight');
```

Similarly, the following example statement selects the even elements (numbered 0,2,...) and applies the CSS class boundary to them:

```
$('div:even').addClass('boundary');
```

Finally, the example statement here uses the custom selector :eq to select the second paragraph (because the first paragraph is numbered 0) and applies the CSS class linkstyle to it:

```
$('p:eq(1)').addClass('linkstyle');
```

1-6. Counting the Number of Nodes in the DOM and Displaying Their Text

Problem

You want to access the DOM and its nodes via jQuery.

Solution

In the DOM, a web page is represented in the form of a tree structure with a root node (parent) and several branches (children) where each HTML element is represented in the form of a node. These nodes can be accessed and manipulated as desired with the help of jQuery.

Let's look at the following HTML page:

```
<!DOCTYPE html PUBLIC "-//W3C//DTD XHTML 1.0 Transitional//EN"
        "http://www.w3.org/TR/xhtml1/DTD/xhtml1-transitional.dtd">

<html xmlns="http://www.w3.org/1999/xhtml" xml:lang="en" lang="en">
  <head>
    <meta http-equiv="Content-Type" content="text/html; charset=utf-8"/>
    <title>JQuery Examples</title>
    <script src="jquery-1[1].3.2.js" type="text/javascript"></script>
    <script src="d1.js" type="text/javascript"></script>
  </head>
  <body>
    <div id="root">
      <div>Darjeeling</div>
      <div>Assam</div>
      <div>Kerala</div>
    </div>
  </body>
</html>
```

We can see that the preceding HTML file includes the <script> tags for loading the jQuery library as well as for including the JavaScript file that contains the jQuery code (d1.js). We also see that the HTML file contains a div element with id="root". All the elements inside this div element are its child elements; i.e., the div with id="root" is the parent of all the div elements described inside it. To count the DOM nodes and display their text, we write the following jQuery code:

```
$(document).ready(function() {
  var $nodes = $('#root').children();
  alert('Number of nodes is '+$nodes.length);
  var txt="";
  $('#root').children().each( function() {
    txt+=$(this).text();
  });
  alert(txt);
});
```

How It Works

All the child elements of the div of id="root" are accessed and assigned to a variable $nodes. We display the length of the collection of child nodes using the alert statement. Thereafter, with the help of the each() method, we access all the elements stored in $nodes one at a time. We use the text() method and access and concatenate the text of the elements in a string variable $txt. At the end, the text of all the children is displayed via another alert() method. Let us look at the methods used in the preceding jQuery code one by one.

children()

The children() method is a tree-traversal method that searches for the immediate children of the specified element and returns a new jQuery object. This method travels only a single level down in the DOM tree. In our example, this method accesses all the DOM nodes defined in the root div element and assigns them to the variable $nodes. $nodes is a jQuery object that contains the three div elements defined in the root div element. Using the $nodes object's length attribute, we first display the count of the number of DOM nodes in the HTML file.

each()

each() is a method that is used to iterate over each element in the wrapped collection. It contains an iterator function in which we write the code to be applied to each individual element of the collection.

text()

text() is a method of the jQuery object that accesses the text contents of the selected element(s). The text contents of the selected element(s) are combined and returned in the form of a string. To see the text contents of a paragraph element, we may write following jQuery code:

```
alert($('p').text());
```

Let's assume that the paragraph element appears as shown in the following example:

```
<p>Styles make the formatting job much easier and more efficient. To give an attractive look
to web sites, styles are heavily used.
<span>jQuery is a powerful JavaScript library that allows us to add dynamic elements to our
web sites. </span>Not only is it easy to learn, but it's easy to implement too.<br>
<a href="a1.htm"> jQuery Selectors</a> are used for selecting the area of the document where
we want to apply styles </p>
```

The preceding jQuery code will display the output as shown in Figure 1-1.

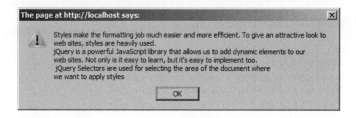

Figure 1-1. The text content of the paragaph element of an HTML file

We can see the text contents of the children of a paragraph element by using the following statement:

```
$(document).ready(function() {
  alert($('p').children().text());
});
```

parent()

The parent() method is a tree-traversal method that searches for the immediate parent of each of the selected elements and returns a new jQuery object. This method travels only a single level up in the DOM tree. To get the text content of the parent of the span element, we may use the following jQuery code:

```
alert($('span').parent().text());
```

1-7. Obtaining the HTML of an Element

Problem

You want to see the HTML code of the selected element(s).

Solution

First assume that the HTML file contains the paragraph element as shown in the following example:

```
<p>Styles make the formatting job much easier and more efficient. To give an attractive look
to web sites, styles are heavily used.
<span>jQuery is a powerful JavaScript library that allows us to add dynamic elements to our
web sites. </span>Not only is it easy to learn, but it's easy to implement too.<br>
<a href="a1.htm"> jQuery Selectors</a> are used for selecting the area of the document where
we want to apply styles </p>
```

The jQuery code to display the HTML code of the paragraph element appears as follows:

```
$(document).ready(function() {
  alert($('p').html());
});
```

How It Works

The contents of the paragraph element are accessed and with the help of the html() method, and its HTML code is displayed. The html() method gets the HTML content of the first element of the selected elements. It returns the HTML contents in the form of a string. The difference between html() and text() is that the text() method can be used in XML as well as in HTML documents, whereas html() can be used only in an HTML document. Another difference is that the html() method displays the tags along with the text.

The output we may get is as shown in Figure 1-2. We can see that the output includes the tags together with the text.

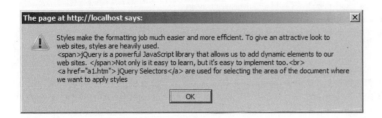

Figure 1-2. The HTML content of the paragaph element of an HTML file

To get the HTML content of the **span** element, we would use following statement:

```
alert($('span').html());
```

To get the HTML content of the parent of the **span** element, we would use the following jQuery code:

```
alert($('span').parent().html());
```

1-8. Changing the Content of a DOM Node

Problem

You want to change the contents of a DOM node dynamically. For example, you have an HTML file in which the **h2** element displays certain text and you want to change the text message using jQuery code.

Solution

Here is an HTML file with a paragraph element and an **h2** element. It also has two elements, a span and an anchor, nested inside the paragraph element. The HTML file appears as shown:

```
<body>
<p>Styles make the formatting job much easier and more efficient. To give an attractive look
to
web sites, styles are heavily used.
<span>jQuery is a powerful JavaScript library that allows us to add dynamic elements to our
web sites. </span>Not only is it easy to learn, but it's easy to implement too.<br/>
<a href="a1.htm"> jQuery Selectors</a> are used for selecting the area of the document where
we want to apply styles </p>
<h2>Using jQuery</h2>
</body>
```

On executing the HTML file without applying any jQuery code, we may get the original output as shown in Figure 1-3.

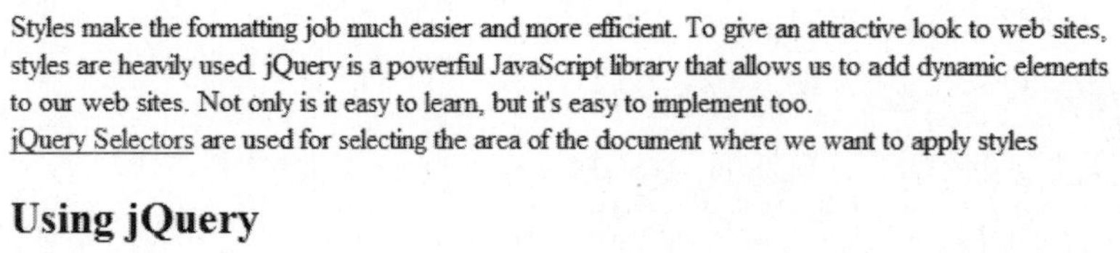

Styles make the formatting job much easier and more efficient. To give an attractive look to web sites, styles are heavily used. jQuery is a powerful JavaScript library that allows us to add dynamic elements to our web sites. Not only is it easy to learn, but it's easy to implement too.
jQuery Selectors are used for selecting the area of the document where we want to apply styles

Using jQuery

Figure 1-3. Original text contents of the h2 element

We can see that currently, the h2 element displays the text *Using jQuery*. This isn't what we want yet, so let's look at two ways of solving our problem and changing the contents using jQuery code.

text(text)

Now we will make use of the `text(text)` method to change the contents of the h2 element on the fly.

```
$(document).ready(function() {
  $('h2').text('JavaScript Libraries');
});
```

html(HTML)

Similar to `text(text)` method is the `.html(HTML)` method. This method sets the HTML contents of the selected element(s).

To set the HTML contents of the h2 element, we would use the following statement:

```
$('h2').html('JavaScript Libraries');
```

How It Works

The `text(text)` method sets the contents of the selected element to the specified text and returns it as a new jQuery object. The jQuery code that uses `text(text)` is for setting the text contents of all h2 elements present in the HTML file to *JavaScript Libraries*. Since there is only one h2 element in the HTML file, its text contents will be replaced and we get the output shown in Figure 1-4.

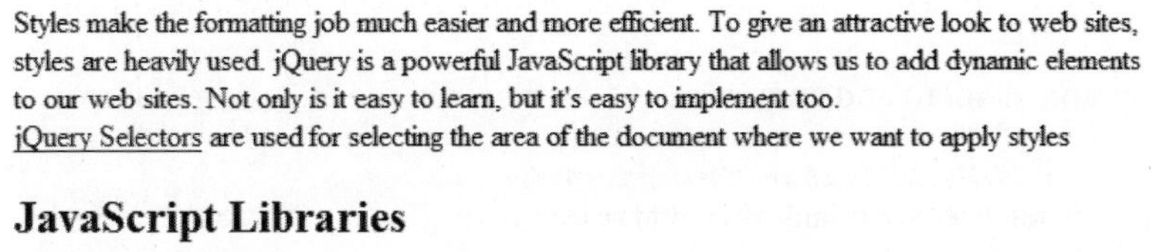

Styles make the formatting job much easier and more efficient. To give an attractive look to web sites, styles are heavily used. jQuery is a powerful JavaScript library that allows us to add dynamic elements to our web sites. Not only is it easy to learn, but it's easy to implement too.
jQuery Selectors are used for selecting the area of the document where we want to apply styles

JavaScript Libraries

Figure 1-4. Setting the text contents of the h2 element by applying the .text(text) method

Unlike the `text(text)` method, in the `html(HTML)` method, we can also specify the HTML tags along with the text. For, example to change the contents of the paragraph element, we can write the following jQuery code:

```
$('p').html('<b>We can create Rich Internet Applications </b><br/>by making AJAX requests');
```

In our example, the `html(HTML)` jQuery code will access the paragraph element of the HTML file and set its contents to two lines, one line to appear in bold with the text as *Rich Internet Applications* and the other line to appear as normal with the text as *by making AJAX requests*. In other words, the original contents of the paragraph element will be replaced by these two lines. The output that we may get is shown in Figure 1-5.

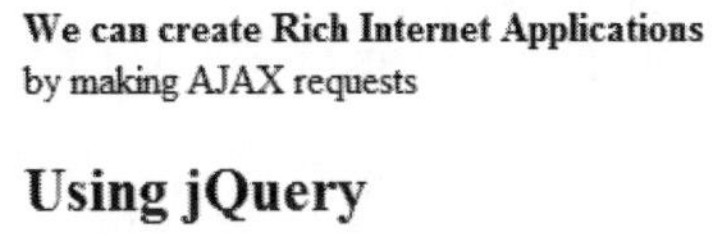

We can create Rich Internet Applications
by making AJAX requests

Using jQuery

Figure 1-5. Setting the HTML contents of the paragraph element

1-9. Creating a DOM Node on the Fly

Problem

You want to create a DOM node dynamically. In this recipe, we will create an h2 element on the fly and add it before an existing paragraph element in an HTML file.

Solution

Our HTML file consists of a paragraph element and an h2 element, as shown in the following example:

```
<body>
<p>Styles make the formatting job much easier and more efficient. To give an attractive look
to
web sites, styles are heavily used.
<span>jQuery is a powerful JavaScript library that allows us to add dynamic elements to our
web sites. </span>Not only is it easy to learn, but it's easy to implement too.<br/>
<a href="a1.htm"> jQuery Selectors</a> are used for selecting the area of the document where
we want to apply styles </p>
<h2>Using  jQuery </h2>
</body>
```

The methods we will use for creating DOM nodes in this solution are: prepend(), prependTo(), and clone(). Other methods that may be used for creating DOM nodes on the fly: append(), appendTo(), before(), insertBefore(), after(), and insertAfter(). Let's look at the prepend() method first.

prepend()

This method inserts the specified content at the beginning of the selected element and returns a jQuery object. The content can be in the form of text, an HTML element, or a jQuery object.

Let's insert an h2 element with the text *Power of selectors* before the paragraph element. The jQuery code for doing so is as follows:

```
$('p').prepend('<h2> Power of selectors </h2>');
```

prependTo()

Similar to prepend(), prependTo() is used for adding DOM nodes dynamically. It inserts the specified element(s) at the beginning of the selected target, where the target can be in the form of an HTML element, a string, or a jQuery object. The method returns a jQuery object. The following is the equivalent of the previous prepend() call.

```
$('<h2> Power of selectors </h2>').prependTo('p');
```

We can see that the contents we want to insert (the h2 element) precede the method.

clone()

When we want to add a DOM node (which is a copy of an existing element) on the fly, we use the clone() method. This method makes a copy of the selected element and returns it as a new jQuery object. To make a copy of the h2 element in the jQuery code and insert it before the paragraph element, the code may be as follows:

```
$('h2').clone().prependTo('p');
```

How It Works

The preceding `prepend()` jQuery code accesses the paragraph element of the HTML file and inserts an `h2` element before it with the text *Power of selectors*. The output that we may get is shown in Figure 1-6.

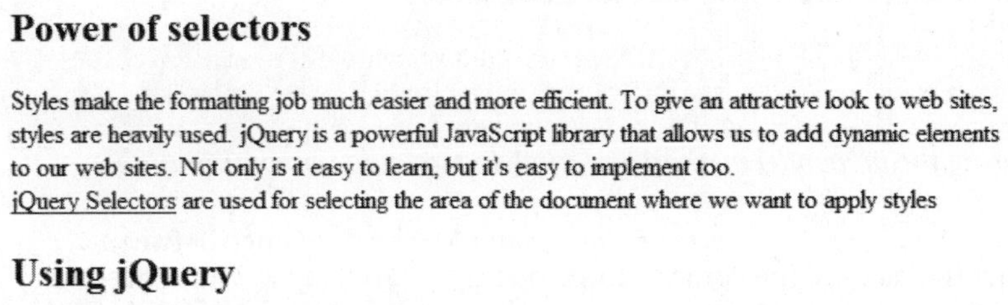

Power of selectors

Styles make the formatting job much easier and more efficient. To give an attractive look to web sites, styles are heavily used. jQuery is a powerful JavaScript library that allows us to add dynamic elements to our web sites. Not only is it easy to learn, but it's easy to implement too.
jQuery Selectors are used for selecting the area of the document where we want to apply styles

Using jQuery

Figure 1-6. DOM node: h2 added on the fly, before the paragraph element

---

■ **Note** By using the `prepend()` method, the inserted contents also appear at the beginning of the element. In other words, if we apply a style to the paragraph element, it will also be applied to the `h2` element.

To see if the style is applied to the combined paragraph and the `h2` element), let us make an external style sheet called `style.css` and write the following CSS class in it:

```
.highlight {
font-style: italic;
background-color: #0f0;
}
```

The preceding style rules make the text appear in italics and change the text color to green. Now let's insert an `h2` element before the paragraph element and apply the style to it. The jQuery code for this will be as follows:

```
$('p').prepend('<h2> Power of selectors </h2>');
$('p').addClass('highlight');
```

We can see that the jQuery code accesses the paragraph element of the HTML file and inserts an `h2` element before it with the text *Power of selectors*. Next, the CSS class `highlight` is applied to the paragraph element (including the newly inserted `h2` element). The output that we may get is shown in Figure 1-7.

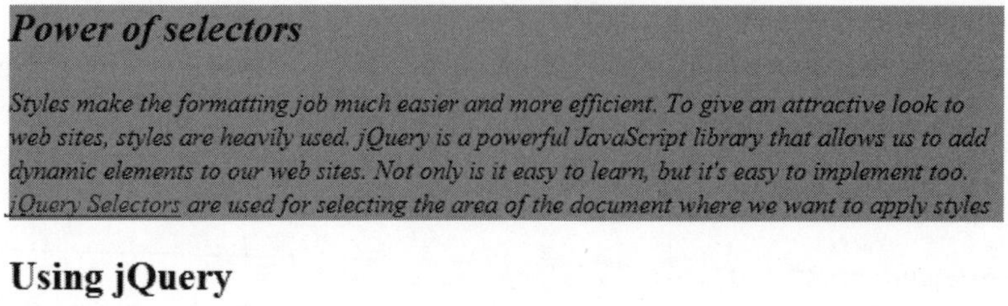

Power of selectors

Styles make the formatting job much easier and more efficient. To give an attractive look to web sites, styles are heavily used. jQuery is a powerful JavaScript library that allows us to add dynamic elements to our web sites. Not only is it easy to learn, but it's easy to implement too. jQuery Selectors are used for selecting the area of the document where we want to apply styles

Using jQuery

Figure 1-7. Inserting contents using the prepend() method and applying styles to the combination

Our `prependTo()` example was very similar to our **prepend()** example. The difference between `prepend()` and `prependTo()` is that the place of the content and target are interchanged. In the **prepend()** method, the target element (which we're prepending to) precedes the method, whereas in **prependTo()**, the content we're prepending precedes the method.

Finally, the `clone()` jQuery code accesses the **h2** element of the HTML file and makes a copy. It then inserts the copy before the paragraph element. The output that we may get is shown in Figure 1-8.

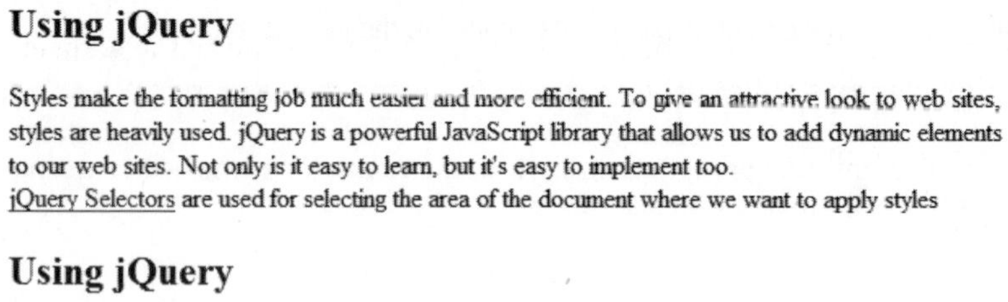

Using jQuery

Styles make the formatting job much easier and more efficient. To give an attractive look to web sites, styles are heavily used. jQuery is a powerful JavaScript library that allows us to add dynamic elements to our web sites. Not only is it easy to learn, but it's easy to implement too.
jQuery Selectors are used for selecting the area of the document where we want to apply styles

Using jQuery

Figure 1-8. Inserting the copy of h2 element before the paragraph element

1-10. Assigning the Same Class Name to Different HTML Elements and Applying Styles to Them

Problem

You want to assign the same class name to two HTML elements and apply styles to them. The two elements can be a paragraph and an **h1** element.

Solution

Let's examine the following HTML file, where the class name **features** is assigned to a paragraph and the h1 element:

```
<!DOCTYPE html PUBLIC "-//W3C//DTD XHTML 1.0 Transitional//EN"
        "http://www.w3.org/TR/xhtml1/DTD/xhtml1-transitional.dtd">

<html xmlns="http://www.w3.org/1999/xhtml" xml:lang="en" lang="en">
  <head>
        <meta http-equiv="Content-Type" content="text/html; charset=utf-8"/>
        <title>JQuery Examples</title>
        <link rel="stylesheet" href="style.css" type="text/css" media="screen" />
        <script src="jquery-1[1].3.2.js" type="text/javascript"></script>
        <script src="d1.js" type="text/javascript"></script>
  </head>
<body>
<p class="features">Styles make the formatting job much easier and more efficient.</p>
To give an attractive look to web sites, styles are heavily used.
<h1 class="features">Using jQuery</h1>
</body>
</html>
```

To apply style to the elements of class **features** in the preceding HTML file, the external style sheet (**style.css**) may be created with the following contents:

```
.features{color:green;font-style:italic}
```

If we want the style rule to be applied to the HTML element via jQuery code (and not automatically), we need to assign some other name to the style rule in the style sheet.

```
.highlight{color:green;font-style:italic}
```

Then we need to write the following jQuery code:

```
$('.features').addClass('highlight');
```

15

How It Works

In the HTML file, the paragraph and `h1` elements both belong to class `features`. In the final style sheet, the style rule has the selector `.highlight`, which means the properties defined in this rule will be applied to all the HTML elements that belong to class `highlight`. The style rule has two properties defined in it, `color` and `font-style, and these properties apply` the green color and `italic` style.

The preceding jQuery code will set the CSS class `highlight` on all HTML elements with class name `features`. The output appears as shown in Figure 1-9.

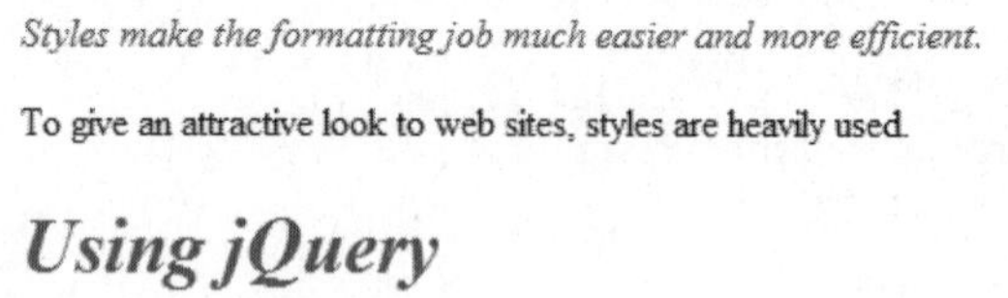

Styles make the formatting job much easier and more efficient.

To give an attractive look to web sites, styles are heavily used.

Using jQuery

Figure 1-9. The same class applied to <p> and <h1> tags

Summary

In this chapter we went over installing jQuery, selecting nodes in the DOM, and applying CSS to elements. We also saw how to select non-standard series of HTML elements, count the number of nodes in the DOM and display their text. We have learned the method of obtaining the HTML of an element, changing the content of a DOM node, creating a DOM node on the fly and assigning the same class name to different HTML elements and applying styles to them. In the next chapter, we will be learning about the different recipes that deal with arrays. We will also learn how to filter, sort, split and manipulate arrays

CHAPTER 2

■ ■ ■

Arrays and Strings

In this chapter we will see how arrays, maps, and strings are dealt with in jQuery. We will be covering the following recipes in this chapter:

- Displaying names in a list using arrays
- Manipulating array elements
- Filtering arrays to show desired data only
- Sorting string and numerical arrays
- Splitting an array
- Combining two arrays
- Converting a numerical array into a string and finding substrings
- Creating an array of objects
- Sorting an array of objects

2-1. Displaying Names in a List Using Arrays

Problem

You want to display a list of names using arrays. That is, assuming that an array containing names exists, you want to display its elements on a web page.

Solution

Let's make an HTML file to display a heading above the names list. The file will also contain an empty paragraph element, as shown here:

```
<body>
<h3> Members of my Group are </h3>
<p></p>
</body>
```

Now add to this paragraph element the names contained in our array. The jQuery code looks something like this:

```
$(document).ready(function() {
  var members = [ "John", "Steve", "Ben", "Damon", "Ian" ];
  $('p').text(members.join(", "));
});
```

Displaying Names One Below the Other

We can also display the names one below the other, as the following jQuery shows:

```
$(document).ready(function() {
  var members = [ "John", "Steve", "Ben", "Damon", "Ian" ];
  $('p').html(members.join("<br/>"));
});
```

Displaying Names with Their Position in the Array

To display the names along with their position in the array, we need to alter the HTML file to contain an empty ordered list element, as shown here:

```
<body>
<h3> Members of my Group are </h3>
<ol id="list">
</ol>
</body>
```

The jQuery code for getting the names from the array and appending to the ordered list looks like this:

```
$(document).ready(function() {
  var memlist = $( "#list" );
  var members = [ "John", "Steve", "Ben", "Damon", "Ian" ];
  $.each(members,function( index, value ){
    memlist.append($( "<li>" + value + "</li>" ));
  });
});
```

Making the Array from HTML Elements and Counting the Array Length

In this solution, we assume that the list of names exists in the HTML file in the form of div elements. We'll get all the names stored in div elements and store them into an array. Then we'll find out the count of the names in the array and display it. The HTML file that contains names of div elements may appear as shown here:

```
<body>
<p></p>
<ul>
  <li>John</li>
  <li>Steve</li>
  <li>Ben</li>
  <li>Damon</li>
  <li>Ian</li>
</ul>
</body>
```

The paragraph element before the div elements is for displaying the count of the names. Currently it has no text but uses jQuery code; we'll assign it some text to display along with the count of the names in the div elements:

```
$(document).ready(function() {
  var names = $("li").get();
  $('p').text("Following are the " + names.length + " members of my Group");
});
```

How It Works

We can see in the first solution that an array by the name members is created that contains five names: John, Steve, Ben, Damon, and Ian. All the elements of the array are assigned to the paragraph element using text(). The elements are joined one after the other with a comma (,) in between using the join() method. In other words, all the names in the array are delimited by a comma and are assigned to the paragraph element. The output will be all the names (separated by a comma) displayed on the web page, as shown in Figure 2-1.

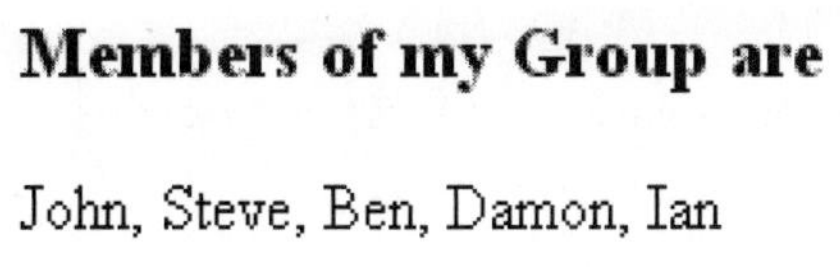

Members of my Group are

John, Steve, Ben, Damon, Ian

Figure 2-1. The names from Array displayed in a row

To display the names one below the other, we use a line break <br/> in between the array elements instead of a comma while using the join() method. Also, to parse the <br/> element as an HTML tag and not as text, we need to assign the array elements to the paragraph element using the html() method instead of `text()`. Otherwise the `<br/>` element will be displayed literally on the screen instead of creating line breaks.

```
$('p').html(members.join("<br/>"));
```

The output in Figure 2-2 shows us how the array elements are now displayed one below the other:

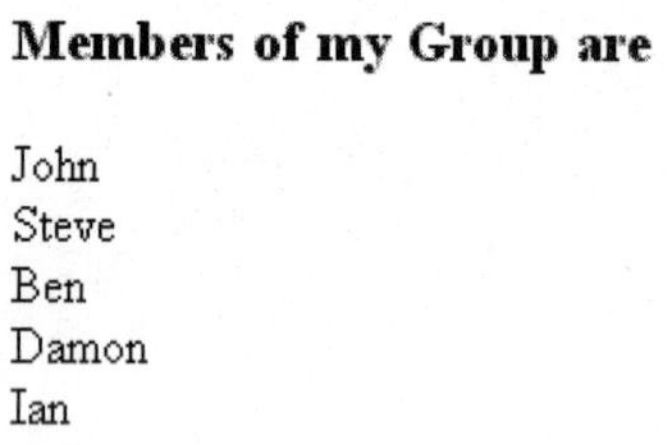

Members of my Group are

John
Steve
Ben
Damon
Ian

Figure 2-2. The names from Array are displayed with a line break between them.

In our ordered-list solution, we have assigned an id of `list` to the ordered list. It is to this ordered list that we will append the names from our array. Recall that ordered lists automatically display numbers for the list items being displayed. In other words, to assign the auto numbering to the names (stored in the array), we will extract one name at a time from the array and will append it to the ordered element `ol`:

```
var memlist = $( "#list" );
var members = [ "John", "Steve", "Ben", "Damon", "Ian" ];
$.each(members,function( index, value ){
  memlist.append($( "<li>" + value + "</li>" ));
});
```

In the preceding jQuery code, we see that the element of id `list` in the HTML file (the ordered list element) is assigned to a variable `memlist`. That is, the `memlist` refers to the `ol` element of the HTML file. An array by name `members` is defined and five names are stored in it. After that, with the help of the `each()` method, every element (name) in the `members` array is extracted and appended to the `ol` element.

The output will be the names with serial numbers assigned to them, as shown in Figure 2-3.

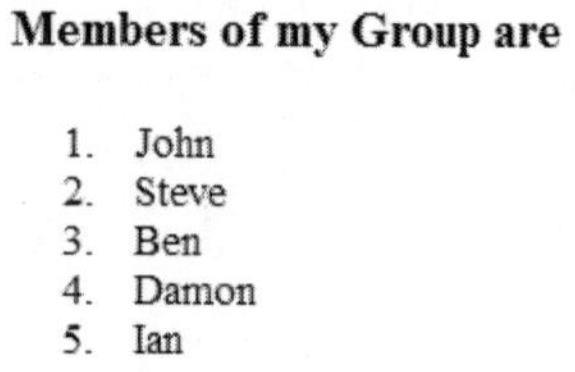

Members of my Group are

1. John
2. Steve
3. Ben
4. Damon
5. Ian

Figure 2-3. The elements of Array appended in the form of list items

Our final example extracted the names from the **div** elements and put them into an array. The following statement does just this: it extracts the text of all the **div** elements with the **get()** method and stores it in an array called **names**:

```
var names = $("div").get();
```

The following statement then assigns text to the paragraph element, inserting the count of the elements in the array **names**:

```
$('p').text("Following are the " + names.length + " members of my Group");
```

The output will display the names along with their count, as shown in Figure 2-4.

Following are the 5 members of my Group
John
Steve
Ben
Damon
Ian

Figure 2-4. The length of Array is used as a count of the div elements (members).

2-2. Manipulating Array Elements

Problem

You want to manipulate array elements for tasks like applying serial numbers to them, converting them to uppercase, and other tasks similar to these.

Solution

Let's assume an HTML file that has a heading element to display the message *Members of my Group are* along with an empty paragraph element, as shown here:

```
<body>
<h3> Members of my Group are </h3>
<p></p>
</body>
```

This blank paragraph element will display names taken from an array, with serial numbers applied. The jQuery code to display the array elements along with the serial number is as shown here:

```
$(document).ready(function() {
  var members = [ "John", "Steve", "Ben", "Damon", "Ian" ];
  members = $.map(members, function(n,i){ return(i+1+"."+n); });
  $('p').html(members.join("<br />"));
});
```

Converting Names to Uppercase

Let's see how we can use other useful methods in the callback method to manipulate members of the array. Our first solution shows how to convert all the names to uppercase with the **toUpperCase()** method:

```
$(document).ready(function() {
  var members = [ "John", "Steve", "Ben", "Damon", "Ian" ];
  members=$.map(members, function(n,i){ return(i+1+"."+n.toUpperCase());});
  $('p').html(members.join("<br/>"));
});
```

Using an Ordered List

Another method of displaying the array elements in capital letters along with serial numbers is to make use of the ordered-list element. Let's make an HTML file that displays a heading element and an empty ordered-list element, as shown here:

```
<body>
<h3> Members of my Group are </h3>
<ol id="list">
</ol>
</body>
```

The jQuery code to display the array elements in uppercase is then as follows:

```
$(document).ready(function() {
  var memlist = $( "#list" );
  var members = [ "John", "Steve", "Ben", "Damon", "Ian" ];
  members=$.map(members, function(n){ return(n.toUpperCase());});
  $.each(members,function( index, value ){
    memlist.append($( "<li>" + value + "</li>" ));
  });
});
```

How It Works

To understand this recipe, you need to know about the `map()` method. This method iterates through each element of the array and invokes a callback function on each of the array elements. The returned elements can be assigned to another array or the same array if you prefer. The `map()` method can also iterate through array-like objects that have a `length` property. Here is the syntax for `map()`:

```
map(array, callback);
```

The callback function here contains the statements for performing the processing task on the array elements. In our first solution, we want to display the names stored in the array along with serial numbers. We can see that an array `members` is defined that contains the names we want to display. We next pass this array to the `map()` method. The callback function in the `map()` method contains two arguments, n and i, where n refers to the elements of the array (names) being passed to the `map()` method, and i is the index of the individual array element (index begins with 0). To make the serial numbers begin with 1 instead of 0, we can add 1 to i in each iteration. The values returned by the callback function thus appear as follows:

```
return(i+1+"."+n)
```

This statement returns all the elements of the array one by one with index beginning from 1. The output that we get is as shown in Figure 2-5.

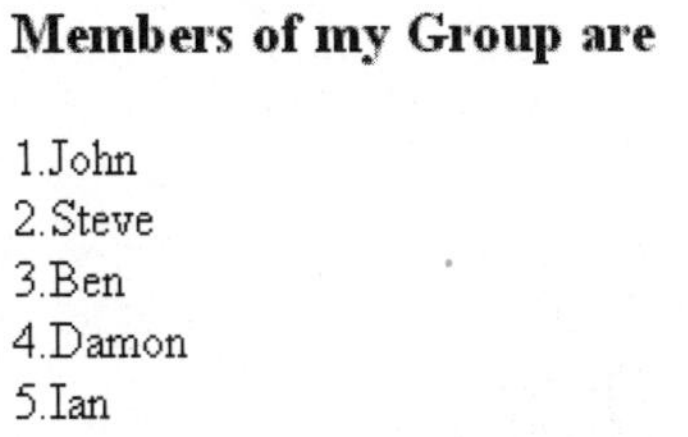

Members of my Group are

1.John
2.Steve
3.Ben
4.Damon
5.Ian

Figure 2-5. Using array mapping to assign serial numbers to elements of the array

In the solution that followed, we then used the `toUpperCase()` method in the callback function to convert into uppercase all the names stored in the array:

```
members=$.map(members, function(n,i){ return(i+1+"."+n.toUpperCase()); });
```

Recall that the arguments n and i in the callback function refer to the array element and index number respectively. We can see that the application of `toUpperCase()` to n (that is, the names stored in the array in the form of array elements) converts the names into uppercase and returns them for displaying in the paragraph element.

The output will be the names converted to uppercase, along with serial numbers, as shown in Figure 2-6.

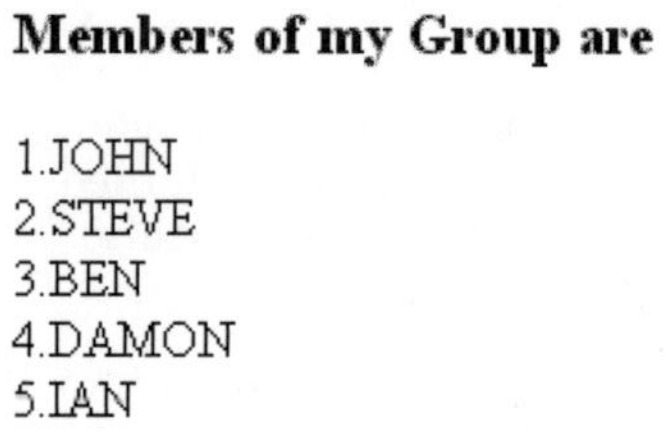

Members of my Group are

1.JOHN
2.STEVE
3.BEN
4.DAMON
5.IAN

Figure 2-6. Using array mappings to convert array elements to uppercase

The ordered-list solution applies auto numbering to its list elements. To the members array, we assign the result of the map() method, which will convert each array element into uppercase. We then append each member of the members array one by one to the ordered list (which has an id of list to identify it through jQuery code). We will get the output shown in Figure 2-7.

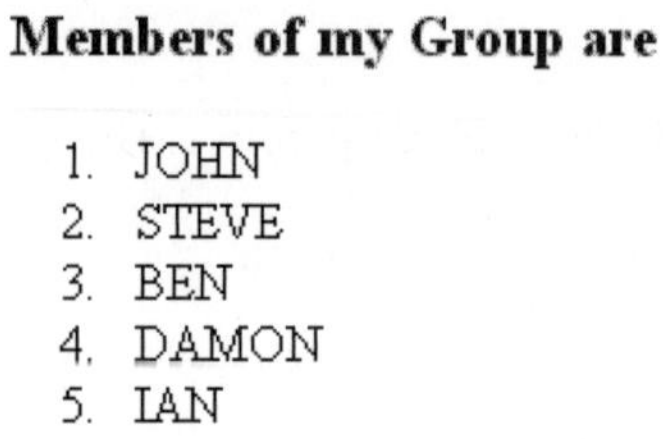

Members of my Group are

1. JOHN
2. STEVE
3. BEN
4. DAMON
5. IAN

Figure 2-7. Displaying array elements in uppercase via list items

2-3. Filtering Arrays to Show Desired Data Only

Problem

You have an array that contains some names and you want to filter it to see only the desired names. For example, you may want to see only those names with a length of more than four characters.

Solution

Let's consider an HTML file that has two heading elements and each is followed by a paragraph element. The first paragraph element is assigned a class name allmem and the other paragraph is assigned the class name selected. The HTML file may appear as shown here:

```
<body>
<h3> Members of my Group are </h3>
<p class="allmem"></p>
<h3> Names with more than 4 characters in length are </h3>
<p class="selected"></p>
</body>
```

We will be using the first paragraph (class `allmem`) to display the whole array; that is, all the names in the list. We'll use the second paragraph (class `selected`) for displaying the filtered names.

Using grep()

Let's write some jQuery code for displaying only the names that have a length of more than four characters using the `grep()` method. (We'll look at how it works a little more in the "How It Works" section.)

```
$(document).ready(function() {
  var members = [ "John", "Steve", "Ben",  "Damon","Ian" ];
  $('p.allmem').html(members.join("<br/>"));
  members = $.grep(members, function(v) { return v.length > 4});
  $('p.selected').html(members.join("<br/>"));
});
```

Using match()

We'll also write some jQuery code to display only those names in the array that begin with any character from A through D using the `match()` method and a regular expression:

```
$(document).ready(function() {
  var members = [ "John", "Steve", "Ben",  "Damon","Ian" ];
  $('p.allmem').html(members.join("<br/>"));
  members = $.grep(members, function(v) { return v.match(/^[A-D]/)});
  $('p.selected').html(members.join("<br/>"));
});
```

How It Works

Our first solution performed filtering on arrays using the `grep()` method. This method parses all the elements of the array and invokes a callback function on each element. In the callback function, we can write statements that filter out undesired elements; that is, only the values that we want in the filtered array are returned by the callback function. Here is the syntax

```
grep(array, callback, boolean)
```

where the parameters in `grep` are as follows:

- `array` is the original array that is passed to this method for performing filtering tasks on it.

- `callback` is the function that performs filtering tasks and returns the values that make up the filtered array. This function can carry two parameters; one is the array element and the second is the index value.

- `boolean` is usually omitted. If it is specified and is set to `false` (which is the default), then it has no effect, but if its value is set to `true`, then the operation of the callback function is inverted. That is, it will return the values that do not match the conditional statements present in the `callback` function.

Using our knowledge of `grep()`, let's dissect the first solution. We can see that `members` is an array that contains some names. The following statement separates each array element with a line break (`<br/>`) and displays them all as the text of the first paragraph (of class `allmem`). This therefore displays the original array on the screen:

```
$('p.allmem').html(members.join("<br />"));
```

The following statement makes use of the `grep()` method and the `members` array is passed to it. Its callback function has the parameter `v`, which represents each array element:

```
members = $.grep(members, function(v) { return v.length >4});
```

We see that the callback function returns only names that have a length greater than four characters. The returned array elements are stored in the original array `members` (replacing its old contents). The following statement displays the filtered array elements with a line break in between (to display them on separate lines) as a text of the paragraph of class `selected`:

```
$('p.selected').html(members.join("<br/>"));
```

On execution of the preceding jQuery code, you will get the output shown in Figure 2-8.

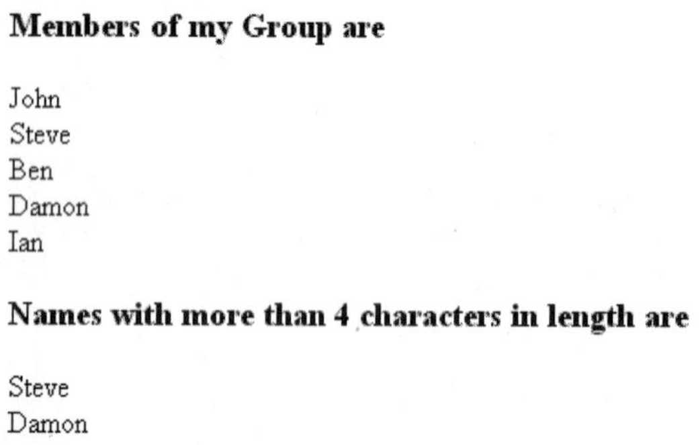

Members of my Group are

John
Steve
Ben
Damon
Ian

Names with more than 4 characters in length are

Steve
Damon

Figure 2-8. Displaying array elements that have a length of more than four characters

Now let's make some changes in our `grep()` method to include the `boolean` parameter, which, as I said before, reverses the operation of the callback function, as shown here:

```
members = $.grep(members, function(v) { return v.length >4}, true);
```

This statement will return those names of the array with a length less than or equal to four characters.

Our second solution used the `match()` method for defining regular expressions, which in our case matched strings starting with A through D, where `match()` is a method of the `String` class that is used for determining whether the regular expression specified matches the specified string object.

Using Regular Expressions

Regular expressions are used as concise methods for specifying patterns of characters that we want in an element. They are a powerful tool for parsing and validating strings.

Here is a list of regular-expression notation:

Character	Matches
\b	Word boundary
\d	Numerical from 0 to 9
\s	Single white space
\w	Character, numeral, or underscore
.	Any character except the newline character
[…]	Any one of the character in the brackets
{n}	Exactly *n* times
{n,}	*n* or more times
{n.m}	Between *n* and *m*
?	Zero or more times

Character	Matches
+	One or more times
^	At the beginning
$	At the end

The following statement uses the grep() method, passing the members array to it:

```
members = $.grep(members, function(v) { return v.match(/^[A-D]/)});
```

Again, the callback function carries an argument v that gets the array elements one by one. The callback function returns only those array elements that begin with any character from A through D. The output we get is shown in Figure 2-9.

Members of my Group are

John
Steve
Ben
Damon
Ian

Members with names beginning from A to D are

Ben
Damon

Figure 2-9. Displaying names that begin with a letter from A through D

Armed with new knowledge, we can now modify the regular expression in match() to display only those names that end with character *n*, like this:

```
members = $.grep(members, function(v) { return v.match(/[n]$/)});
```

Recall that $ is used in a regular expression for specifying the content that we want to see at the end of the line. The output we may get is shown in Figure 2-10.

Members names ending with character n are

John
Ben
Damon
Ian

Figure 2-10. Displaying names ending with the character n

To see all the names in the array that have the character *e* one or more times, we will use the following regular expression:

```
members = $.grep(members, function(v) { return v.match(/[e].+/)});
```

This displays for us only those names that have character *e* one or more times, as shown in Figure 2-11.

Members names having one or more e character in them

Steve
Ben

Figure 2-11. Displaying names having one or more character e

To find out the names that are of exactly five characters in length, we may use following regular expression

```
members = $.grep(members, function(v) { return v.match(/\b.{5}\b/)});
```

which, of course, gives us the output shown in Figure 2-12.

Member names of exactly five characters in length

Steve
Damon

Figure 2-12. Displaying names that are of exactly five characters

2-4. Sorting String and Numerical Arrays

Problem

You have two arrays; one is a string array and the other is a numerical array. You want to sort them individually.

Solution

Let us start with the string array.

Sorting String Arrays

The following is an HTML file that has two heading elements, each followed by a paragraph element. The heading elements are for displaying title messages of *original array* and *sorted array,* respectively. The two paragraph elements are distinguished by assigning them two different class names, `allmem` and `sorted`, respectively. The HTML file may appear as follows:

```
<body>
<h3> Members of my Group are </h3>
<p class="allmem"></p>
<h3> Members of my Group in sorted order </h3>
<p class="sorted"></p>
</body>
```

The paragraph element of class `allmem` will be used for displaying the original array elements and the paragraph element class `sorted` will be used for displaying the sorted array. The actual jQuery code for sorting the string array can then look like this, and you'll see how it works shortly:

```
$(document).ready(function() {
  var members = [ "John", "Steve", "Ben",  "Damon","Ian" ];
  $('p.allmem').html(members.join("<br />"));
  members = members.sort();
  $('p.sorted').html(members.join("<br />"));
});
```

Sorting Numerical Arrays

The sorting of numerical values is done in a different way from sorting strings in jQuery. We again make an HTML file with two heading elements and two paragraphs elements, as shown here:

```
<body>
<h3>Original numerical array is </h3>
<p class="allmem"></p>
```

```
<h3> Array in sorted order </h3>
<p class="sorted"></p>
</body>
```

As with the string solution, the paragraph element class allmem is meant for displaying the original array and the paragraph element class sorted is for displaying the sorted array.

Here is the jQuery code to sort a numerical array:

```
$(document).ready(function() {
  var members = [45, 10,3,22,7 ];
  $('p.allmem').html(members.join("<br>"));
  members = members.sort(function(a,b){
    return a-b;
  });
  $('p.sorted').html(members.join("<br>"));
});
```

How It Works

The statement, which actually sorts the string array in our preceding recipe, looks like this:

```
members = members.sort();
```

Here the sort() method sorts the string array in alphabetical order. This method sorts on the basis of the ASCII values, so it is better to have all uniform names. That is, they must begin with either uppercase or lowercase, but not mixed case. The preceding statement will sort the string array members, and the sorted version is stored in the members array (replacing older values).

Before we use sort(), the members string array method is assigned to the paragraph element class allmem (for the purpose of displaying it) and the same array after the application of sort() is assigned to the paragraph element class sorted. The output is as shown in Figure 2-13.

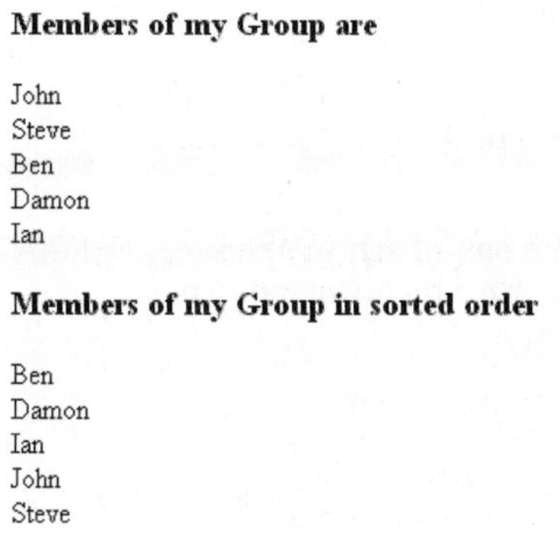

Members of my Group are

John
Steve
Ben
Damon
Ian

Members of my Group in sorted order

Ben
Damon
Ian
John
Steve

Figure 2-13. Displaying names in sorted order

The **sort()** method, as noted earlier, sorts the elements on the basis of ASCII values, so it cannot be used with numerical values, as it will consider 10 smaller than 3 (as the ASCII value of 1 is smaller than that of 3). If we try **sort()** with the numerical array, the jQuery code would be as shown here:

```
$(document).ready(function() {
  var members = [45, 10, 3, 22, 7];
  $('p.a').html(members.join("<br/>"));
  members = members.sort();
  $('p.b').html(members.join("<br/>"));
});
```

We would then get output like that shown in Figure 2-14.

Original numerical array is

45
10
3
22
7

Array in sorted order

10
22
3
45
7

Figure 2-14. Numerical arrays not sorted correctly

As you can see here, the numerical values are not sorted correctly with the **sort()** method because it considers the ASCII value of the first numerical digit of all numerical values for sorting purposes. To sort numerical values correctly, we must therefore define a comparison function with **sort()**.

If we define a comparison function, then a pair of values from the array will be repeatedly sent to the function until all elements of the array are processed. In the comparison function, we thus write a statement considering the pair of values passed to it so that the function returns any of the following three values: <0, =0, or >0.

- When the function returns value <0, the second value (of the pair of array values sent to the function) is larger than the first value and hence must be pushed down the sorting order.

- When the function returns value >0, the first value is larger than the second value, so it must be pushed down the sorting order.

- When the function returns value =0, it means there is no need to change the sort order since the two values are same.

The jQuery code with the comparison function added to the **sort()** method looks like this:

```
members = members.sort(function(a,b){
   return a-b;
});
```

The following statement in the comparison function will sort the numerical values in ascending order:

```
return a-b;
```

We get output much like Figure 2-15.

Original numerical array is

45
10
3
22
7

Array in sorted order

3
7
10
22
45

Figure 2-15. Numerical arrays sorted correctly

Of course, to sort the values in descending order, we just need to change the return value in the comparison function from **a-b** to **b-a**!

2-5. Splitting an Array

Problem

You have an array and you want to divide it into two parts.

Solution

The following is a HTML file that has three heading elements to display the title messages of the original array, and the two pieces we'll be splitting. The file also contains the three paragraph elements of classes **allnum**, **firstp**, and **secondp** for displaying the contents of the original array, the first piece, and the second piece of the array, respectively:

```
<body>
<h3>Original numerical array is </h3>
<p class="allnum"></p>
<h3> First piece of array </h3>
<p class="firstp"></p>
<h3> Second piece of array </h3>
<p class="secondp"></p>
</body>
```

The jQuery code to split the array is as shown here:

```
$(document).ready(function() {
  var members = [45, 10, 3, 22, 7];
  $('p.allnum').html(members.join("<br>"));
  memsecond = members.splice(0,3);
  $('p.firstp').html(memsecond.join("<br />"));
  $('p.secondp').html(members.join("<br />"));
});
```

How It Works

In the jQuery code, we use the `splice()` method for splitting the array. To split the array, this method requires two parameters: the first parameter specifies the index location from where to start splitting, and the second parameter specifies the number of elements to be removed from the original array. The range of array elements defined by the two parameters will be extracted from the original array and will be returned so it can be saved in another array. To recap, one part of the array (defined by the two parameters sent to splice) will be returned; the other remaining array part will be the original array after the first has been removed.

```
subarray = mainarray.splice (m,n);
```

Here `subarray` is the array that will be made after removing the elements from the `mainarray` from index m through n elements.

■ **Note** The `mainarray` will be left with the remaining elements.

We can see in the preceding code that `members` is a numerical array with five numerical values defined in it. The elements of the array will be displayed on the web page in the form of the text of paragraph containing class `allnum`, with the line break (`<br/>`) defined in between. That is, all the elements of the array are displayed one below the other.

The following statement extracts three elements, starting from index location 0, and returns them to be stored in the array `memsecond`:

```
memsecond = members.splice(0,3);
```

As we have planned, the main array members will be left with the remaining elements only. So the memsecond array will contain the first three elements of the members array, and the members array will be left with the last two elements. The first three elements of the array stored in memsecond will be displayed in the paragraph element of the class firstp' and the last two elements left behind in the array members will be displayed as the paragraph element of the class secondp'. Figure 2-16 shows a typical output from all this.

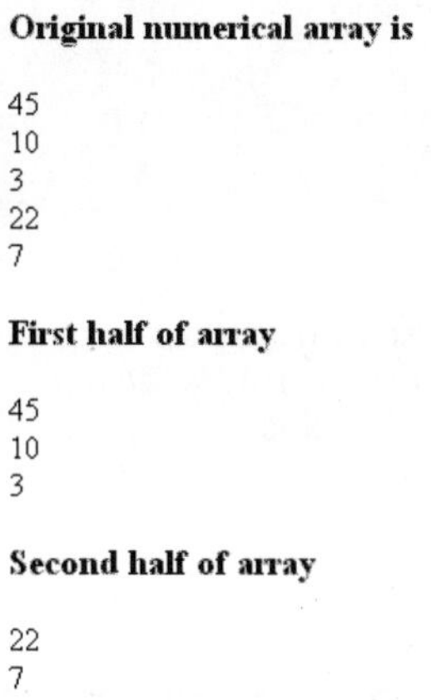

Original numerical array is

45
10
3
22
7

First half of array

45
10
3

Second half of array

22
7

Figure 2-16. *Array split in two halves*

2-6. Combining Two Arrays

Problem

You have two arrays and you want to combine them into a single array.

Solution

Here is an HTML file that has three heading elements to display the title messages of two arrays, and the title message of an array that is a combination of the two arrays. The file here also contains three paragraph elements of the classes firstarr, secondarr, and combinedarr for displaying the elements of two arrays that we want to combine and the total elements of the combined array, respectively:

```
<body>
<h3>First array is </h3>
<p class="firstarr"></p>
<h3> Second array is </h3>
<p class="secondarr"></p>
<h3> Array after combination </h3>
<p class="combinedarr"></p>
 </body>
```

35

The jQuery code to combine two arrays is as follows:

```
$(document).ready(function() {
  var mem1 = [45, 10, 3];
  var mem2 = [22, 7];
  $('p.firstarr').html(mem1.join("<br/>"));
  $('p.secondarr').html(mem2.join("<br/>"));
  members = mem1.concat(mem2);
  $('p.combinedarr').html(members.join("<br/>"));
});
```

How It Works

The `concat()` method is the method of an array object and it is invoked on the first array (the one that we want to concatenate) while a second array is passed to it as a parameter. This returned array is the concatenation (the combination of the two arrays) and is stored in the third array like this:

```
combinedarray = array1.concat(array2);
```

Here `array1` invokes the `concat()` method and `array2` is passed as a parameter. The combined array is the array that will have all the elements of `array1` followed by all the elements of `array2`.

In our solution we start by defining two arrays called `mem1` and `mem2`. Then we display the elements of `array1` and `array2` in the form of paragraph text of the classes `firstarr` and `secondarr`; that is, the contents of two arrays are displayed at the paragraphs of the classes `firstarr` and `secondarr`, respectively. We also see that the `mem1` array invokes the `concat()` method, passing the `mem2` array as a parameter. The resultant combination of the two arrays is stored in the array `members`. The contents of the array `members` are then displayed on the paragraph of the class `combinedarr`.

The output that we get on execution of the preceding jQuery code is as shown in Figure 2-17.

First array is

45
10
3

Second array is

22
7

Array after combination

45
10
3
22
7

Figure 2-17. Combining two arrays

2-7. Converting a Numerical Array into a String and Finding Its Substring

Problem

You have a numerical array and you want it to be converted into a string so that you can apply the `substr()` method to take out a part of the string.

Solution

Here is an HTML file that contains three headings elements to display the titles for the original numerical array we're working with, the array converted into string form, and finally the substring of the string. Also, below each heading element is a paragraph element. The three paragraph elements are assigned class names `origarr`, `arrstring`, and `partstring`. The paragraph of the class `origarr` will be used for displaying elements of the numerical array. The paragraph of the class `arrstring` will be used for displaying the string (the array after converted into string form) and the paragraph of the class `partstring` will be used for displaying the part of the string that we want to take out. The HTML file may appear as shown:

```
<body>
<h3>Original array is </h3>
<p class="origarr"></p>
<h3> Array in form of string </h3>
<p class="arrstring"></p>
<h3> Substring is </h3>
<p class="partstring"></p>
</body>
```

The jQuery code to convert the numerical array into a string, and for then taking out a part of it, is as follows:

```
$(document).ready(function() {
  var members = [45, 10, 3, 22, 7];
  $('p.origarr').html(members.join("<br/>"));
  var str = members.join("");
  $('p.arrstring').text(str);
  var substr = str.substr(0,3);
  $('p.partstring').text(substr);
});
```

How It Works

We define a numerical array `members` of five elements, and display the contents in the paragraph element of the class `origarray`, delimiting each array element with a line break (`<br/>`) so that the array elements are displayed one below the other.

Next we convert the numerical array `members` into a string by joining each of its elements into the string variable `str` without any white space in between. That is, the string `str` will contain all the numerical values of the numerical array joined one after the other, without any space in between. The `str` variable is displayed on the paragraph element of the class `arrstring`.

Finally, we take out a part of the string from the `str` variable, beginning from index location 0. From there, three characters are extracted and stored in a string variable `substr`. The contents of the variable `substr` will be displayed in the paragraph element of the class `partstring`. The output that we will get is shown in Figure 2-18.

Original array is

45
10
3
22
7

Array in form of string

45103227

Substring is

451

Figure 2-18. A numerical array converted to a string

2-8. Creating an Array of Objects

Problem

You want to create an array of objects to store the information about a certain entity, item, person, object, etc. In this solution we will store the information about three students. Each student object is assumed to consist of three attributes: `role`, `name`, and `emailId`.

Solution

We'll make an HTML file that consists of a heading element to display a title and a paragraph element to display the contents of an array:

```
<body>
<h3>List of students is </h3>
<p class="listofstud"></p>
</body>
```

The jQuery code to create an array of objects called `students` with three attributes—`role`, `name`, and `emailId`—is shown here:

```
$(document).ready(function() {
  var students=[
  {
  "role": 101,
  "name": "Ben",
  "emailId":"ben@gmail.com"
  },
  {
  "role": 102,
  "name": "Ian",
  "emailId":"ian@gmail.com"
  },
  {
  "role": 103,
  "name": "Caroline",
  "emailId":"carol@gmail.com"
  }
  ];

  $.each(students,function( index, value ){
    $('p.listofstud').append(value.role+" "+value.name+" "+value.emailId);
  });
});
```

This won't be a very appealing display, so let's display the contents of the array in a table element so that the attributes (`role`, `name`, and `emailId`) will appear aligned, which makes it appear neat and tidy. The HTML file is as shown here:

```
<body>
<h3>List of students is </h3>
<table class="listofstud"></table>
</body>
```

The jQuery code for making an array of objects and assigning it to the table element is as shown here. The file is the same as it was previously, except for the bold lines:

```
$(document).ready(function() {
  ...

  $.each(students,function( index, value ){
    $('table.listofstud').append("<tr><td>"+value.role+"</td><td>"+value.name+
      "</td><td>"+value.emailId+"</td></tr>");
  });
});
```

How It Works

In the first solution above, we see that three elements are created in the array `students`. After that, we make use of the `each()` method, applying a callback function to each of the array elements.

In the callback function, two parameters are passed: `index` and `value`. The parameter `index` refers to the index location of the array element and the parameter `value` refers to the array element itself. Each array element has three attributes: `role`, `name`, and `emailId`. So, the three attributes `role`, `name`, and `emailId` of all the array elements are appended to the paragraph element of the class `listofstud` with a white space in between to display the information of all the students on the screen.

We could also have used a `for` loop for iterating through the elements of the array. The `each()` method in the preceding jQuery code could be replaced by the `for` loop as shown here:

```
for(var i=0;i<students.length;i++){
    $('p.listofstud').append(students[i].role+" "+students[i].name+" "+students[i].emailId);
}
```

As you can see, the `each()` approach iterates automatically and is easier to handle.
Both approaches get the output shown in Figure 2-19.

List of students is

101 Ben ben@gmail.com102 Ian ian@gmail.com103 Caroline carol@gmail.com

Figure 2-19. An array of objects displayed as paragraph text

In the table display version, you can see that after creation of our array of the object `students`, we use `each()` to parse each of the array elements and process it via its callback function. In the callback function each of the array element attributes (that is, `role`, `name`, and `emailId`) are displayed by enclosing them in the `<td>` and `</td>` tags. Each array element is stored in the table element in a separate row, and the attributes of array elements are displayed in columns. This makes the array of objects appear in tabular format, as shown in Figure 2-20.

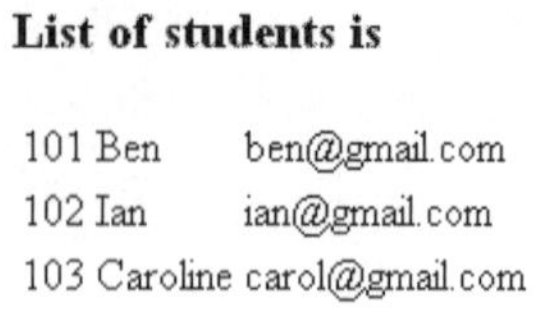

List of students is

101 Ben   ben@gmail.com
102 Ian   ian@gmail.com
103 Caroline carol@gmail.com

Figure 2-20. An array of objects displayed in tabular format

2-9. Sorting an Array of Objects

Problem

You have student information stored in the form of an array of objects. Each student object is assumed to consist of three attributes: `role`, `name`, and `emailId`. You want to sort the array on the basis of its attributes role.

Solution

Let's create an HTML file that displays a heading and an empty `table` element of the class `listofstud`. The `table` element will be used for displaying a sorted array of objects. The HTML file may appear as shown here:

```
<body>
<h3>List of students is </h3>
<table class="listofstud"></table>
</body>
```

We'll now write the jQuery code to create an array of objects to store information of three students with attributes `role`, `name`, and `emailId`. Also, we need to include the code to perform sorting on the `role` attribute of the student object. The jQuery code is shown here, and in the next section we'll look at how it all works:

```
$(document).ready(function() {
  var students=[
  {
  "role": 101,
  "name": "Ben",
  "emailId":"ben@gmail.com"
  },
  {
  "role": 102,
  "name": "Ian",
  "emailId":"ian@gmail.com"
  },
  {
  "role": 103,
  "name": "Caroline",
  "emailId":"carol@gmail.com"
  }
  ];

  students = students.sort(function(a,b){
    return b.role-a.role;
  });

  $.each(students,function( index, value ){
    $('table.listofstud').append("<tr><td>"+value.role+"</td><td>"+value.name+"</td><td>"+
      value.emailId+"</td></tr>");
  });
});
```

41

If we want to sort the array on the basis of alphabetical order of its `name` attribute, we need to replace the preceding `sort()` function with one like this:

```
students = students.sort(function(a,b){
  if(a.name<b.name){ return -1 };
  if(a.name>b.name){ return 1 };
  return 0;
});
```

How It Works

In the `sort()` method we needed to add the comparison function that repeatedly takes a pair of values from the array and returns the values <0, =0, and >0 on the basis of comparison. The basis on which these values are returned is described in Recipe 2-4.

You can see that in the comparison function we are comparing the `role` attributes of the `students` object. In that function, we return the following:

```
return b.role-a.role;
```

This means the function will sort the array in descending order of the attribute `role`.

Thereafter, we use `each()` to parse each of the array elements and process them via their callback function. In the callback function each of the array element's attributes—that is, `role`, `name`, and `emailId,` are displayed by enclosing them in the `<td>` and `</td>` `tags`. This means that each array element is stored in a table data element in a separate row and each of the attributes of the array element is displayed in the form of columns. The result is that now the array of objects appears in tabular format, as shown in Figure 2-21.

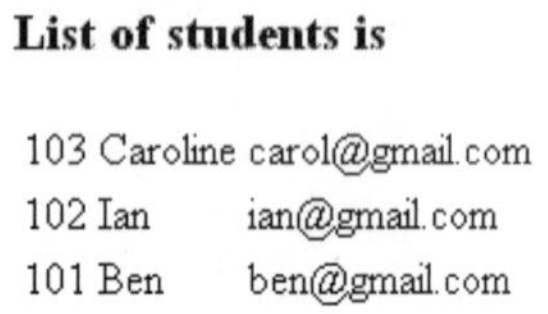

List of students is

103 Caroline carol@gmail.com

102 Ian   ian@gmail.com

101 Ben   ben@gmail.com

Figure 2-21. An array of student objects, sorted in descending order of the role attribute

When we sort on the `name` attribute, you can see that this time in the comparison function we are comparing the `name` attributes of the `students` object. The function returns -1 if the `name` attribute of the first element is smaller (in ASCII value) than the `name` attribute of the second element, and returns 1 in the opposite scenario. The result will be the array of student objects sorted on the basis of the `name` attribute. You'll see output something like Figure 2-22.

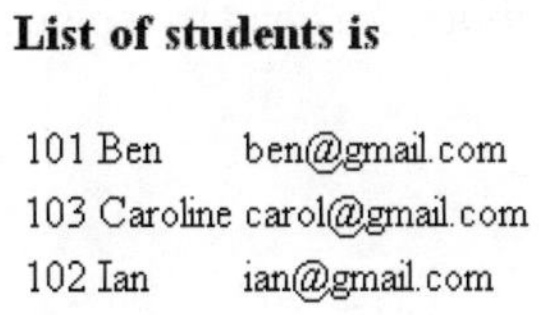

List of students is

101 Ben   ben@gmail.com
103 Caroline carol@gmail.com
102 Ian   ian@gmail.com

Figure 2-22. An array of student objects, sorted in alphabetical order of the name attribute

Summary

In this chapter we discussed the different recipes that deal with arrays, such as how to display names in a list, and how the elements of an array are manipulated. We also went over the recipes that perform the task of filtering arrays.

In the next chapter, we will see several recipes that deal with event handling. We will also learn how to highlight the text dynamically, and how to make an image bright and blur with mouse movements. We will also see the process of creating image-based rollovers, event based addition and removal of text, and more.

CHAPTER 3

■ ■ ■

Event Handling

In this chapter we are going to see how events are handled in jQuery. Events may be in terms of hover, click, double-click, and so on. We will see events related to both mouse and keyboard. Though Chapter 6 covers visual effects and describes how to do animations with images, there are a few animation effects related to text included in this chapter because they are useful when reacting to events. The recipes that we are going to see in this chapter are as follows:

- Finding out which button is clicked
- Triggering events automatically
- Disabling a button after it is clicked once
- Handling mouse events
- Finding out which mouse button is pressed
- Finding the screen coordinates of a mouse-button press
- Highlighting text dynamically
- Making an image bright and blurred with mouse movements
- Finding when an element gains and loses focus
- Applying hover effects on buttons
- Toggling the application of a CSS class
- Creating image-based rollovers
- Adding and removing text in response to events
- Applying styles in response to events
- Displaying word balloons
- Creating "Return to Top" links
- Offering "Read More..." links
- Displaying text with an animation effect

- Replacing text with a sliding effect

- Making an image scroll

- Determining which key was pressed

- Preventing event bubbling

- Chaining multiple activities

3-1. Finding Out Which Button Is Clicked

Problem

On every web page, you find several buttons, each meant for doing different jobs. In order to take the correct action, you need to know which button has been clicked.

Solution

In this recipe, we assume there are two buttons and we want to know which of them is clicked by the user. Let us define an HTML file that contains the text *Bold* and *Italic* to which we will assign the shape of a button by applying different style properties. The HTML file will appear as shown here:

```
<body>
<span class="bold buttons">Bold</span>
<span class="italic buttons">Italic</span>
</body>
```

In the external style sheet `style.css`, we write the CSS class by name `buttons` to give the shape of the button to the text. The CSS class `buttons` may have the following properties:

```
.buttons{
width: 100px;
float: left;
text-align: center;
margin: 5px;
border: 2px solid;
font-weight: bold;
}
```

Let's write the jQuery code to attach the click event on the buttons, using the `bind()` method:

```
$(document).ready(function() {
  $('.bold').bind('click', function(){
    alert('You have clicked the Bold button');
  });
```

```
  $('.italic').bind('click', function(){
    alert('You have clicked the Italic button');
  });
});
```

Applying Click Events to Both the Buttons

Instead of adding a click event to each button individually, we can apply the click event to both buttons simultaneously by adding the click event to the whole button class. For this, we use the following jQuery code:

```
$(document).ready(function() {
  $('.buttons').bind('click', function(){
    alert('You have clicked the ' +$(this).text()+' button');
  });
});
```

Attaching the Event Directly

We can also attach the event to any specified element directly without using the bind() method. Let's see the jQuery code that attaches the click event to the element of the class buttons:

```
$(document).ready(function() {
  $('.buttons').click(function(){
    alert('You have clicked the ' +$(this).text()+' button');
  });
});
```

Using the Target Attribute of the Event Object

The event object is automatically sent to the event-handling function by JavaScript and contains details of the event. One of its attributes, called target, can be used to find out the element where the event has occurred.

The jQuery code using the target attribute of the event object to find out the element where the click event has occurred is as shown here:

```
$(document).ready(function() {
  $('.buttons').click(function(event){
    var $target=$(event.target);
    if($target.is('.bold')){
      alert('You have clicked the Bold button');
    }
    if($target.is('.italic')){
      alert('You have clicked the Italic button');
    }
  });
});
```

Attaching a Double-Click Event

Let's modify our jQuery code a bit to attach the double-click event to our HTML elements of the **buttons** class:

```
$(document).ready(function() {
  $('.buttons').dblclick(function(){
    alert('You have double-clicked the ' +$(this).text()+' button');
  });
});
```

How It Works

In the HTML file, the statement:

```
<span class="bold buttons">Bold</span>
```

This defines the text *Bold* in a **span** element of the classes **bold** and **buttons**. The class **bold** we will be for applying jQuery code to the **span** element and the class **buttons** is for applying the styles defined in the CSS class **buttons** specified in the style sheet.

Similarly, the second statement defines the text *Italic* in a **span** element of the class **italic** and **buttons**. The **italic** class is for applying the jQuery code and the class **buttons** is for applying CSS class.

The style rules in the style sheet apply **width**, **float**, **text-align**, **margin**, **border**, and **font-weight** properties to both the **span** elements of the class **buttons**. It will display two buttons, as shown in Figure 3-1.

The jQuery code makes use of the **bind()** method, so let's see what it is meant for before we go ahead with understanding of jQuery code.

bind()

This method attaches the specific event to the given element.

```
bind(eventType, data, handler)
```

- **eventType**—A string that specifies the type of the event—click, double-click, focus, blur, etc.

- **data**—The data to be passed to the event handler for processing. If it is omitted, the handler function can be used as second argument.

- **handler**—The function that contains the statements to perform on occurrence of the given event.

In the jQuery code, the statement

```
$('.bold').bind('click', function(){
```

binds an inline function as the click event handler for the HTML element of class **bold**; that is, the click event is bound to the **span** element of the class **bold** and hence if the user clicks on the text *Bold*, it will execute the statement stored in the inline function.

The statement

```
alert('You have clicked the Bold button');
```

displays the alert message when the click event occurs on the text.

On execution of the first jQuery code, we find that the text *Bold* and *Italic* appears in the form of buttons. On clicking on the Bold button, we get the alert message "You have clicked the Bold button," as shown in Figure 3-1.

Figure 3-1. *Alert message displayed when a button is clicked*

In the jQuery code that applies click events to both buttons, the statement

```
$('.buttons').bind('click', function(){
```

attaches the click event to all the HTML elements of the class `buttons`. Since the text *Bold* and *Italic* is enclosed in the `span` element of the class `buttons`, the click event will be attached to both pieces of text (the shape of the button will be assigned to these pieces of text by the style rule `buttons` defined in the `style.css` file).

In the statement

```
alert('You have clicked the ' +$(this).text()+' button');
```

the `$(this).text()` will display the text contents of the HTML element on which the click event has occurred; that is, if the Bold button is pressed, `$(this).text()` will display *Bold*. Similarly, if the Italic button is clicked, it will display *Italic*. The output will be exactly same as shown in Figure 3-1.

Now let's look at how the click event works.

click()

This method binds the click event to the selected element. The click event occurs if the mouse pointer is over the element and the mouse button is pressed and released.

```
.click(handler)
.click()
```

Here `handler` is the function that contains the statement we want to execute when the specified element is clicked with the mouse.

When using the `target` attribute of the event object, we get the same output as shown in Figure 3-1. In the jQuery code, we can see that the `target` attribute of the event object is used to find out the target of the element (when the click event has occurred) and is stored in a variable `$target`. After that, via conditional statements, we check whether the element stored in the `$target` variable is of the class `bold` or the class `italic`; that is, whether the Bold button is pressed or the Italic button is pressed. Accordingly, the alert message is displayed on the screen.

One more event that is similar to the click event is the double-click event. Let's take a look at this next.

dblclick()

This method attaches the double-click event to the specified element. Double-click is the event that occurs when the mouse is over the element and is double-clicked.

```
.dblclick(handler)
.dblclick()
```

Here `handler` is the function that contains the statement we want to execute when the element is double-clicked.

In the jQuery code that uses the double-click event, the text *Bold* and *Italic* has the `dblclick()` event attached to them. When either of the buttons is double-clicked we will see the output shown in Figure 3-2.

Figure 3-2. Alert message displayed when a button is double-clicked

3-2. Triggering Events Automatically

Problem

You have a web page with two buttons that say *Bold* and *Italic* and you want the click event to trigger automatically on either button.

Solution

In this recipe, we assume there are two buttons and we want to fire an event automatically. Let us define an HTML file that contains the text *Bold* and *Italic* for the buttons that we want to create. This may appear as shown here:

```
<body>
<span class="bold buttons">Bold</span>
<span class="italic buttons">Italic</span>
</body>
```

In the external style sheet `style.css`, we write the CSS class `buttons` to give the shape of the button to the text:

```
.buttons{
width: 100px;
float: left;
text-align: center;
margin: 5px;
border: 2px solid;
font-weight: bold;
}
```

Let's write the jQuery code to make an event occur automatically; that is, to be triggered by the script instead of by the user. We may require certain events to occur automatically, like autoclick of a button or autosubmission of a form. The method provided by jQuery to trigger an event is `trigger()`. Let's make the click event trigger automatically on the Italic button. The jQuery code for doing so is as follows:

```
$(document).ready(function() {
  $('.buttons').bind('click', function(){
    alert('You have clicked the ' +$(this).text()+' button');
  });
  $('.italic').trigger('click');
});
```

How It Works

In the HTML file, the statement

```
<span class="bold buttons">Bold</span>
```

defines the text *Bold* in a `span` element of the classes `bold` and `buttons`. The class `bold` will be used for applying jQuery code to the `span` element, and the class `buttons` is for applying the styles defined in the CSS class `buttons` specified in the style sheet.

Similarly, the second statement defines the text *Italic* of the `span` element of the classes `italic` and `buttons`. The `italic` class is for applying the jQuery code and the `buttons` class is for applying the CSS class.

In the jQuery code, we have made use of the method **trigger()** to trigger an event. So, let's have a brief introduction to the method.

trigger()

This method invokes the event handler of the specified event type (passed to this method)

```
trigger(eventType)
```

where **eventType** is a string that specifies the type of the event; that is, whether it is a click, double-click, focus, etc.

The method returns a jQuery object. When we trigger the event, the code in the respective event handler will be executed. That means before using the **trigger()** method on any element, we need to confirm that it has an event handler defined.

In the jQuery code, we can see that the click event is attached to the elements of the **buttons** class; that is, to both the Bold and Italic buttons. In addition, the inline functions in the form of event handlers are also defined for them. After that, the statement

```
$('.italic').trigger('click');
```

fires the click event on the Italic button, causing its event handler to be invoked. The event handler displays an alert message that indicates the button is clicked, as shown in Figure 3-3.

Figure 3-3. *Alert message on autotriggering of a click event on the Italic button*

3-3. Disabling a Button After It Is Clicked Once

Problem

Sometimes we want an event to fire only once, or want to disable it when certain conditions are met. For example, we might want to disable the Submit button after it is has been clicked once.

Solution

In this recipe, we assume there are two buttons, and we want to disable a button after it is clicked once. Let us define an HTML file that contains the text *Bold* and *Italic* for the buttons that we want to create, which may appear as shown here:

```
<body>
<span class="bold buttons">Bold</span>
<span class="italic buttons">Italic</span>
</body>
```

In the external style sheet `style.css`, we write the CSS class `buttons` to give the shape of the button to the text. The CSS class `buttons` may have the following properties:

```
.buttons{
width: 100px;
float: left;
text-align: center;
margin: 5px;
border: 2px solid;
font-weight: bold;
}
```

Let's write the jQuery code to disable the event handlers after being clicked once. The code may be as follows:

```
$(document).ready(function() {
  $('.buttons').bind('click', function(){
    alert('You have clicked the ' +$(this).text()+' button');
    $('.buttons').unbind('click');
  });
});
```

How It Works

jQuery provides the `unbind()` method to remove the event type from the specified element. jQuery also supports namespaced events, which allow you to trigger or unbind specific groups of bound handlers without having to reference them directly.

The `unbind()` method removes the previously attached event handler from the specified element:

```
unbind(eventType, handler)
unbind(eventType)
unbind()
```

- `eventType` refers to different events, like click, double-click etc. All the event handlers attached to the specified `eventType` will be stopped from being executed.

- `handler` is the event handler to remove; it should be the same as the one passed to `bind()`.

- If you pass no arguments, all events will be removed.

In the jQuery code, we can see that the click event is bound to the buttons. Clicking on either button will display an alert message showing the text of the button selected. So, if we select the Italic button, we will get the output as shown in Figure 3-2, but after that the statement

```
$('.buttons').unbind('click');
```

unbinds the event handler (inline function) of the click event and hence clicking any button will not display any message.

3-4. Handling Mouse Events

Problem

You want to handle various mouse-related events in your application.

Solution

In this recipe, we assume there are two buttons over which we test different mouse events to take place. Let us define an HTML file that contains the text *Bold* and *Italic* for the buttons that we want to create, which may appear as shown here:

```
<body>
<span class="bold buttons">Bold</span>
<span class="italic buttons">Italic</span>
</body>
```

In the external style sheet `style.css`, we write the CSS class `buttons` to give the shape of the button to the text. The CSS class `buttons` has the following properties:

```
.buttons{
width: 100px;
float: left;
text-align: center;
margin: 5px;
border: 2px solid;
font-weight: bold;
}
```

Let's write the jQuery code to display the message when the mouse button is pressed on any of the buttons:

```
$(document).ready(function() {
  $('.buttons').bind('mousedown', function(){
    alert('The mouse button is pressed over ' +$(this).text()+' button');
  });
});
```

Responding to the Mouseup Event

The jQuery code to respond to the mouseup event may be as follows:

```
$(document).ready(function() {
  $('.buttons').mouseup(function(){
    alert('The mouse button is released over ' +$(this).text()+' button');
  });
});
```

Responding to the Mouseover Event

The jQuery code to respond to the mouseover event may be as follows:

```
$(document).ready(function() {
  $('.buttons').mouseover(function(){
    alert('The mouse is over ' +$(this).text()+' button');
  });
});
```

How It Works

In the preceding jQuery code, we have used the method `mousedown()`, so let's first have a brief introduction to this. Then we'll examine the `mouseup()`, `mouseover()`, and `mouseout()` methods.

mousedown()

This method executes the attached event handler when the mousedown event occurs on the specified element. The mousedown event means the mouse pointer is over the specified element and the mouse button is pressed.

```
.mousedown(handler)
.mousedown()
```

Here `handler` is the function that executes on occurrence of the mousedown event.

The second syntax is for invoking the `mousedown()` event manually. The following example invokes the `mousedown()` event on `button2` (the HTML element of the class `button2`) when `button1` (the HTML element of the class `button1`) is clicked:

```
$(' .button1').click(function(){
  $('.button2').mousedown();
});
```

In the jQuery code in our example, we bind the mousedown event to the HTML elements of the class `buttons`, so we may get the output as shown in Figure 3-4 when the mouse button is pressed over the Bold button.

Figure 3-4. Alert message displayed when the mouse button is pressed on the Bold button

Let's take a look at the methods of handling mouse events, one by one.

mouseup()

This method binds the mouseup event to the specified element. The mouseup event occurs when the mouse pointer is over an element and the mouse button is released.

```
.mouseup(handler)
.mouseup()
```

Here `handler` is the inline function that we want to execute on occurrence of the event. The second syntax is for invoking the mouseup event manually.

mouseover()

This method binds the mouseover event to the specified element. The mouseover event occurs when the mouse pointer enters the specified element.

```
.mouseover(handler)
.mouseover()
```

Here `handler` is the inline function that we want to execute on occurrence of the event. The second syntax is for invoking the mouseover event manually.

In the jQuery code that responds to the mouseover event, the output that we may get when the mouse pointer enters the region of the Bold button will be as shown in Figure 3-5.

Figure 3-5. Alert message displayed when the mouse pointer enters the Bold button region

mouseout()

This method binds the mouseout event to the specified element. The mouseout event occurs when the mouse pointer leaves the specified element.

```
.mouseout(handler)
.mouseout()
```

Here `handler` is the inline function that we want to execute on occurrence of the event. The second syntax is for invoking the mouseout event manually.

3-5. Finding Out Which Mouse Button Is Pressed

Problem

You have a button on the web page and you want to detect which mouse button is pressed on it: whether it is the left or right mouse button.

Solution

Let's say we have an HTML file that has the text *Click Me* (to be represented as a button) and an empty paragraph element, as shown here:

```
<body>
<span class="buttons">Click Me</span><br/><br/>
<p></p>
</body>
```

The class selector **buttons** is as given here:

```
.buttons{
width: 100px;
float: left;
text-align: center;
margin: 5px;
border: 2px solid;
font-weight: bold;
}
```

The jQuery code to detect which mouse button is pressed on the Click Me button is as follows:

```
$(document).ready(function() {
  $('.buttons').mousedown(function(event){
    if(event.button==1){
      $('p').text('Left mouse button is pressed');
    }
    else
    {
      $('p').text('Right mouse button is pressed');
    }
  });
});
```

How It Works

In the HTML file, the text *Click Me* is enclosed in a **span** element of class **buttons** so that the properties defined in the class selector **buttons** defined in the style sheet can be applied to it to give it the shape of a button. The empty paragraph element will be used to display the message showing which mouse button is pressed.

In the jQuery code, we can see that the mousedown event is attached to the element of the class **buttons**; that is, to the *Click Me* text (that is given the shape of a button). Also we know that when an event occurs, the event object is sent to the event-handling function by JavaScript. So, when any mouse button is pressed on the Click Me button, the event object will be automatically passed to the event-handling function.

We use the **button** attribute of the event object to determine which mouse button is pressed. For the left mouse button the value of the **button** attribute is **1**, and for the right mouse button the value is **2**. If the value returned by the **button** attribute of the event object is **1**, we assign the text *Left mouse button is pressed* to the paragraph element, as shown in Figure 3-6.

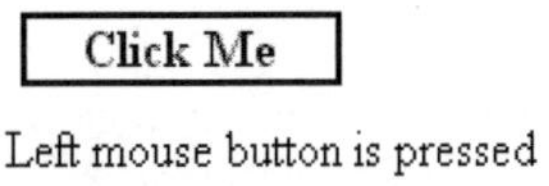

```
Click Me
```

Left mouse button is pressed

Figure 3-6. The text message displayed when the left mouse button is pressed on the Click Me button

If the value returned by the **button** attribute of the event object is not **1**, we assign the text *Right mouse button is pressed* to the paragraph element, as shown in Figure 3-7.

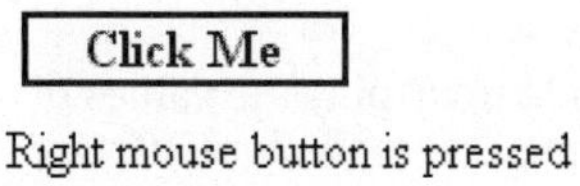

Click Me

Right mouse button is pressed

Figure 3-7. *The text message displayed when the right mouse button is pressed on the Click Me button*

3-6. Finding the Screen Coordinates of a Mouse-Button Press

Problem

You have an image on the web page and want to display the screen coordinates of the location where the mouse button is pressed on the image.

Solution

Let's make an HTML file that displays an image and an empty paragraph element, as shown here:

```
<body>
<img src="cell.jpg"/>
<p></p>
 </body>
```

The empty paragraph will be used for displaying the screen coordinates.

We will now write the jQuery code to attach the mousedown event to the image to sense if the mouse button is pressed on any part of it. The code is as shown here:

```
$(document).ready(function() {
    $('img').mousedown(function(event){
    $('p').text('Mouse is clicked at horizontal coordinate: '+event.screenX+
            ' and at vertical coordinate: '+event.screenY);
  });
});
```

How It Works

In this recipe, we use the attributes of the event object. The event object is the one that is automatically sent by JavaScript to the event-handling function when an event occurs. The event object has several properties or attributes. The two properties that we are going to use in this solution are as follows:

- screenX—Specifies the horizontal coordinate of the occurrence of the event relative to the screen origin

- screenY—Specifies the vertical coordinate of the occurrence of the event relative to the screen origin

In the event-handling function of the mousedown event, we write the code to display the values of the screenX and screenY attributes of the event object in the form of text of the paragraph element. On execution of the jQuery code, we get the output shown in Figure 3-8.

Mouse is clicked at horizontal cordinate: 122 and at vertical cordinate: 133

Figure 3-8. *The location of screen coordinates displaying where the mouse button is clicked on the image*

3-7. Highlighting Text Dynamically

Problem

You have certain text on a web page along with a button, and you want to highlight the text (by changing its background and foreground colors) when the mouse moves over the button.

Solution

The following is the HTML file that has the text *Highlight* enclosed in a span element of the class buttons, and paragraph text as shown here:

```
<body>
<span class="buttons">Highlight</span><br/><br/>
<p>Styles make the formatting job much easier and more efficient. To give an attractive look
to web sites, styles are heavily used. A person must have a good knowledge of HTML and CSS
and a bit of JavaScript.   </p>
</body>
```

On the text *Highlight*, the style rule buttons defined in the style sheet will be applied to give it the shape of a button. The style sheet has the following properties:

```
.buttons{
width: 80px;
float: left;
text-align: center;
margin: 5px;
border: 2px solid;
font-weight: bold;
}
```

To apply the styles to the text dynamically (when the mouse is moved over the text), we write the following jQuery code:

```
$(document).ready(function() {
  $('.buttons').mouseover(function(){
    $('p').css({
      'background-color':'cyan',
      'font-weight':'bold',
      'color':'blue'
    });
  });
});
```

How It Works

In this recipe, we use a technique by which the style properties defined in the style sheet are overridden and the CSS properties will be applied to the specified element(s) directly. jQuery provides us with a method called `css()` for applying CSS properties to the HTML directly. This method sets CSS properties to the specified elements directly—overriding the styles defined in the style sheet (if any). It allows us to have better control of application of styles on the individual elements as well as a collection of elements:

```
.css(property, value)
```

Here `property` is the CSS property name that we want to set and `value` can be either the property value that we want to assign to the property or it can be a function that returns the property value to set. Here's an example:

```
$('p').css('color':'blue');
```

It sets the color of the paragraph text to blue. The following uses a function that returns the height of the `img` element after incrementing it by 30; that is, it will increase the height of the `img` element by 30px:

```
$('img').css('height',function(){ return $(this).height()+30;});
```

The output of our solution will display the button and the paragraph text as shown in Figure 3-9.

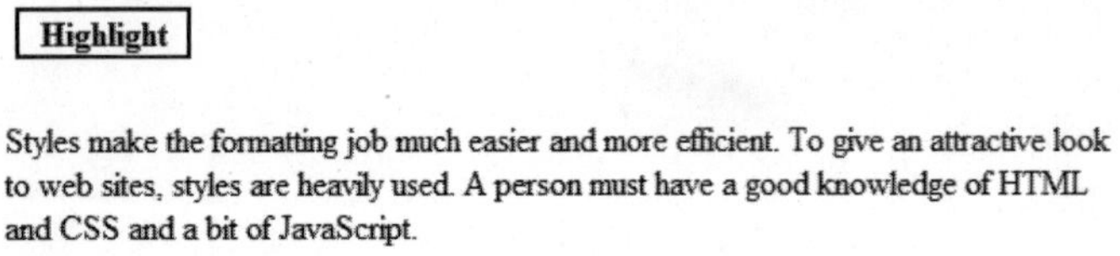

Highlight

Styles make the formatting job much easier and more efficient. To give an attractive look
to web sites, styles are heavily used. A person must have a good knowledge of HTML
and CSS and a bit of JavaScript.

Figure 3-9. The button and the paragraph text

We can see in the jQuery code that `css()` defines several properties, like the `background-color`
property to apply cyan as the background of the paragraph text, `font-weight` to make the text appear in
bold, and `color` to change the foreground color of the paragraph text to blue. The properties in the `css()`
method will be applied to the paragraph text when the mouse is moved over the button and may appear
as shown in Figure 3-10 (despite this being in black and white, you can see the general idea).

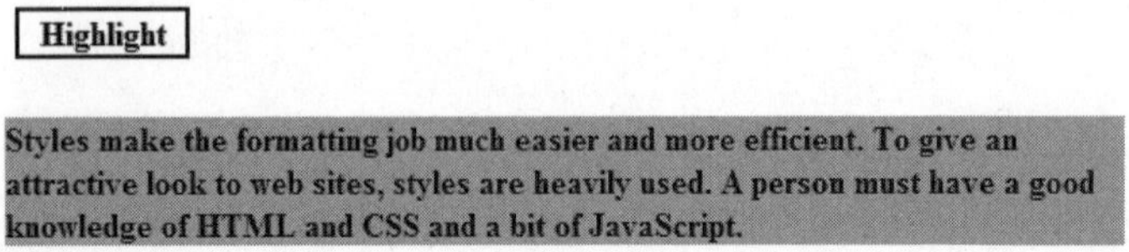

Highlight

**Styles make the formatting job much easier and more efficient. To give an
attractive look to web sites, styles are heavily used. A person must have a good
knowledge of HTML and CSS and a bit of JavaScript.**

Figure 3-10. The paragraph text gets highlighted when the mouse is moved over the button

3-8. Making an Image Bright and Blurred with Mouse Movements

Problem

Imagine you have an image displayed on your web page along with a button. The image is initially
blurred.You want to make it so that when the mouse is moved over the button, the image becomes
bright and when the mouse is moved away from the button, the image again becomes blurred. Also, you
want to increase the height and width of the image when you click on the button.

Solution

In this recipe we will be making use of the different mouse event-handling methods you saw in Recipe 3-
4. So, if you don't know the workings of the different mouse event methods, like `mouseover()`,
`mouseout()`, `mousedown()`, etc., go through Recipe 3-4 before you attempt to work through this recipe.

Let's assume an HTML file that displays a button and an image, as shown here:

```
<body>
<span class="buttons">Bright Image</span>
<img src="cell.jpg"/>
</body>
```

The text *Bright Image* is enclosed within a span element of the class buttons so that the style rule buttons defined in the external style sheet is applied to the text to give it the shape of a button.

```
.buttons{
width: 100px;
float: left;
text-align: center;
margin: 5px;
border: 2px solid;
font-weight: bold;
}
```

The jQuery code to apply effects to the image is as follows:

```
$(document).ready(function() {
  $('img').css('opacity',0.4);

  $('.buttons').bind('mouseover', function(){
    $('img').css('opacity',1.0);
  });

  $('.buttons').bind('mouseout', function(){
    $('img').css('opacity',0.4);
  });

  $('.buttons').bind('mousedown', function(){
    $('img').css('width',function(){ return $(this).width()+50;});
    $('img').css('height',function(){ return $(this).height()+30;});
  });
});
```

How It Works

In this solution, we will be using the opacity CSS property. The value of the opacity property ranges from 0 (transparent) to 1 (opaque) or from 0% to 100%.
Let's examine the code line by line:

```
$('img').css('opacity',0.4);
```

This line makes the image blur at the beginning and when the mouse is moved away from the button.

```
$('img').css('opacity',1.0);
```

This makes the image bright (opaque) when the mouse is over the Bright Image button.

```
$('img').css('width',function(){ return $(this).width()+50;});
```

This increases the width of the image by 50px when the mouse is pressed on the Bright Image button.

```
$('img').css('height',function(){ return $(this).height()+30;});
```

This increases the height of the image by 30px when the mouse is pressed on the Bright Image button.

The image appears blurred initially when the mouse is away from the Bright Image button, as shown in Figure 3-11.

Figure 3-11. The button and a blurred image appear when mouse is away from the button

The image becomes bright—that is, opaque—when the mouse pointer is moved over the Bright Image button, as shown in Figure 3-12.

Figure 3-12. The image becomes bright (opaque) when the mouse is moved over the the Bright Image button.

The width and height of the image are increased by 50 and 30 pixels, respectively, when the mouse button is pressed on the Bright Image button, as shown in Figure 3-13.

Figure 3-13. The height and width of the image increase when the Bright Image button is clicked.

3-9. Finding When an Element Gains and Loses Focus

Problem

You have several text fields in a web page and you want to know when a specified field gets and loses the focus.

Solution

Let's make an HTML file consisting of two text fields—**name** and **age**—as shown here:

```
<body>
Name: <input class="name" type="text" /><br>
Age: <input class="age" type="text" />
</body>
```

The jQuery code to deal with the focus event on the **name** text field is as shown here:

```
$(document).ready(function() {
  $('.name').focus(function(){
    alert('The focus currently is on name field');
  });
});
```

Firing an Event on Losing Focus

The jQuery code to fire an event when the name text field loses the focus is as shown here:

```
$(document).ready(function() {
  $('.name').blur(function(){
    alert('The focus is lost from name field');
  });
});
```

How It Works

In the jQuery code, we will make use of the focus() method to know when the element gets the focus. Let's have a look at how this works.

focus()

This method binds the focus event to the specified element. It contains a function that is fired when the specified element gains the focus:

`.focus(handler)`

Here handler is a function that contains the statements to be executed when the specified element gains the focus, either via the pointing device or via tab navigation.

We can see that the focus() method is bound to the HTML element of the class name and, from the HTML code, we can see that the text field to be used for inserting the name is assigned the class name. That is, the focus event will be fired when the cursor enters the name text field. The focus() method has an inline method attached that displays the alert message *The focus currently is on name field*, as shown in Figure 3-14.

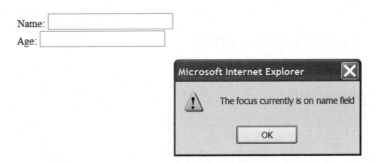

Figure 3-14. Alert message displayed when the name text field gains focus

The method to raise an event when the element loses the focus is called blur(). Let's look at what blur() does.

blur()

This is the event that is fired when the specified element loses the focus. It has an attached event handler that is executed when the focus is moved away from the selected element. The focus can be lost from the element when the user presses the Tab key or clicks the mouse elsewhere on the page.

`.blur(handler)`

Here `handler` is a function containing the statements to be executed when the focus is lost from the specified element.

We can see in the jQuery code that this fires an event on losing focus so that the `blur()` method is attached to the `name` text field, and attached to that is an inline function that will be invoked when the focus is lost from the `name` text field. The inline function will display the alert message *The focus is lost from name field*, as shown in Figure 3-15.

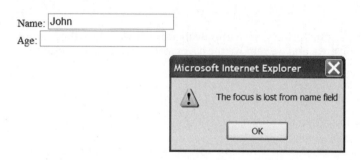

Figure 3-15. Alert message displayed when the focus is lost from the name text field

3-10. Applying Hover Effects on Buttons

Problem

Applying a hover effect means changing the style of an HTML element (such as the shape or color of buttons or images) when the mouse is moved over it. You want the same effect on a few buttons.

Solution

To apply hover effect on buttons, we need to make some text for our HTML file to get the shape of the button. So we will make use of the following HTML file:

```
<body>
<span class="bold buttons">Bold</span>
<span class="italic buttons">Italic</span>
</body>
```

In the external style sheet we write the CSS class **buttons** to give the shape of a button to the text and a class **hover** to apply properties when the buttons are hovered over (that is, when the mouse pointer moves over them). The style sheet file may appear as shown here:

```
.buttons{
width: 100px;
float: left;
text-align: center;
margin: 5px;
border: 2px solid;
font-weight: bold;
}
.hover{
cursor: crosshair;
color: blue;
background-color:cyan
}
```

Let's write the code to add a hover event to the buttons. We apply the **hover** style rule to the button when the mouse pointer enters the button area, and we remove the **hover** style rule when the mouse pointer leaves the button area:

```
$(document).ready(function() {
  $('.buttons').hover(
    function(){
      $(this).addClass('hover');
    },
    function(){
      $(this).removeClass('hover');
    }
  );
});
```

How It Works

The **hover()** method attaches two event handlers to the specified element. One event handler fires when the mouse pointer enters the element, and another handler fires when the mouse pointer leaves the element.

```
.hover(handler1, handler2)
```

handler1 is a function that contains the statements we want to execute when the mouse enters the specified element, and **handler2** is the function that contains statements we want to execute when the mouse leaves the specified element. So, both functions combine to give a hover effect.

In the jQuery code, the selector **$('.buttons')** selects all the elements in the document that have the class name **buttons** and attaches the **hover()** method to them. The CSS class **hover** is applied when the mouse is in the element that has a class of **buttons**, and the hover class is removed from the element when the mouse comes out of that element.

Initially, the buttons may appear as shown in Figure 3-16.

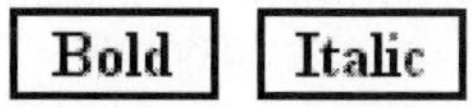

Figure 3-16. Applying a hover style to the buttons class

When the mouse enters the HTML element of class `buttons`, the `hover` class is applied to it and it may appear as shown in Figure 3-17.

Bold   Italic

Figure 3-17. The button changing color when the mouse is moved over it

The `hover` class will be removed from the buttons as the mouse pointer is moved away, and they will appear as normal buttons.

3-11. Toggling the Application of a CSS Class

Problem

When an event occurs on an element, you want to apply the style properties defined in a CSS class on it, and when the same event occurs on the same element, you want to remove the CSS class from the element. That is, you want to toggle the application of the CSS class.

Solution

Let's assume that we have an HTML file that has two pieces of text, *Bold* and *Italic*, enclosed in a `span` of the class `buttons` to apply the class selector `buttons`, which gives the text the button shape. The HTML file appears as shown here:

```
<body>
<span class="bold buttons">Bold</span>
<span class="italic buttons">Italic</span>
</body>
```

The class `buttons` is defined in the following style sheet. It also contains the style rule `hover` that contains the style properties we want to apply and remove with each occurrence of the event.

```
.buttons{
width: 100px;
float: left;
text-align: center;
margin: 5px;
```

```
border: 2px solid;
font-weight: bold;
}

.hover{
cursor: crosshair;
color: blue ;
background-color:cyan
}
```

Now we need to write the jQuery code for using the `toggleClass()` method to toggle the CSS class:

```
$(document).ready(function() {
  $('.buttons').click(function(){
    $(this).toggleClass('hover');
  });
});
```

How It Works

We use the `toggleClass()` method for applying **hover** class to and removing the **hover** class from the buttons. Let's have a look at this first.

toggleClass()

This method removes the class if it is already applied to the selected element and applies the class if it is not already applied to the element.

`.toggleClass(class)`

Here `class` is the class that we want to apply (if it is not already applied) and remove (if it is already applied) on the selected element.

We can see in the jQuery code that we have used `toggleClass()` to apply and remove the CSS class **hover** from the buttons with the occurrence of the click event. That is, when the click event occurs for the first time on a button, the style properties present in the **hover** class will be applied to the button, changing its background color to cyan and its foreground color to blue, as shown in Figure 3-17. When the button is clicked again—that is, when the click event occurs again on the same button—the CSS class **hover** will be removed from the button, giving it the same appearance as it had at the beginning (shown in Figure 3-16).

We can have the same output on application of another method, known as `toggle()`.

toggle()

This method attaches two event-handling functions to the selected element. The first event-handling function is executed with every even occurrence of the event, and the second event-handling function is executed with every odd occurrence of the event, with the count starting at zero. In other words, the first time the event occurs on the element, the first event-handling function will be executed (because the count starts at zero) and when the event occurs for the second time on the element, the second event-handling function will be executed—that is, with every subsequent event, the event-handling functions will cycle.

```
.toggle(handler1, handler2)
```

We can have the same effect of application and removal of the **hover** CSS class (with every click event) as we had in the preceding jQuery code by using the **toggle()** method. Let's have a look at the following jQuery code:

```
$(document).ready(function() {
  $('.buttons').toggle(
    function(){
      $(this).addClass('hover');
    },
    function(){
      $(this).removeClass('hover');
    }
  );
});
```

We can see that in the **toggle()** method, we have used two event-handling functions; the first one applies the **hover** CSS class to the elements of the **buttons** class (that is, on the Bold and Italic buttons), and the second one removes the CSS class from the buttons. Hence, when we click on either button, the **hover** class will be applied to it, changing its background and foreground colors as shown in Figure 3-17. When the click event occurs on the same button again, the **hover** class will be removed from it, making it appear as a simple button (without any foreground or background color applied) as it was at the beginning, as shown in Figure 3-16.

3-12. Creating Image-Based Rollovers

Problem

You want to create an image-based rollover. Image rollovers are those that change shape when the mouse is moved over an image that designates a hyperlink to some web site. The image also changes if it is clicked once, to designate that it has already been visited.

Solution

Let's make an HTML file that contains a hyperlink element:

```
<body>
<a href="abc.com"><span class="roll"></span></a>
</body>
```

In the style sheet we will write style rules called **link**, **hover**, and **active**. The style sheet also contains a type selector **img**, the properties of which will be automatically applied to the **img** element without using jQuery code. The style sheet file may appear as shown here:

```
.link{
display:block;
width:170px;
height:55px;
background-image:url(btn1.bmp);
background-repeat:no-repeat;
background-position: top left;
}

.hover{
display:block;
width:200px;
height:70px;
background-image:url(btn2.bmp);
background-repeat:no-repeat;
background-position: top left;
}

.active{
display:block;
width:170px;
height:55px;
background-image:url(btn3.bmp);
background-repeat:no-repeat;
background-position: top left;
}

img{
border:0;
}
```

The jQuery code to apply the style rules defined in the style sheet to the empty **span** element of the class **roll** is as shown here:

```
$(document).ready(function() {
  $('.roll').addClass('link');
  $('.roll').hover(
    function(){
      $(this).addClass('hover');
    },
    function(){
      $(this).removeClass('hover');
    }
  );
```

```
  $('.roll').click(function(event){
    $(this).addClass('active');
    event.preventDefault();
  });
});
```

How It Works

The preceding HTML file contains a span element of the class roll, which will be filled with images through style rules and jQuery code. We will be using three images in this solution: btn1.bmp, btn2.bmp, and btn3.bmp, shown in Figure 3-18 to 3-20.

In the style sheet, the style rule link contains the properties that will be applied to the image when the web page is loaded. It assigns the width and height of 130px and 35px, respectively, to the image. Also the image btn1.bmp is loaded at the background and the value of the background-repeat property is set to no-repeat so as to avoid repetition of the image and make it appear only once.

Since we want the button to become larger when the mouse pointer is moved over it, the hover style rule contains the second image: btn2.bmp (shown in Figure 3-18). The rest of the properties in this style rule are the same as those in the link style rule.

The third style rule designates the image when the link is visited once, so we use the image named btn3.bmp. The only change between the two images btn1.bmp and btn3.bmp is in the color of the button text. The color of the text on the button in btn3.bmp is set to maroon to represent that its link has been visited.

The style sheet also contains a type selector img that has a single property border with its value set to zero to remove the border from the three images that will be displayed.

In the jQuery code, the statement

```
$('.roll').addClass('link');
```

will apply the link style rule to the span element, making the image in btn1.bmp appear on the screen.

The statements

```
$('.roll').hover(
  function(){
    $(this).addClass('hover');
  },
  function(){
    $(this).removeClass('hover');
  }
);
```

add the hover event to the span element, with two inline functions attached to it. The first function applies the style rule hover to the span element (when the mouse pointer is moved over the image), making btn2.bmp (the enlarged image) appear in place of btn1.bmp. The btn1.bmp image will be hidden by the image in btn2.bmp because the position of the images is set to top left via the background-position property. The second inline function (applied when the mouse pointer is moved away from the image) removes the style rule hover from the image, making it appear as it was previously—that is, just like btn1.bmp.

The statement

```
$(this).addClass('active');
```

applies the property defined in the **active** style rule to the image, setting the background image **btn3.bmp** to appear. This image has the button text set to maroon to make it appear different from the initial image, so as to show that it has been visited already.

The statement

```
event.preventDefault();
```

prevents the browser from navigating to the hyperlinked web site. That is, it makes the hyperlink ignore its default action (which is navigating to the linked web site). As a result, we remain at the same web page even after clicking the image.

Initially the image may appear as shown in Figure 3-18.

Figure 3-18. The usual button that appears in default state

When the mouse pointer is moved over the image, the image becomes enlarged, as shown in Figure 3-19.

Figure 3-19. The button in enlarged state when the mouse moves over it

The image changes if we click on the image link, as shown in Figure 3-20.

Figure 3-20. The color of the button text changes in active state (when it is clicked).

3-13. Adding and Removing Text in Response to Events

Problem

You have two buttons on the web page with the text *Add* and *Remove*, respectively. You want to have certain text be added to the web page when the user selects the Add button, and have the added text removed when the user selects the Remove button.

Solution

Let's begin with making an HTML file that contains the text *Add* and *Remove* enclosed in the span element of class buttons so that the class selector buttons defined in the style sheet can be applied to them:

```
<body>
<span class="add buttons">Add</span>
<span class="remove buttons">Remove</span><br><br>
<div></div>
</body>
```

The style sheet file may appear as shown here:

```
.buttons{
width: 80px;
float: left;
text-align: center;
margin: 5px;
border: 2px solid;
font-weight: bold;
}
```

Following is the jQuery code to add click events to both the buttons along with their inline functions to add and remove text:

```
$(document).ready(function() {
  $('.add').click(function(){
    $('div').prepend('<p>Styles make the formatting job much easier and more efficient. To
give
an attractive look to web sites, styles are heavily used. A person must have a good
knowledge of HTML and CSS and a bit of JavaScript.  </p>');
  });

  $('.remove').click(function(){
    $('p').remove();
  });
});
```

How It Works

We see that the HTML file has an empty `div` element. To this `div` element we will be adding a paragraph element (with some text in it) when the Add button is clicked. Also the newly added paragraph element will be removed from the `div` element when the Remove button is clicked. In order to add the paragraph we use the `prepend()` method that you saw in Chapter 1. To remove the paragraph element, we will be using the `remove()` method.

The `remove()` method removes the set of selected elements from the DOM and returns a JQuery object. It also removes all event handlers and internally cached data. We don't need to pass any parameter with this method.

In the jQuery code, the statement

```
$('div').prepend('<p>Styles...</p>');
```

adds the paragraph element at the beginning of the `div` element when the Add button is clicked, while the statement

```
$('p').remove();
```

accesses the paragraph element(s) in the HTML file and removes them. Since there is only a single paragraph element in the HTML file (added via the Add button), it will be removed when the Remove button is clicked.

On execution of the preceding jQuery code, we will initially get two buttons displayed with the text *Add* and *Remove* on them, as shown in Figure 3-21.

Figure 3-21. Initial two buttons for adding and removing text

On selecting the Add button, the paragraph element with some text appears, as shown in Figure 3-22.

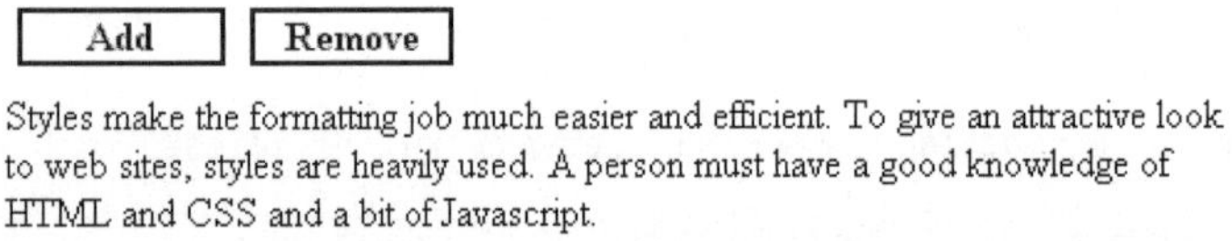

Add   Remove

Styles make the formatting job much easier and efficient. To give an attractive look to web sites, styles are heavily used. A person must have a good knowledge of HTML and CSS and a bit of Javascript.

Figure 3-22. The text appears on selecting the Add button.

On selecting the Remove button, the text disappears.

3-14. Applying Styles in Response to Events

Problem

You have two buttons on the web page, with the text Bold and Italic on them, respectively. Your page also has some text. You want it to work such that when the Bold button is pressed, the text turns bold and when the Italic button is pressed, the text turns italic. Along with all this, you also want a hover effect on the buttons (to change the background and foreground colors of the buttons when the mouse pointer is moved over the buttons).

Solution

Let's make an HTML file that has two buttons and some text, as shown here:

```
<body>
<span class="buttons" id="boldbutton">Bold</span>
<span class="buttons" id="italicbutton">Italic</span><br/><br/>
<div id="info">Creating Rich Internet Applications<br/>
jQuery is an open source project<br/>
Manipulating DOM using jQuery<br/>
</div>
</body>
```

The contents of the style sheet may appear as follows:

```
.buttons{
width: 80px;
float: left;
text-align: center;
margin: 5px;
border: 2px solid;
font-weight: bold;
}

.hover{
cursor: crosshair;
color: blue ;
background-color:cyan
}

.boldmatter
{
   font-weight: bold;
}
```

```
.italicmatter
{
  font-style: italic;
}
```

The jQuery code to make the buttons active is as follows:

```
$(document).ready(function() {
  $('.buttons').hover(
    function(){
      $(this).addClass('hover');
    },
    function(){
      $(this).removeClass('hover');
    }
  );

  $('#boldbutton').bind('click', function(){
    $('#info').removeClass('italicmatter');
    $('#info').addClass('boldmatter');
  });

  $('#italicbutton').bind('click', function(){
    $('#info').removeClass('boldmatter');
    $('#info').addClass('italicmatter');
  });
});
```

How It Works

The span elements are assigned the ids boldbutton and italicbutton respectively, so as to make it possible to apply the styles to convert the text into bold or italic when the appropriate button is clicked. The text to which we will be applying styles, to make it bold or italic, is given an identification by assigning it an id info. The div element consists of three lines of text.

In the jQuery code, we start by selecting all the elements in the document that have a class of buttons, and to those elements the class specified via the hover() method is applied. With the help of two functions, the hover() method applies the CSS class hover when the mouse enters those elements and removes it when the mouse comes out of those elements (that is, the elements that have a class of buttons).

The bind() method allows us to specify any JavaScript event and attach a function (to apply some class) to any element. Using this technique, we select the elements with id boldbutton and bind the click event to it—that is, when a click event occurs on such an element, the function is executed that selects the element with id info (the body of the document other than the buttons), removes the CSS class italicmatter, and applies the class boldmatter to make the selected matter (text) bold.

The final block selects the elements with the id italicbutton and uses bind() to bind the click event to it. So, when anybody clicks on such an element, the function is executed that selects the element with an id info in the document, removes the CSS class boldmatter, and applies the class italicmatter.

Initially, the output may be as shown in Figure 3-23.

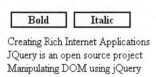

Creating Rich Internet Applications
JQuery is an open source project
Manipulating DOM using jQuery

Figure 3-23. Two buttons: Bold and Italic, with some matter

When we click on the Bold button, the hover effect appears on the button and the body of the document turns bold, as shown in Figure 3-24.

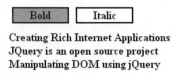

Creating Rich Internet Applications
JQuery is an open source project
Manipulating DOM using jQuery

Figure 3-24. When the mouse is moved over the Bold button, the hover style is applied to it and the bold style is applied to the body of the document

Similarly, when the Italic button is clicked, the hover effect will appear on it and the body of the document will turn italic.

3-15. Displaying Word Balloons

Problem

You have two buttons on the web page, with the text *Bold* and *Italic* on them, respectively. You want to create a word-balloon effect when either of the buttons is clicked. If the Bold button is clicked, you want the text *This is Bold menu* to appear in the word balloon (shown later in Figure 3-27) and if the Italic button is clicked, you want the text *This is Italic menu* to appear in the word balloon (shown later in Figure 3-28).

Solution

We use the following HTML file to display two buttons, Bold and Italic, as was shown in Figure 3-1:

```
<body>
<span class="bold buttons">Bold</span>
<span class="italic buttons">Italic</span>
</body>
```

We will create a style sheet that will contain the class selector **buttons** to apply the properties to the **span** elements so as to give them the shape of the buttons. Besides this, the style sheet also contains two style rules, **hover** and **showtip,** to give the hover effect on the buttons and to display the text in the word balloons. The style sheet file may appear as shown here:

```
.buttons{
width: 150px;
float: left;
text-align: center;
color:#000;
background-color:red;
margin: 5px;
font-weight: bold;
}

.hover{
color:red;
background:url(balloon.jpg);
background-repeat:no-repeat;
background-position:bottom;
}

.showtip{
display:block;
margin:25px;
}
```

The jQuery code to apply the style rules to the buttons is as shown here:

```
$(document).ready(function() {
  $('.buttons').hover(
    function(event){
      $(this).addClass('hover');
      var $txt=$(this).text();
      $('<span class="showtip"> This is '+$txt+' menu </span>').appendTo($(this));
    },
    function(){
      $(this).removeClass('hover');
      $('.showtip').remove();
    }
  );
});
```

How It Works

The image file **balloon.jpg** used in the aforementioned style sheet contains the image shown in Figure 3-25.

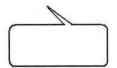

Figure 3-25. The balloon image in the file balloon.jpg

In the style sheet, we can see the `hover` style rule contains the following properties:

- `color`—Sets the foreground color of the button's text to red
- `background`—Displays the word balloon image as the background
- `background-repeat`—Set to `no-repeat` to make the word balloon image appear only once
- `background-position`—Makes the word balloon image appear at the bottom

In the style sheet file, the `showtip` style rule contains the `display` property with its value set to `block` so as to treat the text (that will be displayed in the word balloon) as a block element having white space at the beginning and at the end. It also contains the `margin` property that is set to 25px for setting the gap between the text and the balloon boundaries.

In the jQuery code, we can see that the hover event is assigned to the class `buttons`—that is, to both the buttons. So, when the mouse pointer enters either of the buttons, first the properties defined in the style rule `hover` will be applied, creating a blank word balloon on the screen. Second, the text of the button in question will be stored in the variable `$txt`. Also a `span` element will be appended before the button.

The `span` element is assigned the class `showtip` (so that the properties defined in the class selector `showtip` can be automatically applied to its text). The text content of the `span` element is set to

```
"This is $txt menu"
```

where `$txt` contains the text of the button over which the mouse pointer is hovering, hence making the desired text appear inside the word balloon. The second inline function of the hover event removes the properties defined in both the style rules `hover` and `showtip`.

Initially, the buttons appear as shown in Figure 3-26.

Bold   Italic

Figure 3-26. The Bold and Italic buttons when neither is selected

When the mouse pointer moves over the Bold button, the styles will be applied to change the foreground and background color of the button and to display the word balloon along with the text *This is Bold menu*, as shown in Figure 3-27.

81

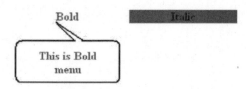

Figure 3-27. The text This is Bold menu appears in a word balloon when the Bold button is moused over.

Similarly, when the mouse pointer is moved over the Italic button, its foreground and background color will be changed and the word balloon with the text *This is Italic menu* will appear, as shown in Figure 3-28.

Figure 3-28. The text This is Italic menu appears in a word balloon when the Italic button is moused over.

3-16. Creating "Return to Top" Links

Problem

You have a web page with lots of text. After every block of text, you want to display a link that says *Return to Top*, which should navigate the user to the beginning of the web page.

Solution

Let's make an HTML file that contains a few blocks of text in the form of paragraph elements, as shown here:

```
<body>
<p>Styles make the formatting job much easier and more efficient.
To give an attractive look to web sites, styles are heavily used.
JQuery is a powerful JavaScript library that allows us to add dynamic elements to our web
sites. Not only it is easy to learn, but it's easy to implement too.</p>
<p> A person must have a good knowledge of HTML and CSS and a bit of JavaScript. jQuery is
an open source project that provides a wide range of features with cross-platform
compatibility</p>
</body>
```

The jQuery code to create a hyperlink with the text *Return to top* after every paragraph element and make that text navigate to the beginning of the web page is shown here:

```
$(document).ready(function() {
  $('<a href="#topofpage">Return to top</a>').insertAfter('p');
  $('<a id="topofpage" name="topofpage"></a>').prependTo('body');
});
```

How It Works

The statement

```
$('<a href="#topofpage">Return to top</a>').insertAfter('p');
```

adds a hyperlink with the text *Return to top* after every paragraph element of the HTML file, and when the link is selected by the user, he will be navigated to the element of id topofpage.

The statement

```
$('<a id="topofpage" name="topofpage"></a>').prependTo('body');
```

adds an anchor element with name and id assigned to it as topofpage before the body of the HTML file. In other words, an anchor element of id topofpage is created at the beginning of the web page.

The output that we may get on execution of the preceding jQuery code is as shown in Figure 3-29.

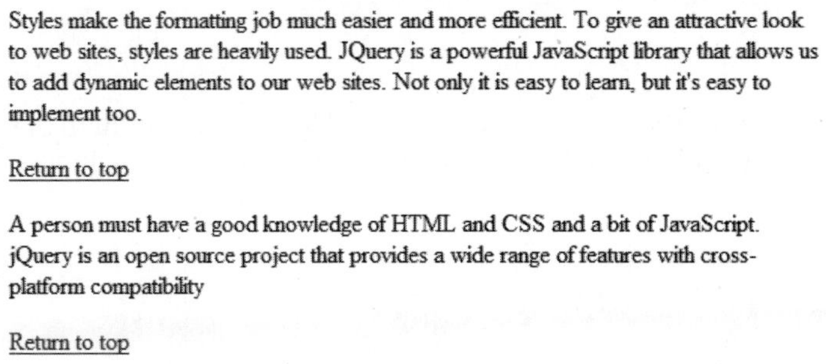

Styles make the formatting job much easier and more efficient. To give an attractive look to web sites, styles are heavily used. JQuery is a powerful JavaScript library that allows us to add dynamic elements to our web sites. Not only it is easy to learn, but it's easy to implement too.

Return to top

A person must have a good knowledge of HTML and CSS and a bit of JavaScript. jQuery is an open source project that provides a wide range of features with cross-platform compatibility

Return to top

Figure 3-29. The text Return to top appears after every paragraph.

If we click any of the "Return to top" links we will be navigated to the beginning of the web page.

3-17. Offering "Read More..." links

Problem

You have a large chunk of text to display, but to keep the screen neat you want to display just a few lines of it along with a link to "Read More..." attached to it. When the user selects this link, the rest of the text (which was hidden) is displayed.

Solution

Let's make an HTML file with two **div** elements and a **span** element of the class **readmore** in between them, as shown here:

```
<body>
<div>
Styles make the formatting job much easier and more efficient.
</div>
<span class="readmore">Read More...</span>
<div class="message">
To give an attractive look to web sites, styles are heavily used.
JQuery is a powerful JavaScript library that allows us to add dynamic elements to our web
sites. Not only it is easy to learn, but it's easy to implement too. A person must have a
good knowledge of HTML and CSS and a bit of JavaScript. jQuery is an open source project
that provides a wide range of features with cross-platform compatibility.
</div>
</body>
```

Let's write the jQuery code to make the lower **div** element invisible and attach the click event to the *Read More...* text along with an inline function that makes the lower **div** element visible on occurrence of the click event:

```
$(document).ready(function() {
  $('.message').hide();
  $('span.readmore').click(function(){
    $('.message').show('slow');
    $(this).hide();
  });
});
```

How It Works

In the HTML file, the text of the upper **div** element will be displayed and the text of the **div** element of the class message (the lower **div** element) will be hidden initially when the web page is loaded. Also, immediately after the text of the upper **div** element, we will display the text *Read More...* that is enclosed in the **span** element of the class **readmore** so that a click event can be applied to it.

We will make the text of the lower **div** element of the class message visible only when the user clicks at the text: *Read More...*.

In the jQuery code, we have used two methods, `show()` and `hide()`, to make text visible and invisible.

■ **Note** We can use `toggle()` to make the matching element visible if it is hidden and vice versa on alternate clicks.

`show()` makes the specified hidden element visible.

```
.show(speed, callback)
```

Here `speed` defines the duration of the animation effect—that is, whether the element has to be displayed immediately or slowly. The speed can be defined in terms of milliseconds or as one of the predefined strings: `slow`, `normal`, or `fast` (which indicate speed values of 600, 400, and 200 milliseconds, respectively). That is, the speed defines how long the animation will run. If it is omitted, the default speed `normal` is used. `callback` is the function that is called when the animation is complete. `hide()` makes the specified element invisible:

```
.hide(speed, callback)
```

`speed` and `callback` have the same meanings here as they did with `show()`.

In our jQuery code, the statement

```
$('.message').hide();
```

makes the `div` element of the class `message` invisible initially (that is, only half the text of the upper `div` element will be displayed), and the statement

```
$('span.readmore').click(function(){
```

attaches the click event to the `span` element of class `readmore` (that is, to the text *Read More...*).
The statement

```
$('.message').show('slow');
```

makes the `div` element of class A visible when the *Read More...* text is clicked, hence displaying the hidden text. The statement

```
$(this).hide();
```

hides the text message *Read More...*, as it is no longer required.

Initially, only half the text is displayed along with a text message *Read More...* at the bottom, as shown in Figure 3-30.

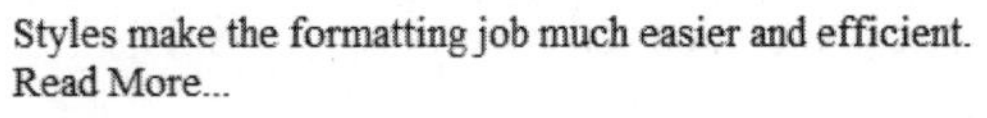

Styles make the formatting job much easier and efficient.
Read More...

Figure 3-30. *The upper half of the text displayed with the Read More... link*

When the text *Read More...* is selected, the hidden text is also displayed, as shown in Figure 3-31.

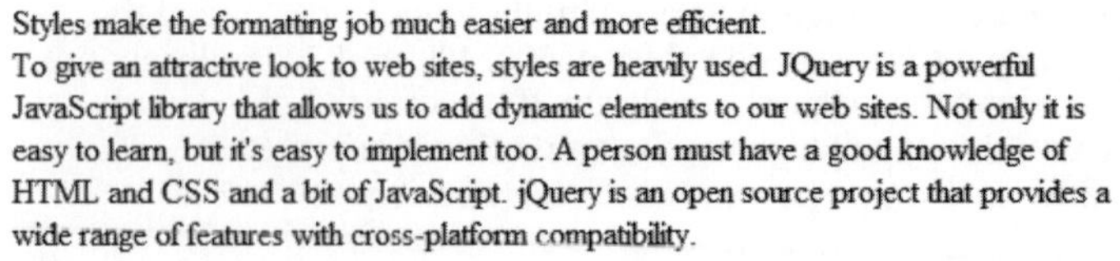

Styles make the formatting job much easier and more efficient.
To give an attractive look to web sites, styles are heavily used. JQuery is a powerful
JavaScript library that allows us to add dynamic elements to our web sites. Not only it is
easy to learn, but it's easy to implement too. A person must have a good knowledge of
HTML and CSS and a bit of JavaScript. jQuery is an open source project that provides a
wide range of features with cross-platform compatibility.

Figure 3-31. *The complete text displayed after selecting the Read More... link*

Reading Less

We can also slightly modify the jQuery code to convert the *Read More...* text to *Read Less...* on displaying the hidden text. Also, we can make the displayed text get back to hidden mode when the *Read Less...* text is selected. The jQuery code for doing so may be as shown here:

```
$(document).ready(function() {
  $('.message').hide();
  $('span.readmore').toggle(function(){
    $('.message').show('slow');
    $(this).text("Read Less…");
  },
  function(){
    $('.message').hide('slow');
    $(this).text("Read More…");
  });
});
```

We can see that in the preceding jQuery code, the `toggle()` method is used to apply the respective event-handling function on each alternate click to the `span` element of the class `readmore`. The first event-handling function will display the hidden text and convert the text *Read More...* to *Read Less....* The second event-handling function hides the displayed text and converts the text again to *Read More....*

Applying an Animation Effect

In the preceding example, on selecting the text *Read More...* the hidden text is displayed. We can also make the hidden text appear slowly, along with an animation effect to make it more attractive. The method to make the hidden text visible with an animation effect is known as `fadeIn()` and the method to make the visible text slowly invisible is known as `fadeOut()`.

■ **Note** The `fadeIn()` and `fadeOut()` methods work by adjusting the opacity of the selected elements.

`fadeIn()` displays the selected elements by converting them to be opaque.

`.fadeIn(speed, callback)`

`speed` decides the duration of the animation. It can be specified in terms of predefined strings `fast`, `normal`, and `slow` or in milliseconds. The higher the number of milliseconds, the longer the animation takes. The default speed is `normal`.

`callback` is the function that is fired on completion of the animation.

`fadeOut()` is for making the selected element invisible by fading it out.

`.fadeOut(speed, callback)`

`speed` and `callback` have the same meaning here as for `fadeIn()`.

The jQuery code to make the hidden text (the `div` element of the class message) appear slowly is shown here:

```
$(document).ready(function() {
  $('.message').hide();
  $('span.readmore').click(function(){
    $('.message').fadeIn('slow');
    $(this).hide();
  });
});
```

3-18. Displaying Text with an Animation Effect

Problem

You have three buttons on the web page, namely Books, Movies, and Music. You want to display the appropriate text when one of these buttons is clicked. You want the text that is displayed on clicking the button to have an animation effect.

Solution

Let's make an HTML file that has three buttons—Books, Movies, and Music—and three paragraphs with class names assigned as books, movies, and music, respectively. These paragraphs contain the text to be displayed when each button is clicked. Initially, the text of these paragraphs will be kept invisible and will be displayed with an animation effect only when its button is clicked. The HTML file appears as shown here:

```
<body>
<span class="buttons" id="booksbutton"> Books </span>
<span class="buttons" id="moviesbutton"> Movies  </span>
<span class="buttons" id="musicbutton"> Music </span><br><br>
<p class="books">Books on a range of different subjects available at reasonable prices.
Ranging from web development, programming languages, and text books, all are available at
heavy discount. Shipping is free. Also available in stock are popular magazines, e-books,
and tutorial CDs at affordable prices.</p>
<p class="movies">Find new movie reviews & the latest Hollywood movie news. Includes new
movie trailers, latest Hollywood releases, movie showtimes, entertainment news, celebrity
interviews etc. Also find Hollywood actresses, actors, videos, biographies, filmography,
photos, wallpaper, music, jokes, and live TV channels at your doorstep.</p>
<p class="music">Find music videos, internet radio, music downloads and all the latest music
news and information. We have a large collection of music and songs classified by type,
language, and region. All downloads are streamed through RealAudio. You can also watch free
music videos, tune in to AOL Radio, and search for your favorite music artists.</p>
</body>
</body>
```

The contents of the style sheet are as follows:

```
.buttons{
width: 100px;
float: left;
text-align: center;
margin: 5px;
border: 2px solid;
font-weight: bold;
}
```

Following is the jQuery code to hide the paragraph text initially and display the contents of the paragraph with an animation effect when its button is clicked:

```
$(document).ready(function() {
  $('.books').hide();
  $('.movies').hide();
  $('.music').hide();

  $('#booksbutton').click(function(){
    $('.books').show('slow');
    $('.movies').hide();
    $('.music').hide();
  });
```

```
$('#moviesbutton').click(function(){
  $('.movies').show('slow');
  $('.books').hide();
  $('.music').hide();
});

$('#musicbutton').click(function(){
  $('.music').show('slow');
  $('.books').hide();
  $('.movies').hide();
});
});
```

How It Works

In the HTML file, we can see that the text *Books, Movies,* and *Music* is enclosed in the span element of the class buttons so that the properties defined in the class selector buttons defined in the style sheet can be automatically applied to it. The class selector buttons contains the properties to give the shape of the button to this text. Also, we see that the buttons are assigned the unique IDs of booksbutton, moviesbutton, and musicbutton so that we can attach click events to them individually and write code for hiding the old text (information from an earlier button click) and for displaying the information related to the clicked button.

In the jQuery code, we start by hiding the text of the paragraphs of class books, movies, and music—that is, only the buttons will be visible initially when the web page is loaded. We then link the click event to the HTML element of id booksbutton—that is, to the Books button. When the Books button is clicked, the contents of the paragraph of the class books becomes visible slowly—giving it an animation effect (it contains the information related to books) and the contents of the paragraph of the classes movies and music are made invisible, hence displaying only the information for the button that is clicked on the screen.

Initially only the three buttons Books, Movies, and Music will be displayed, as shown in Figure 3-32.

Figure 3-32. Thee buttons: Books, Movies, and Music

When the Books button is clicked, it will display the information related to it; that is, the paragraph of the class books will be displayed as shown in Figure 3-33.

Books on a range of different subjects available at reasonable prices. Ranging from web
development, programming languages, and text books, all are available at heavy discount.
Shipping is free. Also available in stock are popular magazines, e-books, and tutorial CDs
at affordable prices

Figure 3-33. Information related to books is displayed when Books button is clicked

Similarly, if the Movies button is clicked, it will hide the information related to the books or music
and will make the information related to movies (that is, the paragraph of class `movies`) appear slowly on
the screen with an animation effect, as shown in Figure 3-34.

Find new movie reviews & the latest Hollywood movie news. Includes new movie trailers,
latest Hollywood releases, movie showtimes, entertainment news, celebrity interviews etc.
Also find Hollywood actresses, actors, videos, biographies, filmography, photos,
wallpaper, music, jokes, and live TV channels at your doorstep.

Figure 3-34. The information related to movies is displayed when the Movies button is clicked

Adding a Mouseover Event

Instead of applying click events to the buttons, we can also attach the mouseover event to them. The
mouseover event will make the appropriate information appear when the mouse pointer enters the
button (there is no need to click the button). The jQuery code for attaching the mouseover event may
appear as follows:

```
$(document).ready(function() {
  $('.books').hide();
  $('.movies').hide();
  $('.music').hide();

  $('#booksbutton').mouseover(function(){
    $('.books').show('slow');
    $('.movies').hide();
    $('.music').hide();
  });

  $('#moviesbutton').mouseover(function(){
    $('.movies').show('slow');
    $('.books').hide();
    $('.music').hide();
  });
```

```
$('#musicbutton').mouseover(function(){
    $('.music').show('slow');
    $('.books').hide();
    $('.movies').hide();
  });
});
```

3-19. Replacing Text with a Sliding Effect

Problem

You want one piece of text to be replaced by another; the first piece is slowly made invisible while the other appears gradually.

Solution

In this solution, we will be applying CSS styles directly to the elements using `css()` instead of picking them from the style sheet (see Recipe 3-6 for details of `css()`).

Let's assume we have an HTML file that has two paragraph elements that are distinguished from each other by assigning them the IDs `message1` and `message2`, respectively.

```
<body>
<p id="message1">jQuery is an open source project</p>
<p id="message2">Manipulating DOM using jQuery</p>
</body>
```

Here is the jQuery code for applying the sliding effect:

```
$(document).ready(function() {
  $('p#message1').css({'border': '2px solid', 'text-align': 'center','font-
weight':'bold'}).hide();
  $('p#message2').css({'backgroundColor': '#f00','color':'#fff','text-align': 'center',
'font-weight':'bold'}).click(
    function(){
      $(this).slideUp('slow');
      $('p#message1').slideDown('slow');
    }
  );
});
```

How It Works

To the paragraph of id `message1`, we assign a solid border of 2px thickness, align its text at the center of the browser window, and set it to appear in bold. The background color of the paragraph of id `message2` is set to red, and the foreground color of the text is set to white and is aligned at the center of the browser window.

In the jQuery code, some text will gradually disappear using the `slideDown()` method and will be replaced with some other text that slowly appears using the `slideUp()` method, so let's take a look at the workings of these two methods.

`slideDown()` displays the selected element with a sliding motion.

```
.slideDown(speed, callback)
```

`speed` decides the duration of the animation. It can be specified in terms of strings as `fast`, `normal`, or `slow`, or in milliseconds. The higher the number of milliseconds, the longer the animation will take.

`callback` is the function that is fired on completion of the animation.

Conversely, `slideUp()` makes the selected element invisible with a sliding motion.

```
.slideUp(speed, callback)
```

`speed` and `callback` have the same meaning as they do for `slideUp()`.

In the jQuery code, we can see that the paragraph of id `message1` is hidden and only the paragraph of id `message2` is set to be visible. So, the output that we get initially is as shown in Figure 3-35. Also, a click event is attached to the visible paragraph. In the inline function of the click event, we have written code to make the visible paragraph (the paragraph of id `message2`) become slowly invisible by sliding up, and the paragraph of id `message1` (which was initially invisible) to become visible slowly by sliding down.

Manipulating DOM using jQuery

Figure 3-35. Applying slideUp() and slideDown()

On clicking the visible paragraph it will slowly become invisible and the paragraph that was initially invisible will start becoming slowly visible, as shown in Figure 3-36.

Figure 3-36. One paragraph in the process of sliding down and another in the process of sliding up

The paragraph is totally replaced by another paragraph, as shown in Figure 3-37.

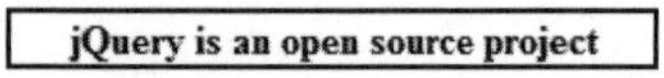

jQuery is an open source project

Figure 3-37. One paragraph totally removed and the other now visible

3-20. Making an Image Scroll

Problem

You want an image to scroll from left to right when it is clicked.

Solution

Let's make an HTML file that displays an image from the file `cell.jpg`, as shown here:

```
<body>
<img src="cell.jpg" />
</body>
```

To make an element move from its current location, we have to apply the `position` property to it. So, we apply the `position` property to the `img` element with its value set to `relative` using the type selector in the style sheet file: `style.css`:

```
img{
position:relative;
}
```

The jQuery code to make the image animate from left to right is as shown here:

```
$(document).ready(function() {
  $('img').click(function(){
    $(this).animate({left:600}, 'slow')
  });
});
```

Hiding the Image After Scrolling

We want the image to scroll from left to right and on reaching the right side of the browser window, the image should become invisible by using the `slideUp()` method.

The jQuery code will be modified as shown here:

```
$(document).ready(function() {
  $('img').click(function(){
    $('img').animate({left: 600}, 'slow')
    $('img').slideUp('slow');
  });
});
```

Fading Out the Image After Scrolling

We want the image to scroll from left to right and on reaching the right side of the browser window, we want it to become invisible—this time by using the fadeTo() method.

The jQuery code will be modified as follows:

```
$(document).ready(function() {
  $('img').click(function(){
    $('img').animate({left: 600}, 'slow')
    $('img').fadeTo('slow',0)
  });
});
```

Making the Image Grow While Scrolling to the Right

As the image scrolls from left to right, we want its width and height to increase. The jQuery code for accomplishing that is as follows:

```
$(document).ready(function() {
  $('img').click(function(){
    $(this).animate({left:600, width:$(this).width()*2,height:$(this).height()*2},'slow');
  });
});
```

Making the Image Scroll to the Right and Again to the Left

We want the image to scroll to the right side of the browser window. On reaching the right side, we want the image to fade out and fade in again (become invisible and visible slowly). After that we want the image to scroll back to the starting location, at the left.

The jQuery code for accomplishing that is as shown:

```
$(document).ready(function() {
  $('img').click(function(){
    $('img').animate(
      {left: 600},
      'slow',
      function(){
        $('img').fadeTo('slow',0);
        $('img').fadeTo('slow',1);
        $('img').animate({left: 0}, 'slow')
      }
    );
  });
});
```

How It Works

In the jQuery code that we are going to use in this solution, we will be making use of the `animate()` method. So let's first understand how the `animate()` method works.

animate()

This method is used for applying custom animation to the selected elements. The custom animation is controlled according to the specified CSS properties and easing parameters used.

```
.animate(properties, speed, easing, callback)
```

In this code

- `properties` refers to CSS properties (the end values) that the element will reach at the end of animation.

- `speed` is in the form of a predefined string or a numerical value in milliseconds to decide the duration of the effect or animation. The predefined strings are `slow`, `normal`, and `fast`. If the `speed` parameter is not used, then the default speed `normal` is used.

- `easing` is an optional function that controls how an animation progresses over time. It requires a plug-in. There are two easing functions: `linear` and `swing`, and `swing` is the default.

- `callback` is the function that is invoked when the animation is complete.

In the jQuery code, the statement:

```
$(this).animate({left:600}, 'slow')
```

makes the image move from its current position to 600px from the left side of the browser window. The movement will be slow and will occur when the click event occurs on the image.

Initially, the image appears to the extreme left, as in Figure 3-38.

Figure 3-38. The image is on the extreme left at the beginning.

When the image is clicked, the image will move right and will stop at a distance of 600px from the left side of the browser window, as shown in Figure 3-39.

Figure 3-39. The image scrolls to the right on being clicked.

We can that the jQuery code hides the image after scrolling, and that clicking the image makes it animate from left to right and stop at the distance of 600px from the left of the browser window. After that the slideUp() method hides the image slowly.

In the jQuery code that makes the image scroll to the right and to the left again, the statement

```
$('img').animate({left: 600}, 'slow', function(){
```

will make the image animate slowly from left to right and make it stop at a distance of 600px from the left boundary of the browser window.

Finally, the statement

```
$('img').animate({left: 0}, 'slow')});
```

will make the image animate back (from right to left) to its starting location. The image will stop when its distance becomes 0px from the left side of the browser window.

fadeTo()

This method adjusts the opacity of the selected elements.

```
.fadeTo(speed, opacity, callback)
```

speed decides the duration of the animation. It can be specified in terms of the predefined strings fast, normal, and slow, or in milliseconds. The higher the number of milliseconds, the longer the animation takes.

opacity is the number between 0 and 1 for deciding the opacity of the selected element at the end of the animation. A value of 0 means the selected element will be invisible, 1 means it will appear sharp, and 0.5 means the selected element will appear dim.

callback is the function that is fired on completion of the animation.

In the jQuery code that fades out the image after scrolling, we can see that when the image is clicked, it moves to the right and stops at a distance of 600px from the left side of the browser window. On reaching the right side, the image slowly vanishes, as its opacity is set to 0.

Let's achieve the same effect using a callback function:

```
$(document).ready(function() {
  $('img').click(function(){
    $('img').animate(
      {left: 600},
      'slow',
      function(){
        $('img').fadeTo('slow',0)
      }
    );
  });
});
```

In the jQuery code that makes the image grow in size while scrolling to the right, we can see that in the event-handling function of the click event, we write the code to animate the image from left to right and set it to stop at a distance of 600px from the left boundary of the browser window and also set its width and height to become twice its original value on reaching the right end. This makes the image slowly scroll to the right, with a gradual increase in its width and height.

At the beginning, the image may appear as shown in Figure 3-38. When the image is clicked, it starts moving to the right, and on reaching the right edge it appears as shown in Figure 3-40.

Figure 3-40. The image becomes twice its original width and height on reaching the right side.

The statement

```
$('img').fadeTo('slow',0);
```

will make the image fade out slowly, as its opacity is set to 0.

Similarly, the statement

```
$('img').fadeTo('slow',1);
```

will make the image fade in—that is, become slowly visible again, as its opacity is set to 1.

3-21. Determining Which Key Was Pressed

Problem

You want to know which key the user pressed while entering data in an input field; that way it can be used for validation checks, etc.

Solution

Let's make an HTML file that contains an input text field and an empty paragraph element, as shown here:

```
<body>
<input type="text" class="infobox" />
<p></p>
</body>
```

The jQuery code to display the numerical code of the key pressed by the user is as shown here:

```
$(document).ready(function() {
  $('.infobox').keypress(function(event){
    $('p').text('Character typed is: '+event.keyCode);
  });
});
```

The jQuery for converting numerical code for the key pressed into character format is as follows:

```
$(document).ready(function() {
  $('.infobox').keypress(function(event){
    $('p').text('Character typed is: '+String.fromCharCode(event.keyCode));
  });
});
```

How It Works

In the HTML file, we will be using the empty paragraph to display what key is pressed by the user. For finding out the key pressed by the user, we will be using the **keypress()** method. So, before we go further with the application of the **keypress()** method, let's understand it and its related methods.

keypress()

keypress() binds the event handler to the specified element that fires when the user presses a key on the keyboard. The difference between **keydown()** and **keypress()** is that if the user repeats any key by pressing and holding a key, the **keydown()** event is executed only once whereas the **keypress()** event is executed for each inserted character (**keydown()** is explained more in a moment). Also, the modifier keys Shift, Ctrl, etc. are recognized by **keydown()**, but **keypress()** is not fired by these modifier keys.

```
.keypress(handler)
.keypress()
```

Here `handler` contains the statements that will be executed every time a key is pressed on the keyboard.

The `keypress()` method with no parameters is used to trigger the keypress event manually. Like in the following example, the keypress event on the input text field of the class `infobox` is invoked manually when an HTML element of the class `button` is clicked:

```
$('.button').click(function(){
  $('.infobox').keypress();
});
```

To serve the `keypress()` event invoked by the preceding code, we need to write the event-handling function to do the desired task.

In order to know which key was pressed, we need to use the event object that is passed to the event-handler function. The event object contains information about the event. The `keyCode` attribute of the event object holds the numerical code of the key pressed.

In the jQuery code, the statement

```
$('.infobox').keypress(function(event){
```

binds the keypress event to the input text field so as to listen to any key that is pressed.

The statement

```
$('p').text('Character typed is: '+event.keyCode);
```

makes use of the `keyCode` attribute of the event object (that is passed to the event handler function) on occurrence of the key press event (in the input text field) to display the numerical code of the key pressed in the paragraph element. The output that we get is shown in Figure 3-41.

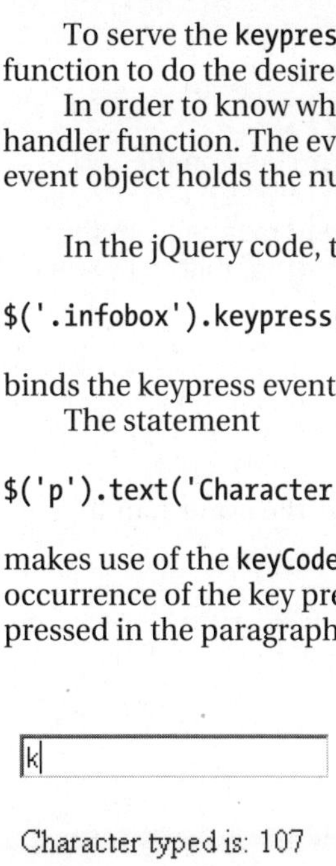

Character typed is: 107

Figure 3-41. The numerical code of the character typed in the text field displayed

We can see in the output that the numerical code of the character *k* is displayed in the paragraph element.

To convert the numerical code of the key pressed into character format, we use the `fromCharCode()` method of JavaScript's `String` object. So let's pass the `keyCode` attribute of the event object to the `fromCharCode()` method to display the key pressed in character format. The output that we get is as shown in Figure 3-42.

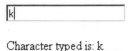

Character typed is: k

Figure 3-42. The character typed in the text field, displayed in character format

keydown()

keydown() binds the event handler to the specified element that fires when the user first presses a key on the keyboard:

```
.keydown(handler)
.keydown()
```

Here handler contains the statements that we want to execute when a key is pressed on the keyboard.

The keydown() method with no parameters is used to trigger the keydown event manually. In the following example, the keydown event on the input text field of class infobox is invoked manually when an HTML element of the class button is clicked:

```
$(' .button').click(function(){
  $('.infobox').keydown();
});
```

To serve the keydown() event invoked by the preceding code, we need to write the event-handling function to do the desired task.

keyup()

keyup() binds the event handler to the specified element that fires when the user releases a key on the keyboard.

```
.keyup(handler)
.keyup()
```

Here handler contains the statements that we want to execute when a key is released.

The keyup() method with no parameters is used to trigger the keyup event manually. In the following example, the keyup event on the input text field of the class infobox is invoked manually when an HTML element of the class button is clicked:

```
$(' .button').click(function(){
  $('.infobox').keyup();
});
```

To serve the keyup event invoked by the preceding code, we need to write the event-handling function to do the desired task.

3-22. Preventing Event Bubbling

Problem

You are facing the problem of event bubbling and want to know how to stop it from giving unexpected results.

Solution

In order to understand event bubbling we have to assume an HTML file that has a few elements nested inside one another in the form of a hierarchy as is shown here:

```
<body>
<div>Div Element
<p>Paragraph Element<br/>
<span>Span Element</span>
</p>
</div>
</body>
```

To understand practically the concept of event bubbling, let's see the following jQuery code that has the click event attached to all three elements of the DOM:

```
$(document).ready(function() {
  $('div').click(function(event){
    alert('You have clicked the div element');
  });

  $('p').click(function(event){
    alert('You have clicked the paragraph element');
  });

  $('span').click(function(event){
    alert('You have clicked the span element');
  });
});
```

To stop event bubbling and to control where an event should take place, we will modify the jQuery code as shown here:

```
$(document).ready(function() {
  $('div').click(function(event){
    var $target=$(event.target);
    if($target.is('div')){
      alert('You have clicked the div element');
    }
```

```
    if($target.is('p')){
      alert('You have clicked the paragraph element');
    }
    if($target.is('span')){
      alert('You have clicked the span element');
    }
  });
});
```

How It Works

In the HTML file, we can see that the topmost element in the DOM (that is, the root element) is the **div** element, followed by the paragraph element (as a child of the **div** element), and finally the **span** element.

When an event occurs on any element, the event-handling mechanism first checks whether the element on which the event has occurred has an event method (with event-handling function) attached to it. If it does, the statements in the event-handling function (of the attached event method) are executed. After that, the event-handling mechanism continues to check the parent of the element to see if it has an event method attached to it and, if so, its event handler is also executed. Again its parent (parent of parent) is checked, and so on. In other words, *event bubbling* refers to the process in which the event that is fired propagates upward in the DOM tree toward the root.

In the first jQuery example, we attach the click event to all three elements. Let's click on the **span** element (lowest node in DOM) in that example; the event-handling function of the **span** element will be executed. But the event-handling mechanism will not stop at that, but rather will propagate to its parent—that is, the paragraph element will be checked and since it also has the click event attached to it, the event-handling function of the paragraph element will also be executed. After the execution of the event-handling function of the paragraph element, the event-handling function of the root of DOM—the **div** element—will also be executed.

Now on execution of the jQuery code, if we click the **span** element, first we will get the alert message because of the execution of the event-handler function of the **span** element, as shown in Figure 3-43.

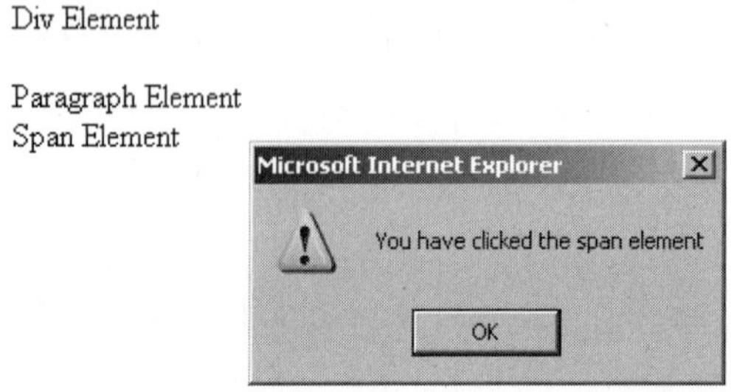

Div Element

Paragraph Element
Span Element

Figure 3-43. Alert message of the span element displayed on clicking the span element

But after that, the event-handling function of the parent of the **span** element (that is, the paragraph element) will also be executed, giving us the alert message shown in Figure 3-44.

Figure 3-44. *Alert message of the paragraph element—executed on account of event bubbling*

Since event bubbling stops at the root of DOM, the event-handling function of the root (that is, the
div element) will also be executed, giving us the output shown in Figure 3-45.

Figure 3-45. *Alert message of the div element—executed on account of event bubbling*

Suppose that we click the paragraph element; we will get the alert message of the paragraph
element followed by the alert message of the **div** element. When we click on the **div** element, only
the alert message of the **div** element will be displayed, as there is no parent of the **div** element to
propagate to.

Now run the jQuery code that stops event bubbling; we have made use of the **target** attribute of the
event object for controlling the events and to stop event bubbling. Using the **target** attribute we can
determine which DOM element first received the event and ensure that the event is not propagated to its
parent elements automatically.

We can see in the modified jQuery code that we determine the target (the element where the click
event has occurred) and store it in the **$target** variable. Then, using **if** statements, we check, one by
one, which element received the click event, and accordingly we send an alert message.

3-23. Chaining Multiple Activities

Problem

Chaining is a procedure for writing jQuery wrapper methods one after the other so as to perform several
activities in a single statement. You want to use this chaining ability.

Solution

Let's assume we have an HTML file that has a few HTML elements, as shown here:

```
<body>
<div>Div Element
<p>Paragraph Element<br>
<span>Span Element</span>
</p>
</div>
</body>
```

Also, we require a style sheet to apply some CSS style to those HTML elements, so let's write a style rule in the style sheet:

```
.hover{
color: blue ;
background-color:cyan
}
```

An example of chaining is as follows:

```
$(document).ready(function() {
  $('div').children().clone().prependTo('div').addClass('hover');
});
```

How It Works

We can see that the preceding HTML file contains three elements, and it will appear as shown in Figure 3-46.

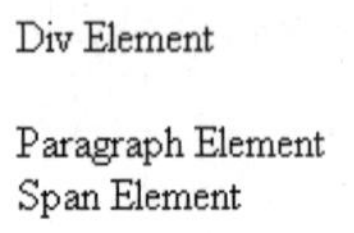

Div Element

Paragraph Element
Span Element

Figure 3-46. *Three elements: div, paragraph, and span*

The preceding style sheet contains a style rule: **hover** to change the foreground and background color of the HTML element to blue and cyan, respectively.

The preceding code selects the children of the **div** element—that is, the paragraph and **span** elements—and makes their clone (copy). This copy of the paragraph and span element is then added before the **div** element. Thereafter, the style rule **hover** is applied to these inserted (paragraph and **span**) elements. So, we see that with chaining ability, we can do so many activities in a single statement. The output of the preceding jQuery code will appear as shown in Figure 3-47.

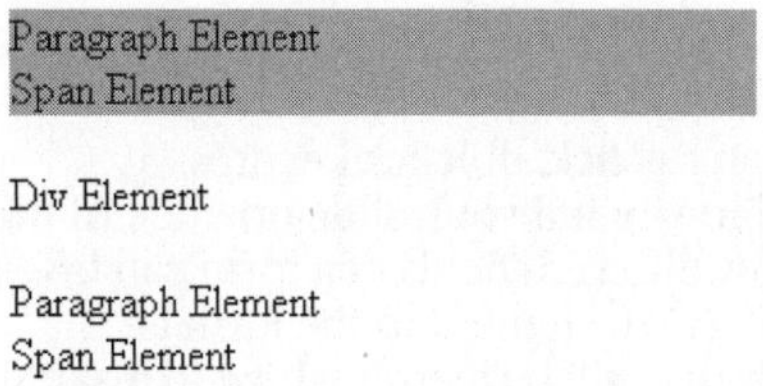

Paragraph Element
Span Element

Div Element

Paragraph Element
Span Element

Figure 3-47. The clone of children of div element inserted beforethe div element, with style applied

Removing Side Effects of Chaining

Chaining deals with the latest wrapped set. As in the preceding jQuery code, we see that the clone of the children of the **div** element is made—the side effect is that there are two wrapped sets now; one is the original child (of the **div** element) and the other is their clone. In this case, the clone of the children will be inserted before the **div** element and the CSS class **hover** is applied to this cloned wrapped set only, not to the original wrapped set. In order to consider the original wrapped set—that is, if we want to apply the CSS style rule to the children of the **div** element (and not to its clone)—we make use of the **end()** method.

The **end()** method, when used in a jQuery chain, backs up to the previous wrapped set and returns it as a value so that the subsequent operations can be applied to it.

Let's modify our earlier jQuery code to apply the **hover** style rule to the actual children of the **div** element (and not to its clone):

```
$(document).ready(function() {
  $('div').children().clone().prependTo('div').end().addClass('hover');
});
```

We can see in the preceding jQuery code that the clone of the children of the **div** element is made—a copy of the paragraph and **span** elements is made and is added at the beginning of the **div** element. However, because of the **end()** command, the original wrapped set (the actual children of the **div** element) is then returned (and not its clone), and the **hover** style is applied to that set instead of to the clone. The output is shown in Figure 3-48.

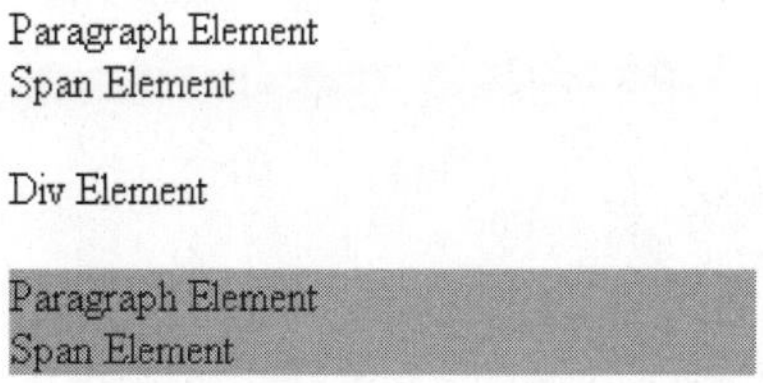

Paragraph Element
Span Element

Div Element

Paragraph Element
Span Element

Figure 3-48. The hover style rule applied to actual children of the div element instead of to their clone

Summary

In this chapter we covered different mouse and keyboard events, such as click, dblclick keypress, keydown, and keyup, and we applied various effects to images (e.g. fade in, fade out, slide up etc.). In the next chapter, we will review Form validation Recipes which show how different fields of a form can be validated. We'll also go over the different techiques of finding which HTML element in the form is selected (e.g. whether it is checked or unchecked by the user). Finally, we will be learning how to disable or enable different form elements.

CHAPTER 4

■■■

Form Validation

In this chapter we'll see different ways of validating forms. We will be covering following recipes, from basic blank-field checking through to more complex password and field-disabling techniques:

- Confirming a required field is not left blank
- Validating a numerical field
- Validating phone numbers
- Validating a user ID
- Validating a date
- Validating an email address
- Checking whether a checkbox is checked
- Finding whether a radio button is selected
- Checking whether an option in a `select` element is selected
- Applying styles to options and a form button
- Checking and unchecking all checkboxes together
- Validating two fields
- Matching the password and confirm password fields
- Disabling certain fields
- Validating a complete form
- Serializing form data

4-1. Confirming a Required Field Is Not Left Blank

Problem

You have a text-input field in a form and you want to ensure its not left blank. The user will get an error message unless he enters the required data in the field.

Solution

Let's make an HTML file that displays a form containing a label, a text field, an error message, and a Submit button, as shown here:

```
<body>
<form id="signup" method="post" action="">
<div><span class="label">User Id *</span><input type="text"  class="infobox" name="userid"
/><span class="error"> This field cannot be blank</span></div>
<input class="submit" type="submit" value="Submit">
</form>
</body>
```

Since the purpose of the HTML form is to validate on the text-input field and not to send the entered data to some other page for processing, the action attribute of the form is left blank. The form is assigned an ID of signup and method is set to post—though it will have no effect on our validation procedure.

The label message User Id is enclosed in a span element of the class label. The text-input field is assigned a class name infobox and the error message (*This field cannot be blank*) is stored as a span element of the class error. Finally, the Submit button is assigned the class submit.

The reasons for assigning the classes to all four items of the form is to apply the properties defined in the class selectors label, infobox, error, and submit (defined in the style sheet style.css) to be applied automatically to the respective four items of the form. The style sheet with the respective class selectors is shown here:

```
style.css
.label {float: left; width: 120px; }
.infobox {width: 200px; }
.error { color: red; padding-left: 10px; }
.submit { margin-left: 125px; margin-top: 10px;}
```

The jQuery code to confirm that the text-input field is not left blank and to display an error message if it is left blank is shown here:

```
$(document).ready(function() {
  $('.error').hide();
  $('.submit').click(function(event){
    var data=$('.infobox').val();
    var len=data.length;
    if(len<1)
    {
```

```
      $('.error').show();
      event.preventDefault();
    }
    else
    {
      $('.error').hide();
    }
  });
});
```

How It Works

The class selector `label` has the `float` property set to `left` so that the next item (text-input field) may appear to its right, and its `width` property is set to 120px to give enough space for the label to display. The class selector `infobox` has its `width` property set to value 200px—the size of the text-input field. The class selector `error` has its color property set to red to highlight it, and padding from left is set to 10px to maintain a good distance from the text-input field. The class selector `.submit` has its `margin-left` and `margin-top` properties set to 125px and 10px, respectively, to set the distance from the left boundary of the browser window and from the text-input field, as we want the Submit button to appear below the text-input field.

In the preceding jQuery code, we can see that initially the error message is hidden and a click event is attached to the Submit button. In the event-handling function of the click event, we extract the data entered by the user in the text-input field (assigned the class name `infobox`) and store it in a variable: `data`. We find out the length of the data, and if it is less than 1 (which means the user has not entered anything in the text field), we make the error message visible on the screen. The method `preventDefault()` of the event object is used to keep the Submit button from sending to the server the data entered by the user.

On execution of the jQuery code, we will get a form displayed with a text label, a text-input field, and a Submit button. If we select the Submit button without entering anything in the text field, we will get an error message—*This field cannot be blank*—displayed in red beside the text field, as shown in Figure 4-1.

Figure 4-1. Error message displayed when the text-input field is left blank

If we enter some name in the text field and select the Submit button, we will not get any error message, as indicated here:

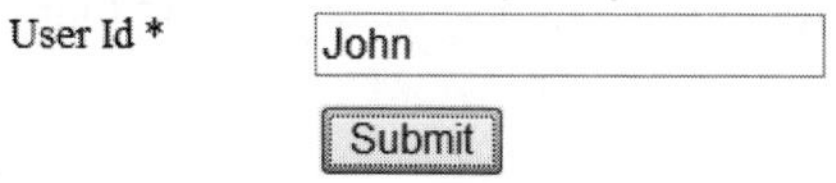

Figure 4-2. No error message appears if data is entered in the text-input field.

4-2. Validating a Numerical Field

Problem

You have a text field for entering the age of the person and you want to confirm that a numerical value is entered in it and no character or symbol is entered.

Solution

The HTML code to display the form that contains a label, a text-input field, an error message, and a Submit button is as shown here:

```
<body>
<form id="signup" method="post" action="">
 <div><span class="label">Enter Age </span><input type="text"  class="infobox" name="age"
/><span class="error"> Only numericals allowed</span></div>
<input class="submit" type="submit" value="Submit">
</form>
</body>
```

Since the purpose of the HTML form is to validate on the text-input field and not to send the entered data to some other page for processing, the `action` attribute of the form is left blank. The form is assigned an ID of `signup` and `method` is set to `post`—though it will have no effect on our validation procedure.

The label message *User Id* is enclosed in a `span` element of the class `label`. The text-input field is assigned a class name `infobox` and the error message ("*This field cannot be blank*") is stored as a `span` element of the class `error`. Finally, the Submit button is assigned the class `submit`.

The reasons for assigning the classes to all four items of the form is to apply the properties defined in the class selectors `label`, `infobox`, `error`, and `submit` (defined in the style sheet `style.css`) to be applied automatically to the respective four items of the form. The style sheet with the class selectors is shown here:

```
style.css
.label {float: left; width: 120px; }
.infobox {width: 200px; }
.error { color: red; padding-left: 10px; }
.submit { margin-left: 125px; margin-top: 10px;}
```

Allowing Only Numerical Values

The jQuery code to check that the age entered in the text field contains only numerical values, and that no text or symbols have been entered, is shown here:

```
$(document).ready(function() {
  $('.error').hide();
  $('.submit').click(function(event){
    var data=$('.infobox').val();
    var len=data.length;
    var c;
    for(var i=0;i<len;i++)
    {
      c=data.charAt(i).charCodeAt(0);
      if(c <48 || c >57)
      {
        $('.error').show();
        event.preventDefault();
        break;
      }
      else
      {
        $('.error').hide();
      }
    }
  });
});
```

Allowing Negative Values

Sometimes while entering numerical values, we come across negative values. In the preceding jQuery code, no symbol is allowed; that is, we cannot use a hyphen or minus sign. Hence we cannot enter a negative value in the text field with the preceding code. Let's modify our jQuery code to accept negative values also:

```
$(document).ready(function() {
  $('.error').hide();
  $('.submit').click(function(event){
    var data=$('.infobox').val();
    var len=data.length;
    var c;
    for(var i=0;i<len;i++)
    {
      c=data.charAt(i).charCodeAt(0);
      if(c==45 && i==0)
      {
        continue;
      }
      if(c <48 || c >57)
      {
        $('.error').show();
        event.preventDefault();
        break;
      }
```

```
    else
    {
      $('.error').hide();
    }
  }
});
});
```

Allowing a Range of Values

You want the allowable age range for your form to be 5 to 99; that is, if an age below or above the given range is entered, you want an error message to be displayed on the screen.

The jQuery code for entering a numerical value between 5 and 99 is shown here:

```
$(document).ready(function() {
  $('.error').hide();
  $('.submit').click(function(event){
    var data=$('.infobox').val();
    var len=data.length;
    var c=0;
    var age=0;
    var flag=0;
    for(var i=0;i<len;i++)
    {
      c=data.charAt(i).charCodeAt(0);
      if(c <48 || c >57)
      {
        $('.error').show();
        flag=1;
        event.preventDefault();
        break;
      }
      else
      {
        $('.error').hide();
      }
    }

    if(flag==0)
    {
      age=parseInt(data);
      if(age<5 || age>99)
      {
        $('.error').show();
        $('.error').text('Invalid Age. Please enter the age within the range 5 to 99');
        event.preventDefault();
      }
    }
  });
});
```

How It Works

We can see in the first HTML file that the label is set to display the text Enter Age and an error message is assigned the text: Only numerals allowed. Also, the label, text-input field, error message, and Submit button are assigned different class names (`label`, `infobox`, `error`, and `submit`) so as to apply the properties defined in the class selectors (defined in the style sheet `style.css`) to them. In this recipe, we use the same external style sheet—`style.css`—that we used in Recipe 4-1.

We can see in the jQuery code in the section "Allowing Only Numerical Values" that the error message is initially set to invisible. The click event is attached to the Submit button so as to execute its event-handling function if the Submit button is clicked. In the event-handling function, we see that the data in the text-input field (the text field is enclosed in the `span` element of class `infobox`) is retrieved and is stored in a variable called `data`. Its length is calculated and a `for` loop is executed up till the length of the input data to parse each of its individual characters.

In the `for` loop, we take one character at a time (of the input data), and with the help of `charCodeAt()`, find its ASCII value. If the ASCII value of the character is below the numeral 0 (ASCII value of 48) or more than the numeral 9 (ASCII value of 57), meaning it is not a numerical value, then we make the error message visible on the screen and exit from the loop. The `preventDefault()` method of the `event` object is used to prevent the data entered by the user from being sent to the server or the user navigating to the target form.

On execution of the program, if we enter some characters after the age, we get the error message "*Only numerals allowed*", as shown in Figure 4-3.

Enter Age   `25a`   Only numericals allowed

Submit

Figure 4-3. Error message displayed if a character appears after the age

Even if the character appears in between the digits, the error will be displayed, as shown in Figure 4-4.

Enter Age   `2a5`   Only numericals allowed

Submit

Figure 4-4. Error message displayed if the character appears between the numerals

Also, if we add any symbol, like a minus sign or an underscore, we get the error message, as shown in Figure 4-5.

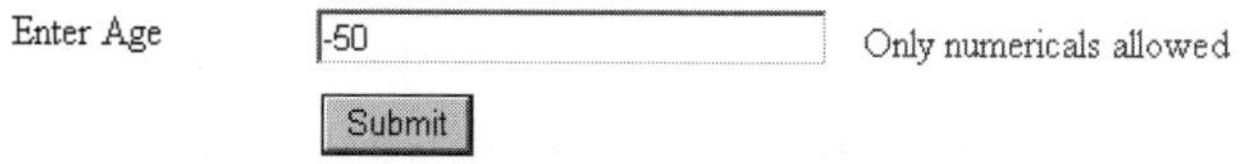

Enter Age   `-50`   Only numericals allowed

Submit

Figure 4-5. Error message displayed on entering symbols

113

We can see in the jQuery code in the "Allowing Negative Values" section that the error message is hidden at the beginning. The event-handling function of the click event attached to the Submit button extracts the data from the text-input field and stores it in variable data. Each individual character stored in data is parsed with the help of a `for` loop. In the loop, we convert each character in the data variable to its ASCII value and check whether the first character has an ASCII value of 45 (which is the ASCII value of the minus sign), then continue checking the rest of the characters without displaying any error message. The second condition in the `for` loop is the one we saw earlier: checking if the characters in the data variable are numerical values and displaying the error message if not.

In the jQuery code in the "Allowing a Range of Values" section, we first make the error message invisible. Then we attach the click event to the Submit button. The event-handling function of the click event does several jobs, such as extracting the numerical value entered in the text-input field (assigned the class name `infobox`) and storing it in the variable data. We then find out the length of the data and execute the loop to parse each of its individual characters. If any of the contents in data has an ASCII value lower than the numeral 0 (ASCII value of 48) or greater than the numeral 9 (ASCII value of 57), it means the data variable contains some value other than a numerical value, so we make the error message visible. Also, we set the value of a variable flag to 1 to indicate that only numbers are allowed, and we exit from the `for` loop. If the value of the flag is set to 1, it means there is no point in checking the range of the numerical value, as it is invalid data.

If the data is a number, we need to check the range of the numerical value; that is, whether it is between 5 and 99. So, if the value of the flag variable is 0 (after the execution of the `for` loop; that is, after inspecting all characters of the data variable), it means the data entered is valid and consist only of numerals; we then apply the conditional statement that that the numeral may not be less than 5 or greater than 99, then make the error message visible and set the error message to *Invalid Age*. The `preventDefault()` method of the event object is used for preventing submission of the entered data in case it is invalid. We may get the error message displayed in Figure 4-6 if the value is not within the range of 5–99.

Figure 4-6. Error message displayed if the value is not within the range 5 to 99.

4-3. Validating Phone Numbers

Problem

You want to use a phone number field and you want the user to be able to enter only numerals and + or – signs, and nothing else.

Solution

Let's make an HTML file that displays a form that consists of label, a text-input field, an error message, and a Submit button. The HTML appears here:

```
<body>
<form id="signup" method="post" action="">
<div><span class="label">Enter Phone number </span><input type="text"  class="infobox"
name="phone" /><span class="error"> Phone number can contain only numbers, + and -
</span></div>
<input class="submit" type="submit" value="Submit">
</form>
</body>
```

All four items of the HTML file are assigned respective class names—label, infobox, error, and submit—so that the style properties defined in the class selectors specified in the external style sheet style.css can be automatically applied to these items.

The class selectors defined in the style sheet file are as shown here:

```
style.css
.label {float: left; width: 150px; }
.infobox {width: 200px; }
.error { color: red; padding-left: 10px; }
.submit { margin-left: 150px; margin-top: 10px;}
```

The jQuery code to confirm that the text-input field accepts only numerals along with – or + signs and nothing else is shown here:

```
$(document).ready(function() {
  $('.error').hide();
  $('.submit').click(function(event){
    var data=$('.infobox').val();
    if(validate_phoneno(data))
    {
      $('.error').hide();
    }
    else
    {
      $('.error').show();
      event.preventDefault();
    }
  });
});

function validate_phoneno(ph)
{
  var pattern=new RegExp(/^[0-9-+]+$/);
  return pattern.test(ph);
}
```

How It Works

The class selector label has the float property set to left so that the next item (text-input field) may appear to its right, and its width property is set to 150px to give enough space for the label message *Enter Phone number* to display. The class selector infobox has its width property set to 200px—that ultimately

115

becomes the width of the text-input field. The class selector `error` has its color property set to red to highlight it, and padding from left is set to 10px to keep the distance from the text-input field. The class selector `.submit` has `margin-left` and `margin-top` properties set to 150px and 10px, respectively, to set the distance from the left boundary of the browser window and from the text-input field, as we want the Submit button to appear just below the text-input field.

We can see in the preceding jQuery code that the error message is made invisible at the beginning. The click event is attached to the Submit button. In the event-handling function of the click event, the phone number entered by the user in the text field (that is enclosed in the `span` element of class name `infobox`) is retrieved and stored in the data variable. The data variable is passed to the `validate_phoneno()` method for validation.

Here, the contents of the data variable are assigned to the `ph` parameter of the `validate_phoneno()` method. In `validate_phoneno()`, an instance of the `RegExp` class is created. The regular expression passed to the `RegExp` constructor is `/^[0-9-+]+$/`, which means the data in the text-input field may begin or end (^ means beginning and $ means end) with any numerical value from 0 to 9 or with a – or + sign. The + sign after closing bracket (]) means that this pattern can repeat one or more times; that is, we can enter the numerals or a – or + sign any number of times in the phone number entered in the text-input field.

`validate_phoneno()` tests the contents of the `ph` parameter with the regular expression and returns `true` if the contents of the `ph` variable match the regular expression supplied; otherwise it returns `false`. On the basis of the Boolean value returned by `validate_phoneno()`, the error message is made visible or invisible. If while entering the phone number we use a symbol other than the + or – sign, we get the error message *Phone number can contain only numbers, + and –*, as shown in Figure 4-7.

Enter Phone number   `91-145(2429193)`   Phone number can contain only numbers, + and -

      Submit

Figure 4-7. Error message displayed when data other than numerals, +, or – is entered

If the phone number consists of numerals and a + or – sign, it will be considered a valid phone number and be accepted without displaying any error message, as shown in Figure 4-8.

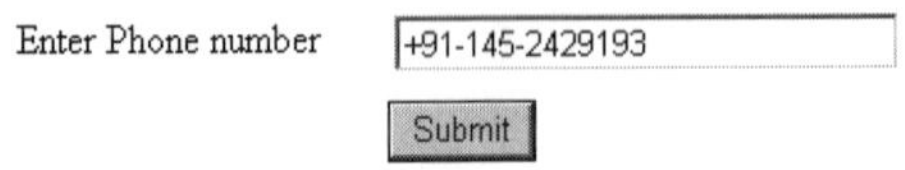

Enter Phone number   `+91-145-2429193`

      Submit

Figure 4-8. The phone number is considered valid if it consists of numerals and + or – signs

4-4. Validating a User ID

Problem

You want to validate a user ID that can consist of characters, numbers, and underscores, and no other symbol.

Solution

Let's make an HTML file that displays a form that contains a label, a text-input field, an error message, and a Submit button. The text of the label is set to *Enter User id* and that of the error message is set to *User id can contain only letters, numbers or underscore*. These four items are also assigned the class names as `label`, `infobox`, `error`, and `submit`, respectively. For these class names, the respective class selectors are written in the external style sheet. The HTML file will appear as shown here:

```
<body>
<form id="signup" method="post" action="">
<div><span class="label">Enter User id </span><input type="text"  class="infobox"
name="userid" /><span class="error"> User id can contain only letters, numbers or
underscore</span></div>
<input class="submit" type="submit" value="Submit">
</form>
</body>
```

The class selectors consist of style properties that are automatically applied to the HTML elements and are defined in the style sheet `style.css`. We use the same style sheet file (`style.css`) that we used in Recipe 4-3.

The jQuery code to accept the user ID that consists of numerals, characters, and underscores only is shown here:

```
$(document).ready(function() {
  $('.error').hide();
  $('.submit').click(function(event){
    var data=$('.infobox').val();
    if(validate_userid(data))
    {
      $('.error').hide();
    }
    else
    {
      $('.error').show();
      event.preventDefault();
    }
  });
});

function validate_userid(uid)
{
  var pattern= new RegExp(/^[a-z0-9_]+$/);
  return pattern.test(uid);
}
```

How It Works

We can see in the preceding jQuery code that the error message is made invisible at the beginning. The click event is attached to the Submit button. In the event-handling function of the click event, the user ID entered by the user in the text field (that is enclosed in the `span` element of the class name `infobox`) is retrieved and stored in the data variable. The data variable is passed to the **validate_userid()** function for validation. The contents of the data variable are assigned to the **uid** parameter of the **validate_userid()** method.

In **validate_userid()**, an instance of the **RegExp** class is created. The regular expression passed to the **RegExp** constructor is **/^[a-z0-9_]+$/**, which means the user ID entered in the text-input field may begin or end (^ means beginning and $ means end) with any character from *a* to *z*, with a numerical value from 0 to 9, or with an underscore (_) symbol. The + sign after the closing bracket (]) means that this pattern can repeat one or more times; that is, we can enter the characters, numerals, or underscore any number of times in the user ID entered in the text-input field.

validate_userid() tests the contents of the **uid** parameter with the regular expression and returns **true** if the contents of the **uid** variable match the regular expression supplied; otherwise it returns **false**. On the basis of the Boolean value returned by the **validate_userid()** function, the error message is made visible or invisible. If while entering the user ID we use a symbol other than the underscore, we may get the error message: *User id can contain only letters, numbers or underscore*, as shown in Figure 4-9.

Enter User id | John-David | User id can contain only letters, numbers or underscore

     Submit

Figure 4-9. *Error message displayed if any symbol other than the underscore is used in the user ID*

If the user ID consists of characters, numbers or an underscore, it is considered a valid user ID and is accepted without any error message displayed, as shown in Figure 4-10.

Enter User id | John_David123 |

     Submit

Figure 4-10. *The user ID is considered valid if it consists of characters, numerals, and the underscore symbol.*

4-5. Validating a Date

Problem

You want to validate a date in the format mm/dd/yyyy or mm-dd-yyyy. If the date entered does not match either format, you want to display an error message.

Solution

Let's make an HTML file that displays a form that contains a label, a text-input field, an error message, and a Submit button. The text of the label is set to *Enter Date of Birth* and that of the error message is set to *Invalid Date*. These four items are also assigned the class names `label`, `infobox`, `error`, and `submit`, respectively. For these class names, the respective class selectors are written in the external style sheet. The HTML file may appear as shown here:

```
<body>
<form id="signup" method="post" action="">
 <div><span class="label">Enter Date of Birth </span><input type="text"  class="infobox"
name="dob" /><span class="error"> Invalid Date. Correct format is mm/dd/yyyy or mm-dd-yyyy
</span></div>
<input class="submit" type="submit" value="Submit">
</form>
</body>
```

The class selectors consist of style properties that are automatically applied to the HTML elements and are defined in the style sheet `style.css`. We use the same style sheet file (`style.css`) that we used in Recipe 4-3.

The jQuery code to accept the date in the format mm/dd/yyyy or mm-dd-yyyy is shown here:

```
$(document).ready(function() {
  $('.error').hide();
  $('.submit').click(function(event){
    var data=$('.infobox').val();
    if(validate_date(data))
    {
      $('.error').hide();
    }
    else
    {
      $('.error').show();
      event.preventDefault();
    }
  });
});

function validate_date(date)
{
  var pattern= new RegExp(/\b\d{1,2}[\/-]\d{1,2}[\/-]\d{4}\b/);
  return pattern.test(date);
}
```

How It Works

The error message is made invisible at the beginning. Then a click event is attached to the Submit button. In the event-handling function of the click event, the date entered by the user in the text-input field (that is enclosed in the `span` element of class name `infobox`) is retrieved and stored in the `data` variable. The `data` variable is passed to the `validate_date()` function for validation. The contents of the `data` variable are assigned to the `date` parameter of the `validate_date()` function. In the `validate_date()` function, an instance of `RegExp` class is created. The regular expression passed to the `RegExp` constructor is `/\b\d{1,2}[\/-]\d{1,2}[\/-]\d{4}\b/`.

The regular expression is explained as follows:

- * \b at the beginning and at the end of a regular expression denotes the word boundary; that is, the pattern must match exactly .

- * \d{1,2} means there can be 1 or 2 digits.

- * [\/-] means the symbols / and – are allowed.

- * \d{4} means there must be exactly 4 digits.

Hence, the date entered in the text-input field must begin with 1 or 2 digits (month) followed by a / or – symbol. Then once more there can be 1 or 2 digits (day), followed by a / or – symbol, and finally there must be exactly 4 digits (year). The `validate_date()` function tests the contents of the `date` parameter with the regular expression and returns `true` if the contents of the `date` variable match with the regular expression supplied; otherwise it returns `false`. On the basis of the Boolean value returned by the `validate_date()` function, the error message is made visible or invisible.

Suppose we make a mistake while entering the date—like instead of four digits, we enter a year of two digits. We would get an error message *Invalid Date*, as shown in Figure 4-11.

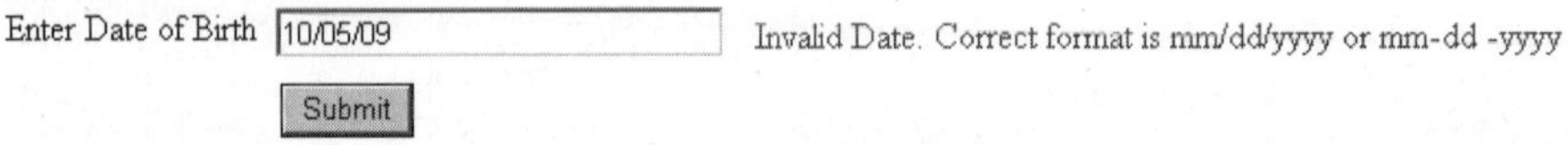

Enter Date of Birth | 10/05/09 | Invalid Date. Correct format is mm/dd/yyyy or mm-dd -yyyy

Submit

Figure 4-11. Error message: Invalid Date is displayed if the date is entered incorrectly.

If the date is entered correctly, with either a / or – delimiter used between day, month, and year, it will be accepted without any error message, as is shown in Figure 4-12

Enter Date of Birth | 10-05-2009

Submit

Figure 4-12. The date is accepted without any error message if it follows the specified pattern.

4-6. Validating an Email Address

Problem

You want to validate an email address; that is, you want to confirm that the email address consists of characters and numbers along with the @ and . (period) symbols.

Solution

Let's make an HTML file that displays a form that contains a label, a text-input field, an error message, and a Submit button. The text of the label is set to *Enter Email Id* and that of error message is set to *Invalid Email Address*. These four items are also assigned the class names label, infobox, error, and submit, respectively. For these class names, the respective class selectors are written in the external style sheet. The HTML file may appear as shown here:

```
<body>
<form id="signup" method="post" action="">
 <div><span class="label">Enter Email Id </span><input type="text"  class="infobox"
name="email" /><span class="error"> Invalid Email Address. Correct email address is the one
that essentially has an @ sign and a . (period) after  @ sign. It should not have any other
special symbol except hyphen or underscore and must be terminated by any letter only
</span></div>
<input class="submit" type="submit" value="Submit">
</form>
</body>
```

The class selectors consist of style properties that are automatically applied to the HTML elements and are defined in the style sheet style.css. We use the same style sheet file (style.css) that we used in Recipe 4-3.

The jQuery code to accept the email address and validate it is shown here:

```
$(document).ready(function() {
  $('.error').hide();
  $('.submit').click(function(event){
    var data=$('.infobox').val();
    if(valid_email(data))
    {
      $('.error').hide();
    }
    else
    {
      $('.error').show();
    event.preventDefault();
    }
  });
});

function valid_email(email)
{
  var pattern= new RegExp(/^[\w-]+(\.[\w-]+)*@([\w-]+\.)+[a-zA-Z]+$/);
  return pattern.test(email);
}
```

How It Works

The error message is made invisible at the beginning. Then a click event is attached to the Submit button. In the event-handling function of the click event, the email address entered by the user in the text-input field (that is, enclosed in the `span` element of class name `infobox`) is retrieved and is stored in the data variable. The data variable is passed to the `validate_email()` function for validation. The contents of the `data` variable are assigned to the `email` parameter of the `validate_email()` function. In the `validate_email()` function, an instance of the `RegExp` class is created. The regular expression passed to the `RegExp` constructor is `/^[\w-]+(\.[\w-]+)*@([\w-]+\.)+[a-zA-Z]+$/` .

The regular expression is explained as follows:

- `/^[\w-]+` means there can be a letter, number, underscore, or hyphen at the beginning of the email address. `^` means at the beginning. `\w` refers to letter, number, and underscore. The `+` sign after the closing bracket (`]`) means one or more times.

- `(\.[\w-]+)*` means the pattern consisting of a . (period) followed by one or more letters, numerals, underscores, and hyphens which can occur for zero or more times. The symbol `*` at the end of the pattern means zero or more times.

- `@` Means the symbol `@` must occur exactly at this point in the email address we are defining: right after the preceding parts of the expression, and right before the part we define after it

- `([\w-]+\.)+` means the letter, numeral, underscore, and hyphen can occur one or more times, followed by a . (period). And this combined sequence (character, numeral, underscore, hyphen and period) can occur one or more times.

- `[a-zA-Z]+$/` is where we define the end of the mail address; so our email address must here be terminated by any uppercase or lowercase letter that may occur one or more times. The `$` means the end.

Hence, the email address entered in the text-input field must begin with letter(s), number(s), underscore(s), or hyphen(s) followed by . (period) and again followed by letter(s), number(s), underscore(s), or hyphen(s) one or more times. After that, there has to be an `@` symbol, which is followed by letter(s), number(s), underscore(s), or hyphen(s) followed by . (period). The email address must then end with any uppercase or lowercase letter.

The `validate_email()` function tests the contents of the email parameter with the regular expression and returns `true` if the contents of the email parameter matches with the regular expression supplied; otherwise it returns false. On the basis of the Boolean value returned by the `validate_email()` function, the error message is made visible or invisible.

Suppose in the email address we don't enter . (period); we will get an error message *Invalid Email Address*, as is shown in Figure 4-13.

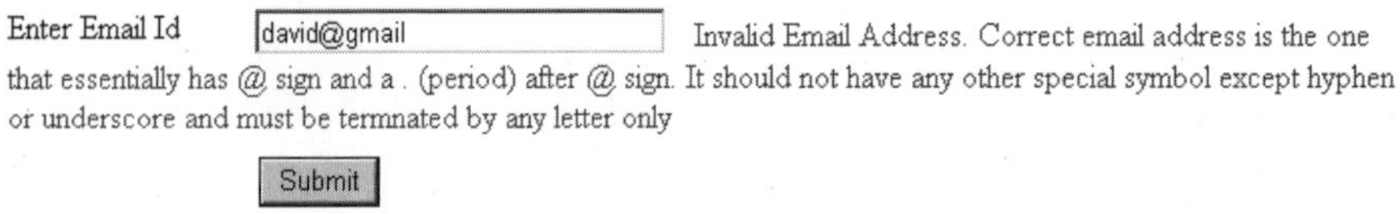

Enter Email Id   david@gmail   Invalid Email Address. Correct email address is the one
that essentially has @ sign and a . (period) after @ sign. It should not have any other special symbol except hyphen
or underscore and must be termnated by any letter only

Submit

Figure 4-13. Error message displayed in case of invalid email address

If the email address is correctly entered that contains @ and . (period), it will be accepted without any error message displayed, as shown in Figure 4-14.

Enter Email Id   david-john_peter123@gmail.com

Submit

Figure 4-14. An email address will be accepted if it contains . and the @ symbol .

4-7. Checking Whether a Checkbox Is Checked

Problem

You have several checkboxes, where each designates an item being sold in a food court. You want to confirm that at least one of the checkboxes is checked when selecting the Submit button. If none of the checkboxes is selected, you want to display an error message.

Solution

Let us make an HTML file that displays four checkboxes, an error message, and an empty paragraph element for displaying the result (total bill of the food items selected). The HTML file may appear as shown here:

```
<body>
<form>
<input type="checkbox"  id="pizza" name="pizza" value=5  class="infobox">Pizza $5 <br>
<input type="checkbox"  id="hotdog" name="hotdog" value=2  class="infobox">HotDog $2<br>
<input type="checkbox"  id="coke" name="coke" value=1  class="infobox">Coke $1<br>
<input type="checkbox"  id="fries" name="fries" value=3  class="infobox">French Fries $3<br>
<p class="error">Select at least one checkbox </p>
<p class="result"></p>
<input class="submit" type="submit" value="Submit">
</form>
</body>
```

The class selectors to apply the style properties automatically to the HTML elements are defined in the external style sheet **style.css**, which may appear as shown here:

```
style.css
.infobox { margin-top: 15px; }
.error { color: red; }
```

The jQuery code to see whether a checkbox is checked or not is as shown here:

```
$(document).ready(function() {
        $('.error').hide();
        $('.submit').click(function(event){
                var count=0;
                var amt=0;
```

```
$('form').find(':checkbox').each(function(){
        if($(this).is(':checked'))
        {
                count++;
                amt=amt+parseInt($(this).val());
        }
});
if(count==0)
{
        $('p.result').hide();
        $('.error').show();
}
else
{
        $('.error').hide();
        $('p.result').show();
        $('p.result').text('Your bill is $ '+amt);
}
event.preventDefault();
        });
});
```

Checking checkboxes with the length Method

In the following jQuery code we confirm whether any of the checkboxes are checked before using the loop to inspect each of them individually:

```
$(document).ready(function() {
        $('.error').hide();
        $('.submit').click(function(event){
                var amt=0;
                var count=$('input:checked').length;
                if(count==0)
                {
                        $('p.result').hide();
                        $('.error').show();
                }
                else
                {
                $('form').find(':checkbox').each(function(){
                        if($(this).is(':checked'))
                        {
                                amt=amt+parseInt($(this).val());
                        }
                });
                $('.error').hide();
                $('p.result').show();
                $('p.result').text('Your bill is $ '+amt);
                }
```

```
                event.preventDefault();
        });
});
```

How It Works

In the HTML file, we can see that the four checkboxes are assigned the class name infobox and represent the four items sold in a food court—pizza, hotdog, Coke, and French fries—along with their price. The paragraph element to display the error message is assigned the class name error and its text displays the error message *Select at least one checkbox.* There is one more paragraph element to display the bill of the food items selected via checkboxes, and it is assigned the class name result and is currently empty. It will be assigned the text to display the bill via jQuery code.

The style sheet defines two class selectors: infobox to be applied to the checkboxes, and the class selector error to be applied to the paragraph element that is meant for displaying the error message. The infobox class selector contains the property margin-top set to 15px to create a sufficient vertical gap among the checkboxes being displayed. The class selector error contains the style property color set to value red so that the error message appears in red (so that it appears highlighted)

In the jQuery code, we first set the error message to be invisible. Then we attach a click event to the Submit button. On selecting the Submit button, its event-handling function will be executed that will do several tasks. In the event-handling function, we first initialize a counter count set to value 0 (which will be used for counting the number of checkboxes that are checked) and another variable amt set to 0 that will be used for totaling the bill of the food items selected. Using the .each() function, we check all the checkboxes of the form one by one and if any of the checkbox is found checked, we increment the value of the counter variable count by 1 and the amount of that food item is added to the amt variable. That is, we are setting the count of the checked checkboxes in the count variable and the total amount of the selected checkboxes in the amt variable. After inspecting all the checkboxes, if we find that the value of the count variable is 0, meaning none of the checkbox is selected, we make the paragraph element meant for displaying the error message visible to display *Select at least one checkbox on the screen.* If the value of the count variable is not 0 (meaning at least one of the checkboxes is selected), we make the paragraph element of the class result visible (and hide the paragraph of the class error) and assign the following text to it: *Your bill is $ +amt,* where amt is the variable in which the total amount for the food items selected is stored.

If we select none of the checkboxes and select the Submit button, an error message *Select at least one checkbox* will appear on the screen, as shown in Figure 4-15.

☐ Pizza $5

☐ HotDog $2

☐ Coke $1

☐ French Fries $3

Select at least one checkbox

[Submit]

Figure 4-15. Error message displayed if no checkbox is selected

If we select one checkbox, the error message will become invisible and the bill for the selected food item will appear as shown in Figure 4-16.

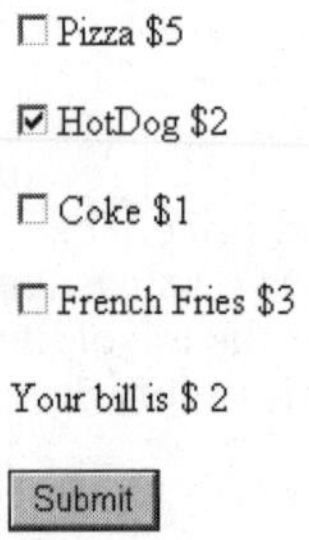

☐ Pizza $5

☑ HotDog $2

☐ Coke $1

☐ French Fries $3

Your bill is $ 2

Submit

Figure 4-16. The bill for the one food item selected is displayed.

If we select more than one checkbox, the total amount for the selected food items will be displayed in the form of a bill, as shown in Figure 4-17.

☑ Pizza $5

☑ HotDog $2

☐ Coke $1

☑ French Fries $3

Your bill is $ 10

Submit

Figure 4-17. The total bill amount of the three food items is displayed.

4-8. Checking Whether a Radio Button Is Selected

Problem

You have several radio buttons and each designates the credit card that the visitor may use to make payments. You want to confirm that one of the radio buttons is selected by the user when selecting the Submit button. If none of the radio button is selected, you want to display an error message.

Solution

What follows is an HTML file that displays three radio buttons. Each radio button is assigned a class name infobox to be used for validation checks and to apply styles. The error message is displayed via a paragraph element with the class name assigned as error, and the Submit button is assigned a class name submit. The HTML code may appear as shown here:

```
<body>
<form>
<input type="radio"  name="paymode" class="infobox" value="MasterCard">MasterCard <br>
<input type="radio"  name="paymode" class="infobox" value="ANZ Grindlay Card">ANZ Grindlay
Card<br>
<input type="radio"  name="paymode" class="infobox" value="Visa Card">Visa Card<br>
<p class="error">Select at least one Option </p>
<p class="result"></p>
<input class="submit" type="submit" value="Submit">
</form>
</body>
```

The external style sheet may contain the following class selectors:

```
style.css
.infobox { margin-top: 15px; }
.error { color: red; }
```

The jQuery code to confirm that at least one radio button is selected is shown here:

```
1.      $(document).ready(function() {
2.            $('.error').hide();
3.            $('.submit').click(function(event){
4.                  var amt=0;
5.                  var count=$('input:checked').length;
6.                  if(count==0)
7.                  {
8.                        $('p.result').hide();
9.                        $('.error').show();
10.          }
11.          else
12.          {
13.                $('.error').hide();
14.                $('p.result').show();
15.                $('p.result').text('You have selected
'+$('input:checked').attr("value"));
16.          }
17.          event.preventDefault();
18.     });
19. });
```

How It Works

In the style sheet file, the class selector `infobox` contains the `margin-top` property set to 15px to keep a good amount of spacing between radio buttons, and the class selector `error` is for assigning the red color to the error messages.

The explanation of the jQuery code statements is shown here line by line:

- Line 2. The error message in the paragraph element of the class `error` is made hidden.

- Line 3. The click event is attached to the Submit button.

- Line 5. Here we're finding out the count of the radio button that is checked (if any) and storing it in the `count` variable.

- Line 8. If no radio button is selected, hide the paragraph element of the class `result` (meant to display the name of the credit card selected).

- Line 9. An error message in the paragraph element of the class `error` is displayed if no radio button is selected.

- Line 15. Assign the text *You have selected n*, where *n* is the value of the radio button selected.

If we select the Submit button without selecting any radio button, we may get the error message *Select at least one Option*, as shown in Figure 4-18.

○ Master Card

○ ANZ Grindlay Card

○ Visa Card

Select at least one Option

Submit

Figure 4-18. Error message displayed if no radio button is selected

If we select a radio button and select the Submit button, a message confirms the name of the credit card selected, as shown in Figure 4-19.

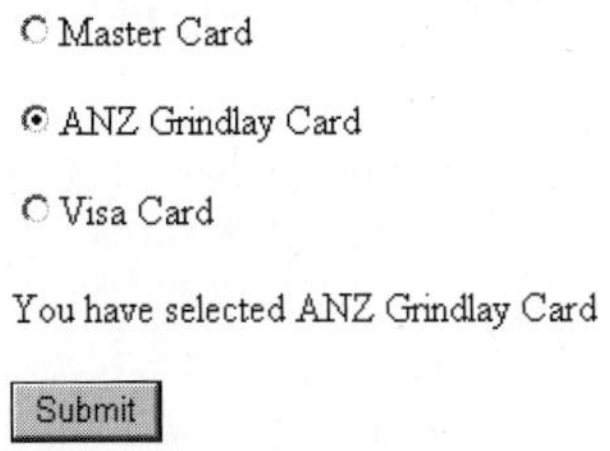

○ Master Card

◉ ANZ Grindlay Card

○ Visa Card

You have selected ANZ Grindlay Card

Submit

Figure 4-19. A message confirms selection of the radio button.

4-9. Checking Whether an Option in a Select Element Is Selected

Problem

You have a drop-down list (`select` element) showing some food items. You want to confirm that the user selected an option from the drop-down list when selecting the Submit button; if no option is selected, an error message is displayed.

Solution

Following is a HTML file that displays a drop-down list box containing a few food items. The `select` element, with the help of which the drop-down list is displayed, is assigned the class name `infobox` so as to apply the style properties defined in the class selector `infobox` (written in the style sheet file `style.css`). The label message *Select the Food Item* is displayed via the `span` element with the class name `label`. The error message is displayed via the paragraph element with the class name assigned as `error`, and the Submit button is assigned a class name *submit*. The HTML code may appear as shown here:

```
<body>
<form>
<span class="label">Select the Food Item </span>
<select id="food" class="infobox">
<option value="0">Select a Food</option>
<option value="Pizza $5">Pizza $5</option>
<option value="HotDog $2">HotDog $2</option>
<option value="Coke $1">Coke $1</option>
<option value="French Fries $3">French Fries $3</option>
</select>
<p class="error">You have not selected any Option</p>
<p class="result"></p>
<input class="submit" type="submit" value="Submit">
</form>
</body>
```

The external style sheet may contain the following class selectors that will be automatically applied to the respective HTML elements of the specified class:

```
style.css
.label {float: left; width: 150px; }
.infobox {width: 150px; }
.error { color: red; padding-left: 10px; }
.submit { margin-left: 150px; margin-top: 10px;}
```

The jQuery code to confirm that the option from the drop-down list is selected is shown here:

```
$(document).ready(function() {
        $('.error').hide();
        $('.submit').click(function(event){
                var count=$('select option:selected').val();
                if(count==0)
                {
                        $('p.result').hide();
                        $('.error').show();
                }
                else
                {
                        $('.error').hide();
                        $('p.result').show();
                        $('p.result').text('You have selected '+$('select
option:selected').text());
                }
                event.preventDefault();
        });
});
```

How It Works

In the style sheet file, the class selector `label` contains the `float` property set to `left` so as to make the label appear on the left (creating space for the drop-down list to appear on the right). The `width` property is set to 150px to define the width that the label can consume. The class selector `infobox` contains the `width` property set to 150px to specify the width for the drop-down list, and the class selector `error` is for assigning the red color to the error message and for making the error message appear at the distance of 10px from the left side of the browser window. The class selector `submit` contains the `margin-left` property set to 150px to make the Submit button appear at the distance of 150px from the left side of the browser window (so that it appears below the drop-down list), and `margin-top` property is set to 10px to keep some spacing from the above element that may appear (error or result message).

In the jQuery code, we initially hide the paragraph element of the class `error` meant to display the error message. Then we attach a click event to the Submit button. The statement

```
var count=$(select option:selected).val();
```

retrieves the value of the option selected from the `select` element and stores it in variable `count`. If the value of `count` is 0, meaning the user has not selected any option, we make the error message appear on the screen by making the paragraph element of the class `error` visible, and if the value of the `count` variable is nonzero, we make the paragraph element of the class `result` display the result using the following statement:

```
You have selected +$(select option:selected).text());
```

which displays the text of the option that is selected from the `select` element.

On execution, if we press the Submit button without selecting any option from the `select` element, we get an error message *You have not selected any Option*, as shown in Figure 4-20.

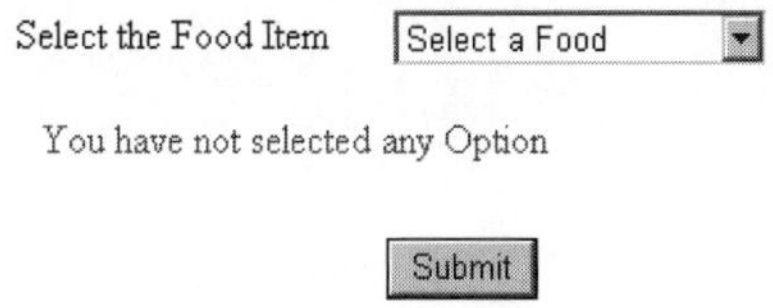

Select the Food Item [Select a Food   ▼]

You have not selected any Option

[Submit]

Figure 4-20. Error message displayed if no option is selected from the select element

If we select any option from the list and select the Submit button, we get the message showing the option selected, as shown in Figure 4-21.

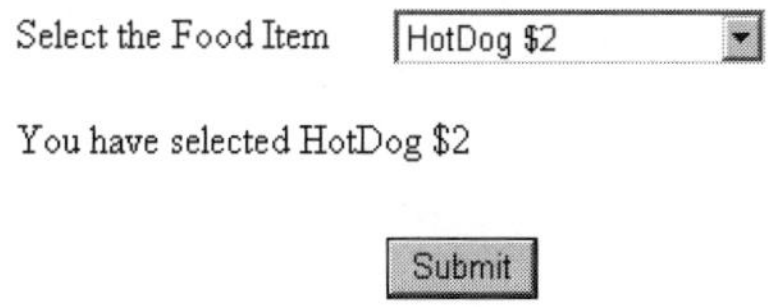

Select the Food Item [HotDog $2   ▼]

You have selected HotDog $2

[Submit]

Figure 4-21. The text of the selected option is displayed.

Multiple Select

Let's modify the preceding solution to allow visitors to select more than one option from the `select` element. To select more than one option from the `select` element, use the `MULTIPLE` attribute along with the `select` element as shown here:

```
<body>
<form>
<span class="label">Select the Food Item </span>
<select id="food" class="infobox" MULTIPLE>
<option value="0" selected="0">Select a Food</option>
<option value="Pizza $5">Pizza $5</option>
<option value="HotDog $2">HotDog $2</option>
<option value="Coke $1">Coke $1</option>
<option value="French Fries $3">French Fries $3</option>
</select>
<p class="error">You have not selected any Option </p>
```

131

```
<p class="result"></p>
<input class="submit" type="submit" value="Submit">
</form>
</body>
```

The MULTIPLE attribute when attached with select element will allow us to select more than one option (making use of the Ctrl or Shift key). Using the same jQuery code and style sheet, we will get a message displaying all the options selected by the user from the select element, as shown in Figure 4-22.

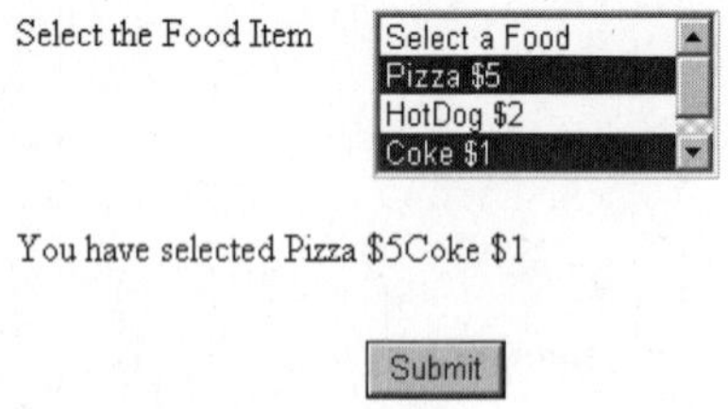

Select the Food Item

Select a Food	▲
Pizza $5	
HotDog $2	
Coke $1	▼

You have selected Pizza $5Coke $1

Submit

Figure 4-22. Text details all selected options, displayed with no space in between.

We can see that the options selected are displayed without any space in between. To separate the options with a comma (,) in between, we modify the jQuery code as shown here:

```
$(document).ready(function() {
  $('.error').hide();
  $('.submit').click(function(event){
    var selectedopts="";
    var count=$('select option:selected').val();
    if(count==0)
    {
      $('p.result').hide();
      $('.error').show();
    }
    else
    {
      $('select option:selected').each(function(){
        selectedopts+=$(this).text()+",";
      });
      $('.error').hide();
      $('p.result').show();
      $('p.result').text('You have selected '+ selectedopts);
    }
    event.preventDefault();
  });
});
```

We have defined a string variable **selectedopts** in the preceding jQuery code and all the options selected from the select element are picked up by using the **.each()** method. We concatenate them to the **selectedopts** variables along with a comma. When the text of all the selected options is added to the **selectedopts** variable, we display its contents via the paragraph element of the class **result**. The output that we may get is shown in Figure 4-23.

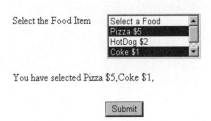

Figure 4-23. Text detalis all selected options, displayed with a comma in between.

In case we don't select any option from the **select** element and we select the Submit button, we may get the error message shown in Figure 4-24.

Figure 4-24. Error message displayed if no option is selected

4-10. Applying Styles to Options and a Form Button

Problem

You have a drop-down list (**select** element) showing food items and you want to apply styles to the options of the **select** element.

Solution

For this recipe, we will be using the same HTML file that we created in Recipe 4-9. In the style sheet we need to add one type selector, **option**, to apply its style properties to all the options of the **select** element automatically, and also a CSS class **.meal** to apply style to the odd-numbered options of the **select** element. The style sheet may appear as shown here:

```
style.css
.label {float: left; width: 150px; }
.infobox {width: 150px; }
.error { color: red; padding-left: 10px; }
.submit { margin-left: 150px; margin-top: 10px;}

option{
background-color:red;
color:white;
}

.meal{
background-color:cyan;
color:blue;
}
```

To make the options appear colorful, we will be applying different styles to even-numbered and odd-numbered options of the select element. The type selector option will apply style properties to all the options of the select element, setting their background color to red and the foreground color to white. The style rule meal will be applied to only odd-numbered options of the select elements via jQuery code, setting their background color to cyan and foreground color to blue.

To apply the style rule meal to the odd-numbered options of the select element, we need to add the following statement in jQuery code:

`$('option:odd').addClass('meal');`

The overall jQuery code may appear as shown here (for details of the validation logic, please see Recipe 4-9):

```
$(document).ready(function() {
  $('.error').hide();
  $('option:odd').addClass('meal');
  $('.submit').click(function(event){
    var selectedopts="";
    var count=$('select option:selected').val();
    if(count==0)
    {
      $('p.result').hide();
      $('.error').show();
    }
    else
    {
      $('select option:selected').each(function(){
        selectedopts+=$(this).text()+",";
      });
      $('.error').hide();
      $('p.result').show();
      $('p.result').text('You have selected '+ selectedopts);
    }
    event.preventDefault();
  });
});
```

How It Works

On execution of the preceding jQuery code, we find that even-numbered and odd-numbered options of the **select** element appear in different foreground and background colors, as shown in Figure 4-25.

Figure 4-25. *Styles applied to options of the select element*

Styling the Form Button

Let us apply styles to the Submit button to make it appear attractive. For this, we need to modify the style properties of the class selector **.submit** defined in the style sheet **style.css**, as shown here:

```
style.css
.label {float: left; width: 150px; }
.infobox {width: 150px; }
.error { color: red; padding-left: 10px; }
.submit { margin-left: 150px; margin-top: 10px;font-size:1.5em;background-
color:green;color:blue;}

option{
background-color:red;
color:white;
}

.meal{
background-color:cyan;
color:blue;
}
```

We can see that the class selector **.submit** contains several properties:

- The **margin-left** property is set to 150px to make it appear at the distance of 150px from the left boundary of the browser window (below the **select** element).

- The **margin-top** property is set to 10px to create some space above the **select** element.

- The font-size property is set to 1.5em to increase the font size to 150% of the default font size.

- The background-color and color properties are set to green and blue, respectively, to create text color over a green background.

The Submit button may appear as shown in Figure 4-26.

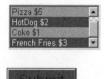

Figure 4-26. Styles applied to the Submit button

Creating an Image Submit Button

Let's now replace the Submit button with an image that will act as Submit button. Before we go ahead with this solution, we need to have an image file **submit.jpg**, as shown in Figure 4-27. We also need to modify the class selector .submit as shown in the following stylesheet file, **style.css**.

```
style.css
.label {float: left; width: 150px; }
.infobox {width: 150px; }
.error { color: red; padding-left: 10px; }
.submit { margin-left: 150px; margin-top: 10px;width:150px;height:40px;}

option{
background-color:red;
color:white;
}

.meal{
background-color:cyan;
color:blue;
}
```

The class selector .submit defines the space of the image (the Submit button) from the left boundary of the browser window as 150px , the distance from the top element to 10px, and the width and height of the image itself to 150px and 40px, respectively.

To apply the image in **submit.jpg** at the place of Submit button, we need to modify the jQuery code as shown here:

```
<body>
<form>
<span class="label">Select the Food Item </span>
<select id="food" class="infobox" MULTIPLE>
<option value="0">Select a Food</option>
<option value="Pizza $5">Pizza $5</option>
<option value="HotDog $2">HotDog $2</option>
<option value="Coke $1">Coke $1</option>
<option value="French Fries $3">French Fries $3</option>
</select>
<p class="error">You have not selected any Option </p>
<p class="result"></p>
<input class="submit" type="image" value="Submit" src="submit.jpg">
</form>
</body>
```

We can see in the boldface code that by specifying the **type** attribute as **image** and specifying the image file name in the **src** attribute, we make the Submit button appear in the form of an image, as shown in Figure 4-27.

Figure 4-27. Image applied to the Submit button

4-11. Checking and Unchecking All Checkboxes Together

Problem

You have several checkboxes, where each designates an item being sold in a food court. You want a Check All checkbox, which, if checked, should check all the other **checkboxes**; if the Check All box is unchecked, it must uncheck all the other checkboxes.

Solution

Let's make an HTML file that displays five checkboxes (four for the food items and one for collectively checking and unchecking them). The HTML file may appear as shown here:

```
<body>
<form>
<div class="infobox"><input type="checkbox" id="checkall">Check/Uncheck all Checkboxes</div>
<div class="infobox"><input type="checkbox"  id="pizza" name="pizza" value=5>Pizza $5</div>
<div class="infobox"> <input type="checkbox"  id="hotdog" name="hotdog" value=2>HotDog
$2</div>
<div class="infobox"><input type="checkbox"  id="coke" name="coke" value=1>Coke $1</div>
<div class="infobox"><input type="checkbox"  id="fries" name="fries" value=3>French Fries
$3</div>
</form>
</body>
```

In the style sheet, we define the class selector: infobox that may appear as shown here:

```
.infobox{ padding: 5px; }
```

The padding property is set to 5px to create spacing among the checkboxes.

The jQuery code to check and uncheck all the checkboxes on selecting the Check All checkbox and to display the bill for the selected food items is shown here:

```
$(document).ready(function() {
        $('#checkall').click(function(){
                $("input[type='checkbox']").attr('checked', $('#checkall').is(':checked'));
        });
        $('form').find(':checkbox').click(function(){
                var amt=0;
                $('div').filter(':gt(0)').find(':checkbox').each(function(){
                        if($('div:gt(0)'))
                        {
                                if($(this).is(':checked'))
                                {
                                        amt=amt+parseInt($(this).val());
                                }
                        }
                });
                $('p').remove();
                $('<p>').insertAfter('div:eq(4)');
                $('p').text('Your bill is $ '+amt);
        });
});
```

How It Works

In the HTML file, we can see that the five checkboxes are assigned the class name infobox, out of which four checkboxes represent the four items sold in a food court: pizza hot dog, Coke, and French fries, along with their prices.

In the jQuery code, we attach a click event to the Check All checkbox (checkall):

```
$("input[type='checkbox']").attr('checked', $('#checkall').is(':checked'));
```

To understand the preceding statement, let's look at the `.attr()` and `.is()` methods that are used in this statement:

`.attr()`

The `.attr()` method is used for setting the attributes of the selected element(s).

```
Syntax:
.attr(attribute, value)
.is()
```

The `.is()` method checks the selected element(s) with a selector and returns `true` if the any of the selected elements match with the selector; otherwise it returns `false`.

```
Syntax:
.is(selector)
```

The `$(#checkall).is(:checked)` part of the preceding statement checks if the checkbox of `id:checkall` is checked. If the checkbox (`id: checkall`) is checked, the `.is()` method will return `true`; otherwise it will return `false`. If the `.is()` method returns `true`, all the input elements of `type:checkbox` (that is, all the checkboxes) are set to checked mode; all of them will be set to unchecked mode if the `.is()` method returns `false`. Since the user is allowed to check any individual check box, we check the status of each checkbox that has an index value greater than 0 (because the checkbox with index value 0 is the Check All checkbox). The value of all the checkboxes is added to the `amt` variable. To display the bill, we create a paragraph element and add the text *Your bill is amt* (where `amt` is the numerical value contained in the `amt` variable), and insert this paragraph element after the `div` element of index value 4; that is, after the last checkbox.

If we select the Check All checkbox, all the following checkboxes will be checked and the sum of their values is displayed in the form of a bill, as shown in Figure 4-28.

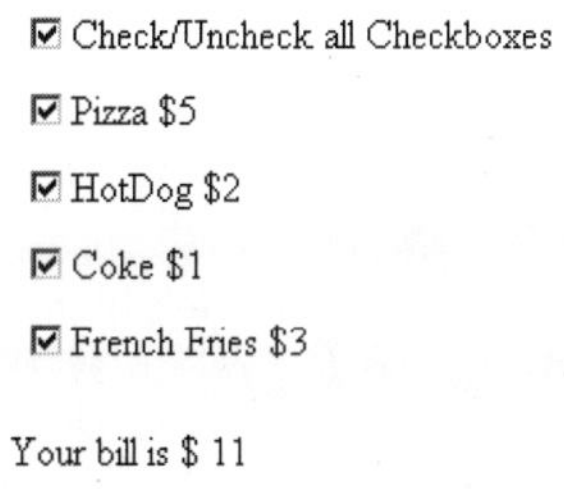

☑ Check/Uncheck all Checkboxes

☑ Pizza $5

☑ HotDog $2

☑ Coke $1

☑ French Fries $3

Your bill is $ 11

Figure 4-28. *All checkboxes selected by selecting Check/Uncheck all Checkboxes*

If the Check All checkbox is unchecked, all the following checkboxes will be unchecked and hence the bill of amount $0 will be displayed, as shown in Figure 4-29.

☐ Check/Uncheck all Checkboxes

☐ Pizza $5

☐ HotDog $2

☐ Coke $1

☐ French Fries $3

Your bill is $ 0

Figure 4-29. All checkboxes unselected by unchecking Check/Uncheck all Checkboxes

Users can also select any of the individual checkboxes. The total amount of the selected checkboxes will appear, as shown in Figure 4-30.

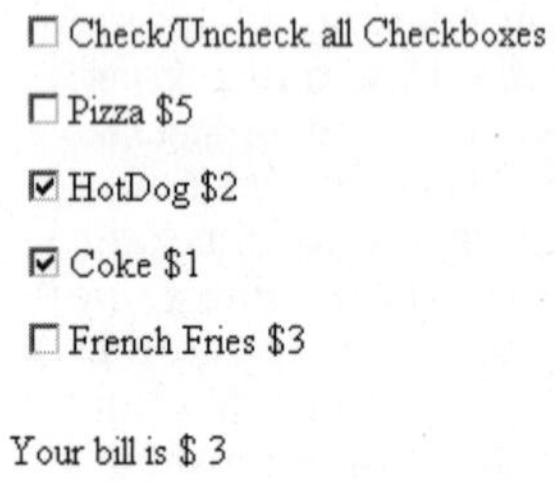

☐ Check/Uncheck all Checkboxes

☐ Pizza $5

☑ HotDog $2

☑ Coke $1

☐ French Fries $3

Your bill is $ 3

Figure 4-30. Bill of the individually selected food items

4-12. Validating Two Fields

Problem

You have two fields, User Id and Password, and you want to confirm that none of the fields are left blank. If any of them are left blank, you want an error message to appear on the screen.

Solution

Let's make an HTML file that displays two labels and two text fields, as shown here:

```
<body>
<div><span class="label">User Id *</span><input type="text"  class="infobox" name="userid"
/><span class="error"> This field cannot be blank</span></div>
<div><span class="label">Password *</span><input type="password" class="infobox"
name="password" /><span class="error"> This field cannot be blank</span></div>
</body>
```

The style sheet with the respective class selectors may appear as shown here:

```
style.css
.label {float: left; width: 120px; }
.infobox {width: 200px; }
.error { color: red; padding-left: 10px; }
div{padding: 5px; }
```

The jQuery code to test that none of the fields are left blank is as shown here:

```
$(document).ready(function() {
  $('.error').hide();
  $('.infobox').each(function(){
    $(this).blur(function(){
      var data=$(this).val();
      var len=data.length;
      if(len<1)
      {
        $(this).parent().find('.error').show();
      }
      else
      {
        $(this).parent().find('.error').hide();
      }
    });
  });
});
```

How It Works

In the HTML file, the label messages *User Id** and *Password** are enclosed in span elements that are assigned the class name label. The text-input fields are assigned the class name infobox and the error message (*This field cannot be blank*) is stored as a span element of the class error. The reasons for assigning the classes to all the three items—the label, the text-input field, and the error message—is to automatically apply the properties defined in the class selectors label, infobox, and error (defined in the style sheet style.css).

In the style sheet file, the class selector label contains the float property set to left so as to make the label appears on its left (creating space for the text-input field to appear on its right) and the width property set to 120px to define the width that the label can consume. The class selector infobox contains the width property set to 200px to specify the width for the drop-down list, and the class selector error for assigning a red color to the error messages and for making the error message appear at the distance of 10px from the left side of the element. The type selector div has the padding property set to 5px for creating some space among the two div elements, where each div element contains a combination of label, text-input field, and error message.

In the jQuery code, initially we hide all the error messages (span elements of the class error), then with the use of the .each() method, we test that if a blur event occurs on any of the text fields, (that is, if the user loses focus on that field), the value in that text-input field is retrieved and stored in the variable data. If the data variable is empty—that is, if its length is less than 1—we display the error message related to that field.

If we leave the focus from the first text field (User Id) and move on to the next field, we get the error message on first field, as shown in Figure 4-31.

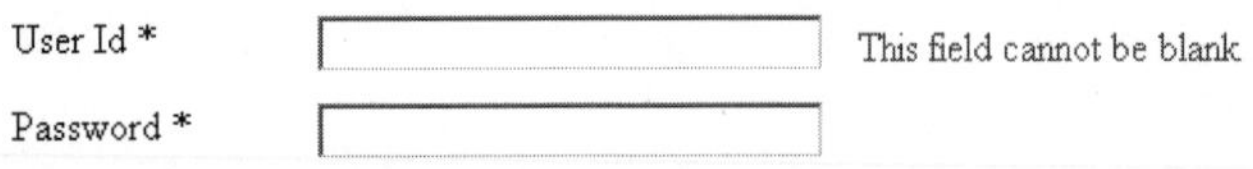

| User Id * | | This field cannot be blank |
| Password * | | |

Figure 4-31. Error message displayed if the first field is left blank

And if the second text field is left blank and the focus is lost on it, the error message appears for it, as shown in Figure 4-32.

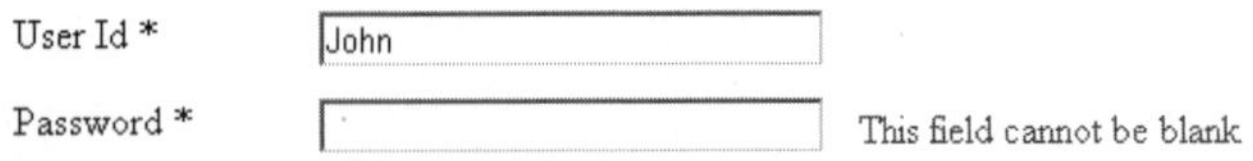

| User Id * | John | |
| Password * | | This field cannot be blank |

Figure 4-32. Error message displayed if the second field is left blank

No error appears if data is provided in both the text-input fields, as shown in Figure 4-33.

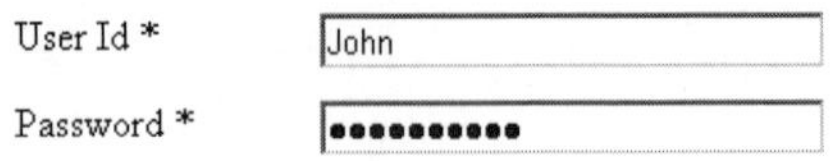

| User Id * | John | |
| Password * | •••••••••• | |

Figure 4-33. No error message appears if data is provided in both the text-input fields.

Adding a Submit Button

In the preceding solution, we didn't add a Submit button. So let's add a Submit button now and validate the text-input fields one by one when the user selects the Submit button. Let us add a Submit button to the preceding HTML file as shown here:

```
<body>
<form>
<div><span class="label">User Id *</span><input type="text"  class="infobox" name="userid"
/><span class="error"> This field cannot be blank</span></div>
<div><span class="label">Password *</span><input type="password" class="infobox"
name="password" /><span class="error"> This field cannot be blank</span></div>
<input class="submit" type="submit" value="Submit">
</form>
</body>
```

We need to add a class selector `.submit` in the style sheet file (`style.css`) so as to apply the style properties to the Submit button automatically to make it appear below the text-input fields with a small bit of spacing from the element just above it. The `style.css` file may now appear as shown here:

```
style.css
.label {float: left; width: 120px; }
.infobox {width: 200px; }
.error { color: red; padding-left: 10px; }
.submit { margin-left: 125px; margin-top: 10px;}
div{padding: 5px; }
```

The jQuery code will be modified to perform validation on occurrence of the click event on the Submit button, as shown here:

```
$(document).ready(function() {
  $('.error').hide();
  $('.submit').click(function(event){
    $('.infobox').each(function(){
      var data=$(this).val();
      var len=data.length;
      if(len<1)
      {
      $(this).parent().find('.error').show();
      }
      else
      {
        $(this).parent().find('.error').hide();
      }
    });
    event.preventDefault();
  });
});
```

Since we are interested in performing validation and not in sending the data (entered in the text-input field) to the server on selecting the Submit button, we invoke the `.preventDefault()`method of the **event** object to stop sending the data to the server . The **event** object is automatically sent by JavaScript to the event-handling function of the click event.

If we leave both the fields blank and select the Submit button, we get two error messages displayed, as shown in Figure 4-34.

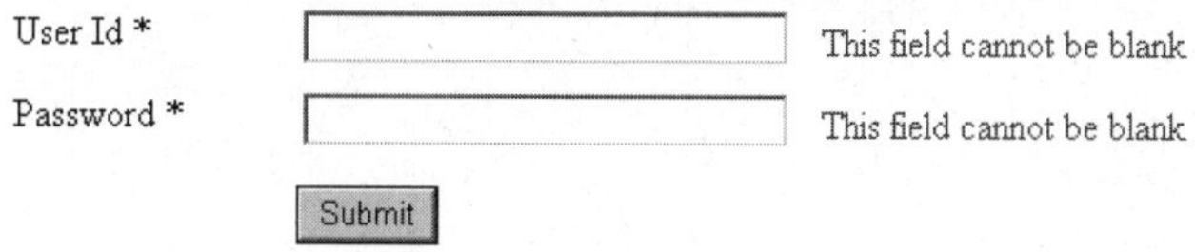

User Id *   [   ]   This field cannot be blank

Password *   [   ]   This field cannot be blank

                [Submit]

Figure 4-34. Error messages for both the fields appear if both are left blank.

If one of the fields is left blank, its error message will be displayed on selecting the Submit button, as shown in Figure 4-35.

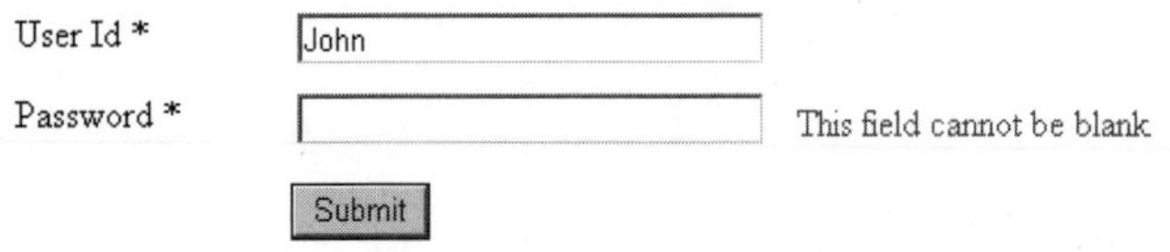

User Id *   [John   ]

Password *   [   ] This field cannot be blank

                 [Submit]

Figure 4-35. An error message for the first text-input field appears if it is left blank.

4-13. Matching the Password and Confirm Password Fields

Problem

You want to assure that password entered in the Password and Confirm Password fields match exactly.

Solution

Let us make an HTML file that displays three labels and three text fields for Userid, Password, and Confirm Password, as shown here:

```
<body>
<form>
<div ><span class="label">User Id </span><input type="text"  class="userid" name="userid"
/></div>
<div ><span class="label">Password </span><input type="password" class="password"
name="password" /><span class="error"> Password cannot be blank</span></div>
<div ><span class="label">Confirm Password </span><input type="password" class="confpass"
name="confpass" /><span class="error"> Password and Confirm Password don't
match</span></div>
<input class="submit" type="submit" value="Submit">
</form>
</body>
```

The style sheet with the respective class selectors may appear as shown here:

```
style.css
.label {float: left; width: 120px; }
.error { color: red; padding-left: 10px; }
.submit { margin-left: 125px; margin-top: 10px;}
div{padding: 5px; }
```

The jQuery code to test that data entered in the Password and Confirm Password fields are exactly same is as shown here:

```
$(document).ready(function() {
  $('.error').hide();
  $('.submit').click(function(event){
    data=$('.password').val();
    var len=data.length;
    if(len<1)
    {
      $('.password').next().show();
    }
    else
    {
      $('.password').next().hide();
    }
    if($('.password').val() !=$('.confpass').val())
    {
      $('.confpass').next().show();
    }
    else
    {
      $('.confpass').next().hide();
    }
    event.preventDefault();
  });
});
```

How It Works

In the HTML file, the label messages *User Id, Password,* and *Confirm Password* are enclosed in `span` elements that are assigned the class name `label`. The text-input fields are assigned the respective class names `userid`, `password`, and `confpass` for retrieving the data entered in them via jQuery. Finally, all the text-input fields are followed by the error message nested inside the `span` element of the class `error`.

The reasons of assigning the classes to all the items—label, error message, and Submit button—is to automatically apply the properties defined in the class selectors `label`, `error`, and `.submit` (defined in the style sheet `style.css`). Also, the combination of label, text-input field, and error are nested inside the `div` element so that we can apply the `style` property to the `div` element to create spacing among each combination of label, text-input field, and error message.

In the style sheet file, the class selector `label` contains the `float` property set to `left` so as to make the label appears on the left side of the browser window (creating space for the text-input field to appear on its right), and the `width` property is set to 120px to define the width that the label can consume. The class selector `error` assigns the red color to the error messages and makes the error message appear at the distance of 10px from the element on its left. The class selector `.submit` contains the `margin-left` property set to 125px and the `margin-top` property set to 10px to make it appear at the distance of 125px from the left border of the browser window (to appear below the text-input fields), and with a gap of 10px from the element just above it. The type selector `div` has the `padding` property set to 5px for creating some space among the `div` elements, where each `div` element contains a combination of label, text-input field, and error message.

Before you can understand the jQuery code, you must understand the usage of the `.next()` method that is used in it, so we'll look at that right now.

.next()

This method returns the very next sibling for each element, and not all next siblings like the `nextAll()` method does.

```
Syntax:
.next(selector)
```

Here selector is an optional parameter used for specifying the selector expression for matching with the specified elements.

In the jQuery code, initially we hide the error messages (elements nested inside the `span` element of the class `error`). Thereafter, we attach a click event to the Submit button. In the event-handling function of the click event, we retrieve the data in the Password field (text-input field of the class `password`) and store it in variable data. If the length of the contents in variable data is found to be less than 1—that is, if the user has not entered anything in the Password field—we make the element next to the password field (which is the `span` element of the class `error`) appear on the screen; that is, we display the error message *Password cannot be blank* on the screen.

If the user has not left the password empty, we check whether the data entered in the Password field and the Confirm Password field (data in elements of class `.password` and `.confpass`) are exactly the same. If the two don't match, we display the error message (which is the element next to the Confirm Password field) *Password and Confirm Password don't match*. We also invoke the `preventDefault()` method of the event object to prevent the data entered by the user from sending it to the server, as we are mainly interested in confirming that the data entered in Password and Confirm Password fields match.

On execution of the jQuery code, if we leave the Password field blank and select the Submit button, we get the error message *Password cannot be blank*, as shown in Figure 4-36.

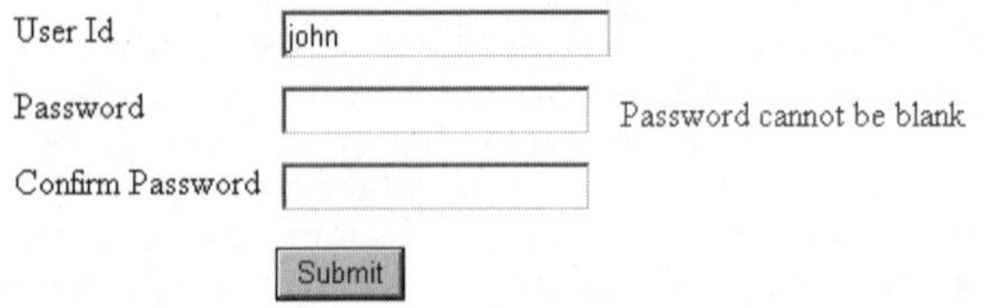

Figure 4-36. The error message that appears if a password is not entered

If the contents of the Password and Confirm Password fields don't match, we get the error message *Password and Confirm Password don't match*, as shown in Figure 4-37.

Figure 4-37. The error message that appears if Password and Confirm Password don't match

4-14. Disabling Certain Fields

Problem

You want the user to fill the User Id, Password, and Confirm Password fields. If the user enters invalid data or leaves any field blank, you want not only to display the error message but also to disable the rest of the fields until the error is corrected.

Solution

Let's make use of the same HTML and style sheet file (`style.css`) that we used in Recipe 4-13. The only change we will make in that HTML file is to remove the Submit button, as we are going to validate fields in this example by using the `blur()` event rather than the `click()` event. The HTML code is provided here for reference:

```
<body>
<form>
<div ><span class="label">User Id </span><input type="text"  class="userid" name="userid"
/><span class="error"> User id cannot be blank</span></div>
<div ><span class="label">Password </span><input type="password" class="password"
name="password" /><span class="error"> Password cannot be blank</span></div>
<div ><span class="label">Confirm Password </span><input type="password" class="confpass"
name="confpass" /><span class="error"> Password and Confirm Password don't
match</span></div>
</form>
</body>
```

The style sheet file `style.css` will be exactly same as the one used in Recipe 4-13. Following is the jQuery code that does these things:

- Validates the data entered by the user

- Displays the error messages

- Disables the rest of the fields if data is skipped or some invalid data is entered in any field

```
$(document).ready(function() {
  $('.error').hide();
  $('.userid').blur(function(){
    data=$('.userid').val();
    var len=data.length;
    if(len<1)
    {
      $('.userid').next().show();
      $('.password').attr('disabled',true);
      $('.confpass').attr('disabled',true);
    }
```

```
      else
      {
        $('.userid').next().hide();
        $('.password').removeAttr('disabled');
        $('.confpass').removeAttr('disabled');
      }
    });

  $('.password').blur(function(){
    data=$('.password').val();
    var len=data.length;
    if(len<1)
    {
      $('.password').next().show();
      $('.confpass').attr('disabled',true);
    }
    else
    {
      $('.password').next().hide();
      $('.confpass').removeAttr('disabled');
    }
  });

  $('.confpass').blur(function(){
    if($('.password').val() !=$('.confpass').val())
    {
      $('.confpass').next().show();
    }
    else
    {
      $('.confpass').next().hide();
    }
  });
});
```

How It Works

Initially we hide the error messages (elements nested inside the **span** element of the class **error**). Thereafter, we check if the **blur()** event has occurred on the text-input field of class **userid**; that is, whether the focus is lost on the User Id field. If yes, we retrieve the data entered by the user in that field and store it in variable data. If the length of the contents in the variable data is found to be less than 1— that is, if the User Id field is left blank—we make the element next to the User Id field (which is the **span** element of the class **error**) appear on the screen; we display the error message *User id cannot be blank* on the screen. Beside this, we also use the following two statements:

```
$('.password').attr('disabled',true);
$('.confpass').attr('disabled',true);
```

to disable the Password and Confirm Passwords fields (two input fields of the classes **password** and **confpass**); that is, until and unless the user enters the User ID, both of the fields will be disabled. When the user enters some data in the User Id field, both of the disabled fields will be enabled with the following two statements:

```
$('.password').removeAttr('disabled');
$('.confpass').removeAttr('disabled');
```

Similarly, we check if the Password field is left empty. If yes, again we see the error message *Password cannot be blank* and the Confirm Password field will be disabled until the user enters some data in the Password field.

Finally, we check if the data entered in the Password and Confirm Password fields (data in elements of the `.password` and `.confpass` classes) are exactly same. If the two don't match, we display the error message (which is the element next to the Confirm Password field) *Password and Confirm Password don't match.*

On execution of the jQuery code, if we leave the User Id field blank and lose focus from it, we get the error message *User id cannot be blank*, as shown in Figure 4-38. Also, the rest of the fields will be disabled; the user will not be able to enter anything in them until the user enters something in the User Id field:

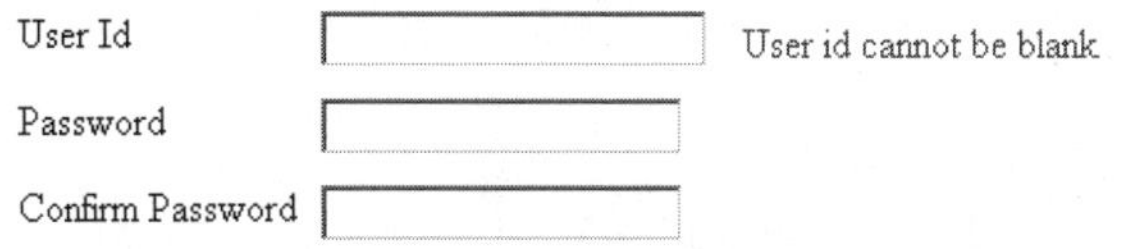

User Id   [ ]   User id cannot be blank

Password   [ ]

Confirm Password [ ]

Figure 4-38. If a user ID is not provided, an error message appears and the remaining fields are disabled.

If the Password field is left blank and we lose focus on it, we get the error message *Password cannot be blank* on the screen and also the Confirm Password field will be disabled until something is entered in the Password field, as shown in Figure 4-39.

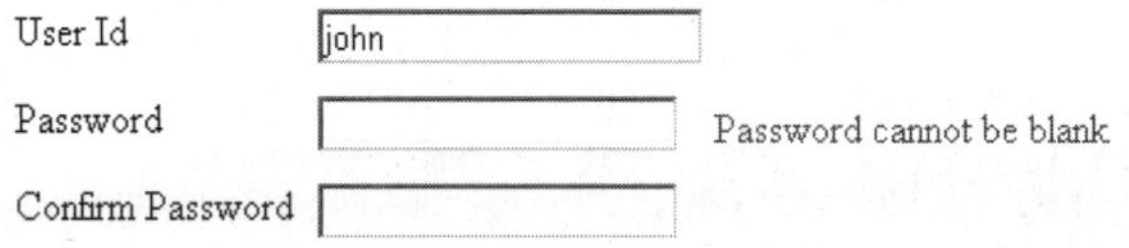

User Id   [john]

Password   [ ]   Password cannot be blank

Confirm Password [ ]

Figure 4-39. An error message appers and the Confirm Password field is disabled if a password is not entered.

4-15. Validating a Complete Form

Problem

You have a form where the user is supposed to provide a lot of information, including user ID, password, and email address. The user also is supposed to select the food items he want to purchase and select the mode of payment (specify the credit card) and designate in which country he lives. You want each field to be validated as follows:

- The user ID should consist of only characters, numerals, and underscores.

- The password cannot be left blank.

- The email address must contain a period and the @ symbol.

- At least one check box (food item) must be selected.

- The user must select one of the modes of payment.

- The country in which user lives must be selected.

Solution

Let's make an HTML file that displays labels and fields, as shown in Figure 4-40. We can see that there are six labels, three text-input fields, four checkboxes, three radio buttons, and one **select** element. The HTML code may appear as shown here:

```
<body>
<form>
<div>    <span class="label">User Id </span><input type="text"  class="userid" name="userid"
/><span class="error">User id can contain only numeral, character or
_(underscore)</span></div>
<div><span class="label">Password </span><input type="password" class="password"
name="password" /><span class="error"> Password cannot be blank</span></div>
<div><span class="label">Email Address </span><input type="text" class="emailadd"
name="emailid" /><span class="error"> Invalid email address</span></div>
<div><span class="label">Select Food items</span><br><input type="checkbox"  id="pizza"
name="pizza" value=5 class="chkb">Pizza $5 <br>
<input type="checkbox"  id="hotdog" name="hotdog" value=2  class="chkb">HotDog $2<br>
<input type="checkbox"  id="coke" name="coke" value=1  class="chkb">Coke $1<br>
<input type="checkbox"  id="fries" name="fries" value=3  class="chkb">French Fries $3<br>
<span class="fooderror">You have not selected any food item</span></div>
<div><span class="label">Mode of  Payment</span><br><input type="radio"  name="paymode"
class="radiobtn" value="MasterCard">MasterCard <br>
<input type="radio"  name="paymode" class="radiobtn" value="ANZ Grindlay Card">ANZ Grindlay
Card<br>
<input type="radio"  name="paymode" class="radiobtn" value="Visa Card">Visa Card<br>
<span class="payerror">You have not selected any payment method</span></div>
<div><span class="label">Country</span><select id="country" class="infobox">
<option value="0">Select a Country</option>
<option value="USA">USA</option>
<option value="United Kingdom">United Kingdom</option>
<option value="India">India</option>
<option value="China">China</option>
</select>
```

```
<span class="error"> Please select the country</span></div>
<input class="submit" type="submit" value="Submit">
</form>
</body>
</html>
```

The style sheet file to apply style properties to the HTML elements may appear as shown here:

```
style.css
.label {float: left; width: 120px; }
.infobox {width: 120px; }
.error { color: red; padding-left: 10px; }
.submit { margin-left: 125px; margin-top: 10px;}
div{padding: 5px; }
.chkb { margin-left: 125px; margin-top: 10px;}
.radiobtn { margin-left: 125px; margin-top: 10px;}
```

The jQuery code to validate all of the fields is shown here:

```
$(document).ready(function() {
  $('.error').hide();
  $('.fooderror').addClass('error');
  $('.fooderror').hide();
  $('.payerror').addClass('error');
  $('.payerror').hide();

  $('.submit').click(function(event){
    var data=$('.userid').val();
    if(validate_userid(data))
    {
      $('.userid').next().hide();
    }
    else
    {
      $('.userid').next().show();
    }

    data=$('.password').val();
    var len=data.length;
    if(len<1)
    {
      $('.password').next().show();
    }
    else
    {
      $('.password').next().hide();
    }
```

```
data=$('.emailadd').val();
if(valid_email(data))
{
   $('.emailadd').next().hide();
}
else
{
   $('.emailadd').next().show();
}

var count=0;
$('div').find(':checkbox').each(function(){
   if($(this).is(':checked'))
   {
      count++;
   }
});
if(count==0)
{
   $('.fooderror').css({'margin-left':250}).show();
}
else
{
   $('.fooderror').hide();
}

count=0;
$('div').find(':radio').each(function(){
   if($(this).is(':checked'))
   {
      count++;
   }
});
if(count==0)
{
   $('.payerror').css({'margin-left':250}).show();
}
else
{
   $('.payerror').hide();
}

count=$('select option:selected').val();
if(count==0)
{
   $('.infobox').next().show();
}
```

```
    else
    {
      $('.infobox').next().hide();
    }

    event.preventDefault();
  });
});


function valid_email(email)
{
  var pattern= new RegExp(/^[\w-]+(\.[\w-]+)*@([\w-]+\.)+[a-zA-Z]+$/);
  return pattern.test(email);
}

function validate_userid(uid)
{
  var pattern= new RegExp(/^[a-z0-9_]+$/);
  return pattern.test(uid);
}
```

How It Works

The meaning of the jQuery code statements is as follows, line by line:

- 2. Hides all the errors related to userid, password, email address, and country. All these error messages are nested inside the span element of the class error.

- 3-4. Applies the style properties contained in the class selector error to the error message related to the checkboxes displaying different food items. The style properties in class selector error apply the red color to the error message. The error message is made hidden for the time being.

- 5-6. Applies the style properties of the class selector error to the error related to the radio buttons displaying different modes of payment (it will appear in red). The error message is made invisible at the beginning.

- 7. Attaches the click event to the Submit button.

- 8. Retrieves the data entered in the User Id field (text-input field of class userid) and stores it in the variable data.

- 9-16. Validates the user ID in the data variable by passing it to the validate_userid() function to compare it with the regular expression that tests to see that the user ID consists only of characters , numerals, or underscores and nothing else. If the user ID matches with the regular expression supplied, no error message will be displayed; otherwise, the error message (which is the element next to the text-input field) *User id can contain only numeral, character, or _ (underscore)* will be displayed on the screen.

- 17-26. Retrieves the data entered in the Password field (text-input field of the class `password`) and stores it in the variable `data`. We find out the length of the contents in the `data` variable. If the length is less than 1—that is, if the Password field is left empty—then the error message (which is the element next to the text-input field) *Password cannot be blank* will be displayed on the screen; otherwise, the error message is kept in hidden mode.

- 27-35. Retrieves the data entered in the email address field (text-input field of the class `emailadd`) and stores it in the variable `data`. Then we validate the email address in the `data` variable by passing it to the `validate_email()` function to compare it with the regular expression that tests to see that the email address begins with an alphanumeric character and contains a period and an @ symbol. If the email address matches with the regular expression supplied, no error message will be displayed; otherwise, the error message (which is the element next to the text-input field) *Invalid email address* will be displayed on the screen.

- 36-42. Initializes a variable `count` to 0. Finds out all the checkboxes in the `div` element that are checked by making use of the `.each()` function. The value of the variable `count` is incremented by 1 on finding any checked checkbox. In other words, we are counting the number of checked checkboxes.

- 43-50. If the value in the `count` variable is 0, meaning no checkbox is selected, the error message defined by the `span` element of the class `fooderror` will be displayed and the `margin-left` property will be applied to it with a value of 250px using the `.css()` method to make it appear at the distance of 250px from the left border of the browser window (below other error messages, if any). If the value in the `count` variable is not zero, the error message is kept in hidden mode.

- 51-57. Initializes a variable `count` to 0. Finds out all the radio buttons in the `div` element that are checked (selected) by making use of the `.each()` function. The value of the variable `count` is incremented by 1 on finding any checked radio button.

- 58-65. If the value in the `count` variable is 0, meaning no radio button is selected, the error message defined by the `span` element of the class `payerror` will be displayed and the `margin-left` property will be applied to it with the value 250px using the `.css()` method to make it appear at the distance of 250px from the left border of the browser window (below other error messages, if any). If the value in the `count` variable is not zero, the error message is kept in hidden mode.

- 66-74. Finds the number of options that are selected in the `select` element. The count of the selected options is stored in the variable `count`. If the value in the `count` variable is 0—that is, if no option is selected from the `select` element—then an error message (which is the element next to the `select` element of the class `infobox`) *Please select the country* will be displayed on the screen; otherwise, the error message is kept in hidden mode.

- 75. Invokes the `preventDefault()` method of the event object to prevent the data entered or selected by the user from being sent to the server, as we are only interested here in validation of data.

154

- 78-82. Validates the email address.

- 83-87. Validates the user ID.

On execution of the jQuery code, if we leave all the fields blank and select the Submit button, we will get the error message shown in Figure 4-40.

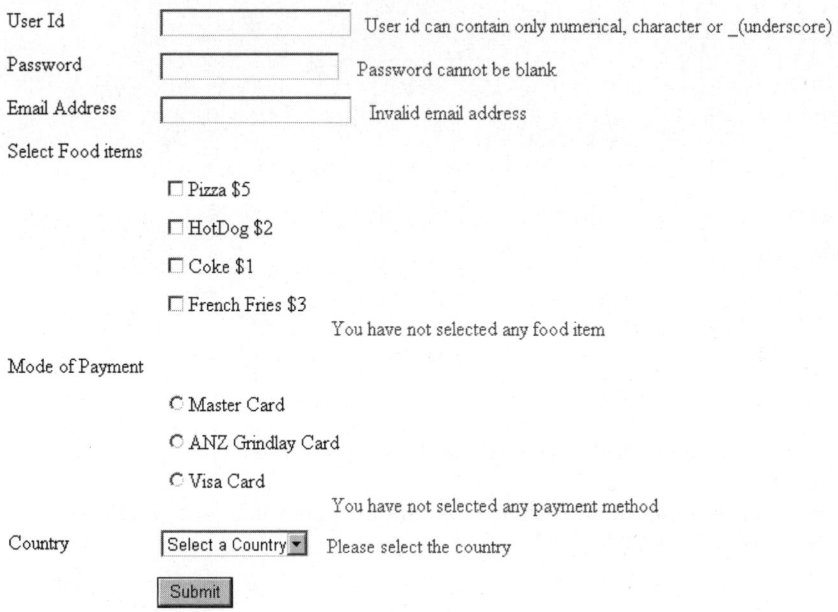

User Id	_____	User id can contain only numerical, character or _(underscore)
Password	_____	Password cannot be blank
Email Address	_____	Invalid email address
Select Food items		

☐ Pizza $5

☐ HotDog $2

☐ Coke $1

☐ French Fries $3

        You have not selected any food item

Mode of Payment

    ○ Master Card

    ○ ANZ Grindlay Card

    ○ Visa Card

        You have not selected any payment method

Country   [Select a Country ▼]   Please select the country

     [Submit]

Figure 4-40. *Error messages appear if no field is filled.*

If we enter an invalid user ID or email address and don't select any checkbox or any option from the **select** element, we will get error messages, as shown in Figure 4-41.

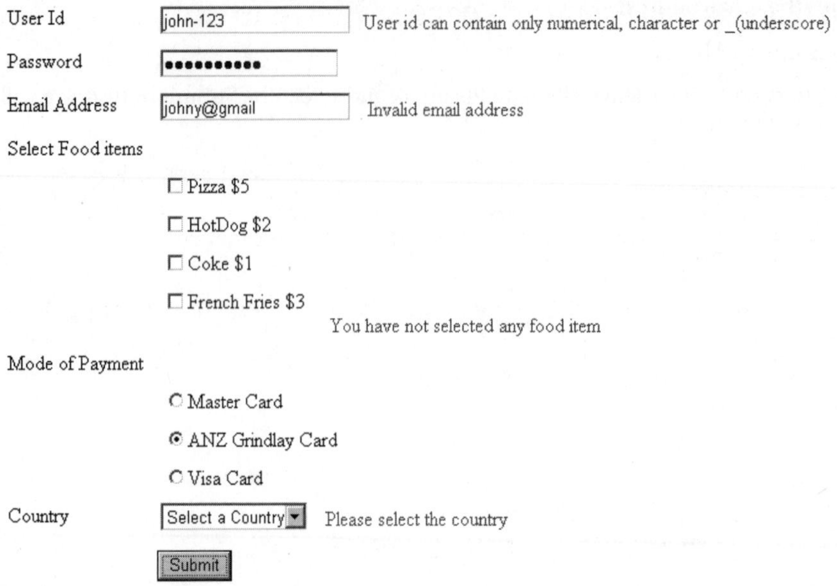

User Id	john-123	User id can contain only numerical, character or _(underscore)
Password	••••••••••	
Email Address	johny@gmail	Invalid email address

Select Food items

☐ Pizza $5

☐ HotDog $2

☐ Coke $1

☐ French Fries $3

You have not selected any food item

Mode of Payment

○ Master Card

◉ ANZ Grindlay Card

○ Visa Card

Country   [Select a Country ▾]   Please select the country

[Submit]

Figure 4-41. Error messages if no data or invalid data is provided

On entering all valid data and selecting all the essential options, the data will be accepted without displaying any error message, as shown in Figure 4-42.

User Id	john_123
Password	••••••••••
Email Address	johny@gmail.com

Select Food items

☑ Pizza $5

☐ HotDog $2

☑ Coke $1

☐ French Fries $3

Mode of Payment

○ Master Card

◉ ANZ Grindlay Card

○ Visa Card

Country   [USA ▾]

[Submit]

Figure 4-42. Valid data is accepted.

Highlighting the Input Fields and Grouping Common Form Elements

Let's now group some related elements of the form and also highlight the input fields when they receive focus. For grouping the form elements and applying captions to them, we need to use two HTML elements: Fieldset and Legend:

- The <fieldset> tag is used for grouping a few form elements together. It draws a box around the grouped elements.

- The <legend> tag is used for defining a caption for the form elements that are grouped by fieldset element.

Let's apply the fieldset elements to make three groups of the preceding form and apply the legend element to add a caption *Enter Your Information* to the form. The modified HTML form may appear as shown here:

```
<body>
<form>
<fieldset>
<legend>Enter Your Information</legend>
<div id="u">    <span class="label">User Id </span><input type="text"  class="userid"
name="userid" /><span class="error">User id can contain only numeral, character, or
_(underscore)</span></div>
<div  id="p"><span class="label">Password </span><input type="password" class="password"
name="password" /><span class="error"> Password cannot be blank</span></div>
<div><span class="label">Email Address </span><input type="text" class="emailadd"
name="emailid" /><span class="error"> Invalid email address</span></div>
</fieldset>
<fieldset>
<div><span class="label">Select Food items</span><br><input type="checkbox"  id="pizza"
name="pizza" value=5  class="chkb">Pizza $5 <br>
<input type="checkbox"  id="hotdog" name="hotdog" value=2  class="chkb">HotDog $2<br>
<input type="checkbox"   id="coke" name="coke" value=1  class="chkb">Coke $1<br>
<input type="checkbox"   id="fries" name="fries" value=3  class="chkb">French Fries $3<br>
<span class="fooderror">You have not selected any food item</span></div>
<div><span class="label">Mode of  Payment</span><br><input type="radio"  name="paymode"
class="radiobtn" value="Master Card">Master Card <br>
<input type="radio"  name="paymode" class="radiobtn" value="ANZ Grindlay Card">ANZ Grindlay
Card<br>
<input type="radio"  name="paymode" class="radiobtn" value="Visa Card">Visa Card<br>
<span class="payerror">You have not selected any payment method</span></div>
</fieldset>
<fieldset>
<div><span class="label">Country</span><select id="country" class="infobox">
<option value="0">Select a Country</option>
<option value="USA">USA</option>
<option value="United Kingdom">United Kingdom</option>
<option value="India">India</option>
<option value="China">China</option>
</select>
</fieldset>
<span class="error"> Please select the country</span></div>
```

```
<input class="submit" type="submit" value="Submit">
</form>
</body>
```

The `<fieldset>` marks the beginning of the group and `</fieldset>` marks the ending of the group.

To define a border for the grouped elements, we define a style property for the type selector `fieldset`, and to apply border, foreground, and background color to the caption and to make it appear bold, we define style properties for the type selector `legend`. To highlight the text-input field on gaining focus, we define a style rule `.inputs` in the style sheet. The style sheet may appear as shown here:

```
style.css
.submit { margin-left: 125px; margin-top: 10px;}
.label {float: left; width: 120px; }
.infobox {width: 120px; }
.error { color: red; padding-left: 10px; }
div{padding: 5px; }
.chkb { margin-left: 125px; margin-top: 10px;}
.radiobtn { margin-left: 125px; margin-top: 10px;}
.inputs{background-color:cyan}

fieldset{
border:1px solid #888;
}

legend{
border:1px solid #888;
background-color:cyan;
color:blue;
font-weight:bold;
padding:.5em
}
```

To apply the style properties defined in the style rule `inputs` to the text-input fields User Id, Password, and Email Address, we add few statements to the preceding jQuery code. Those statements are shown in bold in the following jQuery code. The rest of the code is exactly the same.

```
$(document).ready(function() {
  $('.error').hide();
  $('.userid').focus(function(){
    $(this).addClass('inputs');
  });

  $('.password').focus(function(){
    $(this).addClass('inputs');
  });

  $('.emailadd').focus(function(){
    $(this).addClass('inputs');
  });
```

```
$('.fooderror').addClass('error');
$('.fooderror').hide();
$('.payerror').addClass('error');
$('.payerror').hide();

$('.submit').click(function(event){
  var data=$('.userid').val();
  if(validate_userid(data))
  {
    $('.userid').next().hide();
  }
  else
  {
    $('.userid').next().show();
  }

  data=$('.password').val();
  var len=data.length;
  if(len<1)
  {
    $('.password').next().show();
  }
  else
  {
    $('.password').next().hide();
  }

  data=$('.emailadd').val();
  if(valid_email(data))
  {
    $('.emailadd').next().hide();
  }
  else
  {
    $('.emailadd').next().show();
  }

  var count=0;
  $('div').find(':checkbox').each(function(){
    if($(this).is(':checked'))
    {
      count++;
    }
  });
  if(count==0)
  {
    $('.fooderror').css({'margin-left':250}).show();
  }
```

```
        else
        {
        $('.fooderror').hide();
        }

        count=0;
        $('div').find(':radio').each(function(){
          if($(this).is(':checked'))
          {
            count++;
          }
        });
        if(count==0)
        {
          $('.payerror').css({'margin-left':250}).show();
        }
        else
        {
          $('.payerror').hide();
        }

        count=$('select option:selected').val();
        if(count==0)
        {
          $('.infobox').next().show();
        }
        else
        {
          $('.infobox').next().hide();
        }

        event.preventDefault();
    });
});


function valid_email(email)
{
  var pattern= new RegExp(/^[\w-]+(\.[\w-]+)*@([\w-]+\.)+[a-zA-Z]+$/);
  return pattern.test(email);
}

function validate_userid(uid)
{
  var pattern= new RegExp(/^[a-z0-9_]+$/);
  return pattern.test(uid);
}
```

On execution of preceding jQuery code, we may get the output shown in Figure 4-43.

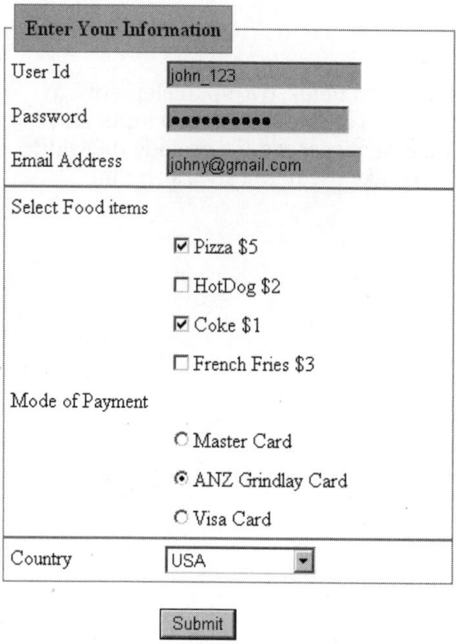

Figure 4-43. Grouping common elements of the form

4-16. Serializing Form Data

Problem

You need to see how form elements are actually encoded in a project.

Solution

For this recipe, we will make use of an HTML file and style sheet file as shown here.

```
<body>
    <form>
        <span class="label">Enter user id</span>
        <input type="text"  name="userid" class="userid"/>  <span class="usrerror">
</span><br/>
        <span class="label">Enter email address</span>
        <input type="text"  name="emailadd" class="emailadd"/>  <span class="emerror">
</span><br/>
            <input type="submit" id="submit"/>
        </form>
```

```
<div id="message"></div>
</body>
```

You can see that the above form contains two labels, two input text fields, two span elements, a submit button and an empty div element. We will expose how the data entered in the two input text fields is encoded. The encoded data will be displayed in the div element message. To provide the width, position, and margin spacing details of these HTML elements, we make use of the style sheet file containing the style rules as shown here:

```
style.css
.label {float: left; width: 120px; }
.userid {width: 200px; }
.emailadd {width: 200px; }
.usrerror { color: red; padding-left: 10px; }
.emerror { color: red; padding-left: 10px; }
#submit { margin-left: 125px; margin-top: 10px;}
```

The jQuery code to invoke the serialize() method, and display the encoded data, looks like this:

```
$(document).ready(function() {
$('.usrerror').hide();
$('.emerror').hide();
    $('#submit').click(function () {
    var info = $("form").serialize();
$('#message').text('The format when input elements are serialized:  '+info);
return false;
});
});
```

How It Works

First of all in our jQuery code we hide the errors related to userid and emailadd and then attach a click event to the submit button. In the event handling function of the click event, we serialize all the form elements (encode them in the form of a query string) and store that query string in the variable info. The query string in info is then assigned to the div element message for display. We return false in the click event because we don't want the browser to send the information entered in the input text fields to the server – instead, of course, we want to run the code assigned to its event handling function

The query string generated on entering the userid and email address should appear something much like you see in Figure 4-44.

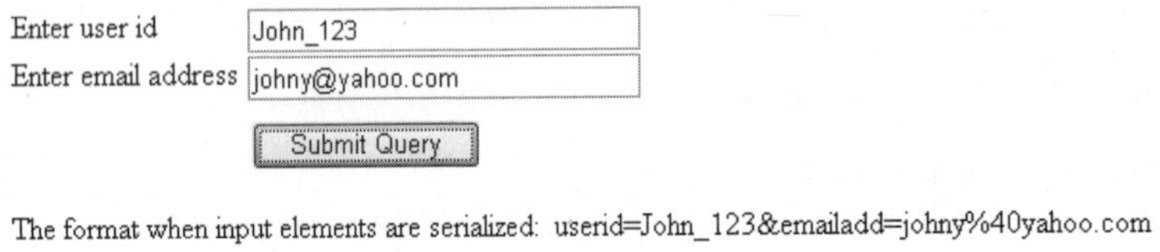

Enter user id   John_123

Enter email address johny@yahoo.com

Submit Query

The format when input elements are serialized: userid=John_123&emailadd=johny%40yahoo.com

Figure 4-44. Serialized output of the input text box

We can see in the query string generated:

```
userid=John_123&emailadd=johny%40yahoo.com
```

Here we can see that `userid` and `emailadd` are the names assigned to the input text fields, and that `John_123` and `johny%40yahoo.com` are the values entered by the user. The value `%40` in the email address represents the @ symbol.

Serializing the Checkboxes, Radio Button and Select Element

In the above solution, we saw how the input text fields were encoded. Let's now see how the options selected in the checkboxes, radio buttons and select element, are encoded. The HTML file to display few checkboxes, radio buttons and select element is as shown here:

```
<body>
    <form>
        <div><span class="label">Select Food items</span><br><input type="checkbox"
id="pizza" name="pizza" value=5 class="chkb">Pizza $5 <br/>
<input type="checkbox" id="hotdog" name="hotdog" value="2" class="chkb">HotDog $2<br/>
<input type="checkbox" id="coke" name="coke" value="1" class="chkb">Coke $1<br/>
<input type="checkbox" id="fries" name="fries" value="3" class="chkb">French Fries $3<br/>
</div>h
<div><span class="label">Mode of  Payment</span><br/><input type="radio" name="paymode"
class="radiobtn" value="Master Card">Master Card <br/>
<input type="radio" name="paymode" class="radiobtn" value="ANZ Grindlay Card">ANZ Grindlay
Card<br/>
<input type="radio" name="paymode" class="radiobtn" value="Visa Card">Visa Card<br/>
</div>
<div><span class="label">Country</span><select id="country" name="country">
<option value="0">Select a Country</option>
<option value="USA">USA</option>
<option value="United Kingdom">United Kingdom</option>
<option value="India">India</option>
<option value="China">China</option>
</select>
<br/>
        <input type="submit" id="submit"/>
        </form>
<div id="message"></div>
</body>
```

A quick glance at Figure 4-5 below will give you the layout in a glance that this creates. Now the class and ID selectors defined in style sheet file `style.css` should appear as shown here:

```
style.css
.label {float: left; width: 120px; }
#submit { margin-left: 125px; margin-top: 10px;}
div{padding: 5px; }
.chkb { margin-left: 125px; margin-top: 10px;}
.radiobtn { margin-left: 125px; margin-top: 10px;}
```

The jQuery code to display the serialized information of the options selected in the checkboxes, radio buttons and select element is as shown below:

```
$(document).ready(function() {
    $('#submit').click(function () {
    var info = $("form").serialize();
$('#message').text('The format when input elements are serialized:  '+info);
return false;
});
});
```

How It Works

The key part of our code executes as a click event that is attached to the submit button: when it's clicked we access all the form elements and encode them in the form of a query string with the help of the serialize() method, and store the query string in the variable info, which is then displayed to the user by assigning it to the div element message. We return false in the click event because we don't want the browser to send the options selected to the server - but once again, to run the code assigned to our event handling function

Depending on exactly what you select of course, you may see the encoded query string as shown in Figure 4-45.

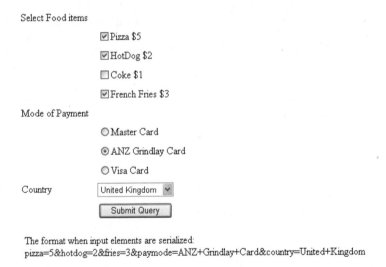

The format when input elements are serialized:
pizza=5&hotdog=2&fries=3&paymode=ANZ+Grindlay+Card&country=United+Kingdom

Figure 4-45. *Serialized output of checkbox, radio button and select element*

We can see the returned query string contains the names and value pairs of the selected options

Using the serializeArray() Method

In above example, we have used .serialize() method for accessing form elements. Now, we will make use of the .serializeArray() method, which allows us to access the form elements and returns them in the form of an array of objects (that contains the names and values pairs) of the selected elements. The array of objects appears somewhat like JSON data. The JSON data takes the following format of name, value pair as shown below:

```
[
    {name: 'pizza', value: '5'},
    {name: 'hotdog', value: '2'},
    {name: 'paymode', value: 'ANZ Grindlay Card'}
]
```

Considering the same HTML file and style sheet that we used above, the jQuery code to return the selected options in the form of an array of objects and displaying the values (of the selected options) is as shown below:

```
$(document).ready(function() {
$('#submit').click(function () {
var selectedopts="";
var info = $("form").serializeArray();

$.each(info, function(i, d){
selectedopts+=d.value+" ";
});

$('#message').text('The options chosen are:  '+selectedopts);
return false;
});
});
```

Let's run through this code line by line now:

- Line 2. Attaches the `click` event to the `submit` button.

- Line 3. Initializes a variable `selectedopts` that we'll use for storing the values of the selected options.

- Line 4. This line collects all the options selected in the form as an array of objects, using `serializeArray()` and stores the information about those selections in our `info` variable, which is an array of objects where each element has two attributes: `name` and `value`.

- Line 5. Using each function to parse each element in array `info`. In the call back function, we use two parameters: `i` and `d` where `i` refers to index location of element and `d` refers to data contained in it. The data will be in the form of `name`, `value` pair. For example: `{ name: 'paymode', value: 'ANZ Grindlay Card'}`.

- Line 6. Concatenates the `value` attribute of the data (that is, of the selected checkbox, radio button or selected options) ready to be stored in the `selectedopts` variable.

- Line 8. Displays the values of the selected options (in the `selectedopts` variable) in the `div` element `message`.

- Line 9. We return 'false' in the click event because we don't want the browser to send the options selected to the server, but rather to run the code assigned to its event handling function

The values of the selected options may appear as shown in Figure 4-46:

Select Food items

☑ Pizza $5

☑ HotDog $2

☐ Coke $1

☑ French Fries $3

Mode of Payment

○ Master Card

◉ ANZ Grindlay Card

○ Visa Card

Country   United Kingdom ▾

Submit Query

The options chosen are: 5 2 3 ANZ Grindlay Card United Kingdom

Figure 4-46. Displaying values of the checkbox, radio button and select element using serializeArray() method

Summary

In this chapter, we saw simple validation checks like a field is not left blank, a numerical is entered within a given range etc. We also saw the recipe confirming the validity of phone number, date, email address etc. We also met the technique to establish via jQuery whether a checkbox or radio box is selected or not. Finally, we learned how a complete form is validated and how to serialize form data. In the next chapter we will be learning different navigation techniques, including how to make contextual menus, accordion menus, dynamic visual menus, and so on.

CHAPTER 5

■ ■ ■

Page Navigation

In this chapter you'll learn how to make different types of menus that you'll find useful to let users navigate your websites. The recipes we'll cover in this chapter are as follows:

- Writing a breadcrumb menu
- Adding a hover effect to menu items
- Creating contextual menu
- Creating a navigation menu with access keys
- Creating a context menu on right-click
- Creating two menus with separate menu items
- Creating two menus with submenu items
- Making an accordion menu
- Making a dynamic visual menu

5-1. Writing a Breadcrumb Menu

Problem

You want to represent a menu of links in the form of breadcrumbs.

Solution

Let's represent a few menu items: Web Development, Programming, and RDBMS of the menu **Books** in the form of an unordered list element. The HTML file will appear as shown here:

```
<body>
        <ul id="menu">
                <li><a href="http://example.com">Books</a>
        <ul>
        <li><a href="http://example.com">Web Development</a></li>
        <li><a href="http://example.com">Programming</a></li>
        <li><a href="http://example.com">RDBMS</a></li>
                        </ul>
                </li>
        </ul>
</body>
```

To give the shape of breadcrumbs to the list items, we define two style rules which are `liststyle` and `ulistyle`, which contain a set of style properties, as shown in the following style sheet file, `style.css`:

```
style.css
.liststyle {
background-image:url(arrow.jpg);
background-repeat:no-repeat;
background-position:left;
padding-left:30px;
display: inline;
}

.ulistyle {
list-style:none;
margin:0;
padding:0;
display: inline;
}
```

The jQuery code to apply the two style rules `.ulistyle` and `.liststyle` to unordered list and their elements is a shown here:

```
$(document).ready(function() {
  $('ul').addClass('ulistyle');
  $('ul li ul li').addClass('liststyle');
});
```

How It Works

In the HTML file, you can see that the unordered list is assigned the ID `menu` and consists of a single list item, `Books`, which itself is an unordered list of three elements: `Web Development`, `Programming`, and `RDBMS`. Also, all the menu items point at a hypothetical web site, `example.com`, which is the target website where the user will be navigated to on clicking any link in the breadcrumb.

In the style sheet file, the `.liststyle` rule contains the `background-image` property set to `url(arrow.jpg)` to display the arrow images (refer to Figure 5-1). The `background-repeat` property is set to `no-repeat` to make the image appear only once. The `background-position` property is set to `left` to make the image appear on the left side of the element to which it is applied. The `padding-left` property is set to 30px to create the distance of 30px on the left, and the `display` property is set to `inline` to remove any space in the block elements to make them appear in a row (without spaces).

The style rule `uliststyle` contains the `list-style` property set to value `none` to remove the traditional bullets from the unordered list. The `margin` and `padding` properties are set to value 0 to remove traditional white spaces. The `display` property is set to `inline` to make the block element appear on the same line.

In the jQuery code, the style rule `.ulistyle` is applied to the unordered list element and `.liststyle` is applied to the list items of the unordered list that is nested inside the first list item of the unordered list.

On execution of the jQuery code, we get the output shown in Figure 5-1.

Books ▶▶   Web Development ▶▶   Programming ▶▶   RDBMS

Figure 5-1. Anchor elements in the form of breadcrumbs

5-2. Adding a Hover Effect to Menu Items

Problem

You want to display a menu with a few menu items in it. You also want to have a hover effect over a menu and its items.

Solution

Let's make an HTML file to represent the menu heading and its menu items. We do so with the help of two unordered lists, one nested inside the other. The HTML file may appear as shown here:

```
<body>
        <ul>
                <li><a href="http://example.com">Books</a>
                        <ul>
                                <li><a href="http://example.com">Web Development</a></li>
        <li><a href="http://example.com">Programming</a></li>
        <li><a href="http://example.com">RDBMS</a></li>
        </ul>
                </li>
        </ul>
</body>
```

We can see in the preceding HTML file that there's an unordered list element with a list item `Books`, which itself is an unordered list element of three list items to represent hyperlinks of *Web Development*, *Programming*, and *RDBMS*. These hyperlinks point at some hypothetical web site, `http://example.com`, where the user will be navigated if any of the menu items are clicked.

To give the appearance of a menu to the unordered list element, we need to apply certain styles to all three elements <u>, <li>, and <a>. We write their type selectors in the style sheet file so that the properties in it can be automatically applied to these three elements. The style sheet file may appear as shown here:

```
style.css
ul {
 width: 200px;
}

ul li ul {
 list-style-type:none;
 margin: 5;
 width: 200px;
}

a {
        display:block;
 border-bottom: 1px solid #fff;
 text-decoration: none;
        background: #00f;
 color: #fff;
        padding: 0.5em;
}

li {
        display:inline;
}

.hover {
 background: #000;
}
```

The jQuery code to apply the hover event to anchor elements is shown here:

```
$(document).ready(function() {
  $('a').hover(
    function(event){
      $(this).addClass('hover');
    },
    function(){
      $(this).removeClass('hover');
    }
  );
});
```

How It Works

The type selector `ul` contains the `width` property set to 200px to define the width of the menu heading: `Books`. The type selector `ul li ul` will be applied to the menu items. It contains the `list-style`-type property set to `none` to remove the traditional bullets from the unordered list elements. The margin property is set to 5 to make the menu items appear a bit indented as compared to the menu heading. The `width` property is set to 200px to define the width of the menu item to accommodate.

The type selector `a` contains the display property set to `block` to make the anchor element appear as a block and not as individual elements. The `border-bottom` property is set to `1px solid #fff` to make a solid white border of thickness 1px to appear below every anchor element (to act as a separator). The `text-decoration` property is set to `none` to remove the traditional underline that appears below hyperlinks. The background color is set to blue and the foreground color is set to white for all the anchor elements. The padding property is set to .5em (that is, 50% of the default font size) to define the spacing between the anchor text and its border.

The type selector `li` is set to `inline` to remove any white space between the list items. The CSS class `.hover` contains the `background` property to set the background color of the menu item (anchor element) to black when the user hovers on any anchor element.

In the jQuery code, we can see that the hover event is applied to the anchor elements. Recall the hover event contains the two event-handling functions, one that is invoked when a mouse pointer is moved over any anchor element and the other when a mouse pointer is moved away from the anchor element. In the event-handling function that is invoked when a mouse is moved over the anchor element, we apply the CSS class `hover` (defined in the style sheet file), making the background color of the anchor element turn black. In the event-handling function that is invoked when the mouse pointer is moved away from the anchor element, we remove the CSS class `hover` from the anchor element to make it appear as it was initially.

On execution of the jQuery code, the menu may appear as shown in Figure 5-2.

Figure 5-2. *Books menu with three menu items*

When we hover on any menu item, its background color changes to black, as shown in Figure 5-3.

Figure 5-3. *Menu item changes to black when hovered over*

5-3. Creating a Contextual Menu

Problem

You want to display a menu with a few menu items in it. When any menu item is hovered over (mouse pointer is moved over it), you want to display the information related to it and also want that menu item to be highlighted. When the menu item is clicked, the user is navigated to the related web site.

Solution

Let's make an HTML file to represent the menu heading **Books**, along with three menu items. We create the menu and its three menu items with the help of two unordered lists, one nested inside the other. The list items contain the anchor elements to represent menu items and refer to the target web site, `http://example.com`, where the user is supposed to be navigated on selecting any menu item. Also, we will write information about the three menu items in three paragraphs. The HTML file appears as shown here:

```
<body>
  <table>
    <td>
      <ul>
        <li><a href="http://example.com">Books</a>
          <ul>
            <li><a href="http://example.com" id="webd">Web Development</a></li>
            <li><a href="http://example.com" id="pgmng">Programming</a></li>
            <li><a href="http://example.com" id="datab">RDBMS</a></li>
          </ul>
        </li>
      </ul>
    </td>
    <td valign="top">
      <p class="web" >The wide range of books that includes how Web development can be done
        with ASP.NET, PHP, JSP etc.</p>
      <p class="prog" >The wide range of books that includes developing Programming skills
        in C, C++, Java etc.</p>
      <p class="rdbms" >The wide range of books that includes how Data Base Management is
        done via Oracle, MySQL, SQL Server etc.</p>
    </td>
  </table>
</body>
```

To make menus to appear on the left side and contents on the right side, we make a table and place the menu in the first column, and the paragraphs containing information of the related menu items in the second column.

To give the appearance of a menu to the unordered list element, we need to apply certain styles to all the elements <u>, <li>, and <a>. We write their type selectors in the style sheet file so that the properties in it can be automatically applied to these three elements. The style sheet file may appear as shown here:

```
style.css
ul {
        width: 200px;
}

ul li ul {
        list-style-type:none;
        margin: 5;
        width: 200px;
}

a {
        display:block;
        border-bottom: 1px solid #fff;
        text-decoration: none;
        background: #00f;
        color: #fff;
        padding: 0.5em;
}

li {
        display:inline;
}

.hover {
        background: #000;
}
```

The jQuery code to display information of the hovered-over menu item is shown here:

```
$(document).ready(function() {
  $('.web').hide();
  $('.prog').hide();
  $('.rdbms').hide();

  $('#webd').hover(function(event){
    $('.web').show();
    $('.prog').hide();
    $('.rdbms').hide();
    $('#webd').addClass('hover');
    }, function(){
      $('#webd').removeClass('hover');
  });
```

```
$('#pgmng').hover(function(event){
    $('.web').hide();
    $('.prog').show();
    $('.rdbms').hide();
    $('#pgmng').addClass('hover');
    }, function(){
       $('#pgmng').removeClass('hover');
});

$('#datab').hover(function(event){
    $('.web').hide();
    $('.prog').hide();
    $('.rdbms').show();
    $('#datab').addClass('hover');
    }, function(){
       $('#datab').removeClass('hover');
    });
});
```

How It Works

In the style sheet file, the type selector `ul` contains the `width` property set to 200px to define the width of the menu heading: `Books`. The type selector `ul li ul` will be applied to the menu items. It contains the `list-style`-type property set to `none` to remove the traditional bullets from the unordered list elements. The margin property is set to 5 to make the menu items appear a bit indented compared to the menu heading. The `width` property is set to 200px to define the width of the menu item to accommodate. The type selector `a` contains the display property set to `block` to make the anchor element appear as a block and not as individual elements. The `border-bottom` property is set to `1px solid #fff` to make a solid white border of thickness 1px to appear below every anchor element (to act as a separator). The `text-decoration` property is set to `none` to remove the traditional underline that appears below hyperlinks. The background color is set to blue and the foreground color is set to white for all the anchor elements. The padding property is set to .5em (that is, 50% of the default font size) to define the spacing between the anchor text and its border.

The type selector `li` is set to `inline` to remove any white space between the list items.

The CSS class `.hover` contains the background property to set the background color of the menu item (anchor element) to black when the user clicks on it.

The meaning of the jQuery code statements is explored here: Initially, we hide the information stored in all the three paragraphs (of the respective menu items). That is, we hide the information stored in the three paragraph of the classes `web`, `prog`, and `rdbms`, as we will display them only when the related menu item is hovered over.

We then attach a hover event to the first menu item: `Web Development`; that is, to the anchor element of ID `webd`. In the first event-handling function of the hover event (which is executed when this menu items is hovered over), we set the paragraph of the class `web`, which contains the information of the `Web Development` element, to visible mode, thus displaying information related to the books on web development. We keep the rest of the paragraph elements hidden. That is, the paragraph elements of the classes `prog` and `rdbms` will be kept hidden. Also, we apply the properties defined in the style rule `.hover` to the hovered-over menu item to highlight it, and we remove the hover style rule in the second event-handling function of the hover event that is executed when mouse pointer is moved away from the menu item.

We attach a hover event to the second menu item: `Programming`; that is, to the anchor element of ID `pgmng`. In the first event-handling function of the hover event (that is executed when this menu items is hovered over), we set the paragraph of the class `prog` (that contains the information of the programming subject) to visible mode, displaying information related to the books about programming. We keep the rest of the paragraph elements hidden. That is, the paragraph elements of the classes `web` and `rdbms` will be kept hidden. Also, we apply the properties defined in the style rule `.hover` to the hovered-over menu item to highlight it, and we remove the hover style rule in the second event-handling function of the hover event that is executed when mouse pointer is moved away from the menu item.

Finally, we attach a hover event to the third menu item: `rdbms`; that is, to the anchor element of ID `datab`. In the first event-handling function of the hover event (that is executed when this menu items is hovered over), we set the paragraph of the class `rdbms` (that contains the information of the database subject) to visible mode, displaying information related to the books about RDBMS. We keep the rest of the paragraph elements hidden. That is, the paragraph elements of the classes `web` and `prog` will be kept hidden. Also, we apply the properties defined in the style rule `.hover` to the hovered-over menu item to highlight it, and we remove the hover style rule in the second event-handling function of the hover event that is executed when mouse pointer is moved away from the menu item.

On execution of the preceding jQuery code, we will get a menu along with three menu items in it. When we hover over any menu item, that menu item will be highlighted and the information related to it will be displayed as shown in Figure 5-4.

The wide range of books that includes how Web development can be done with ASP.NET, PHP, JSP etc.

Figure 5-4. Menu item remains highlighted on being hovered over, and related information is displayed

5-4. Creating a Navigation Menu with Access Keys

Problem

You want to display a menu with a few menu items in it. You want to display the access keys of the menu items. Access keys represent the shortcut keys to represent any menu item. Also, you want to make sure that when any menu item is hovered over, the information related to it is displayed. The information must be displayed in both cases: when the menu item is hovered over as well as when the access key of any menu item is pressed. When user clicks on any menu item, he should be navigated to the related web site.

Solution

Let's make an HTML file to represent the menu heading **Books**, along with three menu items. We create the menu and its three menu items with the help of an unordered list. The list items contain the anchor elements to represent menu items. Also, we will write information about the three menu items in terms of three paragraphs. To make the character of the menu item (that we want to represent as an access key) appear underlined, we nest it inside a **span** element of the class **hot**. The HTML file may appear as shown here:

```
<body>
  <table>
    <td>
      <ul>
        <li><a href="http://example.com">Books</a>
          <ul>
            <li><a href="http://example.com" id="webd"><span class="hot">W</span>eb
              Development</a></li>
            <li><a href="http://example.com" id="pgmng"><span class="hot">P</span>
              rogramming</a></li>
            <li><a href="http://example.com" id="datab" ><span class="hot">R</span>DBMS
              </a></li>
          </ul>
        </li>
      </ul>
    </td>
    <td valign=top>
      <p class='web' >The wide range of books that includes how Web development can be
        done with ASP.NET, PHP, JSP etc.</p>
      <p class='prog' >The wide range of books that includes developing Programming
        skills in C, C++, Java etc.</p>
      <p class='rdbms' >The wide range of books that includes how Data Base Management
        is done via Oracle, MySQL, Sql Server etc.</p>
    </td>
  </table>
</body>
```

To give the appearance of a menu to the unordered list element, we need to apply certain styles to all the three elements: <u>, <li>, and <a>. We write their type selectors in the style sheet file so that the properties in it can be automatically applied to these three elements. The style sheet file may appear as shown here:

```
style.css
ul {
 width: 200px;
}

ul li ul {
 list-style-type:none;
 margin: 5;
 width: 200px;
}
```

```css
a {
        display:block;
 border-bottom: 1px solid #fff;
 text-decoration: none;
        background: #00f;
 color: #fff;
        padding: 0.5em;
}

li {
        display:inline;
}

.hover {
 background: #000;
}

.hot{
        text-decoration:underline;
}
```

The following jQuery code displays the information of the menu item whose access key is pressed or when the menu item is hovered over. Also, the hovered-over menu item is highlighted by application of certain style rules:

```javascript
$(document).ready(function() {
  $('.web').hide();
  $('.prog').hide();
  $('.rdbms').hide();

$('body').keypress(function(event){
  if(String.fromCharCode(event.keyCode)=="w" || String.fromCharCode(event.keyCode)=="W")
  {
    $('#webd').hover();
  }
  if(String.fromCharCode(event.keyCode)=="p" || String.fromCharCode(event.keyCode)=="P")
  {
    $('#pgmng').hover();
  }
  if(String.fromCharCode(event.keyCode)=="r" || String.fromCharCode(event.keyCode)=="R")
  {
    $('#datab').hover();
  }
});

  $('#webd').hover(function(event){
    $('.web').show();
    $('.prog').hide();
    $('.rdbms').hide();
```

```
      $('#webd').addClass('hover');
    }, function(){
      $('#webd').removeClass('hover');
  });

  $('#pgmng').hover(function(event){
    $('.web').hide();
    $('.prog').show();
    $('.rdbms').hide();
    $('#pgmng').addClass('hover');
    }, function(){
      $('#pgmng').removeClass('hover');
  });

  $('#datab').hover(function(event){
    $('.web').hide();
    $('.prog').hide();
    $('.rdbms').show();
    $('#datab').addClass('hover');
    }, function(){
      $('#datab').removeClass('hover');
  });
});
```

How It Works

In the HTML file, observe that the first character of the anchor element is to be highlighted and to act as an access key. Like the access key for the anchor element, `Web Development` is set to the character *w* so that this menu item can be directly accessed by just pressing the *w* key (or *W*). To make the user know that *w* is the access key, it needs to be underlined. To underline the first character *W* of the menu item `Web Development`, we nest it inside the `span` element and assign the class name `hot` to the `span` element to identify it in the style sheet file. Similarly, all the characters that we want to be represented as access keys are nested inside the `span` element of the class `hot`.

Also, to make menus appear on left side and contents on the right side, we create a table and place the menu in the first column, and the paragraphs containing information about the related menu items in the second column.

In the style sheet file, the type selector `ul` contains the `width` property set to 200px to define the width of the menu heading `Books`. The type selector `ul li ul` will be applied to the menu items. It contains the `list-style-type` property set to `none` to remove the traditional bullets from the unordered list elements. The margin property is set to 5 to make the menu items appear a bit indented compared to the menu heading. The `width` property is set to 200px to define the width of the menu item to accommodate.

The type selector `a` contains the `display` property set to `block` to make the anchor element appear as a block and not as individual elements. The `border-bottom` property is set to `1px solid #fff` to make a solid white border of thickness 1px to appear below every anchor element (to act as a separator). The `text-decoration` property is set to `none` to remove the traditional underline that appears below hyperlinks. The background color is set to blue and the foreground color is set to white for all the anchor elements. The `padding` property is set to .5em (that is, 50% of the default font size) to define the spacing between the anchor text and its border.

The type selector `li` is set to `inline` to remove any white space between the list items.

The CSS class .hover contains the background property to set the background color of the menu item (anchor element) to black when user clicks on it.

The CSS class .hot contains the text-decorate property set to underline to make all the access characters of each menu item (nested inside the span element of the class hot) appear underlined.

In the jQuery code, we see that initially the three paragraph elements are made hidden, as we want to display the related information only when any access key is pressed or when any menu item is hovered over. We also attached a keypress event on the body of the HTML file to sense if any key is pressed. If any keypress event occurs, we use conditional statements to check if the pressed key is any of the following characters: w, W, p, P, r, or R. If the any of the said character is pressed, we invoke the hover event on the respective anchor element. For instance, if character w or W is pressed, the hover event on the anchor element Web Development (ID webd) is invoked to display the related information. We also attach a hover event to all the three menu items. We know that the hover event includes two event-handling functions. In the first event-handling function of the hover event (that is executed when this menu items is hovered over), we set the paragraph that contains the related information to visible mode, displaying the desired information. We keep the rest of the paragraph elements hidden. Also, we apply the properties defined in the style rule .hover to the hovered-over menu item to highlight it, and we remove the hover style rule in the second event-handling function of the hover event that is executed when mouse pointer is moved away from the menu item.

On execution, we find that each of the three menu item appears along with its access key (underlined), as shown in Figure 5-5. On pressing the access key or on hovering over the menu item, the information related to it will be displayed as shown in Figure 5-4.

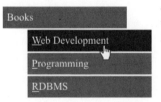

The wide range of books that includes how Web development can be done with ASP.NET, PHP, JSP etc.

Figure 5-5. Menu items with access keys underlined

5-5. Creating a Context Menu on Right-Click

Problem

You want to display a paragraph of text, and when you right-click on it, you want a context menu to appear on the screen. Also, you want the menu items of the context menu to have a hovering effect (that is, menu items get highlighted when the mouse pointer is moved over them). On pressing the Esc key, you want the context menu to disappear.

Solution

Let's make an HTML file that contains a paragraph element and an unordered list for the menu. The list items of the unordered list represent the menu heading and the menu items. The menu items are written in the form of the anchor elements nested inside the list items. The anchor elements point at some hypothetical web site `http://example.com`, where the user will be navigated if any menu item is clicked. The HTML file may appear as shown here:

```
<body oncontextmenu="return false">
  <p class="info">
    Books are the world of information. Books are our best friends. A wise man
    always has a library of several books</p>
  <ul id="contextmenu">
    <li><a href="http://example.com">Books</a>
      <ul>
        <li><a href="http://example.com">Web Development</a></li>
        <li><a href="http://example.com">Programming</a></li>
        <li><a href="http://example.com">RDBMS</a></li>
      </ul>
    </li>
  </ul>
</body>
```

We need to define few style rules in the style sheet to give the unordered list the shape of a menu and also to highlight the menu items when the mouse pointer hovers over them. The style rules in the style sheet may appear as shown here:

```
style.css
ul {
 width: 200px;
}

ul li ul {
 list-style-type:none;
 margin: 5;
 width: 200px;
}

a {
        display:block;
 border-bottom: 1px solid #fff;
 text-decoration: none;
        background: #00f;
 color: #fff;
        padding: 0.5em;
}

li {
        display:inline;
}

.hover {
 background: #000;
}
```

The jQuery code to initially hide the menu and to display it when the user clicks the right mouse button on the paragraph element is as shown below. The jQuery also makes the context menu disappear when the Esc key is pressed:

```
$(document).ready(function() {
  $('#contextmenu').hide();
  $('.info').mousedown(function(event){
    if(event.button==2){
      $('#contextmenu').show();
      $('#contextmenu').css({'position': 'absolute', 'left':event.screenX,
        'top':event.screenY-70});
    }
  });
  $('a').hover(function(event){
    $(this).addClass('hover');
    },function(){
      $(this).removeClass('hover');
  });
  $('body').keypress(function(event){
    if(event.keyCode==27)
    {
      $('#contextmenu').hide();
    }
  });
});
```

How It Works

The usual problem while displaying a context menu is that when we right-click on the paragraph element to display the context menu, the browser's context menu also appears as default along with our context menu. In order to disable the default browser's context menu, we use the attribute oncontextmenu="return false" in the body element. The paragraph element is assigned a class name info so as to access it in jQuery with the help of selectors. The unordered list that will be used to display the context menu is assigned the ID contextmenu . We can see that the first list item of the unordered list represents the text Books (which will act as a menu heading). This list item will contain an unordered list in itself, which will represent the menu items.

In the style sheet file, the type selector ul contains the width property set to 200px to define the width of the menu heading Books. The type selector ul li ul will be applied to the menu items. It contains the list-style-type property set to none to remove the traditional bullets from the unordered list elements. The margin property is set to value 5 to make the menu items appear a bit indented as compared to the menu heading. The width property is set to 200px to define the width of the menu item to accommodate.

The type selector a contains the display property set to block to make the anchor element appear as a block and not as individual elements. The border-bottom property is set to 1px solid #fff to make a solid white border of thickness 1px appear below every anchor element (to act as a separator). The text-decoration property is set to none to remove the traditional underline that appears below hyperlinks. The background color is set to blue and the foreground color is set to white for all the anchor elements. The padding property is set to .5em (that is, 50% of the default font size) to define the spacing between the anchor text and its border. The type selector li is set to inline to remove any white space between the list items. The CSS class .hover contains the background property to set the background color of the menu item (anchor element) to black when the user clicks on it.

In the jQuery code, we start by hiding the menu represented by the unordered list of ID contextmenu. We then check if the mouse button is pressed on the paragraph element of the class info. Recall that we have assigned the class name info to the paragraph element in the HTML file. If it has been pressed, we check if the mouse button pressed is the right mouse button. The button attribute of the event object contains the value 1 if the left mouse button is pressed, and the value 2 if the right mouse button is pressed. If it is the right mouse button, we make the menu visible on the screen that is represented by the unordered list element of ID contextmenu.

Using the css() method, we make the context menu appear at the location specified by the screenX and screenY attributes of the event object that represents the location where the mouse button is pressed. We subtract the value 70 from the coordinate values stored in the screenY attribute to make the context menu appear closer to the paragraph; that is, we reduce the gap between the menu and the paragraph.

Also, we attach the hover() event to the anchor elements (menu and menu items). We apply the style properties defined in the style rule .hover to the anchor elements when the mouse pointer moves over any menu item (making the background color of the menu item turn black). The style properties in the style rule .hover will be removed from the anchor element, making them as they were initially when the mouse pointer is moved away from the menu item.

Finally, we attach a keypress event to the body element to sense if any key is pressed. If any key is pressed, we check if it is the Esc key (the key code of the Esc key is 27). If the Esc key is pressed, we hide the context menu.

On right-clicking the mouse button on the paragraph text, the context menu will appear on the screen. The menu items in the menu will have the hovering effect, as shown in Figure 5-6.

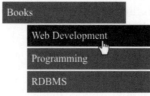

Figure 5-6. Context menu appears on right-clicking the paragraph text

5-6. Creating Two Menus with Separate Menu Items

Problem

You want to display two menus, each with respective menu items. You also want to have a hovering effect over the menus and their items.

Solution

Let's make an HTML file to represent two menu headings, along with their menu items. We do so with the help of unordered lists, one nested inside the other. The HTML file may appear as shown here:

```html
<body>
<ul id="dropdownmenu">
<li class="mainmenu">
        <a href="example.com">Books</a>
         <ul>
          <li><a href="example.com">Web Development</a></li>
          <li><a href="example.com">Programming</a></li>
          <li><a href="example.com">RDBMS</a></li>
         </ul>
         </li>
          <li class="mainmenu">
          <a href="example.com">Movies</a>
         <ul>
          <li><a href="example.com">Latest Movie Trailers</a></li>
          <li><a href="example.com">Movie Reviews</a></li>
          <li><a href="example.com">Celebrity Interviews</a></li>
         </ul>
 </li>
</ul>
</body>
```

You can see in the preceding code that there is an unordered list of ID dropdownmenu with two list items that are assigned the class name mainmenu. These two list items represent the menus Books and Movies. Both the list items in turn consist of unordered list with three elements each. The Books menu has three list items: Web Development, Programming, and RDBMS. Similarly, the list item Movies consists of an unordered list of three elements: Latest Movie Trailers, Movie Reviews, and Celebrity Interviews.

The code apply the styles to the preceding unordered list to give them the appearance of two menus along with menu items is shown here:

```css
.mainmenu {float:left; width:200px; list-style-type:none; margin-right:5px;}
li.mainmenu ul {margin: 0;  }
a  {width: 200px;display:block; text-decoration: none; background: #00f;  color:
#fff;padding: 0.5em;   border-bottom: 1px solid #fff; }
ul#dropdownmenu li a:hover {  background: #000;}
```

The jQuery code to display one set of menu items out of the two when the mouse pointer moves over the respective menu heading is shown here:

```javascript
$(document).ready(function(){
  $('li.mainmenu').hover(
    function() {
      $('ul', this).show();
    },
```

```
    function() {
      $('ul', this).hide();
    }
  );
});
```

How It Works

In the style sheet file, the class selector `.mainmenu` contains the properties that are to be automatically applied to the two menu headings: Books and Movies. It contains the `float` property set to `left` to make the first menu heading float to the left in the browser window (making space for the second menu heading to appear on its right). The `width` property is set to 200px to make the menu headings 200px wide, The `margin-left` property is set to 5px to create spacing of 5px between the two menu headings.

The type selector `li.mainmenu ul` contains the style property to be applied automatically to the unordered list that is nested inside the list items of the class `.mainmenu`; that is, to the unordered lists that acts as menu items of the list items with text *Books* and *Movies*. It contains the `margin` property set to 0 to make the list items of the unordered list (menu items like `Web development`, `Programming`, etc. of the menu headings Books and Movies) appear one below the other (without any hierarchical gap on the left side).

The type selector `a` contains the properties that are to be applied to all the anchor elements; that is, to the menus as well as to all the menu items. The `width` property is set to 200px to specify the width of each menu item. The `display` property is set to `block` to make the anchor element act as an independent block. The `text-decoration` property is set to `none` to remove the traditional underline from the hyperlinks. The `background` property sets the background color of the menu headings and menu items to blue and the `color` property sets the foreground color of the text on the menus (menu headings and menu items) to white. The `padding` property is set to .5em to create the spacing of the 50% of the default font size between the menu text and its border. The `border-bottom` property is set to `1px solid #fff` to create a solid white line of thickness 1px below every anchor element to act as a separator between the menu items.

The type selector `ul#dropdownmenu li a:hover` contains the style property that will be automatically applied to the menu headings as well as menu items on hovering on them. It contains the `background` property that changes the background color of the menu headings as well as menu items to black when the mouse pointer moves over them.

We can see in the jQuery code that when the mouse pointer moves over the list item of the class `mainmenu` (that is, on any menu heading), the unordered list (containing the menu items) nested in that list item will be displayed. Moving away the mouse pointer from a menu heading will make its menu items invisible, as the unordered list of that list item is set to hidden mode.

Initially the two menu headings will appear as shown in Figure 5-7.

Figure 5-7. Two menu headings: Books and Movies

On moving the mouse pointer over the menu heading Books, its menu items (the unordered list that is nested inside the list item with text *Books*) will be displayed as shown in Figure 5-8.

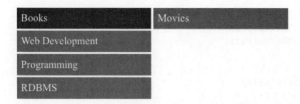

Figure 5-8. Menu items of the Books menu displayed with the hovering effect

On moving the mouse pointer over the menu heading **Movies**, its menu items will be displayed and those of the menu heading **Books** will become invisible as shown in Figure 5-9.

Figure 5-9. *Menu items of the Movies menu with a hovering effect*

5-7. Creating Two Menus with Submenu Items

Problem

You want to display two menus, each with menu items, and attach submenu items to a few of the menu items. You also want to have a hovering effect over the menu, its items, and its submenu items.

Solution

Let us make an HTML file to represent two menu headings along with their menu items. We will also define the submenu items. We do so with the help of unordered lists, one nested inside the other. The HTML file may appear as shown here:

```
<body>
  <ul class="dropdown">
    <li><a href="http://example.com">Books</a>
      <ul>
        <li><a href="http://example.com">Programming</a></li>
        <li><a href="http://example.com">Web Development</a>
```

```
        <ul>
          <li><a href="http://example.com">.Net</a></li>
          <li><a href="http://example.com">JSP</a></li>
        </ul>
      </li>
      <li><a href="http://example.com">RDBMS</a></li>
      <li><a href="http://example.com">Web Services</a></li>
      <li><a href="http://example.com">Open Source</a></li>
    </ul>
  </li>
  <li><a href="http://example.com">Movies</a>
    <ul>
      <li><a href="http://example.com">Movie Reviews</a></li>
      <li><a href="http://example.com">Celebrity Interviews</a></li>
      <li><a href="http://example.com">Latest Hollywood Movies</a>
        <ul>
          <li><a href="http://example.com">Arnold Schwarzenegger</a></li>
          <li><a href="http://example.com">Sylvester Stallone</a></li>
          <li><a href="http://example.com">Bruce Willis</a></li>
        </ul>
      </li>
      <li><a href="http://example.com">Action Movies</a>
        <ul>
          <li><a href="http://example.com">Casino Royale</a></li>
          <li><a href="http://example.com">Rambo III</a></li>
        </ul>
      </li>
      <li><a href="http://example.com">Comedy Movies</a></li>
    </ul>
  </li>
 </ul>
</body>
```

The style properties to be assigned to the unordered list to make them appear in the form of menu headings, menu items, and submenu items are shown here:

```
style.css
a{ text-decoration: none; color: #000;}
ul{ margin: 0; list-style: none; }
ul.dropdown li {  float: left;  background: cyan; }
ul.dropdown a:hover {background: #0f0; color: #00f; }
ul.dropdown li a { display: block; padding: 4px; border-right: 1px solid #000; }
ul.dropdown ul { width: 200px; visibility: hidden; position: absolute;  }
ul.dropdown ul li {background: yellow; border-bottom: 1px solid #000; }
ul.dropdown ul li a { border-right: none; width: 100%; }
ul.dropdown ul ul { left: 100%; top: 0; }
.hover {position: relative; }
```

The jQuery code to apply to make the menu items and submenus appear on the screen is shown here:

```
$(document).ready(function(){
        $("ul.dropdown li").hover(function(){
        $(this).addClass("hover");
                        $('ul:first',this).css('visibility', 'visible');
                }, function(){
                        $(this).removeClass("hover");
                        $('ul:first',this).css('visibility', 'hidden');
        });
        $("ul.dropdown li ul li:has(ul)").find("a:first").append("  >");
});
```

How It Works

Let's look first and in detail at the HTML file, where you can see that an unordered list is created and is assigned the class name dropdown. It contains two list items with text assigned as Books and Movies. These two list items in turn contain unordered list items that are assigned the class name submenu. The unordered list of the list item with text Books contains five list items with text: Programming, Web Development, rdbms, Web Services, and Open Source. Out of these list items, the one with the text *Web Development* contains an unordered list to represent submenu items that contain two submenu items with text *.Net* and *JSP*.

Similarly, the unordered list contained in the list tem with text *Movies* contains four list items: Movie Reviews, Celebrity Interviews, Latest Hollywood Movies, and Action Movies. Out of these list items, the one with text *Latest Hollywood Movies* contains an unordered list to represent submenu items that contain three submenu items: Arnold Schwarzenegger, Sylvester Stallone, and Bruce Willis. Also, the list item with text *Action Movies* contains an unordered list to represent submenu items that contain three submenu items: Casino Royale, Rambo III, and Comedy Movies.

In the style sheet file, the type selector a has the property text-decoration set to none to remove the traditional underline from all the anchor elements; that is, from menu headings, menu items, and submenu items. The color property is set to black to make the text on all menus to appear in black.

The type selector ul contains the margin property set to value 0 to remove the hierarchical margin from the left side in the list items and to make the menu items appear one below the other. The list-style property is set to none to remove the traditional bullets from the unordered list.

The styles defined in the type selector ul.dropdown li will be automatically applied to the list items that belong to the unordered list of the class drop-down; that is, to the menu headings Books and Movies. The float property is set to left to make one menu heading appear on the left side of the browser window, creating space for the next menu heading to appear on its right. Its background color is set to cyan.

The attribute selector ul.dropdown a:hover contains the background and color properties to set the background and foreground color of the anchor elements (all menu items) that are been hovered over to the colors green and blue, respectively.

The type selector : ul.dropdown li a contains the style properties that will be applied to the anchor elements that represent the menu headings Books and Movies. It contains the display property set to block to make the anchor element act as an independent block element; the padding property is set to 4px to create some spacing in between the menu text and its border. The border-right property is set to 1px solid #000 to make a black border of 1px on the right of each menu heading (to show them separately).

The type selector ul.dropdown ul contains the styles that will be applied to the unordered list containing menu items. The width property set to 200px will make each menu item be 200px wide. The visibility property set to hidden will keep the whole menu-items block hidden and make it visible only when the menu headings are hovered over. The `position` property set to `absolute` makes the menu-items block appear below the respective menu headings.

The type selector `ul.dropdown ul li` contains the properties that will be applied to all the list items representing the menu items. The `background` property will set the background color of all menu items and submenu items to yellow; the `border-bottom` property is set to `1px solid #000` to make a black border of thickness 1px appear below each menu item to separate them.

The type selector `ul.dropdown ul li a` contains the properties that will be applied to all the anchor elements representing the menu items and submenu items. The `border-right` property is set to `none` to remove the border on right of the menu items, as we will be displaying submenu items on the right of the menu items. The `width` property is set to 100% to make the anchor element take up all of the 200px width assigned.

The type selector `ul.dropdown ul ul` will be applied to the unordered list representing the submenu items. The `left` property is set to 100% to separate the submenu items by 100% of the width of the menu items (otherwise there will be an overlap with the menu items). The `top` property is set to 0 to make the submenu items the same distance from the top border of the browser as the menu item whose submenu items are being displayed.

The style rule `.hover` is applied via jQuery code to the list items to make the submenu items appear at a location relative to their menu items.

Next we're going to look at the actual jQuery code in detail. But first, let's establish what `:first` does, as it appears in the code:

:first

This is the custom selector that returns the first instance of the specified element.

```
Example:
$('p:first)
```

Which will return the first paragraph element.

Now let's look at the actual jQuery code for our solution. You'll notice that when the mouse pointer is moved over the menu heading `Books` or `Movies` (list items of the unordered list of ID `dropdown`), the properties defined in the CSS class `.hover` (defined in the stylesheet file) will be applied to it and to the first unordered list (menu items of the respective menu heading) in visible mode. Similarly, when any menu item is hovered over (that has an unordered list in the form of submenu items), then that unordered list will also be displayed (that is, submenu items will be displayed). The menu items or submenu items are made hidden when the mouse pointer is away from the menu item or menu heading. Also, for all the list items that have unordered lists nested in them, a symbol `>` is appended to the anchor element to designate that it has submenu items attached.

Initially, the two menu headings `Books` and `Movies` may appear as shown in Figure 5-10.

Figure 5-10. Menu headings Books and Movies

On moving the mouse pointer on the menu heading `Books`, its menu items will be displayed as shown in Figure 5-11.

Books
Movies
Programming
Web Development>
RDBMS
Web Services
Open Source

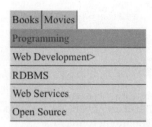

Figure 5-11. Menu items of the Books menu (the menu items that have submeneu items appear with the > symbol).

On moving the mouse pointer over the menu item that has submenu attached, its submenu items will be displayed as shown in Figure 5-12.

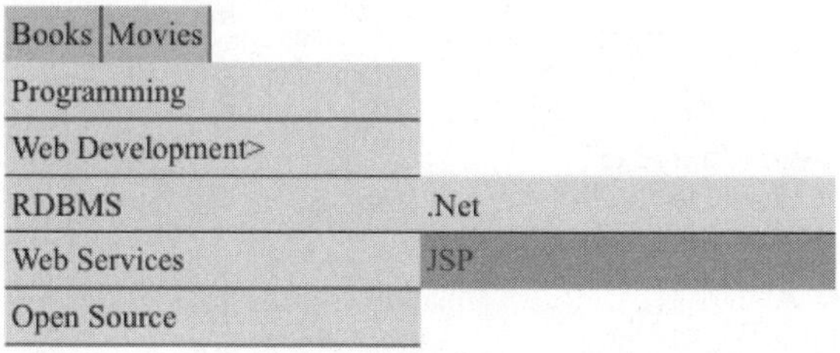

Books
Movies
Programming
Web Development>
RDBMS
.Net
Web Services
JSP
Open Source

Figure 5-12. The submenu item of the menu item (of the Books menu) being highlighted)

The same thing applies to second menu heading, `Movies`. Its menu items will be made visible when the mouse is hovered over it. Also, the submenu items will be displayed when the mouse is hovered over it ,as shown in Figure 5-13.

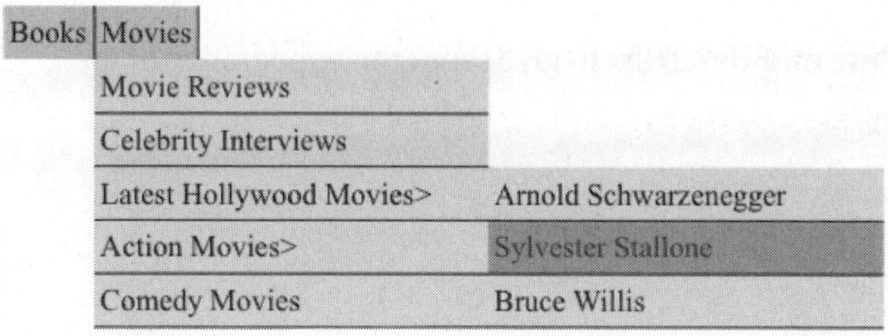

Books
Movies
Movie Reviews
Celebrity Interviews
Latest Hollywood Movies>
Arnold Schwarzenegger
Action Movies>
Sylvester Stallone
Comedy Movies
Bruce Willis

Figure 5-13. The submenu items of the Movies menu being highlighted)

5-8. Making an Accordion Menu

Problem

You want to display two menus in the form of an accordion menu; that is, the submenu items of the menu that is hovered over will be made visible, and the submenu items of other menu heading(s) will be made invisible by using the slide-up or slide-down technique. You also want the menu items to disappear when the mouse pointer is away from both the menus.

Solution

Let us make an HTML file to represent two menu headings, along with their menu items. We do so with the help of unordered lists, one nested inside the other. The HTML file may appear as shown here:

```
<body>
  <p class="menus">Books</p>
    <div class="menuitems">
        <ul>
         <li><a href="example.com">Web Development</a></li>
         <li><a href="example.com">Programming</a></li>
         <li><a href="example.com">RDBMS</a></li>
        </ul>
    </div>
  <p class="menus">Movies</p>
    <div class="menuitems">
        <ul>
         <li><a href="example.com">Latest Movie Trailers</a></li>
         <li><a href="example.com">Movie Reviews</a></li>
         <li><a href="example.com">Celebrity Interviews</a></li>
        </ul>
    </div>
</body>
```

The code to apply the styles to the preceding unordered list to give them the appearance of an accordion menu is shown here:

```
style.css
.menus{
        width: 200px;
        padding:5px;
        margin:1px;
        font-weight:bold;
        background-color: #0ff;
}

.menuitems{
        display:none;
}
```

```
a{
  display:block;
  border-bottom: 1px solid #fff;
  text-decoration: none;
        background: #00f;
  color: #fff;
  padding:10px;
  font-weight:bold;
        width: 190px;
}

.menuitems a:hover {
  background: #000;
}

li {
        display:inline;
}

ul{display:inline;}
```

The jQuery code to display the menu items of the hovered-over menu headings and to hide the menu items of other menu headings (from where the mouse pointer is moved away) with a sliding effect is shown here:

```
$(document).ready(function() {
  $('p.menus').mouseout(function(){
    $("div.menuitems'").slideUp("slow");
    $('p').css({backgroundImage:""});
  });

  $('p.menus').mouseover(function(){
    $(this).css({'background-image':"url(down.png)", 'background-repeat':"no-repeat",
      'background-position':"right"}).next("div.menuitems").slideDown(500)
      .siblings("div.menuitems").slideUp("slow");
    $(this).siblings().css({backgroundImage:""});
  });
});
```

How It Works

In the HTML file, we can see that there are two paragraph elements of the class menus with the text *Books* and *Movies* to represent the two menu headings. Each paragraph element is followed by a div element of the class menuitems that contains an unordered list with three list items, each to represent submenu items of each menu heading. The unordered list (below the paragraph element Books) has three list items: Web Development, Programming, and RDBMS. Similarly, the unordered list that is below the paragraph element Movies has three list items: Latest Movie Trailers, Movie Reviews, and Celebrity Interviews.

In the style sheet file, the properties defined in the class selector `.menus` will be automatically applied to the paragraph elements of the class `.menu` to give them the shape of menu headings. The `width` property is set to 200px to define the menu heading to be 200px wide, and the `padding` property is set to 5px to keep some space between the border and the menu text. The `margin` property is set to 1px to keep space of 1px between the two menu headings. The `font-weight` property is set to `bold` to make the menu headings appear in bold, and the background of the menu heading is set to cyan by applying the code #0ff to the `background-color` property.

The properties in the class selector `.menuitems` will be applied to the `div` elements of the class `menuitems` automatically. It contains the display property set to `none` to hide the menu items initially.

The properties defined in the type selector `a` will be applied to all anchor elements (to all menu items). The display property is set to `block` to make the anchor element act as a block. The `border bottom` property is set to value `1px solid #fff` to create a solid white line of 1px thickness below every anchor element to separate all menu items. The `text-decoration` property is set to `none` to remove the traditional underline from the anchor elements. The `background` and `color` properties are used to set the background and foreground colors of the menu items to blue and white, respectively. The `padding` property is set to 10px to define the spacing between the menu-item text and its border. The `font-weight` property is set to `bold` to make the menu items appear in bold, and the `width` property is set to 190px to make the menu items 190px wide.

The properties defined in the attribute selector `.menuitems a:hover` will be automatically applied to the anchor elements nested inside the `div` element of the class `menu element` when the mouse pointer hovers over the menu items. It contains the `background` property that makes the background color of the hovered-over menu items turn black.

The type selector `li` contains the `display` property set to value `inline` to remove any spacing between the list items. Similarly, the type selector `ul` has the display property set to value `inline` to remove the spacing above and below the unordered list.

Now let's examine the actual jQuery code. We attach the `mouseout` event to the paragraph elements of the class `menus`; that is, to the menu headings `Books` and `Movies`. The reason for doing so is that we want to hide the menu items if the mouse pointer is away from both the menus.

Then we attach the `mouseover` event to the paragraph element of the class `menus`; that is, to the menu headings `Books` and `Movies`. Next we display an image of a down pointer to the hovered-over menu heading using the `.css()` method (to show that currently it is in expanded mode). The `background-repeat` property is set to `no-repeat` to make it appear once, and the `background-position` property is set to `right` to make the down pointer appear on the right end of the menu heading.

The contents of the next element (which matches the selector for us), is nothing but a `div` element of the class `menuitems`, containing the menu items of the hovered-over paragraph element. This is made visible with a slide-down effect. Its siblings (menu items of another menu heading: the `div` element of the class `menuitems`) are made invisible by using slide-up effect. Finally, the background image is removed from the menu item that has lost focus.

On execution of the preceding jQuery code, the menu headings will appear one below the other, as shown in Figure 5-14.

Books
Movies

Figure 5-14. Two menu headings: Books and Movies

On hovering over the first menu heading, `Books`, its menu items will be displayed with the slide-down effect, as shown in Figure 5-15. We can see that the menu heading has a down pointer attached to it to designate that it is in expanded mode now. Also, these menu items will have a hovering effect; that is, they will be highlighted on when the mouse pointer moves over them.

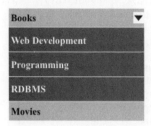

Figure 5-15. Menu Items of the Books menu appear with the slide-down effect

Similarly, on moving the mouse pointer over another menu heading, `Movies` we see that its menu items appear and those of the `Books` menu disappear with the slide-up effect, as shown in Figure 5-16.

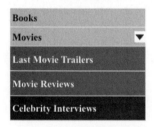

Figure 5-16. Submenu items of the Movies menu appear with the slide-up effect.

5-9. Making a Dynamic Visual Menu

Problem

You want to make a curved tab navigation menu that has three menus: `Books`, `Movies`, and `Music`. You want the menu tabs to have a hovering effect (highlighted when the mouse moves over them). You also want information related to the menu tab be displayed when a tab is hovered over.

Solution

Let's make an HTML file to define the anchor elements with the text *Books*, *Movies*, and *Music* nested inside the `span` element of the class `buttons`. The anchor elements are assigned the IDs `booksbutton`, `moviesbutton`, and `musicbutton`, respectively (to be accessed via jQuery code) and point at some hypothetical web site, `http://example.com`, where the user will be navigated if the menu item is selected. The HTML file may appear as shown here:

```
<body>
<span class="buttons"><a href="example.com" id="booksbutton"> Books </a></span>
<span class="buttons"><a href="example.com" id="moviesbutton"> Movies </a> </span>
<span class="buttons"><a href="example.com" id="musicbutton"> Music </a></span><br><br>
<p class="books">Books of different subjects available at reasonable prices. Ranging from
web development to programming languages and text books, all are available at heavy
discount. Shipping is free. Also available in stock are popular Magazines, E-books and
Tutorial CDs at affordable prices.</p>
<p class="movies">Find new movie reviews & latest hollywood movie news. Includes new movie
trailers, latest hollywood releases, movie showtimes, entertainment news, celebrity
interviews etc. Also find Hollywood actresses, actors, videos, biographies, filmographies,
photos, wallpapers, music, jokes, and live tv channels at your doorstep</p>
<p class="music">Find music videos, internet radio, music downloads and all the latest music
news and information. We have a large collection of music and songs classified by type,
language and region. All downloads are streamed through RealAudio. You can also watch free
music videos, tune in to AOL Radio, and search for your favorite music artists.</p>
</body>
```

Below the span elements we find three paragraph elements with three different class names assigned: Books, Movies, and Music. The paragraphs contain the information related to the three menu tabs. For this solution, we will be requiring two tab images. One tab image is for the left side of the menu tab to give it a curved slope as shown in Figure 5-17.

Figure 5-17. Image for the left side of the menu tab

The image for the left side is saved as tabl.jpg and the image for the right side of the menu tab is saved as tabr.jpg and may appear as shown in Figure 5-18.

Figure 5-18. Image for the right side of the menu tab

The two images in Figures 5-17 and 5-18 are in black. We need the same two images in green too (which will be used while hovering over the menu tabs). The two images with the green color are saved as tablselect.jpg and tabrselect.jpg.

The style sheet file style.css contains several style rules to make the span element appear as a tab navigation menu. The style.css file may appear as shown here:

```
style.css
.buttons{
background-image:url(tabl.jpg);
background-repeat:no-repeat;
background-position: left;
```

```
background-color:#000;
width: 80px;
float: left;
text-align: center;
}

a{
display:block;
background-image:url(tabr.jpg);
background-repeat:no-repeat;
background-position: right;
padding:3px;
text-decoration:none;
font-weight:bold;
color:#fff;
}

.rightselectfig{
display:block;
background-image:url(tabrselect.jpg);
background-repeat:no-repeat;
background-position: right;
padding:3px;
text-decoration:none;
font-weight:bold;
color:#fff;
}

.leftselectfig{
background-image:url(tablselect.jpg);
background-repeat:no-repeat;
background-position: left;
background-color:#0f0;
width: 80px;
float: left;
text-align: center;
}
```

The jQuery code to apply a hovering effect to the menu tabs and to display their related information is shown here:

```
$(document).ready(function() {
  $('.books').hide();
  $('.movies').hide();
  $('.music').hide();

  $('a').hover(
    function(event){
      $(this).addClass('rightselectfig');
      $(this).parent().addClass('leftselectfig');
    },
```

```
      function(){
        $(this).removeClass('rightselectfig');
        $(this).parent().removeClass('leftselectfig');
      }
    );

  $('#booksbutton').click(function(event){
    event.preventDefault();
    $('.books').show('slow');
    $('.movies').hide();
    $('.music').hide();
  });

  $('#moviesbutton').click(function(event){
    event.preventDefault();
    $('.movies').show('slow');
    $('.books').hide();
    $('.music').hide();
  });

  $('#musicbutton').click(function(event){
    event.preventDefault();
    $('.music').show('slow');
    $('.books').hide();
    $('.movies').hide();
  });
});
```

How It Works

The class selector .buttons contains the style properties that will be automatically applied to the span elements of the class buttons; that is, to Books, Movies, and Music. The background image property is set to url(tab1.jpg) to make the image shown in Figure 5-17 appear along with the menu text; the background-repeat property is set to no-repeat to make the image appear only once; the background-position property is set to left to make the image appear on the left side of the menu text to assign it a slope on the left side.

The background color of the menu tab is set to black and the width assigned to the menu tab is 80px. The float property is set to left to make the menu tab appear on left side of the browser window, making space on its right (for other menu tabs to appear on its right). The text-align property is set to center to make the menu text appear at the center of the defined width of 80px.

The properties defined in the type selector a will be automatically applied to the anchor elements. The display property is set to block to make the anchor element act as a block element instead of an individual element. The background-image property is set to tabr.jpg to apply the image shown in Figure 5-18 on the right side of the menu tab. The background-repeat property is set to no-repeat to make the image appear only once. The background-position is set to right to make the image appear on right side to assign it a slope shape on its right. The padding property is set to 3px to have spacing of 3px between the menu text and its border. The text-decoration property is set to none to remove the traditional underline that appears below the anchor elements. The font-weight property is set to bold to make the menu text appear in bold, and color is set to white to make the menu text appear in white.

The style rule `.rightselectfig` contains the properties will be applied to the anchor elements when the mouse pointer is moved over them. It contains the `display` property set to value `block` to make the anchor element act as a block element instead of an individual element. The `background-image` property is set to `tabrselect.jpg` to apply the image shown in Figure 5-18 in green on the right side of the menu tab. The `background-repeat` property is set to `no-repeat` to make the image appear only once. The `background-position` is set to `right` to make the image appear on right side to assign it a slope shape on its right. The `padding` property is set to 3px to have the spacing of 3px between the menu text and its border. The `text-decoration` property is set to `none` to remove the traditional underline that appears below the anchor elements. The `font-weight` property is set to `bold` to make the menu text appear in bold, and `color` is set to `white` to make the menu text appear in white.

The style rule `.leftselectfig` contains the properties that will be applied to the menu tab buttons when the mouse pointer is moved over them. It contains the background image property set to `url(tablselect.jpg)` to make the image shown in Figure 5-17 in green appear along with the menu text. The `background-repeat` property is set to `no-repeat` to make the image appear only once, and the background-position property is set to `left` to make the image appear on the left side of menu text to assign it a slope on left side. The background color of the menu tab is set to green to give it a hovering effect. The width assigned to the menu tab is 80px. The `float` property is set to `left` to make the menu tab appear on left side of the browser window, making space on its right (for other menu tabs to appear on is right). The `text-align` property is set to `center` to make the menu text appear at the center of the defined width of 80px.

Now in the jQuery code itself, all the paragraph elements of the classes `Books`, `Movies`, and `Music` are made invisible, as we will be displaying them only when we hover over the respective menu tab. We then attach the hover event to the anchor element and apply the properties defined in the style rule `.rightselectfig` to the menu tab (that has been hovered over) to apply green to it. We also add the image (`tabrselect.jpg`) on the right side for the right slope of the menu tab; we deal with the left side in the same way.

When the mouse is no longer hovering over the tab, we remove the style properties of the style rules `.rightselectfig` and `.leftselectfig` to make the menu tabs appear as they did initially when the mouse is moved away from the menu tabs.

Next we have the click events for the tabs. In these, we prevent the form from being submitted to the server. We also prevent the user from being navigated to the target web site on clicking the menu tab. We then display the information associated with the tab that was clicked, and hide the contents of the paragraph elements associated with the other tabs.

When we hover over the Books menu tab, its background color changes to green and the information related to books will be displayed as shown in Figure 5-19.

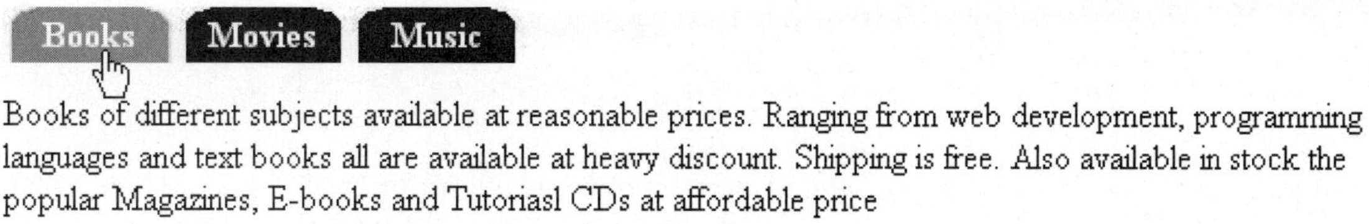

Books of different subjects available at reasonable prices. Ranging from web development, programming languages and text books all are available at heavy discount. Shipping is free. Also available in stock the popular Magazines, E-books and Tutoriasl CDs at affordable price

Figure 5-19. The menu tab becomes highlighted when it's hovered over, and the associated information is displayed.

In order to give the animation effect to the text being displayed, we can use `slideDown()` and `slideUp()` methods instead of simple `show()` and `hide()` methods, as shown in the following jQuery code:

```
$(document).ready(function() {
  $('.books').hide();
  $('.movies').hide();
  $('.music').hide();

  $('#booksbutton').mouseover(function(){
    $('.books').slideDown('slow');
    $('.movies').slideUp('slow');
    $('.music').slideUp('slow');
  });

  $('#moviesbutton').mouseover(function(){
    $('.movies').slideDown('slow');
    $('.books').slideUp('slow');
    $('.music').slideUp('slow');
  });

  $('#musicbutton').mouseover(function(){
    $('.music').slideDown('slow');
    $('.books').slideUp('slow');
    $('.movies').slideUp('slow');
  });
});
```

Summary

In this chapter, you saw how to create different types of menus, such as breadcrumb menus, contextual menus, accordion menus, and dynamic visual menus. You also saw how to access menu items using access keys and how to make menus with hovering menu items.

The next chapter includes a wide variety of examples concerning animation effects. You will learn how to make image sliders, horizontal and vertical image scrollers, image shufflers, etc. You will also see how to make news scrollers and how to display images on a page.

CHAPTER 6

Visual Effects

In this chapter you'll discover many recipes that deal with different animation effects. The solutions that we'll be covering in this chapter are as follows:

- Displaying images horizontally and vertically
- Creating a horizontal image slider
- Displaying an image that scrolls left and becomes invisible when clicked
- Creating an image that scrolls left, disappears, and reappears at the right
- Scrolling an image at the center of the browser window
- Showing an image one after the other on hover
- Scrolling an image vertically
- Scrolling an image horizontally
- Making a news scroller
- Displaying the enlarged image on mouse over
- Showing images pagewise
- Shuffling images in either direction
- Writing a pendulum scroller
- Scrolling images using arrays

6-1. Displaying Images Horizontally and Vertically

Problem

You have five images and you want to display them horizontally, one after the other, with a small distance between them.

Solution

Let's start out by making an HTML file to display all the five images in the form of a hyperlink, so that if any visitor clicks on the image, he will be navigated to the target web site (assuming any hypothetical web site:). The HTML file should appear as shown here:

```
<body>
<div id="images">
<a href="http://example.com" ><img src="image1.jpg" width=150px height=150px /></a>
<a href="http://example.com"><img src="image2.jpg"  width=150px height=150px /></a>
<a href="http://example.com"><img src="image3.jpg"  width=150px height=150px /></a>
<a href="http://example.com" ><img src="image4.jpg"  width=150px height=150px /></a>
<a href="http://example.com" ><img src="image5.jpg"  width=150px height=150px /></a>
</div>
</body>
```

All the images in the form of anchor elements are stored within a `div` element of ID `images`. We can see in the preceding HTML file that the width and height of all images is set to 150px to give them a uniform appearance.

The jQuery code to display the images one after the other in a row is shown here:

```
$(document).ready(function() {
  var $pic = $('#images a');
  $pic.hide();
  var imgs = $pic.length;
  var next;
  for (i=0;i<imgs;i++){
    next=$pic.eq(i);
    next.css({'position': 'absolute','left':160*i});
    next.show();
  }
});
```

How It Works

Before we examine the code statements, let's first explore the two methods that are used in the preceding code: `.eq()` and `.length`.

.eq()

`.eq()` is one of the filtering methods that retrieves the element at the specified index position from the specified selection and returns it in the form of a jQuery object.

Syntax:
`.eq(index)`

Here `index` specifies the location in the selection (begins t 0 and goes to length –1). If an out-of-range index is supplied, then an empty jQuery object is returned.

.length

This method returns the count of the matched elements.

Syntax:
`.length`

Looking now at the actual jQuery solution, we start by collecting and storing all the anchor elements (a) of the `div` element of ID `images` in an array, `$pic`. Since all the images are part of the anchor element, the information of all five images will be stored in the `$pic` array. We also hide all the images using `$pic.hide()`.They will be displayed one by one with the help of a `for` loop.

The length of the `$pic` array is then computed and is stored in the variable `imgs`. Since there are in all five images that are stored in the `$pic` array, the value that is stored in the `imgs` variable will be 5. One image at a time from the `$pic` array is then retrieved and stored in the `next` variable to display.

Finally, with the help of the `.css()` property, the image referred to by the `next` variable is assigned the absolute position from the left boundary of the browser window. The first image is assigned the position 0px from the left side, the second image is at a distance of 160px from the left, the third image is at a distance of 320px from left, and so on. Hence all the images are assigned positions, keeping a gap of 10px between them.

On execution of preceding jQuery code, we may get the output shown in Figure 6-1.

Figure 6-1. All images displayed in a horizontal row

Display Images Vertically

We can make the preceding jQuery code display the images vertically, one below the other, by just altering a single statement. If we alter this statement,
```
next.css({'position': 'absolute','left':160*i});
```

to the following:

```
next.css({'position': 'absolute','top':160*i});
```

then the images will appear at the specified distance from the top boundary of the browser window instead of the left boundary. The preceding statement, depending on the value of i, will make the image appear at the distance of 0px, 160px, 320px, and so on from the top boundary of the browser window. The overall code should appear as shown here:

```
$(document).ready(function() {
  var $pic = $('#images a');
  $pic.hide();
  var imgs = $pic.length;
  var next;
  for (i=0;i<imgs;i++){
    next=$pic.eq(i);
    next.css({'position': 'absolute','top':160*i});
    next.show();
  }
});
```

The output that you will get with this code is shown in Figure 6-2.

Figure 6-2. All images displayed vertically, one below the other

6-2. Creating a Horizontal Image Slider

Problem

You want to make an image gallery (consisting of five images) in which initially three images will be displayed. On using the horizontal scroll bar, you can scroll and see the rest of the images.

Solution

Let's make an HTML file to define all five images of the image gallery in the form of a hyperlink. If we click on any image, it is supposed to navigate us to the target web site that displays the complete information about the image. Here we assume the target web site is some hypothetical web site. The HTML file should appear as shown here:

```
<body>
<div id="scroller">
<div id="images">
<a href="http://example.com" ><img src="image1.jpg" width=150px height=150px /></a>
<a href="http://example.com"><img src="image2.jpg"  width=150px height=150px /></a>
<a href="http://example.com"><img src="image3.jpg"  width=150px height=150px /></a>
<a href="http://example.com" ><img src="image4.jpg"  width=150px height=150px /></a>
<a href="http://example.com" ><img src="image5.jpg"  width=150px height=150px /></a>
</div>
</div>
</body>
```

We see that there are two `div` elements, nested one inside the other, with IDs `scroller` and `images`. Inside the `div` element of ID `images` we define five anchor elements, each containing an image. All the images are assigned the uniform width and height of 150px.

To the `div` element of ID `scroller`, we will apply the style rule `.imageslider`, and to the `div` element of ID `images` we will apply the style rule `.pics`. The style rule `.imageslider` contains the style properties to define a window of the specified width so as to display at most three images and a scroll bar—allowing us to view the hidden images. The style rule `.pics` contains the `width` property for specifying the total width required to display all five images. The width defined in this style rule decides the space in which we can scroll. Both the style rules are defined in the external style sheet file `style.css`. The jQuery code to apply the `style.css` properties to the `div` elements of ID `scroller` and `images` is shown here:

```
$(document).ready(function() {
$('#scroller').css({'margin':auto, 'width':'490px', 'height':'170px', 'overflow':'scroll'});
$('#images').css({'width':'790px'});
});
```

How It Works

In the style properties applied to the `div` element of ID `scroller`, we find that the value of the `margin` property is set to `auto` to adjust the margin of the image-slider window automatically on the basis of the size of the browser window; as a result, the window will appear at the center of the browser window. The width property is set to 490px to accommodate three images of 150px each, plus some distance in between them. The height property is set to 170px. The value of the overflow property is set to scroll, which makes a horizontal scroll bar appear in the window.

Similarly, the style properties applied to the div element of ID images has the width property set to 790px (to define the total width of all the five images). In other words, the style rule to be applied to the outside div element (of ID scroller) is for specifying the width of the window (to define the number of images that we want to see at in it), and the style rule of the internal div element (of ID images) is for defining the complete width required to see all the images.

We get a window at the center of the browser window showing three images, with a horizontal scroll bar to scroll and see the hidden images, as shown in Figure 6-3.

Figure 6-3. Images displayed in a window with a horizontal scroll bar

We can modify the values of the properties in the style rules to make the window scroll vertically instead of horizontally. The modification in jQuery code may be as shown here:

```
$(document).ready(function() {
$('#scroller').css({'margin':auto, 'width':'170px', 'height':'490px', 'overflow':'scroll'});
$('#images').css({'height':'790px'});
});
```

We can see in the preceding style properties that the values of the width and height properties are modified to reduce the width and increase the height. The image slider may appear as shown in Figure 6-4.

Figure 6-4. All images displayed vertically, one below the other, with a vertical scroll bar

6-3. Displaying an Image that Scrolls Left and Becomes Invisible When Clicked

Problem

You have an image that is displayed on the left side of the browser window. When the image is clicked, it will scroll to the left and become invisible.

Solution

Let's make an HTML file to define the image element to display the image that we want to appear on the screen. The HTML file should appear as shown here:

```
<body>
<img src="image1.jpg" width=150px height=150px class="image"/>
</body>
```

We can see in the preceding HTML code that the img element is assigned the class name image that will be used to attach a click event to it. Also the width and height of the image are set to 150px. An image is set to scroll by using its position property. By setting the value relative to the position property, we can make an image scroll.

Now let's write the class selector .image in the external style sheet file style.css to apply the position property automatically to the HTML element of the class image; that is, to the img element. The style sheet may appear as shown here:

```
style.css
.image{
position:relative;
}
```

We can see that the .image class selector assigns relative value to the position property. Let's write the jQuery code to attach the click event to the HTML element of the class image; that is, to the img element. We also need to define the code for animating the image in the event-handling function of the click event. The code may appear as shown here:

```
$(document).ready(function() {
  $('.image').click(function (event){
    $(this).animate({'left': -160}, 'slow' );
  });
});
```

How It Works

We can see that the animate() method defined in the event-handling function (of the click event) makes the images scroll to the left and stop at the distance of –160px from the left boundary of the browser window so as to make the whole image of width 150px disappear completely. Thus the value assigned to left represents to what end the image will be animated, and the image will be transitioned from its current state to the value specified. Initially, the image will appear completely, as shown in Figure 6-5.

Figure 6-5. Image that appears on loading the web page

On clicking the image, it will start scrolling to the left and will disappear slowly, as shown in Figure 6-6.

Figure 6-6. Image partially visible as it is being scrolled to the left

Making the Scrolling Image Appear at the Center of the Browser Window

In the previous solution, we saw that the image initially appears at the left side of the browser window. Now we want the image to appear at the center of the browser window. We also want the image to be surrounded by an invisible window so that when the image is clicked, it scrolls to the left (in the boundary of the invisible window) and disappears gradually.

The HTML file should be modified as shown here:

```
<body>
<div id="scroller">
<img src="image1.jpg" width=150px height=150px class="image"/>
</div>
</body>
```

In the HTML code, you can see that the img element is enclosed within a div element, which is assigned the ID scroller. The reason of making use of the div element is to assign the width and height to the invisible window for the image (within which we want it to scroll).

We write the ID selector #scroller in the style sheet so that the style properties defined in it can be automatically applied to the div element of ID scroller without any need for jQuery code. The style sheet will also contain the class selector .image to assign the relative property to the position property of the img element, which is necessary to make the image scroll.

The style sheet style.css may appear as shown here:

```
style.css
#scroller{
width:155px;
height:155px;
margin:auto;
overflow:hidden;
position:relative;
}

.image{
position:relative;
}
```

The jQuery code to attach the click event to the image, and the `animate` method (defined in the event-handling function) to make the image scroll to the left and stop at the distance of –160px from the left side of the enclosing window (to become completely invisible) are shown here:

```
$(document).ready(function() {
  $('.image').click(function (event){
    $(this).animate({'left': -160}, 'slow');
  });
});
```

How It Works – Part 2

We can see that the ID selector `#scroller` contains the `width` and `height` properties set to 155px to define the width and height of the invisible window for the image. The `margin` property is set to `auto` so that window takes the margin space from the browser window, automatically making the window appear at the center of the width of the browser window. The value of the `overflow` property is set to `hidden` to make the region of the image that has scrolled out of the boundary of the window become invisible. The `position` property is assigned the value `relative` to make the image scroll relative to the enclosed window.

The class selector `.image` contains the `position` property set to `relative` to make the image scroll from its current position. Initially, the image will appear as shown in Figure 6-5, but of course it will appear at the center of the browser window instead at the left side, and on clicking the image, it will scroll to the left and will become invisible slowly, as shown in Figure 6-6.

6-4. Creating an Image that Scrolls Left, Disappears, and Reappears at the Right

Problem

You have an image that is displayed at the center of the browser window (enclosed in an invisible window). On clicking the image, it scrolls to the left (inside the enclosed window) and disappears. When the image totally disappears, it reappears form the right side of the window and stops where it started.

Solution

We need to write the HTML code to display an image. We also need to enclose the image element within a `div` element as shown here:

```
<body>
<div id="scroller">
<img src="image1.jpg" width=150px height=150px class="image"/>
</div>
</body>
```

In the HTML code, we can see that the `img` element is enclosed within a `div` element, which is assigned the ID `scroller`. The reason for making use of the `div` element is to assign the width and height to the invisible window for the image (within which we want it to scroll).

We write the ID selector `#scroller` in the style sheet so that the style properties defined in it can be automatically applied to the `div` element of ID `scroller` without using jQuery code. The style sheet will also contain the class selector `.image` to assign the `relative` property to the `position` property of the `img` element, which is very necessary to make the image scroll.

The style sheet `style.css` may appear as shown here:

```
style.css
#scroller{
width:155px;
height:155px;
margin:auto;
overflow:hidden;
position:relative;
}

.image{
position:relative;
}
```

The jQuery code to make the image scroll is shown here:

```
$(document).ready(function() {
  $('.image').click(function (event){
    $(this).animate(
      {'left': -160}, 'slow',
      function(){
        $(this).css('left',150);
        $(this).animate({'left': 0}, 'slow');
      }
    );
  });
});
```

How It Works

We can see that the ID selector `#scroller` contains the `width` and `height` properties set to 155px to define the width and height of the invisible window for the image. The `margin` property is set to `auto` so that window takes the margin space from the browser window, automatically making the window appear at the center of the width of the browser window. The `overflow` property is set to `hidden` to make the area of the image that has scrolled out of the boundary of the window become invisible. The `position` property is assigned the value `relative` to make the image scroll relative to the enclosed window. The class selector `.image` contains the `position` property set to `relative` to make the image scroll from its current position.

We can see in the preceding jQuery code that a click event is attached to the image. In the event-handling function of the click event, the `animate` method is used to make the image scroll to the left slowly (in the boundary of the window in which the image is enclosed) and stop at the distance of –160px from the left side of the window; that is, the image completely disappears. In the callback function of the `animate` method (which is invoked when the animate method is over; that is, when the image is completely invisible), we use the `.css()` method to make the image appear at the distance of 150px from the left side of the invisible window, making a small portion of the left edge of the image appear. In the same callback function, we again make use of the `animate` method to make the image scroll to the left and stop at the distance of 0px (from the left side of the invisible window); that is, the image will stop where it started.

Initially, the image will appear as shown in Figure 6-7.

Figure 6-7. *Image on loading the web page*

And upon clicking the image, it will scroll to the left and will become invisible slowly, as shown in Figure 6-8.

Figure 6-8. *Image scrolling to the left*

After the image completely disappears, it appears again at the right side of the window and scrolls left, as shown in Figure 6-9:

Figure 6-9. Image appearing from the right border of the invisible window

6-5. Scrolling an Image at the Center of the Browser Window

Problem

You have an image that is displayed at the center of the browser window (enclosed in an invisible window). You want the image to keep scrolling; that is, it should scroll toward the left boundary of the window and disappear, then reappear from the right side of the window, and again scroll toward the left, and so on.

Solution

We need to write the HTML code to display an image. We also need to enclose the image element within a div, as shown here:

```
<body>
<div id="scroller">
<img src="image1.jpg" width=150px height=150px class="image"/>
</div>
</body>
```

In the HTML code, we can see that the img element is enclosed within a div element, which is assigned the ID scroller. The reason for making use of the div element is to assign the width and height to the invisible window for the image (within which we want it to scroll).

We write the ID selector #scroller in the style sheet so that the style properties defined in it can be automatically applied to the div element of ID scroller without using jQuery code. The style sheet will also contain the class selector .image to assign the relative property to position property of the img element, which is necessary to make the image scroll.

The style sheet **style.css** may appear as shown here:

```
style.css
#scroller{
width:155px;
height:155px;
margin:auto;
overflow:hidden;
position:relative;
}

.image{
position:relative;
}
```

The jQuery code to make the image scroll is shown here:

```
$(document).ready(function() {
  scroll();
});

function scroll()
{
  $('.image').animate(
    {'left': -160}, 'slow',
    function(){
      $('.image').css('left',150);
      $('.image').animate({'left': 0}, 'slow');
    }
  );
  setTimeout(scroll, 1200);
}
```

How It Works

We can see that the ID selector **#scroller** contains the **width** and **height** properties set to 155px to define the width and height of the invisible window for the image. The **margin** property is set to **auto** so that window takes the margin space from the browser window, automatically making the window appear at the center of the width of the browser window. The value of the **overflow** property is set to hidden to make the area of the image that has scrolled out of the boundary of the window to become invisible. The **position** property is assigned the value **relative** to make the image scroll relative to the enclosed window. The class selector **.image** contains the position property set to **relative** to make the image scroll from its current position.

Before we explore the workings of the preceding jQuery code, let's first examine the method **setTimeout()**, which is used in the following section.

setTimeout()

This method is used to make an event appear after a certain amount of time has passed.

```
Syntax:
setTimeout(action, time)
```

The `setTimeout()` method takes two arguments: the action that we want to take, and the time in milliseconds that we want to wait before taking the specified action.

We can see in the preceding jQuery code that a function `scroll` is defined that contains an `animate` method used to make the image to scroll to the left slowly (in the boundary of the window in which the image is enclosed) and stop at the distance of –160px from the left side of the window; that is, the image completely disappears. In the callback function of the animate method (which is invoked when the animate method is over (that is, when the image is completely invisible), we use the `.css()` method to make the image appear at the distance of 150px from the left side of the invisible window, making a small portion of the left edge of the image appear. In the same callback function, we again make use of the `animate` method to make the image scroll to the left and stop at the distance of 0px (from the left side of the invisible window); that is, the image will stop where it started.

The function `scroll` doing all the aforementioned things is invoked when the web page is loaded, making the image have one complete round in the window. After that, within the `scroll` function we call it again (recursively) after the delay of 1200 milliseconds. In other words, the image will keep scrolling infinitely after a gap of 1200 milliseconds after each round. Initially, the image will appear as shown in Figure 6-7. The image will scroll to the left and will become invisible slowly, as shown in Figure 6-8. When the image completely disappears, it reappears from the right side of the window and scrolls left as shown in Figure 6-9, and so the process continues.

6-6. Showing Images One After the Other on Hover

Problem

You have several images to be displayed and you want to display them one by one. The first image is displayed and when you hover over it, and you want it to fade out and another image to fade in. Then you want the second image to fade out on hover and the third image to fade in, and so on. After the last image, you want the first image to reappear.

Solution

Let's make an HTML file to display all the five images in the form of a hyperlink, so that if any visitor clicks on the image, he will be navigated to the target web site displaying complete information of the object that image represents. Currently we assume the target web site as any hypothetical web site. The HTML file should appear as shown here:

```
<body>
<a class="imge" href="http://example.com" ><img src="image1.jpg" width=300px
height=300px></a>
<a class="imge" href="http://example.com"><img src="image2.jpg" width=300px
height=300px></a>
```

```
<a class="imge" href="http://example.com"><img src="image3.jpg" width=300px
height=300px></a>
<a class="imge" href="http://example.com" ><img src="image4.jpg" width=300px
height=300px></a>
<a class="imge" href="http://example.com" ><img src="image5.jpg" width=300px
height=300px></a>
</body>
```

All the anchor elements are assigned the class name `imge` so as to automatically apply to them the style properties that are defined in the class selector `.imge` defined in the external style sheet (`style.css`). The class names are also used to identify the elements to which we want to apply jQuery code. Also, all the images are assigned an identical width and height of 300px to give them a uniform appearance.

The style sheet `style.css` may appear as shown here:

```
style.css
.imge{
position:absolute;
top:10px;
left:10px;
}
```

The jQuery code for making an image fade out (become invisible) slowly and replacing it with another image that fades in (becomes visible) slowly is shown here:

```
$(document).ready(function() {
  $(".imge").hide();
  $('.imge:first').fadeIn('slow');
  $('.imge').hover(
    function(){
      $(this).fadeIn('slow');
    },
    function(){
      var next = ($(this).next().length) ? $(this).next() :$('.imge:first');
      $(this).fadeOut('slow');
      next.fadeIn('slow');
    }
  );
});
```

How It Works

We want it so that when we hover on one image, it will be replaced by another image at the same place, so we have used the `position` property and set the class selector `.imge` to `absolute` to define the exact location of the image to appear on the web page. Also, the `top` and `left` properties are set to 10px to assure that the image appears at the distance of 10px from the top and left boundaries of the browser window.

Now looking at the jQuery code itself, we make all the images disappear initially, as we want them to appear one by one. We then make the first element of all the HTML elements of the class `imge` to appear slowly on the web page. That is, the first image (of all the images) will appear slowly on opening the web page. This is the initial image that will appear first on the web page. Once this is complete, we attach the hover event to all the images (all HTML elements of the class imge).

In the hover event, we make the current image appear slowly when the mouse is over the image. When the mouse pointer is moved away from the image being displayed, we see the next image to be displayed. We first check that we are not on the last image (of elements of the class imge), then we assign the next image in sequence to the variable next. And if we *are* at the last image, the first image (of the HTML elements of the class imge) is assigned to the variable next. In other words, the variable next will be set to refer either to the next image in sequence or to the first image (if we have reached the last image of the class imge).

Once we have decided on the image to display next, the image that is currently visible is made to fade out slowly. Finally, the image in the variable next (referring to the next image in sequence) is set to appear slowly on the web page (fade in).

Initially, we get the first image of the five images on the screen, as shown in Figure 6-10.

Figure 6-10. The first image displayed on loading the web page

On hovering over the image (that is, on moving the mouse over the image and taking it away), the next image in sequence will appear slowly, as shown in Figure 6-11. Similarly, all the images will be displayed one by one. When the last image is reached, the first image will reappear:

Figure 6-11. The first image is replaced by the next image in sequence on hover.

Making a Slide Show

So let' make a slide show. We'll display an image that, when clicked, will be replaced by another image in sequence, and so on. The only modification that we will make to the preceding jQuery code is that instead of the hover event, we will attach the click event to the images. The Query code may appear as shown here:

```
$(document).ready(function() {
    $(".imge").hide();
    var next;
    $('.imge:first').fadeIn('slow');
    $('.imge').click(function(event){
        $(this).fadeIn('slow');
        next = ($(this).next().length) ? $(this).next() :$('.imge:first');
        $(this).fadeOut('slow');
        next.fadeIn('slow');
        event.preventDefault();
    });
});
```

We can see that all the images are initially made invisible. The first image is made visible by a fade-in effect. A click event is attached to the images and if the click event occurs on any of the image, the next image in sequence is retrieved and stored in the variable **next**. The image that was visible earlier is made invisible slowly with a fadeout effect, and the next image in sequence (which is retrieved in the **next** variable) is made visible with the fade-in effect. To stop from migrating to the target web page on clicking the image, the **preventDefault** method of the **event** object (that is automatically passed to the event-handling function by JavaScript) is used.

6-7. Scrolling an Image Vertically

Problem

You have several images, one below the other, which you want to scroll down the browser window slowly. When all of an image disappears, you want it to reappear from the top border of the browser window and continue scrolling downward.

Solution

Let's make an HTML file to define all five images that we want to scroll, in the form of a hyperlink. If we click on any image, it will navigate us to the target web site that displays the complete information about the image. Here we assume the target web site as some hypothetical web site. The HTML file should appear as shown here:

```
<body>
<div id="scroller">
<a href="http://example.com" ><img src="image1.jpg" width=150px height=150px /></a>
<a href="http://example.com"><img src="image2.jpg"  width=150px height=150px /></a>
<a href="http://example.com"><img src="image3.jpg"  width=150px height=150px /></a>
<a href="http://example.com" ><img src="image4.jpg"  width=150px height=150px /></a>
<a href="http://example.com" ><img src="image5.jpg"  width=150px height=150px /></a>
</div>
</body>
```

All the anchor elements are enclosed within the **div** element of ID : **scroller** so as to apply the style properties defined in the ID selector **#scroller** to all the anchor elements and images. The ID selector is defined in the external style sheet **style.css**. Also, all the images are assigned an identical width and height of 150px to give them a uniform appearance. The style sheet **style.css** may appear as shown here:

```
style.css
#scroller {
  position: relative;
  height: 760px;
  width: 150px;
}

#scroller a img { border:0; }
```

The jQuery code for making the images scroll is shown here:

```
$(document).ready(function() {
  var $wrapper=$('#scroller');
  $wrapper.css({overflow: 'hidden'});
  var animator = function(imgblock) {
    imgblock.animate(
      {bottom:"-" + imgblock.height() + "px"}, 5000,
      function() {
        $(this).css({ bottom:imgblock.height()});
        animator($(this));
      }
    );
  }
  animator($wrapper);
});
```

How It Works

We can see in the **style.css** file that the ID selector **#scroller** contains a **position** property set to **relative**—a necessary condition to make the image scroll (images scroll by assigning them some position relative to their current location). The height and width are set to 760px and 150px, respectively. The height of 760px is required to display all five images of height 150px each (one below the other), plus some distance between them.

Also, the style sheet contains a type selector **#scroller a img** to apply the style properties to the **img** element nested inside the anchor element, which in turn is enclosed with an HTML element of ID **scroller**. That is, the **style** property with value 0 will be applied to the **img** elements to make the borders of the images invisible.

Now in the jQuery code itself, we see that all the contents in the **div** element of ID **scroller** are retrieved and stored in a variable wrapper. That is, all the images are now contained in the **wrapper** variable. Using the **.css()** method, we apply the **overflow** property set to **hidden** to the wrapper variable (to the block of images) so as to make the images that scroll down the browser window invisible. Also, a function named **animator** is defined, which is invoked by the statement

```
animator($wrapper);
```

This statement invokes the **animator** function, and the **wrapper** variable containing the block of images is passed to it that will be assigned to its parameter **imgblock**. In the **animator** function itself, the code animates the image block toward the bottom of the browser window and stops it at the height of −760px from the bottom of the browser window. Since 760px is the total height of the image block, the whole image block will disappear. The image block will scroll down slowly, as we have defined the duration of animation as 5000 milliseconds. In the callback function of the animate method (that is invoked when the animate method is over), we make use of the **.css()** method to make the image block appear at the distance of 760px from the bottom border of the browser window, making the whole block visible. After that the animator function is recursively called to invoke itself to make the image block again scroll down toward the bottom of the browser window, and the process is repeated.

The part of the image block visible while scrolling may appear as in Figure 6-12.

Figure 6-12. Block of images scrolling vertically

Making the Images Scroll in a Small Window at the Center of the Browser Window

The solution that we just saw makes the images scroll to take up the whole browser window. We can make the images appear within a smaller invisible window so as to take less space. Also, we can make them appear at the center of the browser window's width instead of being left-aligned.

We'll use the HTML file the same as the one we created at the beginning of this recipe. We need to add some more properties to the ID selector **#scroller** and to the type selector **#scroller a img**, as shown here:

```
style.css
#scroller {
  height: 460px;
  width: 150px;
  overflow:hidden;
  position: relative;
  margin:auto;
}
```

```
#scroller a img { border:0; position:relative;}
```

The jQuery code to make the vertical scroller scroll in the window of width and height 150px and 460px, respectively, is as shown here:

```
$(document).ready(function() {
  var $wrapper=$('#scroller a img');
  $wrapper.css({bottom:750});
  var animator = function(imgblock) {
    imgblock.animate(
      {bottom:-460}, 5000,
      function() {
        imgblock.css({bottom:750});
        animator($(this));
      }
    );
  }
  animator($wrapper);
});
```

How It Works

The ID selector `#scroller` contains the `height` property set to 460px, which is sufficient to display three images of height 150px, one below the other (we want to see at most three images at a time). The `width` property is set to 150px (that is the width of an image). The `overflow` property is set to `hidden` to make invisible those images that cross this window boundary. The value of the `position` property is set to `relative` to make it possible for the images to scroll, and the `margin` property is set to `auto` to make the invisible window (displaying a vertical scroller) appear a the center of the browser window's width.

The style properties defined in the type `#scroller a img` will be automatically applied to the `img` element (images of the HTML file). It contains the `border` property set to 0 (to make the borders of the images invisible), and the `position` property is set to `relative` to make the images scroll.

Looking now at the jQuery code itself, first up all the `img` elements of the HTML file enclosed in the anchor element of the `div` element of ID `scroller` are retrieved, and stored, in the variable `wrapper`. Then the block of these images stored in `wrapper` is set to appear at the distance of 750px from the bottom of the invisible window (it makes the bottom edge of the last image of the image block appear within the invisible window.

Next, in the `animator` method the image block is set to animate toward the bottom of the invisible window and stop at the distance of –460px; that is, when the image block disappears. The image block will animate slowly, as the duration of animation is set to 5000 milliseconds.

In the callback function of the `animator` method (that executes when animation is done), we set the image block to appear at the distance of 750 pixels from the bottom of the invisible window, making the bottom edge of the last image appear. The `animator` method is then called recursively to make the vertical scroller scroll infinitely.

Finally, the `animator` method is invoked and all the images that were stored in the variable `wrapper` are passed to it.

Making the Scroller Scroll Upward

The preceding scroller was moving downward. We can alter the jQuery code to make it scroll upward; that is, toward the top border of the invisible window. The jQuery code to accomplish that is as follows:

```
$(document).ready(function() {
  var $wrapper=$('#scroller a img');
  $wrapper.css({top:0});
  var animator = function(imgblock) {
    imgblock.animate(
      {top:-770}, 5000,
      function() {
        imgblock.css({top:450});
        animator($(this));
      }
    );
  }
  animator($wrapper);
});
```

All the images (`img` elements nested inside the anchor element, which in turn is nested inside the `div` element of ID `scroller`) are retrieved and stored in the variable `$wrapper`. Using the `.css()` method, the images are set at the distance of 0px from top border; that is, three images of height 150px each will appear initially, one below the other. The `animator` function is invoked and all the images stored in the `$wrapper` variable are sent to it and are assigned to its `imgblock` parameter. The image block is then set to animate toward the top border of the invisible window. The animation will stop at the distance of – 770px; that is, it will stop when whole of the image block disappears! The scrolling will be slow, as the delay is set to 5000 milliseconds. After the animation effect, the block is then set to appear at the distance of 450px from the top border; that is, the top edge of the first image in the image block will reappear from the bottom border of the invisible window. The `animator` function is called recursively to continue the scrolling…

6-8. Scrolling an Image Horizontally

Problem

You have several images and you want them to be displayed in the form of a scroller. That is, you want the images to scroll from right to left one by one in an invisible window. When all the images are scrolled to the left, you want the first image to reappear from the right side of the window and scroll toward the left side, followed by other images behind it.

Solution

Let's make an HTML file to define the five images that we want to scroll, in the form of a hyperlink. If we click on any image, it is supposed to navigate us to the target web site that displays the complete information about the image. Here we assume the target web site as some hypothetical web site. The HTML file should appear as shown here:

```
<div id="scroller">
<div id="images">
<a href="http://example.com" ><img src="image1.jpg" width=150px height=150px /></a>
<a href="http://example.com"><img src="image2.jpg"  width=150px height=150px /></a>
<a href="http://example.com"><img src="image3.jpg"  width=150px height=150px /></a>
<a href="http://example.com" ><img src="image4.jpg"  width=150px height=150px /></a>
<a href="http://example.com" ><img src="image5.jpg"  width=150px height=150px /></a>
</div>
</div>
</body>
```

We can see that the anchor elements containing the `img` elements are enclosed within two `div` elements, one inside the other. The outer `div` element is assigned the ID `scroller` and the inner `div` element is assigned the ID `images`. To the outer `div` element we will apply the style properties to define the width of the invisible window; it decides how many images we want to see at a time. To the inner `div` element, we will apply the style properties that decide the total width of the complete image block. All the images are assigned an identical width and height of 150px to give them a uniform appearance. We define the style properties for the `div` elements and the `img` elements in the style sheet `style.css` that may appear as shown here:

```
style.css
#scroller {
   position: relative;
   height:150px;
   width: 460px;
   overflow:hidden;
   margin:auto;
}

#images{
   width: 770px;
}

#images a img {border:0; position:relative;}
```

The jQuery code to make the horizontal scroller appear at the center of the browser window is as shown here:

```
$(document).ready(function() {
  var $wrapper=$('#scroller a img');
  $wrapper.css({left:0});
  var animator = function(imgblock) {
    imgblock.animate(
      {left:-770}, 5000,
```

```
    function() {
      imgblock.css({left:450});
      animator($(this));
    }
  );
}
animator($wrapper);
});
```

How It Works

We can see in the `style.css` file that the ID selector `#scroller` contains a `position` property set to `relative`—a necessary condition to make the image scroll (images scroll when we assign them some position relative to their current location). The height and width are set to 150px and 460px, respectively. The width of 460px is required to display at most three images at a time (the width includes the width of three images of 150px width, with some space in between). The `overflow` property is set to hidden to make the region of the images invisible that falls outside the width of this invisible window. The `margin` property is set to `auto` to make the horizontal scroller appear at the center of the width of browser window.

The ID selector #images contains the `width` property that will be applied to the inner `div` element. The `width` property is set to770px, which is the total of the width of all the images that we want to be displayed in the scroller (with some distance in between the images). The `width` property here decides the number of images that we want to see in the horizontal scroller. Also, the style sheet contains a type selector `#images a img` to apply the style properties to the `img` element nested inside the anchor element, which in turn is enclosed with an HTML element of ID `images`. It contains the border property set to 0 (to make the borders of the images invisible) and the position property is set to `relative` to make the images scroll.

Looking now at the jQuery code itself, all the `img` elements of the HTML file that are enclosed in the anchor element of the `div` element of ID `scroller` are retrieved and stored in the variable `wrapper`. The block of images stored in the `wrapper` variable is then set to appear at the distance of 0px from the left boundary of the invisible window (it makes the first three image of the image block appear within the invisible window initially).

Then, in the `animator` method, the image block is set to animate toward the left edge of the invisible window and stop at the distance of –770px; that is, when all five images in the image block have scrolled to the left. The image block will animate slowly, as the duration of animation is set to 5000 milliseconds.

In the callback function of the `animator` method (that executes when the animation is done), we set the image block to appear at the distance of 450px from the left boundary of the invisible window, making the left edge of the first image (in the image block) appear from the right boundary of the invisible window. The `animator` method is then called recursively to make the horizontal scroller scroll infinitely. When all the images are scrolled to the left side, the first image reappears from the right boundary of the invisible window.

Finally, the `animator` method is invoked and all the images that were stored in the variable `wrapper` are passed to it. On execution of the preceding jQuery code, three images appear, as shown in Figure 6-13.

223

Figure 6-13. Images that appear on loading the web page

These images start scrolling to the left, making the rest of the images (that were hidden behind the invisible window) appear as shown in Figure 6-14.

Figure 6-14. Images scrolling to the left, and the hidden images appearing from the right

Pausing the Scroll on Hover

Say we also want the image scroller to pause when the mouse pointer moves over any of its images, and resume scrolling when the mouse pointer moves away from the images. We can modify the jQuery code as shown here:

```
$(document).ready(function() {
  var $wrapper=$('#scroller a img');
  $wrapper.css({left:0});
  var animator = function(imgblock) {
    imgblock.animate(
      {left:-770}, 5000,
      function() {
        imgblock.css({left:450});
        animator($(this));
      }
    );
  }
  animator($wrapper);

  $wrapper.hover(
    function(){
      $wrapper.stop();
    },
```

```
    function(){
      animator($wrapper);
    }
  );
});
```

Before we explore what this jQuery code is doing, please note the `stop()` method that we have used in this code, which stops all the currently running animations on all the specified elements.

So in the jQuery code itself, all the images (`img` elements nested inside the anchor element, which in turn is nested inside `div` element of ID `scroller`) are retrieved and stored in the variable `$wrapper`. Using the `.css()` method, the images are set at the distance of 0px from left border; that is, three images of width 150px each will appear initially, one after the other, in the invisible window (the width of the invisible window is set to 360px in style sheet).

The `animator` function is invoked and all the images stored in the `$wrapper` variable are sent to it and are assigned to its `imgblock` parameter. The image block is set to animate toward the left border of the invisible window. The animation will stop at the distance of –770px; that is, it will stop when whole of the image block disappears into the left border of the window. The scrolling will be slow, as the delay is set to 5000 milliseconds. After the animation effect, the block is set to appear at the distance of 450px from the left border; that is, the left edge of the first image in the image block will reappear from the right border of the invisible window. The `animator` function is called recursively to continue the scrolling.

To the image block—that is, to the `$wrapper` variable—we attach the `hover` event. Recall that the `hover` event has two event-handling functions: one is invoked when the mouse pointer is over the object, and the other is invoked when the mouse pointer is moved away from the object. In the event-handling function that is invoked when the mouse pointer is moved over the image block, it invokes the `.stop()` method to stop the scrolling; and in the event-handling function that is invoked when the mouse pointer is moved away from the image block, the animator function is invoked to resume scrolling.

Scrolling to the Right

The preceding scroller is scrolling to the left. To make the scroller scroll to the right, we have to alter the jQuery code as shown here:

```
$(document).ready(function() {
  var $wrapper=$('#scroller a img');
  $wrapper.css({right:0});
  var animator = function(imgblock) {
    imgblock.animate({
      right:-460}, 5000,
      function() {
        imgblock.css({ right:770});
        animator($(this));
      }
    );
  }
  animator($wrapper);
});
```

All the images (`img` elements nested inside the anchor element, which in turn is nested inside the `div` element of ID `scroller`) are retrieved and stored in the variable `$wrapper`. Using the `.css()` method, the images are set at a distance of 0px from right border; that is, the first three images of width 150px each will appear, one after the other, in the invisible window (the width of the invisible window is of 360px).

The `animator` function is invoked and all the images stored in `$wrapper` variable are sent to it that are assigned to its `imgblock` parameter. The image block is set to animate toward the right border of the invisible window. The animation will stop at the distance of –460px; that is, it will stop when whole of the image block disappears into the right border of the window. The scrolling will be slow as the delay is provided of 5000 milliseconds.

After the animation effect the block is set to appear at the distance of 770px from the right border; that is, the right edge of the last image in the image block will reappear from the left border of the invisible window. The `animator` function is called recursively to continue the scrolling.

6-9. Making a News Scroller

Problem

You have some news in the form of text to be displayed to the visitor of your web site. You want the news to scroll upward in an invisible window. When the news is completely scrolled up, you want it to appear again at the bottom of the window and continue scrolling upward. We will be writing the solution of this problem using two methods: first we'll use the `.animate()` method and then we'll use the `.css()` method.

Solution

Let's start out with an HTML file to display the news in the form of a paragraph element. The paragraph element is enclosed within the `div` element of ID `scroller`. The HTML file should appear as shown here:

```
<body>
<div id="scroller">
<p>Styles make the formatting job much easier and more more efficient. To give an attractive
look to web sites, styles are heavily used. A person must have a good knowledge of HTML and
CSS and a bit of JavaScript.
jQuery is a powerful JavaScript library that allows us to add dynamic elements to our web
sites. Not only is it easy to learn, but it's easy to implement too.
jQuery is an open source project that provides a wide range of features with cross-platform
compatibility. jQuery has hundreds of plug-ins to extend its features. jQuery helps in
increasing interactions with a web site.
</div>
</body>
```

The idea of defining the `div` element is to apply certain style properties to it automatically via the ID selector `#scroller` to define the size of the news window within which the news will scroll. This ID selector `#scroller` is defined in the style sheet `style.css`. Also, the style sheet contains the type selector `#scroller p` that contains the style properties to be applied to the text of the paragraph element representing the news text. The style sheet `style.css` file may appear as shown here:

```
style.css
#scroller {
height: 250px;
width: 230px;
overflow:hidden;
position: relative;
margin:auto;
border:2px solid ;
padding:10px;
}

#scroller p {font-weight:bold;position:relative;}
```

The jQuery code to make the news scroll is shown here:

```
$(document).ready(function() {
  var $wrapper=$('#scroller p');
  $wrapper.css({top:0});
  var animator = function(imgblock) {
    imgblock.animate(
      {top:-350}, 5000,
      function() {
        imgblock.css({top:250});
        animator($(this));
      }
    );
  }
  animator($wrapper);
});
```

How It Works

The ID selector `#scroller` contains the properties `height` and `width` set to 250px and 230px, respectively, to define the height and width of the news window (within which we want the news text to scroll). By setting the value `hidden` to the `overflow` property, we make the text that falls outside the height of the news box become invisible. The value of the `position` property is set to `relative`—it is a necessary condition for any text or image to scroll, as scrolling happens on positioning an element relative to its current position. The `margin` property is set to `auto` to make the news scroller appear at the center of the width of the browser window. The `border` property will create a solid border of 2px thickness around the news text, and the `padding` property is set to 10px to define some spacing between the text and the news box's border. The type selector `#scroller p` contains the `font-weight` property set to `bold` to make the paragraph text appear in bold, and the position property is set to `relative` to make the paragraph text scroll.

In the jQuery code itself, you can see that the whole of the paragraph text that is enclosed in the `div` element of ID `scroller` is retrieved and is stored in the variable `$wrapper`. The text is initially set to appear at the distance of 0px from the top border of the window; that is, the upper region of the text is made visible. The overflow text (that goes beyond the height of the news box) will not be visible. An `animator` function is defined and all the paragraph text (stored in the variable `$wrapper`) is passed to this function and is assigned to its `imgblock` parameter. The `imgblock`—that is, all the paragraph text—is set to animate toward the top boundary of the window and is set to stop at the distance of –350px from the top boundary of the news box, when all the paragraph text is scrolled up (becomes invisible). This scrolling will happen quite slowly, as the duration of animation is set to 5000 milliseconds. In the callback function of the `animate` method (that is executed when the animation is over), we make the paragraph text appear at the distance of 250px from the top border of the window, making only the first line of the paragraph text appear from the bottom boundary of the window. After that, the `animator` function is called recursively to make the paragraph text scroll infinitely.

Initially the paragraph text that is able to fit in the height and width of the window will be visible, as shown in Figure 6-15.

Styles make the formatting job much easier and efficient. To give an attractive look to web sites, styles are heavily used. A person must have a good knowledge of HTML and CSS and a bit of Javascript. jQuery is a powerful JavaScript library that allows us to add dynamic elements to our web sites. Not only it is easy to learn but easy to implement too. jQuery is an open source project that provides a wide range of features with cross platform compatiblity.

Figure 6-15. The news text scrolling toward the top border of the news box

Then the news will start scrolling toward the top border of the news box slowly, and vanish as it crosses the top border, as shown in Figure 6-16.

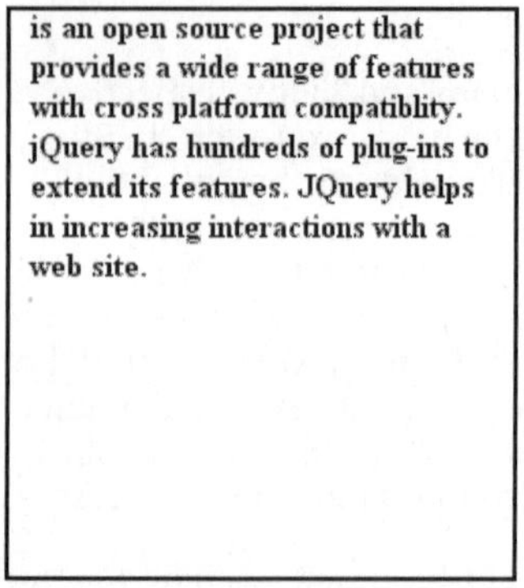

is an open source project that provides a wide range of features with cross platform compatiblity. jQuery has hundreds of plug-ins to extend its features. JQuery helps in increasing interactions with a web site.

Figure 6-16. The news text that is scrolled up disappears

When all the news text is scrolled up, the first line of the news will appear at the bottom border of the window and will continue scrolling upward.

News Scroller Using the .css() Method

In this second approach to our solution, we will make use of `.css()` method in a loop to create an animation effect. We will be making a new HTML file for trying out this method. So, let's make an HTML file to display the news in the form of a paragraph element. The paragraph element is enclosed within the `div` element of ID `news_scroller` to define the width and height of the news box window in which we want the news to scroll. The HTML file should appear as shown here:

```
<body>
<div id="news_scroller">
<p>Styles make the formatting job much easier and more efficient. To give an attractive look
to web sites, styles are heavily used. A person must have a good knowledge of HTML and CSS
and a bit of JavaScript.
jQuery is a powerful JavaScript library that allows us to add dynamic elements to our web
sites. Not only it is easy to learn, but it's easy to implement too.
jQuery is an open source project that provides a wide range of features with cross-platform
compatiblity. jQuery has hundreds of plug-ins to extend its features. jQuery helps in
increasing interactions with a web site.
</div>
</body>
```

We will write an ID selector `#news_scroller` and a type selector `p` to apply the style properties automatically to the `div` element and the text of paragraph element. The contents of the external style sheet `style.css` should look like this:

```
style.css
#news_scroller{position:relative; height:200px; width:200px; overflow:hidden; border:2px
solid ; padding:10px;}
p{position:relative;}
```

The jQuery code to make the text scroll is as shown here:

```
$(document).ready(function() {
  ticker_height = $('#news_scroller').height();
  news_height=$('#news_scroller p').height();
  no_oflines = 0;
  scroll();
});

function scroll() {
  no_oflines -= 2;
  $('#news_scroller p').css( 'top', ''+no_oflines+"px" );
  if( no_oflines<-1*news_height ) no_oflines = ticker_height;
  setTimeout( scroll, 50 );
}
```

How It Works

The ID selector `#news_scroller` contains the `position` property set to `relative` to make the text inside it scroll. The height and `width` properties are set to 200px each to define height and width of the news box, and the value of over `flow` property is set to `hidden` to make the text that is not able to fit in the given width and height of the news box disappear. The `border` property is set to display the solid border of 2px thickness. The `padding` property is set to 10px to keep some spacing between the paragraph text and the news box's boundary. The property in the type selector `p` contains the `position` property set to `relative`—a necessary condition to make the text (inside the news box) scroll.

In the jQuery code itself, we first find out the total height of the `news_scroller` (`div` element) and the height of the text (paragraph) element, and store them in variables `ticker_height` and `news_height`, respectively. In this solution, we are going to scroll the text toward the top border of the news box by using the `.css()` method repetitively instead of using the `animate()` method. That is, we initially set some lines to scroll and then gradually increment the quantity of lines to scroll; for doing so, we need the help of the variable `no_oflines`. We initialize it to 0. Then we invoke the scroll function.

In the scroll function, we decrement the value of `no_oflines` variable by 2 (every time we call this function). Assuming the value of `no_oflines` =–2, we use the `.css()` method to make the paragraph text (enclosed in the `div` element of ID `news_scroller`) to be set at the distance of -2 pixels from the top boundary of the news box; that is, the paragraph text will scroll up the top border by 2px and will not be visible now (as the `overflow` property is set to `hidden`). In the next call of the `scroll` function, the value of the `no_oflines` variable will become –4 (decremented by 2 every time), making the text to go inside the top border by 4px (that is, 2px more of paragraph text is scrolled up and made invisible), and the process is repeated. When the value of the variable `no_oflines` becomes equal to the size of `news_height`—that is, when the whole news text is scrolled up—we set the value of the `no_oflines` variable equal to the size of the `ticker_height`—the height of the `news_scroller` box—to make the text again appear from the bottom border of the news box.

The `scroll` function is set to call itself recursively at the time delay of 50 milliseconds to make the text scroll infinitely.

Making the News Scroller Pause on Hover

Let's add a bit more jQuery code this time to pause the news scroller when the mouse is moved over the text and to resume scrolling when the mouse is moved away from the news scroller. We need to add one Boolean variable, `rotate`, that decides when to stop scrolling and when to begin scrolling. Initially the value of the `rotate` variable is set to `true`, as shown in the following jQuery code:

```
$(document).ready(function() {
  ticker_height = $('#news_scroller').height();
  news_height=$('#news_scroller p').height();
  no_oflines = 0;
  rotate = true;

  $('#news_scroller').hover(
    function(){
      rotate = false;
    },
    function(){
      rotate = true;
    }
  );

  scroll();
});
```

```
function scroll() {
  no_oflines += rotate ? -2 : 0;
  $('#news_scroller p').css( 'top', ''+no_oflines+"px" );
  if( no_oflines<-1*news_height ) no_oflines = ticker_height;
  setTimeout( scroll, 50 );
}
```

In this jQuery code, as we have done before, we first find out the total height of the `news_scroller` (`div` element) and the height of the text (paragraph) element and store them in the variables `ticker_height` and `news_height`, respectively. We also initialize the value of the variable `no_oflines` to 0 (which we are going to use in scrolling the text). We'll set the news text to scroll by gradually decreasing the value in the `no_oflines` variable). We also make use of the Boolean variable `rotate`, which is initially set to `true`. We will stop scrolling the news text when the value of the rotate variable is set to `false`, and resume scrolling when its value is `true`. Also, we apply the `hover()` event to the `div` element of ID`news_scroller` so that when the mouse is over the news box, we set the value of the `rotate` variable to `false` so as to pause the news scroller; when the mouse pointer is moved away from the news box, we set the value of the Boolean variable `rotate` to `true` to resume the scrolling. Then we invoke the `scroll` function.

Now in the scroll function, we decrement the value of the `no_oflines` variable by 2 if the value of the `rotate` variable is `true`; otherwise, we don't change its value (in which case the news text will remain at its current position and will not scroll). Assuming the value of `no_oflines` =–2, we use the `.css()` method to set the paragraph text (enclosed in the `div` element of ID `news_scroller`) at the distance of –2 pixels from the top boundary of news box,; that is, the paragraph text will scroll up the top border by 2px and will disappear (as the `overflow` property is set to `hidden`).

In the next call of the `scroll` function, the value of the `no_oflines` variable will become –4 (decremented by 2 every time), making the text to go inside the top border by 4px (that is, 2px more of the paragraph text will be scrolled up and hence disappear), and the process is repeated. When the value of the variable `no_oflines` becomes equal to the size of `news_height`—that is, when the whole news text is scrolled up—we set the value of the `no_oflines` variable equal to the size of the `ticker_height`—the height of the `news_scroller` box—to make the news text again appear from the bottom border of the news box.

The `scroll` function is set to call itself recursively at the time delay of 50 milliseconds to make the text scroll infinitely.

6-10. Displaying an Enlarged Image on Mouseover

Problem

You want to display several items to be sold on your web page and to efficiently use the space, so you plan to display the images of these items in the form of icons. You want things to work so that when the mouse pointer is moved over the icons, an enlarged image of the item itself is displayed to give a better view to the visitor.

Solution

Let's start out with an HTML file to display four icons of the items that we want to display. The icons, as usual, will be displayed via `img` elements and will be enclosed in the anchor element. The anchor element refers to the enlarged view of the icon. That is, if the visitor clicks on any icon, he will be navigated to the web page that displays the enlarged view of the icon. Also, all the anchor elements will be written within a `div` element of the class `small` so that styles can be applied via jQuery code or style sheet to the whole collection. The HTML file should appear as shown here:

```
<body>
  <div class="small">
            <a href="a1.jpg"><img src="a1.jpg"  /></a>
            <a href="a2.jpg"><img src="a2.jpg"  /></a>
            <a href="a3.jpg"><img src="a3.jpg"  /></a>
            <a href="a4.jpg"><img src="a4.jpg"  /></a>
  </div>
            <img src="a1.jpg" class="large" />
</body>
```

In the preceding HTML file, we can also see that anchor elements and `img` elements both refer to the same image file; that is, the anchor element and the `img` element will display the image of the same size, whereas we want the `img` element to display the small image (in the form of an icon) and the anchor element to display an enlarged view. Though images in the anchor elements and in `img` elements are actually of the same size, by applying style properties to the `img` element (of `div` element of the class `small`), we will reduce the images' width and height to make them appear as icons. The image displayed via the `img` element of the class `large` will be displayed in its actual size, so it will be used to display the enlarged view. By default it will show the enlarged view of the first icon.

The style properties applied to the `img` element enclosed in the `div` element of the class `small` can be written in the external style sheet file `style.css` that may appear as shown here:

```
style.css
.small img { border:none;margin:10px;width:60px; height:60px; }
```

The jQuery code to display the enlarged view of the icon when the mouse is moved over it is shown here:

```
$(document).ready(function() {
  $(".small a").hover(
    function(){
      var imgname = $(this).attr('href');
      $(".large").fadeTo(
        "slow", 0,
        function() {
          $('.large').attr('src',imgname);
        }
      ).fadeTo("slow", 1);
    }
  );
});
```

How It Works

You can see that the properties defined in the type selector `.small img` will be automatically applied to the `img` elements enclosed in the `div` element of the class `small`. The border property set to `none` will make the border of the images invisible; the margin property set to 10px will create the spacing of 10px between icons; the width and height properties are set to 60px to reduce the width and height of the images to make them appear as icons.

Looking now at the jQuery code itself, we first we attach the hover event to all the anchor elements enclosed in the div element of the class small. Then in the hover event, the value of the href attribute of the anchor element being hovered over is retrieved and stored in the variable imgname; that is, the respective image file name (whether it is a1.jpg, a2.jpg, etc.) of the icon (on which the mouse pointer is hovering) will be stored in the imgname variable. The current enlarged image (assigned to the img element of the class large) is then made invisible slowly with the help of the .fadeTo() method.

In the callback function of the .fadeTo() method (that is called when the animation effect is over), we set the value of the src attribute (the image source value of the img element of the class large) equal to the value stored in the variable imgname. Thus the image file name stored in the variable imgname (on which the mouse pointer is hovering) is assigned to the img element of the class large to display the enlarged view of the icon. In the second fadeTo() call, the enlarged view of the image is made to appear gradually on the screen. Finally, the second function of the hover event (which is invoked when the mouse pointer moves *away* from the icon) is left empty, as we don't want to take any action but to make the enlarged view of the icon persist on the screen.

On execution of the jQuery code, if we take the mouse pointer on the first icon, its enlarged view will be displayed as shown in Figure 6-17.

Figure 6-17. The list of icons, along with the enlarged image of the first icon

Similarly, if we take the mouse pointer to some other icon, again its enlarged view will be displayed as shown in Figure 6-18.

Figure 6-18. Enlarged image of the icon over which the mouse pointer is moved

Enlarging the Icon Itself on Hover

What if you only want to enlarge the icon itself? Let's modify the preceding solution so that we enlarge the icon in place when the mouse pointer is over it. When the mouse pointer is moved away from the icon, we want it to return to its original size. The HTML file will be modified to display only the icons and the div block to show that the large image below the small ones is removed, as shown here:

```
<body>
  <div class="small">
          <a href="a1.jpg"><img src="a1.jpg"  /></a>
          <a href="a2.jpg"><img src="a2.jpg"  /></a>
          <a href="a3.jpg"><img src="a3.jpg"  /></a>
          <a href="a4.jpg"><img src="a4.jpg"  /></a>
  </div>
</body>
```

You can see that the four icon images are displayed via img elements that are nested inside the div element of the class small. To define the width, height, and border properties of the img element, we define a type selector in the style sheet file style.css, which may appear as shown here:

```
style.css
.small img { border:none;margin:10px;width:60px; height:60px; }
```

The jQuery code to enlarge the icon in place when the mouse pointer is over it is shown here:

```
$(document).ready(function() {
  $(".small a").hover(
    function(){
      $(this).find('img').css({'width':200,'height': 200});
    },
    function(){
      $(this).find('img').css({'width':60,'height': 60});
    }
  );
});
```

How It Works – Enlarging the Icon Itself

We can see that the preceding style sheet file contains the type selector img, the properties of which will be automatically applied to the element of the class small. The type selector contains the border property set to none to make the border of the images invisible, the margin property is set to 10px to create the spacing of 10px among icons, and the width and height properties are set to 60px each to reduce the width and height of the images to make them appear as icons.

In the jQuery code itself, we attach the hover event to all the anchor elements (and the img elements) that are nested inside the div element of the class small. In the event-handling function (that is executed when the mouse pointer moves over the images), we use the .css() method to enlarge the icon's width and height to 200px, and in the event-handling function (that is executed when mouse pointer is moved away from the image block), we again make use of the .css() method to reduce the icon's size back to its original width and height of 60px each.

Initially the icons will appear as shown in Figure 6-19.

Figure 6-19. *All icons that appear initially on loading the web page*

When the mouse pointer moves over any icon, it will be enlarged in place, as shown in Figure 6-20. The icon will regain its original shape when the mouse pointer is moved away from it.

Figure 6-20. *The icon turns into the enlarged image on hovering over it.*

Making a Content Slider

Let's now go a step further and modify the preceding solution to use a content slider. That is, a few items in the form of icons will be displayed, one below the other, and when the mouse pointer is moved over any icon, its enlarged view will appear on the right side, as shown in Figure 6-21.

```
<body>
<table border="1">
<tr><td width=150 align=center> <a href="a1.jpg" class="small"><img src="a1.jpg"  /></a><p>
"Model: M1001. Price 100$"</td><td rowspan="4" width=350 align=center><img src="a1.jpg"
class="large" /></td></tr>
<td width=150 align=center><a href="a2.jpg" class="small"><img src="a2.jpg"/></a><p>
"Model: M1002. Price 150$"</p></td></tr>
 <td width=150 align=center><a href="a3.jpg" class="small"><img src="a3.jpg"/></a><p>
"Model: M1003. Price 90$"</td></tr>
<td width=150 align=center> <a href="a4.jpg" class="small"><img src="a4.jpg"/></a><p>
"Model: M1004. Price 200$"</td></tr>
</table>
</body>
```

In the preceding HTML file, we see that anchor elements and img elements (both refer to the same image files) are both nested inside the `<td>` element to make them appear in the form of a column of a table element. Also in the column, below the icons, we have included a paragraph element to display the model number and price of the product that it represents. The second column of the table is set to take the size equal to the size of all four rows; that is, the image that will be displayed in the second column of the table will be as large as the size of all four rows together. The border of the table element is set to 1 to make it appear as shown in Figure 6-21. The image displayed via the img element of the class large will display the enlarged image of the icon that is hovered over.

The style properties applied to the img element enclosed in the div element of the class small can be written in the external style sheet file **style.css**. Also, the style sheet file contains the CSS class that we want to be applied to the enlarged image and to the icons when they are hovered over. The style sheet file may appear as shown here:

```
style.css
.small img { border:none;margin:10px;width:60px; height:60px; }
.large{width:200px; height:200px;}
.hover{color: blue ; background-color:cyan }
```

The jQuery code to apply the hover effect and to display the enlarged view of the icon when the mouse is moved over it is shown here:

```
$(document).ready(function() {
  $('td').find('p').css({'font-size':12, 'font-weight':'bold'});
  $(".small").hover(
    function(){
      $(this).parent().addClass('hover');
      var imgname = $(this).attr('href');
      $(".large").fadeTo(
        "slow", 0,
        function() {
          $('.large').attr('src',imgname);
        }
      ).fadeTo("slow", 1);
    },
    function(){
      $(this).parent().removeClass('hover');
    }
  );
});
```

How It Works – The Content Slider

The properties defined in the type selector .small img (to be automatically applied to the img elements nested inside the div element of the class small) includes the border property set to none to remove the border of the images, the margin property set to 10px to create spacing of 10px between the icons, and width and height properties set to 60px each to reduce the width and height of the images to make them appear as icons. The class selector .large contains the width and height properties set to 200px to display the enlarged view of the image being displayed via the img element of the class .large. The CSS class hover contains the background-color and color properties set to cyan and blue, respectively, to apply the background and foreground colors to the element that is hovered over.

Now let's take a look at the jQuery code itself. We start by finding the paragraph elements in the td elements and applying to them the font-size property set to 12px, and the font-weight property set to bold with the help of the .css() method. Next we attach the hover event to all the elements of the class small; that is, to all the anchor elements (and subsequently to the nested img element).

In the hover event handler, the CSS class hover is applied to the element that is hovered over; that is, the foreground and background colors of the image and paragraph element change. The value of the href attribute of the anchor element is then retrieved and stored in the variable imgname; that is, the respective image file name (whether it is a1.jpg, a2.jpg, etc.) of the icon on which the mouse pointer is hovering will be stored in the imgname variable. With that done, the enlarged image (assigned to the img element of the class large) is made invisible slowly with the help of the .fadeTo() method.

In the callback function of the .fadeTo() method (that is called when the animation effect is over), we set the value of the src attribute (image source value of the img element of the class large) equal to the value stored in the variable imgname. In other words, the image file name stored in the variable imgname (on which the mouse pointer is hovering) is assigned to the img element of the class large to display the enlarged view of the icon. The second fadeTo() method makes the enlarged view of the image appear gradually on the screen.

The second function of the hover event, which is invoked when the mouse pointer moves away from the icon, is used for removing the hover class from the image and paragraph element to make them appear as they were before the mouse pointer moved over them. On execution of the jQuery code, if we take the mouse pointer on the first icon, its background and foreground color change and its enlarged view is displayed, as shown in Figure 6-21.

Figure 6-21. Enlarged image of the hovered-over item

6-11. Showing Images Pagewise

Problem

You have several images on the web page and you want to display them pagewise, where a page may contain one or more images (depending on the space on the web page). At the top of the image, you want the numbers to represent the page numbers. You want the image of the selected page number to be displayed on the screen.

Solution

Let's create an HTML file to define five images that we want to be displayed. Also, since we want the images to act as hyperlinks that navigate the visitor to the target web page (one that will display more detailed information of the image that's been selected) we need to nest the image elements inside the anchor elements. The HTML file should appear as shown here:

```
<body>
<div id="images">
<a href="http://example.com" ><img src="image1.jpg" width=150px height=150px /></a>
<a href="http://example.com"><img src="image2.jpg" width=150px height=150px /></a>
<a href="http://example.com"><img src="image3.jpg" width=150px height=150px /></a>
<a href="http://example.com" ><img src="image4.jpg" width=150px height=150px /></a>
<a href="http://example.com" ><img src="image5.jpg" width=150px height=150px /></a>
</div>
</body>
```

We can see in the HTML page that all the `img` elements are assigned the same width and height of 150px to give them a uniform appearance, and the anchor elements target at some hypothetical website to which the visitor will be navigated on selecting any image.

Now let's define the CSS classes in the external style sheet file `style.css`, as shown here:

```
style.css
.page{
margin:5px;
}
.hover{
color: blue ;
background-color:cyan
}
```

The jQuery code to divide the images into pages and display the image of the selected pages is shown here:

```
$(document).ready(function() {
  var $pic = $('#images a');
  $pic.hide();
  var imgs = $pic.length;
  var next=$pic.eq(0);
```

```
next.css({'position': 'absolute','left':10});
next.show();
var $pagenumbers=$('<div id="pages"></div>');
for(i=0;i<imgs;i++)
{
    $('<span class="page">'+(i+1)+'</span>').appendTo($pagenumbers);
}
$pagenumbers.insertBefore(next);

$('.page').hover(
    function(){
        $(this).addClass('hover');
    },
    function(){
        $(this).removeClass('hover');
    }
);

$('span').click(function(event){
    $pic.hide();
    next=$pic.eq($(this).text()-1);
    next.show();
});
});
```

How It Works

We find that the CSS class page contains the style property margin set to 5px to define the space between the page numbers, and the class hover contains two properties, color and background-color, set to blue and cyan, respectively, to change the background and foreground colors of the page numbers when mouse pointer moves over them.

Now let's look at the jQuery code itself. First, all the anchor elements (that is, all the images enclosed in the anchor elements) nested in the div element of ID images are retrieved and stored in the variable $pic. The object $pic will contain all the images. We then hide all the images and set some variables; the count of the images is stored in the variable imgs, and the first image in the $pic object is stored in the variable next.

To the first image stored in variable next, some style properties are applied using the .css() method. The position property is set to absolute and the left property is set to 10px to make the image stored in the variable next to appear at the distance of 10px from the left boundary of the browser window. With that done, the image in the next variable is made visible on the screen and we define a variable $pagenumbers, and a div element of ID pages is assigned to it.

A for loop is then used to create several span elements (equal to the number of images) of the class pages. The text in the span element will be 1,2... (to serve as page numbers). The span elements are assigned the class name pages so that the properties defined in the class selector .pages (in style.css file) can be applied to them automatically. The span elements are appended to the div element of ID pages that we assigned to the variable $pagenumbers.

The whole div element of ID pages containing the span elements (which contain the page numbers) is inserted before the first image displayed via the variable next, and we apply and remove the CSS class hover to the page numbers (span elements of the class page) when the mouse pointer is moved over the page numbers. We then need to attach the click event to the span elements (that is, to the page numbers).

Here we make all the images invisible, including the current one that is displayed if the user selects any of the page numbers. Finally, we retrieve the image from the $pic object (containing an array of images), depending on the value of the page number selected; we store it in variable next and display the image retrieved in the variable next.

On execution of the jQuery code, initially the first image will be displayed with page numbers at its top, as shown in Figure 6-22.

Figure 6-22. The first image, along with the page-number list above it

On selecting the page number, the image of that page number will be displayed as shown in Figure 6-23.

Figure 6-23. The image that appears on clicking the page number 4

6-12. Shuffling Images in Either Direction

Problem

You want to display a few images on the web page within an invisible window, along with left and right arrow buttons below them. You want it to work so that when the left arrow button is pressed, the images shuffle toward the left side (making the images that were hidden scroll left), and when the right arrow button is selected, all the images scroll right to display any hidden images.

Solution

Let's create an HTML file to define the images that we want to be displayed. The images are nested inside the **div** element of ID **images** (to apply styles and codes via jQuery code), which in turn is nested inside the **div** element of ID **scroller**. The HTML file you want to create is shown here:

```
<body>
<div id="scroller">
<div id="images">
<a href="http://example.com" ><img src="image1.jpg" width=150px height=150px /></a>
<a href="http://example.com"><img src="image2.jpg"  width=150px height=150px /></a>
<a href="http://example.com"><img src="image3.jpg"  width=150px height=150px /></a>
<a href="http://example.com" ><img src="image4.jpg"  width=150px height=150px /></a>
<a href="http://example.com" ><img src="image5.jpg"  width=150px height=150px /></a>
</div>
</div>
<div id="direction">
<img src="leftarrow.jpg" class="leftarrow"/>
<img src="rightarrow.jpg" class="rightarrow"/>
</div>
</body>
```

The images are enclosed within the anchor elements so as to navigate the visitor to the target web page to display the detailed information about the image that's been selected. For the time being, we assume the target web site as some hypothetical web site. The anchor elements containing the **img** elements are enclosed within the two **div** elements, one inside the other. The outer **div** element is assigned the ID **scroller** and the inner **div** element is assigned the ID **images**. To the outer **div** element, we will apply the style properties to define the width of the invisible window; that is, it decides how many images we want to see at a time. To the inner **div** element, we will apply the style properties that decide the total width of the complete image block. All the images are assigned an identical width and height of 150px to give them a uniform appearance.

Also, we make use of the **img** element to display the two left and right arrow buttons. These **img** elements are assigned the class names **leftarrow** and **rightarrow**, respectively, so that the style properties defined in the class selectors can be applied to them respectively. The two arrows are nested inside the **div** element that is assigned the ID **direction**. We define the style properties for the **div** elements and the **img** elements in the style sheet **style.css**, which may appear as shown here:

```
style.css
#scroller {
  position: relative;
  height:150px;
  width: 460px;
overflow:hidden;
margin:auto;
}

#images{
  width: 770px;
}

#images a img { border:0; position:relative;}
```

```
#direction
{
width: 460px;
margin:auto;
}

.leftarrow{margin-top:10px;}
.rightarrow{margin-left:390px;margin-top:10px;}
```

The jQuery code to make the images scroll on selecting the left and right arrow images is shown here:

```
$(document).ready(function() {
  var $wrapper=$('#scroller a img');

  var leftanimator = function(imgblock) {
    imgblock.animate({left:-310 }, 2000);
  }

  var rightanimator = function(imgblock) {
    imgblock.animate({left:0 }, 2000);
  }

  $('.leftarrow').click(function(event){
    leftanimator($wrapper);
    event.preventDefault();
  });

  $('.rightarrow').click(function(event){
    rightanimator($wrapper);
    event.preventDefault();
  });
});
```

How It Works

You can see in the `style.css` file that the ID selector `#scroller` contains the `position` property set to `relative`—a necessary condition to make the image scroll (images scroll when you assign them some position relative to their current location). The height and width are set to 150px and 460px, respectively. The width of 460px is required to display at most three images at a time (the width includes the width of three images of 150px each, with some space in between). The `overflow` property is set to `hidden` to make invisible the region of the images that falls outside the width of this invisible window. The `margin` property is set to `auto` to make the horizontal scroller appear at the center of the width of the browser window.

The ID selector `#images` contains the `width` property that will be applied to the inner `div` element. The `width` property is set to 770px, which is the total of the width of all the images that we want to be displayed in the scroller (with some distance in between the images). The `width` property here decides the number of images that we want to see in the horizontal scroller. Also, the style sheet contains a type selector `#images a img` to apply the style properties to the `img` element nested inside the anchor element, which in turn is enclosed with an HTML element of ID `images`. As you'll notice, `images` contains the

border property set to 0 (to make the borders of the images invisible) and the **position** property is set to **relative** to make the images scroll.

The ID selector **#direction** contains the style properties that will be applied to the block of left and right arrow images. The **width** property set to 460px assigns the maximum width that this block (of the two arrow images) can occupy, and the **margin** value set to **auto** makes the block (of two images) appear at the center of the browser window, just below the images block.

The class selector **.leftarrow** contains the properties that will be automatically applied to the left arrow image. It has **margin-top** property set to 10px to keep the left arrow at a distance of 10px from the images block at its top. Meanwhile, the class selector **.rightarrow** contains the style properties that will be automatically applied to the right arrow image. It contains the **margin-left** property set to 390px to make the right arrow image be right-justified in the assigned width of 460px, and the **margin-top** property is set to 10px to keep it 10px from the images block at its top.

Now turning to the jQuery code in our solution, you'll notice that all the images that are nested inside the anchor element of the **div** element of ID **scroller,** are retrieved and stored in a variable **$wrapper**.

We continue by defining a function **leftanimator** that takes in the parameter **imgblock**, which it animates toward the left slowly and stops at the distance of –310px from the left border (310px inside the left border). As a result, the two images on the left of the image block will disappear inside the left border of the invisible window, making two images on the right (which were hidden earlier) become visible.

The **rightanimator** method takes in the parameter **imgblock**, which it animates toward the right slowly and stops at the distance of 0px from the left border. That is, it will make the image block scroll toward the right border and stop when the first image of the block becomes visible—the scrolling will stop when the first three images are visible in the invisible window. It will make the two images on the right side become invisible.

Next we attach a click event to the left arrow image, and when the click event occurs on it, the **leftanimator** function is invoked and the **$wrapper** variable containing the block of all five images is sent to it, which will be assigned to its parameter **imgblock**. The function will make the image block scroll to the left, displaying last three images. The **preventDefault** method is invoked of the **event** object to avoid navigating to the target web site to which the image (nested inside the anchor element) is pointing.

Finally, we attach a click event to the right arrow image, and when the click event occurs on it, the **rightanimator** function is invoked and the **$wrapper** variable containing the block of all five images is sent to it and will be assigned to its parameter **imgblock**. The function will make the image block scroll toward the right, making the first three images reappear on the screen. The **preventDefault** method of the **event** object is invoked to avoid navigating to the target web site to which the image (nested inside the anchor element) is pointing.

So how does all this look? Well initially, the first three images will be displayed along with the left and right arrows below them, as shown in Figure 6-24.

Figure 6-24. Three images appear initially, along with the left and right arrows at the bottom.

On selecting the left arrow button, the images will scroll left and we will be able to see the last three images (of the five-image block), as shown in Figure 6-25.

Figure 6-25. Images scrolled to the left on selecting the left arrow

Similarly, if we select the right arrow button, the images will scroll right, making the first three images reappear.

6-13. Writing a Pendulum Scroller

Problem

You have a block of five images and you want it to work so that initially three of the five images appear in an invisible window. Then these images should scroll left and disappear out of the window, as if they're swinging on a pendulum. When the last image also disappears, you want the images to appear from the left border and scroll toward the right border (making the last image appear first, followed by the fourth, and so on). All the images will scroll toward the right border and disappear from the window. When the first image disappears, you want the images to again scroll toward the left border, and the process continues.

Solution

Let's set up an HTML file to define the images that we want to be displayed. The images are nested inside the div element of ID images (to apply styles and codes via jQuery code), which in turn is nested inside the div element of ID scroller. The HTML file should appear as shown here:

```
<body>
<div id="scroller">
<div id="images">
<a href="http://example.com" ><img src="image1.jpg" width=150px height=150px /></a>
<a href="http://example.com"><img src="image2.jpg"  width=150px height=150px /></a>
<a href="http://example.com"><img src="image3.jpg"  width=150px height=150px /></a>
<a href="http://example.com" ><img src="image4.jpg"  width=150px height=150px /></a>
<a href="http://example.com" ><img src="image5.jpg"  width=150px height=150px /></a>
```

```
</div>
</div>
</body>
```

The images are enclosed within the anchor elements so as to navigate the visitor to the target web page to display the detailed information of the image that's been selected. For the time being, we assume the target web site as some hypothetical web site.

The anchor elements containing the img elements are enclosed within the two div elements, one inside the other. The outer div element is assigned the ID scroller and the inner div element is assigned the ID images. To the outer div element, we will apply the style properties to define the width of the invisible window; that is, it decides how many images we want to see at a time. To the inner div element, we will apply the style properties that decide the total width of the complete image block. All the images are assigned an identical width and height of 150px to give them a uniform appearance.

We define the style properties for the div elements and the img elements in the style sheet style.css that may appear as shown here:

```
style.css
#scroller {
  position: relative;
  height:150px;
  width: 460px;
overflow:hidden;
margin:auto;
}

#images{
  width: 770px;
}

#images a img { border:0; position:relative;}
```

The jQuery code to make the images scroll as if on a pendulum is shown here:

```
$(document).ready(function() {
  var $wrapper=$('#scroller a img');

  var left_rightanimator = function() {
    $wrapper.animate(
      {left:-770}, 5000,
      function() {
        $wrapper.animate({left:465 }, 5000);
        left_rightanimator();
      }
    );
  }

  left_rightanimator();
});
```

How It Works

You can see in the `style.css` file that the ID selector `#scroller` contains a `position` property set to `relative`—a necessary condition to make the image scroll (images scroll when you assign them some position relative to their current location). The height and width are set to 150px and 460px, respectively. The width of 460px is required to display at most three images at a time (the width includes the width of three images of 150px width, with some space in between). The `overflow` property is set to `hidden` to make invisible the region of the images that falls outside the width of this invisible window. The `margin` property is set to `auto` to make the horizontal scroller appear at the center of the width of browser window.

The ID selector `#images` contains the `width` property that will be applied to the inner `div` element. The `width` property is set to 770px, which is the total of the width of all the images that we want to be displayed in the scroller (with some distance in between the images). The `width` property here decides the number of images that we want to see in the horizontal scroller.

Also, the style sheet contains a type selector `#images a img` to apply the style properties to the `img` element nested inside the anchor element, which in turn is enclosed with an HTML element of ID `images`.

It contains the `border` property set to 0 (to make the borders of the images invisible) and the `position` property set to `relative` to make the images scroll.

Looking now at our jQuery code, all images that are nested inside the anchor element and the `div` element of ID `scroller` are retrieved and stored in the `$wrapper` variable. That is, the `$wrapper` variable contains the whole block of five images.

Next we define a function `left_rightanimator`, which animates the images block toward the left border (of the invisible window) and stops at the distance of –770px from the left border—that is, 770px inside the left border—which will make the whole block of vive images disappear (recall that each image is 150px wide and there is some space between images). So again, the image block is set to appear from the left border and set to animate toward the right (making the last image appear first), and scrolling will stop when the first image also disappears out of the window (from the right border) at the distance of 465px from the left border, which is when the first image also disappears in the right border of the invisible window.

The last action of this method is to make a recursive call to the `left_rightanimator()` function to make the image block keep scrolling left and right. Finally, we invoke the `left_rightanimator()` function to get the process going.

The images scroll toward the left border, disappear, reappear from the left border, and scroll toward the right border. The last two images may appear as shown in Figure 6-26 while scrolling left.

Figure 6-26. Images scrolling to the left and disappearing

6-14. Scrolling Images Using Arrays

Problem

You have a block of five images and you want it to work so that initially three of the five images appear in the invisible window. Then these images should scroll toward the left border (making the last two hidden images appear in the invisible window). All the images should disappear out of the left border. You want to do this with the help of arrays.

Solution

We will be making use of the same HTML file and style sheet file (**style.css**) that we used in Recipe 6-13. The jQuery code to make each image scroll toward the left border and become invisible one by one is shown here:

```
$(document).ready(function() {
  var $pic = $('#scroller a img');
  var imgs = $pic.length;
  var next;
  for (var i=0;i<imgs;i++){
    next=$pic.eq(i);
    scroll(next);
  };
});

function scroll(im)
{
  im.animate({'left': -770}, 5000);
};
```

Here, we start by retrieving all the images nested inside the anchor elements, which are in turn nested inside the **div** element of ID **scroller**, and storing them in the variable **$pic**. **$pic** is now an array of five images. We then find out the number of images in **$pic** array and store the count in the **imgs** variable.

In the **for** loop we get one image from the **$pic** array and store it in the variable **next**. That is, all the images will be assigned to the variable **next** one by one. To scroll, we invoke the function **scroll**, and the image stored in the variable **next** is passed to it (that is, the variable **next** is assigned to its parameter **im**).

In the **scroll()** method, the image is set to animate toward the left and stop at a distance of –770px from the left border—that is, 770px inside the left border—to make even the last (fifth) image disappear.

The image while scrolling may appear as in Figure 6-27.

Figure 6-27. All images scrolling to the left

Scrolling an Image over Other Images

Say you want to adapt the solution above, because you want three images to appear stationary and one image (the fourth) to scroll over this block of three images. The jQuery code for that solution is here:

```
$(document).ready(function() {
  var $pic = $('#scroller a img');
  var next;
  next=$pic.eq(3);
  scroll(next);
});

function scroll(im)
{
  im.animate({'left': -770}, 5000);
};
```

We can see that the variable next is assigned to the fourth image (at index location 3) in the $pic array in the fourth statement, and is passed to the scroll function for scrolling over the images. Initially, we have three images that appear in the invisible window, as shown in Figurer 6-28.

Figure 6-28. Initial images on loading the web page

The fourth image will begin from the right border and will scroll toward the left border (of the invisible window) over the three images, as shown in Figure 6-29, where that fourth image is over the second and third images.

Figure 6-29. An image scrolling to the left on top of the other images

Scrolling Only the Image that Is Hovered Over

You have three images that appear initially in the invisible window, and you want functionality so that any image that is hovered over will scroll toward the left border and disappear. The jQuery code may appear as shown here:

```
$(document).ready(function() {
  var $pic = $('#scroller a img');
  $pic.hover(
    function(){
      $(this).animate({'left': -770}, 5000);
    },
    function(){
    }
  );
});
```

We can see that the third statement attaches the hover event to the block of images (stored in the $pic array) and in its event-handling function we are animating the hovered image toward the left border and making it stop at the distance of –770px from the left border; that is, 770px inside the left border (to make it completely invisible). If we hover over the middle image, it will start scrolling toward the left, as shown in Figure 6-30.

Figure 6-30. An image that is hovered over starts scrolling left.

When the middle image is completely scrolled in the left border, we're left with a blank space in the middle of the image block, as shown in Figure 6-31.

Figure 6-31. The middle image scrolled to the left, creating an empty space.

Fading Out and Replacing an Image

You have three image that appear initially in the invisible window, and you want any image that is hovered over to slowly become invisible with a fadeout effect, and its space to be filled by the next image (making a hidden image visible). The jQuery code may appear as shown here:

```
$(document).ready(function() {
  var $pic = $('#scroller a img');
  $pic.hover(
    function(){
      $(this).fadeOut(5000);
    },
    function(){
    }
  );
});
```

A `hover` event is attached to the `$pic` variable, which is nothing but the array of five images. In the event-handling function of the `hover` event, we make the image that is being hovered on fade out in 500 milliseconds. The moment the image becomes completely invisible, the next image in the `$pic` array will fill up the vacant space.

Initially, we have three images visible in the window, as was shown in Figure 6-28. When the first image is hovered over, it will fade out slowly and its place will be occupied by the next image in sequence.

Scrolling One Image Left and One Image Right, and Fading Out the Middle

Okay so we'll end this set of recipes with a final rather fancy modification on our current recipe – just to give you more ideas of what's possible now you have the core solutions around scrolling and fading!

Now let's say you have three images that appear initially in the invisible window, and you want the first image to scroll toward the left border and disappear, the third image to scroll toward the right border of the invisible window and disappear, and the middle image to remain at its position and slowly fade out. This time, the jQuery code would appear as shown here:

```
$(document).ready(function() {
  var $pic = $('#scroller a img');
  $pic.eq(0).animate(
    {'left': -155}, 5000,
    function(){
      $pic.eq(2).animate(
        {'right': -155}, 5000,
        function(){
          $pic.fadeOut(5000);
        }
      );
    }
  );
});
```

All the image elements that are nested inside the anchor elements of ID `scroller` are retrieved and stored in the variable `$pic`. The first image (the image at the index location 0 in the `$pic` array) is set to animate toward the left border and stop at a distance of –155px from the left border; that is, 155px inside the left border (which is sufficient for the image of 150px width to disappear). Similarly, the third image is set to animate toward the right border and stop at a distance of –155px from the right border; that is, 155px inside the right border (to make the image disappear). The middle image that is left behind is set to fade out slowly, in 5000 milliseconds. The code is probably now very familiar to you if you've followed the earlier recipes, but the sky is the limit to what you can do to keep your user's attention where you want it on your web site.

Summary

In this chapter we covered the recipes for applying visual effects to our web site, including developing image sliders, horizontal and vertical image scrollers, and news scrollers. We also explored the technique of displaying images pagewise and enlarging images on hovering over their icons.

The next chapter will present recipes dealing with tables, such as highlighting table rows and columns, filtering out the desired rows, erasing the contents of selected columns, and expanding and collapsing rows of the tables. You will also see how a table is sorted on the basis of the selected column and how the rows of tables can be paginated.

■ ■ ■

CHAPTER 7

Dealing with Tables

In this chapter, we'll explore the following recipes, which are useful when you're dealing with tables:

- Highlighting a table row on hover
- Highlighting alternate columns
- Filtering rows
- Hiding the selected column
- Paginating a table
- Expanding and collapsing list items
- Expanding and collapsing table rows
- Sorting list items
- Sorting a table
- Filtering rows from a table

7-1. Highlighting a Table Row on Hover

Problem

You have a table consisting of a few rows and columns. You want a row to be highlighted when the mouse pointer is moved over it.

Solution

Let's make an HTML file that contains a table element with some rows and columns elements (th, td, tr) defined in it. The HTML file appears as shown here:

```
<body>
<table border="1">
<thead>
<tr><th>Roll</th><th>Name</th><th>Marks</th></tr>
</thead>
<tbody>
<tr><td>101</td><td>John</td><td>87</td></tr>
<tr><td>102</td><td>Naman</td><td>90</td></tr>
<tr><td>103</td><td>Chirag</td><td>85</td></tr>
</tbody>
</table>
</body>
```

Let's define a style rule `.hover` in the style sheet file `style.css` to apply style properties to the hovered-on row. The style rule may appear as shown here:

```
style.css
.hover { background-color: #00f; color: #fff; }
```

The jQuery code to apply the hovering effect to the table rows is shown here:

```
$(document).ready(function() {
  $('tbody tr').hover(
    function(){
      $(this).find('td').addClass('hover');
    },
    function(){
      $(this).find('td').removeClass('hover');
    }
  );
});
```

How It Works

In the preceding HTML file we see that a table with a border of 1px is defined that has three column headings (defined using the th element): `Roll`, `Name`, and `Marks`. Also it contains three rows of student records. The table headings are nested inside the `thead` element and the body of the table (the rows that contain information) is nested inside `tbody` element

In the style sheet file, the `.hover` style rule contains the `background-color` property set to `#00f` and the `color` property set to `#fff` to change the background and foreground color of the hovered-on row to blue and white, respectively.

In the jQuery code, we attach the `hover()` event to the `tr` (row elements) that are nested inside the `tbody` element, as we want only the rows that contain student information to be hovered on, and not the row that contains column headings. In the event-handling function of the `hover` event, we search for the `td` elements of the hovered-on row and apply the properties defined in the style rule `.hover` (that exists in the style sheet file `style.css`) to change their background and foreground colors to blue and white, respectively, so as to highlight them.

Initially, the table may appear as shown in Figure 7-1

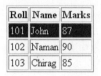

Roll	Name	Marks
101	John	87
102	Naman	90
103	Chirag	85

Figure 7-1. Table consisting of a few rows and columns

When the mouse pointer moves over any row, that row will be highlighted as shown in Figure 7-2.

Roll	Name	Marks
101	John	87
102	Naman	90
103	Chirag	85

Figure 7-2. The highlighted row on being hovered on

7-2. Highlighting Alternate Columns

Problem

You have a table consisting of a few rows and columns. You want alternate columns of the table to be highlighted.

Solution

For this solution, we will make use of the same HTML and style sheet file (`style.css`) that we used in the Recipe 7-1.

The jQuery code to apply style properties defined in the style rule `.hover` to the alternate columns of the table is shown here:

```
$(document).ready(function() {
  $('td:nth-child(odd)').addClass('hover');
});
```

How It Works

Since we use the `:nth-child()` method in the jQuery code, let's take a quick look at what it does and how you can use it.

:nth-child()

This method is used for retrieving all elements that are the *n*th child of their parent. This method is one-based; that is, it begins counting from 1, and not 0. This method is different from the `:eq()` method in the following two ways:

- The `:eq()` method matches only a single element, whereas `:nth-child()` matches one for each parent with the specified index.

- The `:eq()` method is zero-based; that is, it begins counting from zero, whereas `:nth-child()` is one-based (it begins counting from one).

For example,

```
$('tr:nth-child(3)');
```

will select all the **tr** elements that are third child of their parent (which may be the **tbody** or **table** element); that is, it will select the third row of the table.

Similarly, the statement

```
$('tr:nth-child(even)');
```

will select all the even rows of the table.

In the preceding jQuery code, the statement

```
$('td:nth-child(odd)').addClass('hover');
```

will select all the odd columns of the table (in other words, each **td** that is an odd child of its parent) and apply the style properties defined in the style rule **hover** to them, changing their background color to blue and their foreground color to white, as shown in Figure 7-3.

Figure 7-3. Table with odd-numbered columns highlighted

Highlighting Alternate Rows

To highlight alternate rows of the table, we will modify the jQuery code as shown here:

```
$(document).ready(function() {
  $('table tr:odd').addClass('hover');
});
```

The preceding jQuery code will select all the odd rows of the table and apply the style properties defined in the style rule .hover to them so as to highlight them as shown in Figure 7-4.

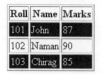

Figure 7-4. Table with alternate rows highlighted

Highlighting the Column that Is Hovered On

You want to highlight only columns whose headings are hovered on; that is, when the mouse pointer moves over any column heading, you want that column to be highlighted. The jQuery code may appear as shown here:

```
$(document).ready(function() {
  $('th').hover(
    function(){
      var colindex=$(this).parent().children().index(this);
      $('table td:nth-child('+(colindex+1)+')').addClass('hover');
    },
    function(){
      $('table tr').children().removeClass('hover');
    }
  );
});
```

Before we delve into the jQuery code, let's look at the .index() method that is used in the code:

.index()

This method searches every matched element for the element that's passed within its parameter, and returns the ordinal index of that passed element, if found, starting with 0. The index() function returns –1 if the passed element is not found in the matched set. If a jQuery object is passed as a parameter to index(), then only the first element of that object is checked.

Syntax:
.index(element)

Now let's look at the jQuery code itself. We first attach the hover event to the table heading (th) elements. When the user hovers over a table heading, we find out the index (column number) of its column and store that index location in a variable colindex. The .index() method uses zero-based counting, which means it begins counting from zero. So an index of 0 means the first column heading is hovered over, an index of 1 means the second column heading is hovered over, and so on.

We can then apply the style properties defined in the style rule `.hover` to the column whose index location is stored in the variable `colindex`. Since the `:nth-child()` method is one-based; that is, it begins counting from one (as compared to the `.index()` method, which begins from zero), we need to increment the value stored in variable `colindex` by one before applying the style rule `.hover` to the column represented by `colindex` in the event-handling function of the **hover** event.

In the event-handling function, which is invoked when the mouse pointer is moved away from the column heading, we remove the style properties defined in the style rule `.hover` from all the rows of the table.

The contents of the hovered-over column are highlighted as shown in Figure 7-5.

Roll	Name	Marks
101	John	87
102	Naman	90
103	Chirag	85

Figure 7-5. Contents of the hover-over column are highlighted.

Highlighting the Column Heading While Hovering

In the preceding example, we see that the column contents are highlighted when the column heading is hovered over, but the column heading is not highlighted; it appears as it was initially. We need to add one more statement (shown in bold in the jQuery code) to highlight the column heading as well:

```
$(document).ready(function() {
  $('th').hover(
    function(){
      var colindex=$(this).parent().children().index(this);
      $(this).addClass('hover');
      $('table td:nth-child('+(colindex+1)+')').addClass('hover');
    },
    function(){
      $('table tr').children().removeClass('hover');
    }
  );
});
```

The statement

```
$(this).addClass('hover');
```

will apply the style properties defined in the style rule `.hover` to the column heading too when it is hovered over, as shown in Figure 7-6.

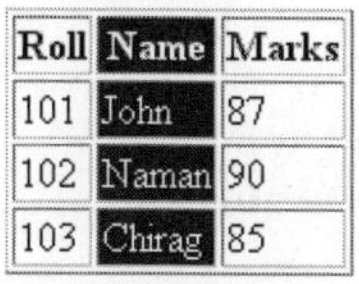

Roll	Name	Marks
101	John	87
102	Naman	90
103	Chirag	85

Figure 7-6. Column contents and column heading are highlighted when the heading is hovered over.

Highlighting Individual Cells of the Table When Hovered On

When any cell of the table except a column heading is hovered over, you want it to be highlighted. The jQuery code for doing this appears as shown here:

```
$(document).ready(function() {
  $('td').hover(
    function(){
      $(this).addClass('hover');
    },
    function(){
      $('table tr').children().removeClass('hover');
    }
  );
});
```

We can see that this time the hover event is attached to the td elements so that if any cell is hovered over (except the column headings), the properties defined in the style rule .hover are applied to it to highlight it as shown in Figure 7-7.

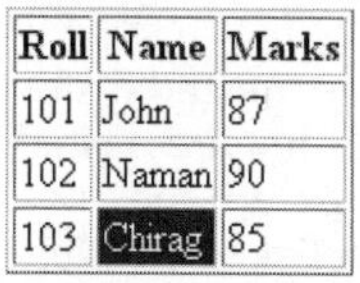

Roll	Name	Marks
101	John	87
102	Naman	90
103	Chirag	85

Figure 7-7. Table cell highlighted on being hovered over

7-3. Filtering Rows

Problem

You have a table consisting of a few rows and columns. You want to make it so that when the mouse pointer moves over any row, that row is highlighted, and when the user clicks on any row, all the other rows disappear.

Solution

For this solution we will use the same HTML and style sheet file (`style.css`) that we used in Recipe 7-1. The jQuery code to highlight the row that is hovered over and to make all the rows become invisible (except the one that is clicked) is shown here:

```
$(document).ready(function() {

  $('tbody tr').hover(
    function(){
      $(this).find('td').addClass('hover');
    },
    function(){
      $(this).find('td').removeClass('hover');
    }
  );

  $('tbody tr').click(function(){
    $('table').find('tbody tr').hide();
    $(this).show();
  });
});
```

How It Works

In the first half of the jQuery code, we attach the **hover()** event to the **tr** (row elements) that are nested inside the **tbody** element, as we want only the rows that contain student information to exhibit the hover behavior, and not the row that contains column headings. In the event-handling function of the **hover** event, we search for the **td** elements of the hovered-over row and apply the properties defined in the style rule **.hover** (that exists in the style sheet file **style.css**) to change their background and foreground colors to blue and white, respectively, to highlight them.

In the second half of the jQuery code, we attach the **click** event to all the **tr** elements (nested inside the **tbody** element), and in its event-handling function, we search for all the **tr** elements (that are nested inside the **tbody** element) and make all of them invisible; that is, all the rows of the table except the column headings will be invisible. Thereafter, we make the contents of the row that was clicked visible, hence making only the clicked row appear in the table.

On hovering over any row of the table, the table may appear as shown in Figure 7-8.

Figure 7-8. *A row gets highlighted when hovered over.*

On clicking any row, all rows will become invisible except the one that was clicked, as shown in Figure 7-9.

Figure 7-9. The selected row is left behind in the table.

Hiding the Selected Row

We can modify the preceding jQuery code to reverse the process; that is, instead of keeping the selected row, we can hide it. The jQuery code is as follows:

```
$(document).ready(function() {

  $('tbody tr').hover(
    function(){
      $(this).find('td').addClass('hover');
    },
    function(){
      $(this).find('td').removeClass('hover');
    }
  );

  $('tbody tr').click(function(){
    $(this).hide();
  });
});
```

We can see in the jQuery code that the selected row is hidden with the `hide()` method. On hovering over the last row, the table may appear as shown in Figure 7-8, and on clicking on that row, it is erased and the remaining table will appear as shown in Figure 7-10.

Roll	Name	Marks
101	John	87
102	Naman	90

Figure 7-10. The selected row is erased from the table.

7-4. Hiding the Selected Column

Problem

You have a table consisting of a few rows and columns. When the mouse pointer moves on any column heading, you want that column (including the column heading) to get highlighted. Also, when the user clicks on any column heading, the complete column along with its heading should become hidden.

261

Solution

For this solution, we will use the same HTML and style sheet file (`style.css`) that we used in Recipe 7-1.

The jQuery code to highlight the column (when its column heading is hovered over) and to make its contents invisible on being clicked is shown here:

```
$(document).ready(function() {
  $('th').hover(
    function(){
      var colindex=$(this).parent().children().index(this);
      $(this).addClass('hover');
      $('table td:nth-child('+(colindex+1)+')').addClass('hover');
    },
    function(){
      $('table tr').children().removeClass('hover');
    }
  );

  $('th').click(function(){
    $(this).hide();
    colindex=$(this).parent().children().index(this);
    $('table td:nth-child('+(colindex+1)+')').hide();
  });
});
```

How It Works

In the jQuery code, we start by attaching the **hover** event to all the column headings of the table. In the event handler we find out the index location of the column heading that is being hovered over, and store it in the variable **colindex**. The **index()** method use zero-based counting; that is, it begins from zero.

We then apply the style properties defined in the style rule **.hover** to the highlighted column heading and to the column whose index location is stored in the **colindex** variable (the one that is hovered over) to highlight them. Since the **:nth-child()** method is one-based, we increment the value of **colindex** by one before highlighting it.

When the mouse pointer is moved away from the column headings, we remove the properties defined in the style rule **.hover** from all the rows of the table. In the **click** event handler we hide the column heading that has been clicked and find out its index, which we store in the **colindex** variable.

Finally, we hide the column contents whose value is stored in the **colindex** variable (the index location of the column heading that is clicked). Hence, the column heading and the complete column contents will be made invisible when any of the column headings are clicked. On hovering over a column heading, it will be highlighted, along with the contents of the column, as shown in Figure 7-11.

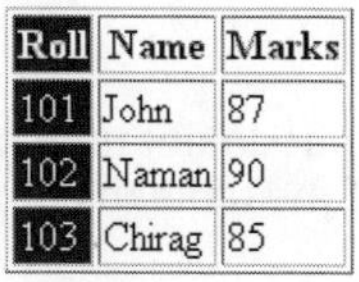

Roll	Name	Marks
101	John	87
102	Naman	90
103	Chirag	85

Figure 7-11. A column's contents and heading get highlighted when the heading is hovered over.

When the column heading is clicked, it will be erased, along with the contents of the column, as shown in Figure 7-12.

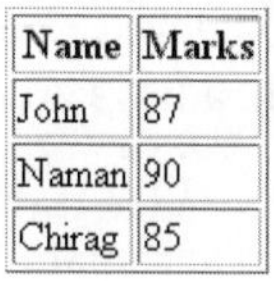

Name	Marks
John	87
Naman	90
Chirag	85

Figure 7-12. The selected column is erased from the table.

Filtering out Columns

You want to make all the columns of the table invisible except the one whose column heading is clicked. That is, you want to keep the clicked column (along with its heading), making the rest of the columns invisible.

The modified jQuery code to highlight the column (when its column heading is hovered over) and to hide all the columns except the one that has been clicked is shown here:

```
$(document).ready(function() {
  $('th').hover(
    function(){
      var colindex=$(this).parent().children().index(this);
      $(this).addClass('hover');
      $('table td:nth-child('+(colindex+1)+')').addClass('hover');
    },
    function(){
      $('table tr').children().removeClass('hover');
    }
  );

  $('th').click(function(){
    colindex=$(this).parent().children().index(this);
    $('table th:not(:nth-child('+(colindex+1)+'))').hide();
    $('table td:not(:nth-child('+(colindex+1)+'))').hide();
  });
});
```

How It Works

Looking at the jQuery code, first notice that the `:not()` selector selects all the elements that do not match the specified selector. It works like this, for example, which will select all the elements of the table that do not belong to the class `student`: `$('table :not(.student)')`.

In the `hover` event handler, we find the index location of the column heading that is hovered over and store it in the variable `colindex`. The `.index()` method uses zero-based counting. We then apply the style properties defined in the style rule `.hover` to the highlighted column heading and to the column whose index location is stored in the `colindex` variable (the one that is hovered over) to highlight it. Since the `:nth-child()` method is one-based, we increment the value of `colindex` by one before highlighting it.

When the mouse pointer is moved away from the column headings, we remove the properties defined in the style rule `.hover` from all the rows of the table. In the `click` event handler, we find out the index of the column heading that has been clicked and store the value in the `colindex` variable. We then hide all the column headings that are not clicked, using the `not` selector; that is, we keep the column heading whose index location is stored in the `colindex` variable, and the rest of the column headings are made invisible.

Finally, we hide all the column contents whose value is not equal to the index location stored in the `colindex` variable (the index location of the column heading that is clicked). The only column to remain visible is the one whose column heading is clicked. On hovering over the column heading, it will be highlighted, along with the contents of the column, as shown in Figure 7-13.

Roll	Name	Marks
101	John	87
102	Naman	90
103	Chirag	85

Figure 7-13. The column heading and column contents get highlighted when the column heading is hovered over.

When any column heading is clicked, that heading (along with its column contents) will be filtered out, making all of the rest of the columns of the table invisible as in Figure 7-14.

Roll
101
102
103

Figure 7-14. The selected column is filtered out.

7-5. Paginating a Table

Problem

You have a table consisting of a few rows and columns. You want the rows of the table to be displayed pagewise. That is, on the top of the table, you want the page numbers to appear and when any page number is clicked, the rows that belong to that page number will be displayed.

Solution

For this solution, we will make use of the same HTML file that we used in Recipe 7-1. We need to define style rules to highlight the page numbers when they're hovered over and to keep some spacing between page numbers. The two style rules that we define are **.hover** and **.page**, as shown in the following style sheet file:

```
style.css
.hover { background-color: #00f; color: #fff; }
.page{ margin:5px; }
```

The jQuery code to divide the rows of the table in to pages (depending on the number of rows that we want to see per page) and to display the respective rows when a page number is clicked is shown here:

```
$(document).ready(function() {
  var rows=$('table').find('tbody tr').length;
  var no_rec_per_page=1;
  var no_pages= Math.ceil(rows/no_rec_per_page);
  var $pagenumbers=$('<div id="pages"></div>');
  for(i=0;i<no_pages;i++)
  {
    $('<span class="page">'+(i+1)+'</span>').appendTo($pagenumbers);
  }
  $pagenumbers.insertBefore('table');

  $('.page').hover(
    function(){
      $(this).addClass('hover');
    },
    function(){
      $(this).removeClass('hover');
    }
  );

  $('table').find('tbody tr').hide();
  var tr=$('table tbody tr');

  $('span').click(function(event){
    $('table').find('tbody tr').hide();
```

```
    for(var i=($(this).text()-1)*no_rec_per_page;
        i<=$(this).text()*no_rec_per_page-1;
        i++)
    {
        $(tr[i]).show();
    }
  });
});
```

How It Works

The style rule `hover` contains the `background-color` and `color` properties set to `#00f` and `#fff`, respectively, to turn the background color of the hovered-over page number to blue and its foreground color to white. The style rule `.page` contains the `margin` property set to 5px to create the space of 5px among page numbers

Our jQuery code starts by counting the number of rows (`tr` elements nested inside the `tbody` element) and storing the count in variable rows. For this example, we'll assume that we want to see only one row per page, so we initialize the value of the variable `no_rec_per_page` equal to 1. We next have to find out the total number of pages by dividing the total count of the rows by the number of records that we want to see per page. The count of the pages is assigned to the variable `no_pages`. The final action to take before we start on the event handlers is to set up the page-number display. We start this by defining a `div` element of ID `pages` and assigning it to the variable `$pagenumbers`.

With the help of a `for` loop, we create a few `span` elements (equal to the number of pages) that contain the sequence of page numbers 1,2… and the `span` element is assigned the class name `page` so that the style properties defined in the class selector `.page` are automatically applied to all the page numbers. Finally, all the `span` elements containing the page numbers are appended to the `div` element of ID `pages`. To finish the job we insert the `div` element of ID `pages` that was stored in the variable `$pagenumbers` before the table element, which makes the page numbers appear above the table.

Next we attach the `hover()` event to the page numbers (`span` element of the class .pages). In the event handler, and we highlight the page numbers when the mouse pointer moves over them. (The properties defined in the style rule `.hover` are applied to the page numbers, changing their background and foreground color to blue and white respectively.) Conversely, when the mouse pointer moves away from them we remove the style properties of the style rule `.hover`.

After the `hover` event handler, because we don't want to see any of the data when the page first loads, we hide all the rows (`tr` elements nested inside the `tbody` element) of the table, keeping only the column headings visible. Only when the user selects a page number will the rows that belongs to that page number be displayed. We then retrieve all the rows of the table and store them in the variable `tr`; that is, now `tr` is an array containing all the rows of the table.

In the `click` event handler of the page numbers, we hide all the rows of the table (keeping only the column visible). We then display the rows that fall within the clicked page number using the `tr` array.

Initially, we get a blank table with only column headings and page numbers at the top, as shown in Figure 7-15.

1 2 3

Roll	Name	Marks

Figure 7-15. Table with column headings and page numbers

On hovering on any page number, the number will be highlighted; on clicking on the page number, the rows of that page number will be displayed as shown in Figure 7-16.

Roll	Name	Marks
101	John	87

Figure 7-16. Displaying rows of page one (assuming one row per page)

We see only one row displayed here because we have set the value of the variable no_rec_per_page (which decides the number of rows to be displayed per page) to 1 (refer to the third statement of the code). Let us set its value to 5. Assuming the HTML file has some more rows added in its table element, we will now see a group of five rows when we select any page number, as shown in Figure 7-17.

Roll	Name	Marks
101	John	87
102	Naman	90
103	Chirag	85
104	David	92
105	Kelly	81

Figure 7-17. Displaying rows of page one (assuming five rows per page)

Also, we can modify the jQuery code to display the rows that belong to page one at the beginning (instead of showing only the column headings as we did in Figure 7-15). The jQuery code that displays the rows of the first page by default is as follows:

```
$(document).ready(function() {
  var rows=$('table').find('tbody tr').length;
  var no_rec_per_page=1;
  var no_pages= Math.ceil(rows/no_rec_per_page);
  var $pagenumbers=$('<div id="pages"></div>');
  for(i=0;i<no_pages;i++)
  {
    $('<span class="page">'+(i+1)+'</span>').appendTo($pagenumbers);
  }
  $pagenumbers.insertBefore('table');

  $('.page').hover(
    function(){
      $(this).addClass('hover');
    },
```

```
      function(){
        $(this).removeClass('hover');
      }
    );

    $('table').find('tbody tr').hide();
    var tr=$('table tbody tr');

    for(var i=0;i<=no_rec_per_page-1;i++)
    {
      $(tr[i]).show();
    }

    $('span').click(function(event){
      $('table').find('tbody tr').hide();
      for(i=($(this).text()-1)*no_rec_per_page;i<=$(this).text()*no_rec_per_page-1;i++)
      {
        $(tr[i]).show();
      }
    });
});
```

We can see that a for loop is added to make the rows of the first page number (depending on the value assigned to the variable no_rec_per_page) visible on the screen.

7-6. Expanding and Collapsing List Items

Problem

You have an unordered list with two list items, and both these list items contain a nested unordered list. You want the two list items to appear with a plus (+) icon to their left (indicating that some items are hidden). When the user selects the plus icon, you want that list item to expand to display all the elements that were hidden, and you want the plus icon to be replaced with a minus (–)icon when in expanded mode.

Solution

Let's start with an HTML file that contains an unordered list with two list items: Tea and Coffee. Both the list items are assigned the class name drink so as to identify and access them via jQuery code. The first list item (Tea) contains an unordered list of three list items: Darjeeling, Assam, and Kerala. The list item Assam has the class name drink and contains an unordered list item with two list items in it: Green Leaves and Herbal.

The second list item, Coffee, contains an unordered list element with two list items: Cochin and Kerala. The HTML file is shown here:

```
<body>
<ul>
  <li class="drink">Tea
    <ul>
      <li>Darjeeling</li>
      <li class="drink">Assam
        <ul>
          <li>Green Leaves</li>
          <li>Herbal</li>
        </ul>
      </li>
      <li>Kerala</li>
    </ul>
  </li>
  <li class="drink">Coffee
    <ul>
        <li>Cochin</li>
        <li>Kerala</li>
    </ul>
  </li>
</ul>
</body>
```

Without applying any style or jQuery code, the HTML file on execution displays the unordered list with its respective list items, as shown in Figure 7-18.

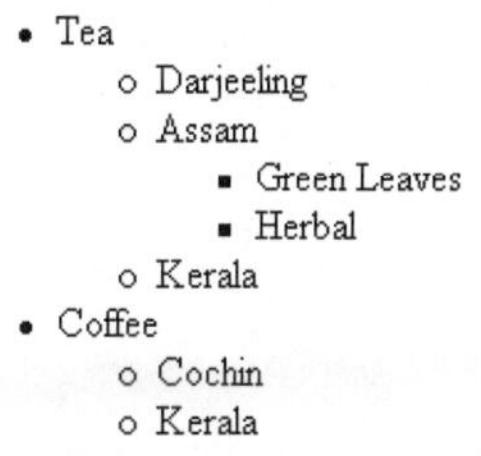

- Tea
  - Darjeeling
  - Assam
    - Green Leaves
    - Herbal
  - Kerala
- Coffee
  - Cochin
  - Kerala

Figure 7-18. Unordered list with its list items

To add the plus and minus icons to the list items, we need to apply certain style rules. The style sheet file `style.css` may contain the following style rules:

```
style.css
.plusimageapply{list-style-image:url(plus.jpg);}
.minusimageapply{list-style-image:url(minus.jpg);}
.noimage{list-style-image:none;}
```

In order to apply the preceding style rules to the list items and to make them expand and collapse on selecting the plus and minus icons on their left, we need to write the following jQuery code:

```
$(document).ready(function() {
  $('li.drink').addClass('plusimageapply');
  $('li.drink').children().addClass('noimage');
  $('li.drink').children().hide();
  $('li.drink').each(
    function(column) {
      $(this).click(function(event){
        if (this == event.target) {
          if($(this).is('.plusimageapply')) {
            $(this).children().show();
            $(this).removeClass('plusimageapply');
            $(this).addClass('minusimageapply');
          }
          else
          {
            $(this).children().hide();
            $(this).removeClass('minusimageapply');
            $(this).addClass('plusimageapply');
          }
        }
      });
    }
  );
});
```

How It Works

The style rule `plusimageapply` will be applied to all the list items (in collapsed mode) that have a nested unordered list in them, and it contains the `list-style-image` property set to `url(plus.jpg)` to replace the traditional bullets symbol with a plus icon (that we assume to exist in an image file named `plus.jpg`). Similarly, the style rule `minusimageapply` will be applied to all the list items in expanded mode, and it contains the `list-style-image` property set to `url(minus.jpg)` to display a minus icon on the left of the list items. We assume that the image file `minus.jpg` contains a minus icon in it. The style rule `noimage` will be applied to all of the list items that do not have unordered list nested in them, and it contains the `list-style-image` property set to `none` to display them with their traditional bullet symbols.

Now looking at our jQuery code, all the list items of the class `drink` (those that have unordered list items nested in them) the style rule `plusimageapply` will be applied, making a plus icon to appear on their left. To all the rest of the list items (that do not have nested list items in them), the style rule `noimage` will be applied to make them appear with their traditional bullet symbols. We initially make all the nested elements of the list items (that have unordered list items in them) invisible. That is, we make all the list items that have unordered list items in them appear in collapsed mode.

To apply the expansion functionality, we attach a `click` event to each of the list items (that has an unordered list item in it), one by one. In the event handler, we check whether the list item on which the `click` event has occurred has the style rule `plusimageapply` applied to it. If it does, we display the hidden contents of the list item.

We then remove the style properties of style rule `plusimageapply` and apply the style properties of the style rule `minusimageapply` to replace the plus icon with the minus icon for the expanded list items. If the list item that was clicked has a minus icon on its left—that is, if the style rule `plusimageapply` is not applied to it—we hide the nested contents. We also remove the style properties of style rule `minusimageapply` and apply the style properties of the style rule `plusimageapply` to replace the minus icon with the plus icon for the list items that is in collapsed mode (we need to collapse the list item that has the `minusimageapply` style rule applied on it and is clicked).

Initially, the list items will appear in collapsed mode with a plus icon on their left, as shown in Figure 7-19.

⊞ Tea
⊞ Coffee

Figure 7-19. Two list items in collapsed mode

When you select the plus icon (or the list item itself), it will be expanded to show the nested unordered list in it, and the plus icon will be replaced with the minus icon, as shown in Figure 7-20. The list item `Assam` has an unordered list item in it, and that is why it has a plus icon on its left.

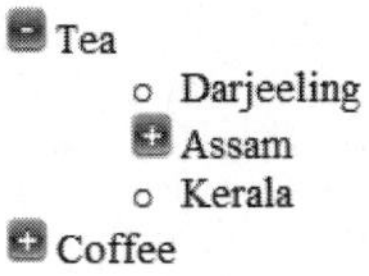

⊟ Tea
    ○ Darjeeling
    ⊞ Assam
    ○ Kerala
⊞ Coffee

Figure 7-20. Contents of first list item displayed when clicked

When you select the plus icon of the `Assam` list item, it will be expanded to show the hidden list items in it, and the plus icon will be replaced with the minus icon.

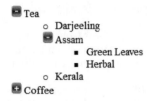

Figure 7-21. The contents of the nested list item (collpased list item) are displayed when the item is clicked.

When you select the plus icon (or the list item itself) of the list item `Coffee`, it will be expanded to show the list items in it, and the plus icon will be replaced with the minus icon, as shown in Figure 7-22.

Figure 7-22. The contents of the second list item are displayed when that item is clicked.

7-7. Expanding and Collapsing Table Rows

Problem

You have a table consisting of 15 rows where each row has 3 columns. The table represents student records. It initially displays three rows: `Roll 101-105`, `Roll 106-110`, and `Roll 111-115`. You want to see at most 5 records at a time; that is, if you hover over the `Roll 101-105` row, it must be expanded to show the student records with roll numbers between 101 and 105.

Solution

Start off by making an HTML file with a table element that has table headings and a table body consisting of 15 row (`tr`) elements, as shown here:

```
<body>
<table border="1">
<thead>
<tr><th>Roll</th><th>Name</th><th>Marks</th></tr>
</thead>
<tbody>
<tr><td colspan=3 class="studgroup" align="center">Roll 101-105</td></tr>
<tr><td>101</td><td>John</td><td>87</td></tr>
<tr><td>102</td><td>Naman</td><td>90</td></tr>
<tr><td>103</td><td>Chirag</td><td>85</td></tr>
<tr><td>104</td><td>David</td><td>92</td></tr>
<tr><td>105</td><td>Kelly</td><td>81</td></tr>
<tr><td colspan=3 class="studgroup"  align="center">Roll 106-110</td></tr>
<tr><td>106</td><td>Charles</td><td>77</td></tr>
<tr><td>107</td><td>Jerry</td><td>91</td></tr>
<tr><td>108</td><td>Beth</td><td>75</td></tr>
<tr><td>109</td><td>Caroline</td><td>82</td></tr>
<tr><td>110</td><td>Hanen</td><td>71</td></tr>
<tr><td colspan=3 class="studgroup"  align="center">Roll 111-115</td></tr>
<tr><td>111</td><td>Douglas</td><td>57</td></tr>
<tr><td>112</td><td>Tim</td><td>86</td></tr>
<tr><td>113</td><td>Michael</td><td>68</td></tr>
<tr><td>114</td><td>Kimbley</td><td>88</td></tr>
<tr><td>115</td><td>Christina</td><td>72</td></tr>
</tbody>
</table>
</body>
```

The table headings are represented by th elements nested inside the thead element, and student records are represented by tr elements nested inside the tbody element. To designate a block of five rows, we define three rows (consisting of a td element spanning three columns): Roll 101-105, Roll 106-110, and Roll 111-115. These rows (td element spanning three columns) are assigned the class name studgroup so as to identify and use them in jQuery.

To highlight the rows, we define a style rule .hover in the style sheet file. The style sheet file style.css is shown here:

```
style.css
.hover { background-color: #00f; color: #fff; }
```

The jQuery code to expand hidden rows when their corresponding row is hovered over is shown here:

```
$(document).ready(function() {
  $('table tbody tr').hide();
  $('table tbody').find('.studgroup').parent().show();
  $('tbody tr').hover(
    function(){
      var tr=$('table tbody tr');
      var rindex=$(this).parent().children().index(this);
      for(var i=rindex;i<=rindex+5;i++)
      {
```

```
        $(tr[i]).show();
      }
      $(this).addClass('hover');
    },
    function(){
      $('table tbody tr').hide();
      $('table tbody').find('.studgroup').parent().show();
      $(this).removeClass('hover');
    }
  );
});
```

How It Works

The `.hover` style rule contains the `background-color` property set to `#00f` and the `color` property set to `#fff` to change the background and foreground colors of the hovered-over row to blue and white, respectively.

    The meaning of the jQuery code statements is as follows:

    We begin by hiding all the rows that are nested inside the `tbody` element of the table; that is, except the table headings, we hide all the rows.

    Then we display the three rows that each represent a block of the five rows, consisting of a `td` element spanning three columns): `Roll 101-105`, `Roll 106-110`, and `Roll 111-115`, respectively). Recall these three rows are assigned the class name `studgroup`.

    We then attach the `hover` event to the visible rows of the table. In the event handler, we highlight the row when the mouse pointer moves over it (the properties defined in the style rule `.hover` are applied to that row, changing its background and foreground colors to blue and white, respectively). Conversely, when the mouse pointer moves away from the row, we remove the style properties (of the style rule `.hover`). Also, in the `hover` event handler, we retrieve all the rows of the table and store them in the variable `tr`—now `tr` is an array containing all the rows of the table—and we find out the index number of the row that is hovered over, and store it in a variable `rindex`. Then, with the help of a `for` loop we display the next five rows; that is, the rows underlying the row heading of the class name `studgroup` are displayed.

    In the event handler of the `hover` event that is executed when the mouse pointer is moved away from the rows, besides removing the properties of the `hover` style rule, we hide all the rows of the table except the heading rows.

    On execution of the preceding jQuery code, we find three rows—`Roll 101-105`, `Roll 106-110`, and `Roll 111-115`—that designate the group of records underneath them, as shown in Figure 7-23.

Roll	Name	Marks
Roll 101-105		
Roll 106-110		
Roll 111-115		

Figure 7-23. Table with rows designating groups of rows underneath them

On hovering over any row, the group of five records nested inside that row will be displayed. For instance, on hovering over the `Roll 101-105` row, we may get the rows shown in Figure 7-24, and the hovered-over row will be highlighted:

Roll	Name	Marks
Roll 101-105		
101	John	87
102	Naman	90
103	Chirag	85
104	David	92
105	Kelly	81
Roll 106-110		
Roll 111-115		

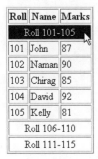

***Figure 7-24.** Student records are displayed when the row designating their group is hovered over.*

Similarly, when the `Roll 111-115` row is hovered over, the row will be highlighted and the student records that belong to that range of roll numbers will be displayed, as shown in Figure 7-25:

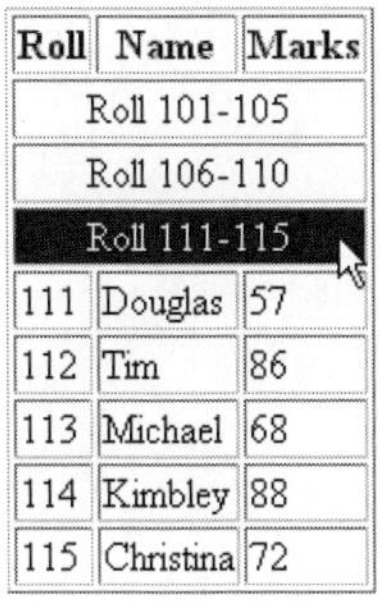

Roll	Name	Marks
Roll 101-105		
Roll 106-110		
Roll 111-115		
111	Douglas	57
112	Tim	86
113	Michael	68
114	Kimbley	88
115	Christina	72

***Figure 7-25.** Once again, student records are displayed when the row designating their group is hovered over.*

Rows with + and – Icons

When the rows shown in Figure 7-23 are hovered over, you want a plus icon to be displayed on their left. When the row is expanded, it should display the records in the respective range and the plus icon should be replaced with a minus icon.

To accomplish this, the jQuery code would be modified as shown here:

```
$(document).ready(function() {
  $('.studgroup').css(
    {'background-image':"url(plus.jpg)",
     'background-repeat':"no-repeat",
     'background-position':"left"}
  );
  $('table tbody tr').hide();
  $('table tbody').find('.studgroup').parent().show();
  $('tbody tr').hover(
    function(){
      $(this).find('.studgroup').css(
        {'background-image':"url(minus.jpg)",
         'background-repeat':"no-repeat",
         'background-position':"left"}
      );
      var tr=$('table tbody tr');
      var rindex=$(this).parent().children().index(this);
      for(var i=rindex;i<=rindex+5;i++)
      {
        $(tr[i]).show();
      }
      $(this).addClass('hover');
    },
    function(){
      $(this).find('.studgroup').css(
        {'background-image':"url(plus.jpg)",
         'background-repeat':"no-repeat",
         'background-position':"left"}
      );
      $('table tbody tr').hide();
      $('table tbody').find('.studgroup').parent().show();
      $(this).removeClass('hover');
    }
  );
});
```

Here, in the rows that display the range of roll numbers (td element spanning three columns and assigned the class name .studgroup), we display a plus icon that is assumed to exist in the image file plus.jpg. We use the background-repeat and background-position properties in the .css() method to make the icon appear only once, on the left side of the row.

We then hide all the rows that are nested inside the tbody element of the table. That is, we hide all the student records (except the table headings), as we want to display them only when the plus icon of the associated row is hovered over. Then we display the three rows that display the range of roll numbers (rows that are assigned the class name studgroup and that have plus icon next to them).

When any row is hovered over, its plus icon is replaced with a minus icon using the .css() method, and the background-repeat and background-position properties are set to no-repeat and left, respectively, to make the minus icon appear only once, on left side of the row. Also, in the hover event handler, we retrieve all the rows of the table and store them in the variable tr (now tr is an array containing all the rows of the table), and we find out the index number of the row that is hovered over and store it in a variable **rindex**. Then, with the help of a **for** loop we display the next five rows; that is, the rows underlying the row heading (of the class name **studgroup**) are displayed. Finally, for the **hover** event we apply the properties defined in the style rule **hover** to highlight the hovered-over row.

When the mouse pointer is moved away from the hovered-over row, its minus icon is replaced with a plus icon using the **.css()** method, and the **background-repeat** and **background-position** properties are set to **no-repeat** and **left**, respectively, to make the plus icon appear only once, on left side of the row. We then hide all of the rows of the table except the rows that show the range of roll numbers, along with a plus icon (this is what we want when the mouse pointer is moved away from the hovered-over row). Finally, we remove the properties defined in the **.hover** style rule to make the row appear as it was initially when mouse pointer is moved away.

On execution of the preceding jQuery code, we find three rows—**Roll 101-105**, **Roll 106-110**, and **Roll 111-115**—that designate the group of records underneath them. Also, we will find that on left of each row is a minus icon indicating that the rows are currently collapsed, as shown in Figure 7-26.

Figure 7-26. Rows designating a group of records underneath them, along with a plus icon on their left

When we hover on any row, that row will be highlighted, the associated student records will be displayed, and the plus icon will be replaced by a minus icon in the hovered-over row, as shown in Figure 7-27.

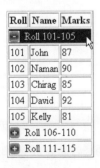

Figure 7-27. The hovered-over row displays its records, and the plus icon is replaced by the minus icon.

Similarly, if we hover over the row **Roll 106-110**, it will be highlighted, the associated student records will be displayed, and the plus icon will be replaced by a minus icon in the hovered-over row; at the same time, the row we hovered over previously (which has now lost focus) will get its plus icon back (see Figure 7-28).

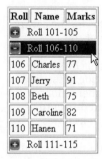

Figure 7-28. The row gets is plus icon back when it returns to collapsed mode

7-8. Sorting List Items

Problem

You have an unordered list consisting of a few list items, which you want to sort.

Solution

Let's make an HTML file that consists of an unordered list:

```
<body>
<ul>
  <li>Tea</li>
  <li>Coffee</li>
  <li>Pepsi</li>
  <li>Energy Drink</li>
  <li>Soup</li>
</ul>
</body>
```

The HTML file, when opened in a browser, will show the list items as in Figure 7-29.

- Tea
- Coffee
- Pepsi
- Energy Drink
- Soup

Figure 7-29. Unsorted list items

The jQuery code to sort the list items is shown here:

```
$(document).ready(function() {
  var drinks = $('ul').children('li').get();

  drinks.sort(function(a, b) {
    var val1 = $(a).text().toUpperCase();
    var val2 = $(b).text().toUpperCase();
    return (val1 < val2) ? -1 : (val1 > val2) ? 1 : 0;
  });

  $.each(drinks, function(index, row) {
    $('ul').append(row);
  });
});
```

How It Works

Looking at our jQuery code, we first get all the list items that are children of the unordered list and store them in a variable `drinks`. That is, `drinks` will become an array containing the list item's text. We then invoke the `.sort()` function on the `drinks` array, which repeatedly takes two elements of the array at a time and assigns them to its parameters `a` and `b` for comparison. The `sort` function will return a value depending on the values assigned to the parameters `drinks` and `b`. Note the following details of th function:

- When the function returns `<0`, it means the second value is larger than the first and is hence pushed down.

- When the function returns `=0`, it means both values are equal and there's no need to change the sort order.

- When the function returns `>0`, it means the first value is larger than the second and must be pushed down.

Before we invoke the sorting algorithm, we convert the two array elements passed to the `sort` function to uppercase. We then use the sorting algorithm to return the values in the bulleted list, which will sort the list items in alphabetical (ascending) order. Finally, the `each()` function operates on the array `drinks` (that contains sorted list items); we extract each element stored in the array and append it to the unordered list element. That is, we're appending the sorted list items to the unordered list element for display.

On execution of the preceding jQuery code, we get the sorted list items shown in Figure 7-30.

- Coffee
- Energy Drink
- Pepsi
- Soup
- Tea

Figure 7-30. Sorted list items

7-9. Sorting a Table

Problem

You have a table consisting of a few rows and columns. When a user selects any column of the table, its contents must be sorted in ascending order.

Solution

Let's make an HTML file that contains a `table` element with some rows and columns defined in it:

```
<body>
<table border="1">
<thead>
<tr><th>Roll</th><th>Name</th><th>Marks</th></tr>
</thead>
<tbody>
<tr><td>103</td><td>Chirag</td><td>85</td></tr>
<tr><td>102</td><td>Naman</td><td>90</td></tr>
<tr><td>101</td><td>John</td><td>87</td></tr>
</tbody>
</table>
</body>
```

We define a table with a border of 1pxand with three column headings (defined using the `th` element): `Roll`, `Name`, and `Marks`. Also, it contains three rows of student records. The table headings are nested inside the `thead` element and the body of the table (rows that contain information) is nested inside the `tbody` element.

We will approach this recipe in three steps:

1. Determining which column heading is clicked

2. Sorting a column in ascending order

3. Sorting a column in both ascending and descending order

Determining Which Column Heading Is Clicked

Before sorting a column in ascending or descending order, you need to know which of the table's column headings is selected. To highlight the column heading that's selected by the user, we need to define a style rule `.hover` in the style sheet file. The style sheet file `style.css` may appear as shown here:

```
style.css
.hover{
cursor: default;
color: blue ;
background-color:cyan
}
```

Here's the jQuery code to display which of the column heading is selected:

```
$(document).ready(function() {
  $('th').each(function() {
    $(this).hover(
      function(){
        $(this).addClass('hover');
      },
      function(){
        $(this).removeClass('hover');
      }
    );

    $(this).click(function(){
      alert($(this).text()+' column is selected');
    });
  });
});
```

How It Works

In the style sheet file, the style rule `.hover` contains the `cursor` property set to `default` to make the mouse pointer appear as it normally does (in the form of a pointer). The `color` and `background-color` properties are set to blue and cyan, respectively, to turn the background color of the highlighted column heading cyan and its foreground color blue.

We can see in the preceding jQuery code that each of the table headings is checked to see if it's been hovered over. If any of the table heading is hovered over, the style properties defined in the style rule `.hover` will be applied to it to highlight it (its background color will change to cyan and its foreground color to blue). When the mouse pointer is moved away from the column heading, the style properties of the `.hover` style rule will be removed, making the column heading appear as it was initially. Also, we check if any table heading is clicked; if so, we display the text of the column heading using the `alert()` method.

On moving the mouse pointer over any column heading, that heading will be highlighted and its name will be displayed via the `alert()` method, as shown in Figure 7-31.

Figure 7-31. Column name displayed when column heading is hovered over

Sorting a Column in Ascending Order

The jQuery code to sort a column in ascending order is shown here:

```
$(document).ready(function() {
  $('th').each(function(column) {
    $(this).hover(
      function(){
        $(this).addClass('hover');
      },
      function(){
        $(this).removeClass('hover');
      }
    );

    $(this).click(function(){
      var rec=$('table').find('tbody >tr').get();
      rec.sort(function(a, b) {
        var val1 = $(a).children('td').eq(column).text().toUpperCase();
        var val2 = $(b).children('td').eq(column).text().toUpperCase();
        return (val1 < val2) ? -1 : (val1 > val2) ? 1 : 0;
      });

      $.each(rec, function(index, row) {
        $('tbody').append(row);
      });
    });
  });
});
```

Before we move on, let's discuss the significance of the > symbol in our code.

The > Symbol

The > symbol is a selector that represents the children of the selected element; for example, in the following example, it selects all the children of the element E1 that are matched by element E2:

```
Syntax:
E1>E2
```

Now looking at our jQuery code in action, each table heading is checked to see if it is hovered over. If any of the table headings are hovered over, the style properties defined in the style rule .hover will be applied to that heading to highlight it. Also when the mouse pointer is moved away from the heading the style properties of the .hover style rule will be removed, making the column heading appear as it was initially.

Then we attach a click event to each of the table headings. In the click event handler, we retrieve all the table rows (nested in the tbody element) and store them in the variable rec. rec will be now an array containing all the table rows. By invoking the sort() function on the rec array, we repeatedly take two elements (rows) of the array at a time and arrange them in ascending order. To do so, the column contents of the first and second parameters (rows) passed to the sort() function are extracted and converted to uppercase before they're compared.

The sort() function then returns any of the values <0, =0, or >0, which helps in deciding which column contents should be moved up in the sort order and which should be pushed down in the sort order. When this sort function is finished, the rec array will have all the rows of the selected column sorted in ascending order. Finally, the sorted rows from the rec array are retrieved and appended to the tbody element of the table for display.

Initially, the table may appear as shown in Figure 7-32.

Roll	Name	Marks
103	Chirag	85
102	Naman	90
101	John	87

Figure 7-32. Unsorted table

On selecting the Roll column, it will be highlighted and the table rows will be sorted in ascending order by roll number, as shown in Figure 7-33.

Roll	Name	Marks
101	John	87
102	Naman	90
103	Chirag	85

Figure 7-33. Table sorted in ascending order by roll number

Similarly, on selecting the Name column, it will be highlighted and the table rows will be sorted in ascending (alphabetical) order by name, as shown in Figure 7-34.

Roll	Name	Marks
103	Chirag	85
101	John	87
102	Naman	90

Figure 7-34. Table sorted in ascending order by name

Sorting a Column in both Ascending and Descending Order

If any of the column heading is clicked for the first time, the table must be sorted in ascending order by that column, and if the column is clicked again, the table must be sorted in descending order by that column. In other words, we want the sort order to toggle on each click. In order to inform the user which sorting order is currently applied on a column, we need to display an up or down arrow in the column heading. The up arrow will denote that the table is sorted in ascending order by that column, and the down arrow will indicate that the table is sorted in descending order by the column.

To display the up and down arrows in the column headings, we need to define two style rules in the style sheet file **style.css**, as shown here:

```
style.css
.asc{
background:url('up.png') no-repeat; padding-left:20px;
}

.desc{
background:url('down.png') no-repeat; padding-left:20px;
}
```

Let's now modify the jQuery code to sort the table in ascending as well as in descending order by the selected column:

```
$(document).ready(function() {
  $('th').each(function(column) {
    $(this).hover(
      function(){
        $(this).addClass('hover');
      },
      function(){
        $(this).removeClass('hover');
      }
    );

    $(this).click(function(){
      if($(this).is('.asc'))
      {
        $(this).removeClass('asc');
        $(this).addClass('desc');
        sortdir=-1;
      }
      else
      {
        $(this).addClass('asc');
        $(this).removeClass('desc');
        sortdir=1;
      }
      $(this).siblings().removeClass('asc');
      $(this).siblings().removeClass('desc');

      var rec=$('table').find('tbody >tr').get();
```

```
    rec.sort(function(a, b) {
      var val1 = $(a).children('td').eq(column).text().toUpperCase();
      var val2 = $(b).children('td').eq(column).text().toUpperCase();
      return (val1 < val2) ? -sortdir : (val1 > val2) ? sortdir : 0;
    });

    $.each(rec, function(index, row) {
      $('tbody').append(row);
    });
   });
  });
});
```

How It Works

The style rule `.asc` contains the background property set to `url(up.png)` to display an up arrow pointer in the column heading. The value `no-repeat` will make the pointer appear only once in the column heading, and the `padding-left` property is set to 20px to create some space on the left. Similarly, the style rule `desc` contains the `background` property to display the down arrow pointer in the column headings.

Then our jQuery code begins by checking each of the table headings to see any of them are hovered over. If any of the table headings are in fact hovered over, the style properties defined in the style rule `.hover` will be applied to it to highlight it. Also, when the mouse pointer is moved away from the column heading, the style properties of the `.hover` style rule will be removed, making the column heading appear as it did initially.

We then attach a `click` event to each of the table headings and check if the selected column heading has the style rule `.asc` applied to it. That is, we check if the table is already sorted in ascending order by the selected column heading. If it is, we remove the style properties defined in the style rule `asc` and apply the style properties defined in the style rule `desc` (when a column heading that's been sorted in ascending order is clicked again). As a result, the column heading will display a down arrow on its left. Also, the value of the variable `sortdir` is set to –1, which will be used to manipulate the return values of the sort function to perform sorting in descending order.

If the selected column had the `desc` style rule already applied to it—that is, if the table is sorted in descending order by the selected column—we remove the style properties defined in the style rule `desc` and apply the properties defined in the style rule `asc`, which will place an up arrow to the left of the column heading. Also, the value of the variable `sortdir` is 1 to make the sort function sort in ascending order.

Once we've sorted the column, we need to remove the properties of the style rules `.asc` and .desc from all the column headings except the one that is selected by the user. We also need to retrieve all the table rows (nested in the `tbody` element) and store them in the variable `rec`, which will be now be an array containing all the table rows.

We can then invoke the `sort` function on the `rec` array. The `sort` function will repeatedly take two elements (rows) of the array at a time and arrange them in sort order as decided by the value in the variable `sortdir`. The `sort` function begins by extracting the column contents of the first and second parameters (rows) passed to the sort function, then converts them to upper case before comparing them.

The function returns any of the values `<0`, `=0`, or `>0`, which helps in deciding which column contents should be moved up in the sort order and which should be pushed down in the sort order. When this `sort` function is complete, the `rec` array will have all the rows sorted in either ascending or descending order by the selected column, depending on the value assigned to the variable `sortdir`. Finally, the sorted rows from the `rec` array are retrieved and appended to the `tbody` element of the table for display.

Initially, the table may appear as shown in Figure 7-35.

Roll	Name	Marks
103	Chirag	85
102	Naman	90
101	John	87

Figure 7-35. Unsorted table consisting of a few rows and columns

If we select the column heading `Name` once, an up arrow will appear on its left (indicating that sorting will be done in ascending order) and the table will be sorted in ascending alphabetical order by name, as shown in Figure 7-36.

Roll	▲ Name	Marks
103	Chirag	85
101	John	87
102	Naman	90

Figure 7-36. Table sorted in ascending order by name

On selecting the `Name` column heading again, a down arrow will appear on its left (indicating that sorting will be done in descending order) and the table will be sorted in descending alphabetical order by name, as shown in Figure 7-37.

Roll	▼ Name	Marks
102	Naman	90
101	John	87
103	Chirag	85

Figure 7-37. Table sorted in descending order by name

7-10. Filtering Rows from a Table

Problem

You have a table consisting of few rows and columns, along with a text-input field preceding the table. You want to filter the rows of the table on the basis of the characters typed in the text-input field. For instance, if the user enters the character *c*, all the rows in the table that have names beginning with *c* will be displayed and the rest of the rows will be filtered out.

Solution

We'll start with an HTML file that contains a table element with some rows and columns. Before the table, let's display the message *Enter the character*, followed by a text-input field. Below the text-input field, we will display a Submit button, which on being clicked will display the filtered information of the table. The HTML file may appear as shown here:

```
<body>
<div><span class="label">Enter a character </span><input type="text"  class="infobox"
/></div>
<input class="submit" type="submit" value="Submit"/><br/><br/>
<table border="1">
<thead>
<tr><th>Roll</th><th>Name</th><th>Marks</th></tr>
</thead>
<tbody>
<tr><td>101</td><td>John</td><td>87</td></tr>
<tr><td>102</td><td>Naman</td><td>90</td></tr>
<tr><td>103</td><td>Chirag</td><td>85</td></tr>
<tr><td>104</td><td>David</td><td>92</td></tr>
<tr><td>105</td><td>Kelly</td><td>81</td></tr>
<tr><td>106</td><td>Charles</td><td>77</td></tr>
<tr><td>107</td><td>Jerry</td><td>91</td></tr>
<tr><td>108</td><td>Beth</td><td>75</td></tr>
<tr><td>109</td><td>Caroline</td><td>82</td></tr>
<tr><td>110</td><td>Hanen</td><td>71</td></tr>
<tr><td>111</td><td>Douglas</td><td>57</td></tr>
<tr><td>112</td><td>Tim</td><td>86</td></tr>
<tr><td>113</td><td>Michael</td><td>68</td></tr>
<tr><td>114</td><td>Kimbley</td><td>88</td></tr>
<tr><td>115</td><td>Christina</td><td>72</td></tr>
</tbody>
</table>
</body>
```

You can see that the text message is nested inside the span element of the class label, the text-input field is assigned the class name infobox, and the Submit button is assigned the class name submit so that the style properties defined in the class selectors .label, .infobox, and .submit (defined in the style sheet file) can be applied to them automatically. The style sheet is shown here:

```
style.css
.label {float: left; width: 120px; }
.infobox {width: 200px; }
.submit { margin-left: 125px; margin-top: 10px;}
```

The jQuery code to filter the table rows to display the names that begin with the character supplied in the text-input field is shown here:

```
$(document).ready(function() {
  var rows;
  var coldata;

  $('.submit').click(function(event){
    $('table').find('tbody tr').hide();
    var data=$('.infobox').val();
    var len=data.length;
    if(len>0)
    {
      $('table tbody tr').each(function(){
        coldata=$(this).children().eq(1);
        if(coldata.text().charAt(0).toUpperCase()==data.charAt(0).toUpperCase())
        {
          $(this).show();
        }
      });
    }
    event.preventDefault();
  });
});
```

How It Works

The properties defined in the class selector `.label` include a `float` property set to `left` to make the label appear on the left of the browser window (making space for the next element to appear on its right). The `width` property is set to 200px to make the label fit within the width of 200px. The class selector `.infobox` contains the `width` property set to 200px to make the text-input field 200px wide, and the class selector `.submit` contains the `margin-left` property set to 125px to make the Submit button appear at the distance of 125px from the left border of the browser window (so that it appears below the text-input field). The `margin-top` property is set to 10px to make the Submit button appear 10px from the text-input field at its top.

Our jQuery code kicks off by attaching a `click` event to the Submit button, where we hide all the rows of the table (`tr` elements nested inside the `tbody` element), displaying only the column headings. We then retrieve the contents typed in the text-input field (that is assigned the class name `infobox`) and store them in a variable `data`.

Next we find the length of the variable `data` and scan each row of the table (`tr` element nested inside the `tbody` element). For each row, we get the contents of the children of the `row` element with an index of 1 (that is, the index of the `Name` column) and store them in the variable `coldata`.

Then we start filtering by comparing the first character of the column content (in `coldata`) with that of the character typed in the text-input field (after converting both of them to uppercase). If they match, we display the row.

Finally, we invoke the `.preventDefault()`method of the `event` object so as to avoid the submission to the server of information entered by the user; that is, avoiding the default behavior of the browser when a button is clicked.

On execution of the preceding jQuery code, we get a text-input field with a Submit button. If we enter a character—say *c*—in the text-input field, all the names in the table that begin with character *c* will be displayed, and the rest of the rows will be filtered out, as shown in Figure 7-38.

Enter the character c

Submit

Roll	Name	Marks
103	Chirag	85
106	Charles	77
109	Caroline	82
115	Christina	72

Figure 7-38. *Table displaying rows that contain a name beginning with the character entered in the text-input field*

Summary

In this chapter, you learned different recipes that perform different functions on tables, including highlighting rows and columns, filtering out a selected row, erasing a selected column, and displaying the rows of a table pagewise. You also saw the method involved in expanding and collapsing rows of a table, and learned how a table can be sorted in a ascending or descending order by a selected column.

In the next chapter, you will see how to make web pages highly responsive by applying AJAX techniques. You'll see how to display a welcome message and perform authentication using Ajax. We'll also look into validating user names and email address with AJAX, and paginating a table using AJAX. You'll also learn to employ an autocomplete feature using Ajax. Finally, you'll see how to get serialized information, JSON data, and XML data using AJAX.

■ ■ ■

CHAPTER 8

Ajax

Ajax is a technique that makes a web page highly responsive because it allows asynchronous requests to be made back to the server without the need to reload pages. In this chapter, you will learn some recipes that make use of Ajax to improve the user experience:

- Displaying a welcome message
- Performing authentication
- Validating a user name
- Validating an email address
- Using auto complete
- Importing HTML
- Getting JSON data
- Getting XML data
- Paginating tables

8-1. Displaying a Welcome Message

Problem

You have a label, an input text field, and a submit button on a form, and you want a welcome message be displayed to the user when they select the submit button – once they have entered their name in the input text field.

Solution

Let's create an HTML file that contains a label element, an input text field, a submit button, and an empty `div` element. The HTML file should look like this:

```
<body>
  <form>
    <label>Enter your Name</label>
    <input type="text" name="uname" class="uname"/>  <br/>
    <input type="submit" id="submit"/>
  </form>
  <div id="message"></div>
</body>
```

You can see that the HTML file contains a label, an input text field, and a submit button nested in a form. The input text field is given the class name uname for the purpose of accessing it via our jQuery code that we're about to write. Below the form is an empty div element of id message which we will use for displaying the welcome message to the user.

The jQuery code for our solution looks like this:

```
$(document).ready(function() {
  $('#submit').click(function () {
    var name = $('.uname').val();
    var data = 'uname=' + name;
    $.ajax({
      type:"POST",
      url:"welcome.php",
      data: data,
      success: function (html) {
        $('#message').html(html);
      }
    });
    return false;
  });
});
```

The script file welcome.php on the server is as follows:

```
<?php
$name = $_POST['uname'];
echo "Welcome ".  $name;
?>
```

How It Works

The ajax() method loads a remote page using an HTTP request. It creates and returns the XMLHttpRequest object. It takes one argument: an object of key/value pairs, which are used to initialize and handle the request.

```
.ajax( object of key/value pairs )
```

A few key/value pairs that we'll be using in this solution are:

- **type** – is a string that defines the HTTP method we will use for the request; that is, whether it is GET or POST. Default type is the GET method.

- **url** – is a string containing the URL of the web page to which we want to send the request

- **data** – is a map or string that we want to be sent to the server along with the request

- **success** – is a callback function that is executed if the request sent to the server succeeds. The returned data (from the server) is assigned to this callback function's parameter

You can look at all these key/value pair options at the following address: http://docs.jquery.com/Ajax/jQuery.ajax#options

In the jQuery code itself, we retrieve the name entered by the user in the input text field (of class uname) and store it in a variable name. We also define a variable data that will store a pair uname=name where name is the name entered by the user. This data variable is sent to the server to be assigned to the script file welcome.php (which is assumed to already exist on the server in this solution) for generating a response.

We invoke the request through ajax() method. In the ajax() method, we specify that the method of request that we are going to use is POST and the name of the script file that will be executed on the server (welcome.php). The parameter to be passed to the script file is contained in the string data(uname=name).welcome.php, and after processing the passed-in data, our solution generates the output which is received by the JavaScript file in the parameter html of the callback function.

The contents of html will be then assigned to the div element of id message so as to display the response (generated by the script file on the server) to the user. We return false in the click event to suppress the default browser click behavior; that is, we want it to take the action specified via jQuery code and not the default action.

The welcome.php script file retrieves the element uname from the $_POST array and stores it in variable $name. Then the string Welcome $name is returned to the jQuery code as the response from the server where $name is the name entered by the user. The HTML file generates the output consisting of label, input text field and a submit button as shown in Figure 8-1:

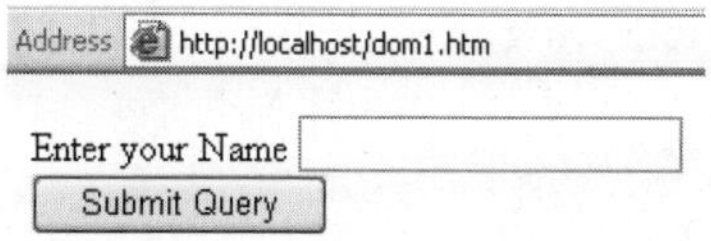

Figure 8-1. *Screen to enter name of the user*

If we enter some name in the input text field and select the Submit button, we will get a welcome message generated from the server as shown in Figure 8-2:

Figure 8-2. *Welcome message displayed on selecting Submit Query button*

Using the GET HTTP method of request

If you want to load data from the server using a GET HTTP request, you have two options: either set the value of the **type** key to GET in the ajax() method (or don't define this key at all as the default request method is GET) or use the $.get() method. Let's try each option in turn now, the first by setting **type** key to GET:

```
$(document).ready(function() {
  $('#submit').click(function () {
    var name = $('.uname').val();
    var data = 'uname=' + name;
    $.ajax({
      type:"GET",
      url:"welcome.php",
      data: data,
      success: function (html) {
        $('#message').html(html);
      }
    });
    return false;
  });
});
```

We can see that except for the **type** key, there is no other modification in the JavaScript file. This **type** key helps when you want to load the data from the server using the GET HTTP request. To make the script on the server retrieve data from the $_GET array, we need to make following alterations in the welcome.php file:

```
<?php
$name = $_GET['uname'];
echo "Welcome ". $name;
?>
```

You can see that instead of the $_POST array, the data will be retrieved from the $_GET array. Let's use the $.get() method now for using GET HTTP request. This method invokes the GET request to the server to fetch data. It executes the script whose URL is specified, along with the parameters passed (if any):

```
$.get(url, parameters, callback)
```

These parameters are as follows:

- `url` is the server-side script that you want to execute via GET method

- `parameters` is key/value pair that you want to be passed to the server-side script for processing

- `callback` is the function that is invoked on completion of the request. It contains two parameters, the first is the response from the server side script and the second parameter is the status of execution

So let's modify the JavaScript that we saw above to now use the `$.get()` method. Your code should look something like this:

```
$(document).ready(function() {
  $('#submit').click(function () {
    var name = $('.uname').val();
    var data = 'uname=' + name;
    $.get(
      "welcome.php",
      data,
      function (html) {
        $('#message').html(html);
      }
    );
    return false;
  });
});
```

You can see that the `$.get()` method invokes the `welcome.php` file on the server and passes `uname=name` to it as a parameter (where `name` stores the name entered by the user) and the callback function displays the response (from the server) by assigning it to the `div` element of id `message`. The output we will get the same as shown in Figure 8-1 and 8-2 above.

Making POST requests

For making POST requests to the server, we make use of the `$.post()` method, which you'll use most generally when you want to make some modification in the information stored on the server. It fetches the data onto the server using `POST HTTP` request. It executes the script whose URL is specified along with the parameters passed (if any). This function also allows a single callback function to be specified that will be executed when the request is complete. Here's the method and parameters:

```
$.post(url, parameters, callback)
```

These parameters are as follows:

- url is the server-side script to which we want to send request (via the POST method)

- parameters is key/value pair that we want to be passed to the server-side script for processing

- callback is the function that is invoked on completion of the request. It contains two parameters, the first is the response from the server side script and the second parameter is the status of execution

The previous JavaScript file can therefore be modified to use the $.post() method as follows:

```
$(document).ready(function() {
  $('#submit').click(function () {
    var name = $('.uname').val();
    var data = 'uname=' + name;
    $.post(
      "welcome.php",
      data,
      function (html) {
        $('#message').html(html);
      }
    );
    return false;
  });
});
```

You can see that the $.post() method invokes the welcome.php file on the server and passes uname=name to it as a parameter (where name stores the name entered by the user) and the callback function displays the response (from the server) by assigning it to the div element of id message. The output that you will get is the same as shown in Figure 8-1 and 8-2.

Finally, please do remember that the server side script welcome.php must access the data from the $_POST array and not from the $_GET array beacuse the request sent this time is via the POST method:

```
<?php
$name = $_POST['uname'];
echo "Welcome ".  $name;
?>
```

8-2. Performing Authentication

Problem

You want to ask the user to enter a name and password in a login form. If the name and password entered by the user matches with the contents in the server side script, your user should get a welcome message, otherwise a message should declare that they are an 'Unauthorized user'.

Solution

Let's create an HTML file that displays two labels: 'Enter your Name' and 'Enter your Password' and two input text fields and a submit button and an empty div element. The HTML file should appear like this:

```
<body>
  <form>
    <label>Enter your Name</label>
    <input type="text"  name="uname" class="uname"/>  <br/>
    <label>Enter your Password</label>
    <input type="password"  name="password" class="passwd"/>  <br/>
    <input type="submit" id="submit"/>
  </form>
  <div id="message"></div>
</body>
```

You can see that the HTML file contains the two input text fields that are assigned class names uname and passwd for the purpose of accessing them via jQuery code. Below the form is an empty div element of id message which we will be using for displaying the response generated by the server side script.

The jQuery code can now appear as shown here:

```
$(document).ready(function() {
  $('#submit').click(function () {
    var name = $('.uname').val();
    var pwd = $('.passwd').val();
    var data='uname='+name+'&password='+pwd;
    $.ajax({
      type:"GET",
      url:"logincheck.php",
      data:data,
      success:function(html) {
        $("#message").html(html);
      }
    });
    return false;
  });
});
```

The script file logincheck.php on the server validates the name and password entered by the user, and looks like this:

```
<?php
$name = trim($_GET['uname']);
$pswd = trim($_GET['password']);
if(($name=="guest") && ($pswd=="jquery"))
  echo "Welcome ".  $name;
else
  echo "Sorry you are not authorized";
?>
```

297

How It Works

We start our jQuery code by attaching a click event to the submit button that is assigned the id `submit`. In this event we retrieve the name and password entered by the user in those input text fields, of class `uname` and `passwd`, and store them in the variables `name` and `pwd` respectively.

We then define a variable `data` that will store `uname=name&password=pwd` where `name` holds the name entered by the user and `pwd` contains the password entered by the user. This `data` variable is sent to the server to be assigned to the script file `logincheck.php` for validating the name and password and accordingly generating response.

In the `ajax()` method, we specify that the method of request that we are going to use is GET and the name of the script file that will be executed on the server is `logincheck.php` and the parameter to be passed to the script file is contained in the string `data`.

After `logincheck.php` processes the data sent to it, it generates the output which is received by the JavaScript file in the parameter `html` of the callback function. The response returned by the script file will be then assigned to the `div` element of id `message` so as to display the response to the user.

Finally, we return `false` in the click event to suppress the default browser click behavior i.e. we want it to take action that is specified via jQuery code and not its default action.

In `logincheck.php` we can see that the parameters sent are accessed through the `$_GET` array i.e. the information stored in the elements `uname` and `password` of the `$_GET` array are retrieved and stored in variables `$name` and `$pswd` respectively. Then, we check if the name entered by the user is `guest` and password is `jquery`, then send back the 'Welcome name' message or else send the 'Sorry you are not authorized' message.

On execution, the HTML file will display a login form to enter name and password. If the name and password entered by the user doesn't matches with what we discussed in the server side script file: logincheck.php, the user gets the message `Sorry you are not authorised` as response from the server as shown in Figure 8-3:

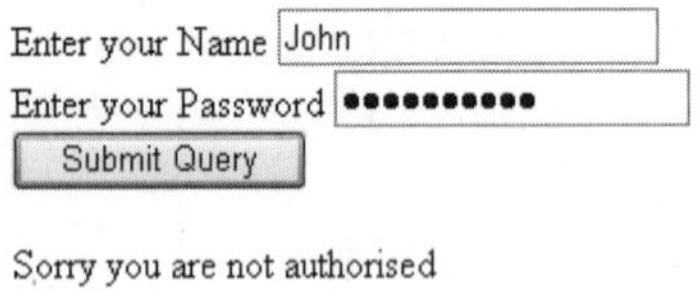

Enter your Name `John`
Enter your Password `••••••••••`
`Submit Query`

Sorry you are not authorised

Figure 8-3. Message displayed when the wrong name or password is entered

If the name and password entered are 'guest' and 'jquery' respectively, the user is greeted with a welcome message as shown in Figure 8-4:

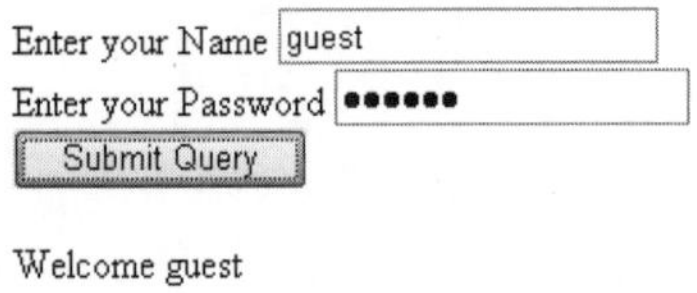

Enter your Name `guest`
Enter your Password `••••••`
`Submit Query`

Welcome guest

Figure 8-4. Welcome message displayed when the correct name and password are entered

8-3. Validating a User Name

Problem

You want to ask the user to enter a name and you want to use a server-side script to confirm that the field is not left blank. If the user does not enter anything in the name field, then he should get an error message.

Solution

Let's start by creating an HTML file that displays a label: 'Enter your Name' and an input text field and a submit button. The HTML file may appear as shown below:

```
<body>
  <form>
    <span class="label">Enter your Name</span>
    <input type="text"  name="uname" class="uname"/>  <span class="error"> </span><br>
    <input type="submit" id="submit"/>
  </form>
</body>
```

You can see here that the input text field is assigned class name uname for the purpose of accessing it via jQuery code. Following the input text field is an empty span element of class error. The text to this span element will be assigned from the server generated response – if the user leaves the input text field blank.

In order to specify a width to the input text field label, and a color to the error message, we need to write some style rules in the style sheet file:

```
.label {float: left; width: 120px; }
.uname {width: 200px; }
.error { color: red; padding-left: 10px; }
#submit { margin-left: 125px; margin-top: 10px;}
```

The jQuery code to invoke the server side script is below, which passes to validateuser.php. the name entered by the user as a parameter, and displays an error message if the name is left blank by the user:

```
$(document).ready(function() {
  $('.error').hide();
  $('#submit').click(function () {
    var name = $('.uname').val();
    var data='uname='+name;
    $.ajax({
      type:"POST",
      url:"validateuser.php",
      data:data,
```

```
    success:function(html) {
      $('.error').show();
      $('.error').text(html);
    }
  });
  return false;
 });
});
```

The script file `validateuser.php` itself, is on the server, and is meant for checking whether the name of the user is not left blank. This code looks like this:

```php
<?php
if($_POST['uname'] == '')
{
  echo "This field cannot be blank";
}
?>
```

Validating user name using a regular expression

In the above solution, the user could enter anything when they were meant to be entering their user name – including symbols. So let's improve the server side script so we will only accept names that consist of alphanumerical and underscore only. The script file `validateuser.php` can be modified as shown here to achieve this for us:

```php
<?php
$name = $_POST['uname'];
if (!eregi("^[a-z0-9_]+$", $name))
{
  echo "Invalid User name";
}
?>
```

How It Works

We start our jQuery code, that you see above, by hiding the span element of class error and attaching a click event to the submit button that is assigned the id submit. We then retrieve the name entered by the user in the input text fields (of class uname) and store it in variable name.

The variable data will store a string, uname=name, where name holds the name entered by the user. This data variable is sent to the server to be assigned to the script file validateuser.php (which is assumed to already exist on the server) for confirming that the name is not left blank.

We invoke the request through the ajax() method, in which we specify that the method of request that we are going to use is POST and that the name of the script file that will be executed on the server is validateuser.php. We also specify that the parameter we're passing to the script file is contained in the string data.

Now the code we have in validateuser.php, after processing the passed data, generates the output which is received by the JavaScript file in the parameter html of the callback function. The response returned by the script file (stored in html) will be then assigned to the span element of class error so as to display the error response to the user, which will be generated by the script file on the server. Before assigning the response `html` to the `span` element of class `error`, however, we first make it visible, because we made it hidden at the beginning of the code. Finally, we return `false` in the click event to suppress the default browser click behavior; that is, we want it to take action that is specified via jQuery code and not its default action.

You can see also how the above PHP script retrieves the name passed via the parameter `data` through the `$_POST` array and, on finding it blank, responds back with an error message `This field cannot be blank` which will be displayed in the span element of class `error`. No response is generated if the name is not blank.

On leaving the input text field blank, if we select the Submit button, we get the error message displayed as shown in Figure 8-5:

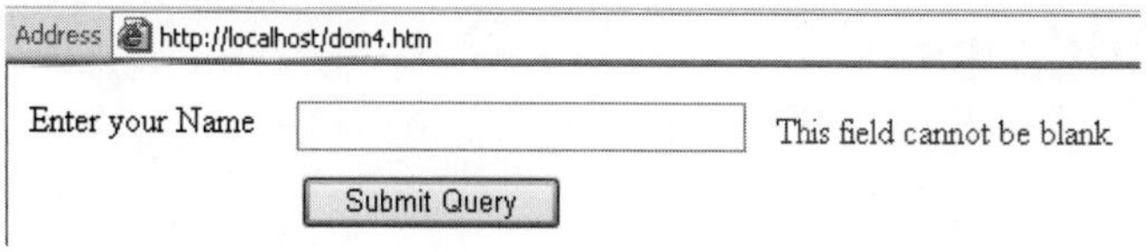

Figure 8-5. Error message displayed when name field is left blank

If a valid name is entered, the name will be accepted without displaying any error message as shown in Figure 8-6:

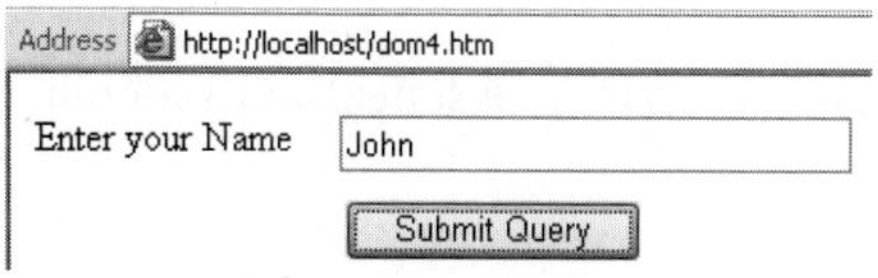

Figure 8-6. Name accepted and no error message displayed

When using a regular expression, you can see that `eregi()` method is used to specify the regular expression for validating the user name. The ^ and $ symbol in regular expression represents 'beginning' and 'at end' respectively. Regular expressions are explained in Chapter 4 – Form Validation.

The '+' symbol means one or more times. Hence the complete regular expression denotes that the name may consists of any character from a to z, number from 0 to 9 and an underscore. These can appear at the beginning or at the end and for one or more times. So if we enter a symbol other than underscore in the user name, we will get the error `Invalid User name` as shown in Figure 8-7:

Figure 8-7. Error message appears on entering an invalid name

No error message will appear and the name will be accepted, if it consists of alphanumerical and underscore only as shown in Figure 8-8:

Figure 8-8. Name accepted and no error message is displayed if it consists of alphanumericals and underscores only

8-4. Validating an Email Address

Problem

You want the user to enter his email address and you want to use a server-side script to confirm that it is a valid email address. This means that it must consist of alphanumericals, no symbols other than - and _ , plus it must contain both symbols . and @. If the email address is invalid, an error message should be displayed to the user.

Solution

Let's make an HTML file that displays a label: 'Enter email address' and an input text field and a submit button. The HTML file may appear as shown below:

```
<body>
  <form>
    <span class="label">Enter email address</span>
    <input type="text" name="emailadd" class="emailadd"/>
    <span class="error"></span><br/>
    <input type="submit" id="submit"/>
  </form>
</body>
```

We can see in above HTML file that the input text field is assigned the class name emailadd for the purpose of accessing it via jQuery code. Following the input text field, is an empty span element of class error. The text to this span element will be assigned from the server generated response, if the user enters an invalid email address.

In order to specify width to the label, input text field and color to the error message, we will make use of the style rules written in the style sheet file from the solution we used in 8-3.

The jQuery code to invoke the server side script: validatemail.php for validating the email address entered by the user is as shown below:

```
$(document).ready(function() {
  $('.error').hide();
  $('#submit').click(function () {
    var em = $('.emailadd').val();
    var data='emailadd='+em;
    $.ajax({
      type:"POST",
      url:"validatemail.php",
      data:data,
      success:function(html) {
        $('.error').show();
        $('.error').text(html);
      }
    });
    return false;
  });
});
```

The script file validatemail.php, on the server, is designed to check whether the email address of the user is valid or not:

```
<?php
$emid = $_POST['emailadd'];
if (!eregi("^[_a-z0-9-]+(\.[_a-z0-9-]+)*@[a-z0-9-]+(\.[a-z0-9-]+)*(\.[a-z]{2,3})$", $emid))
{
  echo "Invalid email address";
}
?>
```

Validating two fields together

Now, let's combine the two recipes together to see how more than one field can be validated through Ajax. We'll make an HTML file that displays two labels: 'Enter user id' and 'Enter email address' and two input text fields for entering a userid and email address respectively, plus a submit button. The HTML file looks like this:

```
<body>
    <form>
        <span class="label">Enter user id</span>
        <input type="text"  name="userid" class="userid"/>
        <span class="usrerror"> </span><br/>
        <span class="label">Enter email address</span>
        <input type="text"  name="emailadd" class="emailadd"/>
        <span class="emerror"> </span><br/>
        <input type="submit" id="submit"/>
    </form>
</body>
```

303

In order to specify a width to the label and input text fields, and a color to the error messages, we'll make use of style rules. So let's write following style rules in the external style sheet file **style.css**:

```
.label {float: left; width: 120px; }
.userid {width: 200px; }
.emailadd {width: 200px; }
.usrerror { color: red; padding-left: 10px; }
.emerror { color: red; padding-left: 10px; }
#submit { margin-left: 125px; margin-top: 10px;}
```

The jQuery code to invoke the server side script **validatedata.php** for validating the userid and email address entered by the user is as shown here:

```
$(document).ready(function() {
  $('.usrerror').hide();
  $('.emerror').hide();
  $('#submit').click(function () {
    var uid = $('.userid').val();
    var em = $('.emailadd').val();
    var data='userid='+uid+'&emailadd='+em;
    $.ajax({
      type:"POST",
      url:"validatedata.php",
      data:data,
      success:function(html) {
        var twomsgs = html.split("\n");
        for ( var i in twomsgs )
        {
          var errmsg = twomsgs[i].split("|");
          if(errmsg[0]=='user')
          {
            $('.usrerror').show();
            $('.usrerror').text(errmsg[1]);
          }
          if(errmsg[0]=='email')
          {
            $('.emerror').show();
            $('.emerror').text(errmsg[1]);
          }
        }
      }
    });
    return false;
  });
});
```

The script file `validatedata.php,` on the server, is used to validate the userid as well as the email address, and looks like this:

```php
<?php
$errors = null;
$name = $_POST['userid'];
if (!eregi("^[a-z0-9_]+$", $name))
{
  $errors .= "user|Invalid User id\n";
}
else
{
  $errors .= "user|\n";
}
$emid = $_POST['emailadd'];
if (!eregi("^[_a-z0-9-]+(\.[_a-z0-9-]+)*@[a-z0-9-]+(\.[a-z0-9-]+)*(\.[a-z]{2,3})$", $emid))
{
  $errors .= "email|Invalid email address\n";
}
else
{
  $errors .= "email|\n";
}
echo $errors;
?>
```

How It Works

We begin by hiding the `span` element of class `error` and attaching a click event to the submit button that is assigned the id `submit`. We then retrieve the email address entered by the user in the input text field (of class `emailadd`) and store it in the variable `em`.

The variable `data` stores a string `emailadd=em` where `em` holds the email address entered by the user. This `data` variable is then sent to the server to be assigned to the script file `validatemail.php` (which is assumed to already exist on the server) for confirming that the email address is valid.

Next we invoke the request through the `ajax()` method, where we specify that the method of request that we are going to use is `POST` and the name of the script file that will be executed on the server is `validatemail.php`. We also assert that the parameter to be passed to the script file is contained in the string `data` (which of course contains the string `emailadd=em`).

Next up, `validatemail.php`, after processing `data` generates the output, received by the JavaScript file in the parameter `html` of the callback function. The response returned by the script file (stored in `html`) will then be assigned to the span element of class `error` to display the error response, which is generated by the script file on the server, to the user. But before assigning the response, here `html`, to the span element of class `error`, we make it visible – because if you note, we made it hidden at the beginning of the code.

We return `false` in the `click` event to suppress the default browser click behavior; we do this because we want to take action that is specified via our jQuery code, and not the default `click` action.

In the PHP script, we can see that `eregi()` method is used to specify the regular expression for validating the email address. The ^ and $ symbols in regular expressions represent 'beginning' and 'at end' respectively. The + symbol means one or more times, and the * symbol means 0 or more times. Let's break down the regular expression to understand it better:

- [_a-z0-9-]+ means that our email address can have _ (underscore), alphabets from a to z, numerical from 0 to 9 and a – (hyphen) for 1 or more time

- (\._a-z0-9-]+)* means the email address can have a . (period) followed by _ (underscore), alphanumerical, - (hyphen) for 0 or more times

- @[a-z0-9-]+ means the email address must have @ symbol followed by alphanumerical and - (hyphen) for 1 or more times

- (\.[a-z]{2,3})$ means the email address must terminate with a . (period) and any alphabet from a to z which should be between 2 to 3 (in count) i.e. after the .(period) we cannot have less than 2 alphabet or more than 3 alphabet

So if we enter the email address that does not match with the regular expression supplied above, we will get the error: 'Invalid email address' as shown in Figure 8-9:

Figure 8-9. Error message displayed if invalid email address is entered

Now if we enter a valid email address that follows the regular expression specified in the server side script file, `validatemail.php`, then it will be accepted without displaying any error message as shown in Figure 8-10:

Figure 8-10. Email address accepted and no error message displayed if it is valid

So in our HTML we have two input text fields assigned class names `userid` and `emailadd` respectively for the purpose of accessing them via jQuery code. After each of these input text fields, we have an empty `span` element that will be used for displaying error messages. The `span` element is to display the error message in case an invalid user id is entered; in which case the `span` element is assigned the class `usrerror` and the `span` element intended for displaying our error message related to invalid email addresses, is assigned the class name: `emailadd`. The text to these `span` elements will be assigned from the response generated by the server side script.

In the style sheet file, we give the class selector `label` a float property set to value `left` so that the next item (the input text field) may appear to its right, and its width property is set to value 120px to give enough space for the label to display. The class selector `userid` has width property set to value 200 px – to define the size of the input text field for entering userid. Similarly, the class selector `emailadd` has width property set to value 200 px – to define the size of the input text field for entering email address. The class selectors `usrerror` and `emerror` have color property set to `red` to highlight them, padding from left is set to 10px to keep the distance from their respective input text field. Finally, the class selector `submit` has margin-left and margin-top property set to 125px and 10px respectively, to set the distance from the left boundary of the browser window and from the input text field, because we want the submit button to appear below the input text fields.

In the jQuery code itself, we begin by hiding the span element of class `usrerror` and `emerror` at the beginning. We will display them when some invalid data is entered. We then attach a click event to the submit button that is assigned the id `submit`.

We next retrieve the user id and email address entered by the user in the input text field (of class `userid` and `emailadd` respectively), and store them in variables `uid` and `em`. To send these to the server, we define a variable `data` that will store a string `userid=uid&emailadd=em` where `uid` and `em` hold the userid and email address entered by the user. This `data` variable is sent to the server to be assigned to the script file `validatedata.php` (which is assumed to already exist on the server) for validating our userid and email address.

We next invoke the request through the `ajax()` method, where we specify that the method of request that we are going to use is `POST` and the name of the script file that will be executed on the server is `validatedata.php`. Meanwhile the parameter to be passed to the script file is contained in the string `data`, which contains the string `userid=uid&emailadd=em`).

The script file (`validatedata.php` on server), after it has processed the passed `data` generates the output which is received by the JavaScript file in the parameter `html` of the callback function.

The response returned by the script file (stored in `html`) is split wherever line feed character ('\n') has occurred (assuming that the two error message generated by the script file are separated by '\n') and the result is stored in variable `twomsgs`. Our variable `twomsgs` is an array of two elements, containing the error message related to userid and the email address itself. We then split each element of the `twomsgs` array (containing data in format: "field|error_message") one by one wherever '|' has occurred, and store the result in another array `errmsg`. The result is that the first element of the `errmsg` array contains either 'user' or 'email' and the errmsg[1] contains the respective error message.

If the `errmsg[0]` contains the string 'user', then we assign the contents of `errmsg[0]` (which contains the error message of userid) to the `span` element of class `usrerror` for displaying the error message to the user. The `span` element of class `usrerror` is made visible first before assigning the error message

If the `errmsg[0]` contains the string 'email', then we assign the contents of `errmsg[1]` (which contains the error message of email address) to the `span` element of class `emerror` for displaying the error message to the user. The span element of class `emerror` is made visible first before assigning the error message. We return 'false' in the click event to suppress the default browser click behavior, because we want it to take action that is specified via our jQuery code and not the default click default action

In the PHP code, we access the userid and email address sent by the Java Script file via parameter `data` containing the information in the format `userid=uid&emailadd=em` through the `$_POST` array (since the data is sent via the HTTP POST request) and store them in variables: `$name` and `$emid` respectively. Then with the help of the `eregi()` method, the regular expressions for both `userid` and the email address are specified as we've seen above. If the `userid` does not match the specified regular expression – meaning the userid is invalid – then we display the text `user|Invalid User id` by assigning it to our `$errors` variable. The contents after the symbol | are designed to be displayed as an error message in the `span` element that exists after the input text fields. If the `userid` is valid (that is, it matches with our regular expression), then the text `user|` is assigned to our `$errors` variable. Thus, no error message is supplied after the |symbol, and so no error message will be displayed for a valid `userid` – just as we wish. The same thing is then repeated with the email address: if it is invalid, then the text `email|Invalid email address` is concatenated to the `$errors` variable.

So, if we enter invalid userid and email address (one that does not match with the regular expressions supplied in the server side script file), we will get the errors shown in Figure 8-11:

Figure 8-11. *Error messages of both userid and email address displayed*

If the `userid` is valid, then its error message will disappear, leaving behind the error message related to email address only as shown in Figure 8-12:

Figure 8-12. *Error message for invalid email address appears*

Finally, if both the `userid` and the email address entered are valid, then they will be accepted without displaying any error message as shown in Figure 8-13:

Figure 8-13. *No Error message appears when both userid and email address are valid*

8-5. Using Auto complete

Problem

You want to ask the user to enter a name in the input text field, so that the moment the user types the first character of a name, a suggestion box will appear that displays all the names beginning with the character typed. You also want the names displayed in the suggestion box to have a hovering effect – so that they become highlighted on moving the mouse pointer over them – and the clicked name to be inserted in the input text field.

Solution

Let's create an HTML file that displays a label: 'Enter userid' and an input text field. Below the input text field, we create two empty div elements that are assigned the class names: `listbox` and `nameslist` respectively. The HTML file may appear as shown below:

```
<body>
    <form>
        <span class="label">Enter user id</span>
        <input type="text"  name="userid" class="userid"/>
        <div class="listbox">
            <div class="nameslist">
            </div>
        </div>
    </form>
</body>
```

The div element of class `listbox` will be used for displaying a box and the div element `nameslist` will be used for displaying the names with hovering effect. We define the style rules to be applied to the two div elements in the style sheet file: style.css as shown here:

```
.listbox {
position: relative;
left: 10px;
margin: 10px;
width: 200px;
background-color: #000;
color: #fff;
border: 2px solid #000;
}

.nameslist {
margin: 0px;
padding: 0px;
list-style:none;
}

.hover {
background-color: cyan;
color: blue;
}
```

The jQuery code to now make our suggestion box appear when the user types the first character in the input text field, and to make the clicked name (in the suggestion box) to appear in the input text field automatically, is as shown here:

```
$(document).ready(function() {
  $('.listbox').hide();
  $('.userid').keyup(function () {
    var uid = $('.userid').val();
    var data='userid='+uid;
```

```
$.ajax({
  type:"POST",
  url:"autocomplete.php",
  data:data,
  success:function(html) {
    $('.listbox').show();
    $('.nameslist').html(html);
    $('li').hover(function(){
      $(this).addClass('hover');
    },function(){
      $(this).removeClass('hover');
    });
    $('li').click(function(){
      $('.userid').val($(this).text());
      $('.listbox').hide();
    });
  }
});
return false;
});
});
```

The script file `autocomplete.php`, on the server, is designed to send the list of names as response, and it should look like this:

```
<?php
echo '<li>Jackub</li>';
echo '<li>Jenny</li>';
echo '<li>Jill</li>';
echo '<li>John</li>';
?>
```

Getting names generated from the database

One drawback in the above server side script is that it only returns the names beginning with character 'j'. Even if the user types any other character, it will still generate names beginning with character 'j'. We want to instead generate names beginning with any character typed by the user. For this, we need to create a database and a table containing hundreds of names in it. I have created a database called `autofill` (using MySQL server) and a table by name `info` in it. The table `info` contains a field `name` and we'll insert a few names in it beginning with characters a to z…

```
<?php
$name = $_POST['userid'];
$connect =
  mysql_connect("localhost", "root", "mce") or die("Please, check your server connection.");
mysql_select_db("autofill");
$query = "SELECT name FROM info WHERE name LIKE '$name%'";
$results = mysql_query($query) or die(mysql_error());
```

```
if($results)
{
  while ($row = mysql_fetch_array($results)) {
    extract($row);
    echo '<li>' . $name. '</li>';
  }
}
?>
```

How It Works

In the style sheet file, the style rule .listbox includes the position property set to value relative so as to assign it a position in relation with its container (which is usually the browser window when not defined). The left property is set to '10px' to make the suggestion box appear at the distance of 10px from the left border of the browser window. The Margin property is set to value 10px to keep the distance of 10px from the input text field above it. The Width property is set to 200px to make the names (that will be displayed in this box) occupy 200px. The background-color and color properties are set to value #000 and #fff respectively to make the background color of the box to turn black, and the names to appear in white color. The border property is set to value 2px solid #000 to make a solid black border of 2px thickness appear around the names displayed in the suggestion box.

Moving along to our jQuery code, we hide the div element of class listbox at the beginning, because we only want to display it when user types a character in the input text field. We attach the keyup() event to the input text field, which is assigned the class name userid, so that its event handling function is fired when the user releases a key on the keyboard

We then retrieve the character typed by the user in the input text field of class userid and store it the variable uid; then define a variable data that will store a string userid=uid where uid holds the first character (of the name) entered by the user. This data variable is sent to the server to be assigned to the script file autocomplete.php (which is assumed to already exist on the server) for displaying the suggestion box to the user.

We invoke the actual request through the ajax() method, where we specify that the method of request that we are going to use is POST and the name of the script file that will be executed on the server is autocomplete.php. The parameter to be passed to the script file is contained in the string data, which itself contains the string userid=uid. The script file (autocomplete.php on server) will, after processing the passed data, generate the output which is received by the JavaScript file in the parameter html of the callback function. We then make the div element of class listbox visible so as to display the names in it. We also assign the response returned by the script file (stored in html) to the div element of class nameslist. The script file will then return few names in the form of list items

We next attach the hover event to the names returned by the script file (which are in form of list items). In this event, we add the style properties defined in the style rule hover to the names (in the form of list items) when the mouse pointer moves over them, making them appear in blue color over the cyan background. We also remove the style properties defined in style rule hover from the names when mouse pointer is moved away from them.

We attach the click event to the names that exist in the form of list items, and make the clicked name appear in the input text field of class: userid and hide the suggestion box containing names. We return false in the click event to suppress the default browser click behavior, because we want it to take action that is specified via jQuery code and not its default action

We can see that the above PHP code just generates a few names in the form of list items to be sent back to the JavaScript file. The script sends a few names beginning with character 'j', assuming that user will enter only this character (as the first character) of course! In order to make this script generate names beginning with any character typed by the user (from a to z), we will need a database with hundreds of names in it. We'll take a look at interacting with such a database soon, but for now, upon execution, we find an input text field with label Enter userid on its left ... and the moment user types a character (any character!), the names sent by the server will be displayed in the form of a suggestion box as shown in Figure 8-14:

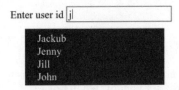

Figure 8-14. *A suggestion box appears on entering a single character in input text field*

We can hover on any name with the mouse pointer. You might also observe that the hovered name gets highlighted as shown in Figure 8-15:

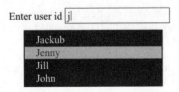

Figure 8-15. *The available options get highlighted on hovering over them*

On clicking on any name, it appears in the input text field as shown in Figure 8-16:

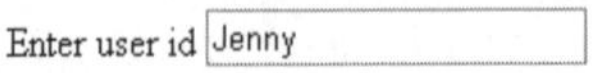

Enter user id Jenny

Figure 8-16. *The clicked option appears in the input text field*

Let's examine the database solution. We start by retrieving the character sent from the JavaScript file (though data parameter) with the help of the $_POST array (since the request was sent via HTTP POST method) and storing it in variable $name. I'll skip the DB connection code, as that will vary according to your setup. The interesting part comes when writing a SQL query to retrieve all the names from the info table that begins with the character stored in $name (which was typed by the user in the input text field).

We execute the SQL query, and the rows returned by the table as the outcome of the query are stored in the $results array. We then retrieve each name stored in the $results array, one by one, using a while loop and sending each nane to the JavaScript file after enclosing them in <li> tags, because of course we want to generate names in the form of list items.

■ **Note** We can also cache the results, and filter on the cache, for each user session.

Now, we get the names beginning with any character that we type in the input text field. So, if we type character 'k', we get all the names beginning with character 'k' as shown in Figure 8-17:

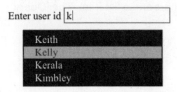

Figure 8-17. *The options in the suggestion box change on the basis of first character typed in input text field*

8-6. Importing HTML

Problem

You want to import some HTML contents from another file into the current web page.

Solution

Let's create an HTML file that contains a paragraph element and a hyper link. We want the contents to be imported only when user selects the hyperlink. The HTML file may appear as shown below:

```
<body>
<p>We are going to organize the Conference on IT on 2nd Feb 2010</p>
<a href="abc.com" class="list">Participants</a>
<div id="message"></div>
</body>
```

The hyperlink is assigned the class name `list` so that we can access it via jQuery code. Below that hyperlink is an empty div element called `message` which we will use for displaying the imported HTML contents. The file from where we want to import HTML contents is named, for example, `namesinfo.htm` and it will likely have the following contents:

```
<p>The list of the persons taking part in conference</p>
<ul>
<li>Jackub</li>
<li>Jenny</li>
<li>Jill</li>
<li>John</li>
</ul>
<p>We wish them All the Best</p>
```

We can see that the above HTML file contains two paragraph elements and a list item. The jQuery code to import the HTML contents is as shown below:

```
$(document).ready(function() {
  $('.list').click(function () {
  $('#message').load('namesinfo.htm');
    return false;
  });
});
```

Importing only desired elements

We can also import only the desired HTML elements from the imported file. So in the following jQuery code, we import only the list items (and no paragraph elements) from the namesinfo.htm file :

```
$(document).ready(function() {
  $('.list').click(function () {
  $('#message').load('namesinfo.htm li');
    return false;
  });
});
```

How It Works

Before we begin understanding the above jQuery code, let's first see what the load() method does, and how it is used in above code. Essentially, this function adds the specified file from the server and returns its HTML contents, like this:

Syntax:

```
.load(url, parameters, callback function)
```

- url is the string defining the location of the server side script file

- parameters contains the data that we want to be passed to the server side script file for some processing

- callback function is the one that is executed when the request succeeds

---

■ **Note** With Internet Explorer, the `load()` method caches the loaded file.

Looking now at our jQuery code, it beings by attaching the click event to the hyper link of class `list` and in its event handling function, we load the HTML contents of the file `namesinfo.htm`, and assign it to the div element `message`. We return `false` in the click event so as to suppress the default browser click behavior, because we want it to take action that is specified via jQuery code and not its default action.

Initially our web page may appear as shown in Figure 8-18 containing a paragraph element and a hyperlink with text: 'Participants':

Figure 8-18. Original web page with hyperlink

On selecting the hyperlink, the contents (consisting of two paragraph elements and list items) gets imported from the `namesinfo.htm` file into the current web page as shown in Figure 8-19:

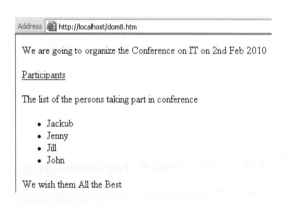

Figure 8-19. Web page after contents imported from other html file

When importing only the desired elements, we can see that in the `load()` method; the `namesinfo.htm` file is followed by `li` to declare that we want to import only the list items present in the file `namesinfo.htm`. As a result, when we select the hyperlink `Participants` we find only the list items imported in the div element `message` as shown in Figure 8-20:

We are going to organize the Conference on IT on 2nd Feb 2010

Participants
- Jackub
- Jenny
- Jill
- John

Figure 8-20. The web page after list items are imported from other HTML file

8-7. Getting JSON Data

Problem

You have a JSON file with some information stored in it. You want to import that information from the JSON file into the current web page asynchronously. The JSON file is a file that contains information regarding 'name' and 'value' pairs.

Solution

We'll start by creating an HTML file that contains a paragraph element, a submit button, and an empty div element. The HTML file should look like this:

```
<body>
<p>For information from JSON file click the button given below :<br>
<input type="submit" id="submit"/>
<div id="message"></div>
</body>
```

The paragraph element just displays a message; our intention is that when the user selects the submit button, the information from the JSON file will be imported and displayed in the div element `message`. For this example, let's assume that the name of the JSON file is `drinkinfo.json` , and that it can have information like this:

```
[
{"optiontext" : "Tea", "optionvalue" : "Tea"},
{"optiontext" : "Coffee", "optionvalue" : "Coffee"},
{"optiontext" : "Juice", "optionvalue" : "Juice"}
]
```

We can see information is stored here in the form of two attributes `optiontext` and `optionvalue`. The jQuery code to import the information from JSON file, and display it in the form of list items in the current web page, is as follows:

```
$(document).ready(function() {
  $('#submit').click(function () {
    $.ajax({
      type:"GET",
      url:"drinkinfo.json",
      dataType:"json",
      success: function (data) {
        var drinks="<ul>";
        $.each(data, function(i,n){
          drinks+="<li>"+n["optiontext"]+"</li>";
        });
        drinks+="</ul>";
        $('#message').append(drinks);
      }
    });
    return false;
  });
});
```

How It Works

In the above jQuery code we attach a **click** event to the submit button that is assigned the id **submit** and we invoke the request through the **ajax()** method, where we specify that the method of request that we are going to use is **GET** and the url of the JSON file on the server is **drinkinfo.json**. We also assert that the value of the **dataType** key is set to **json** to signal that the url contains the data in JSON encoded form.

The information loaded from the JSON file (which is assumed to be present on the server) is returned to the JavaScript file, in the form of response generated from the server, and then received in the parameter **data** of the callback function. Here of course, **data** is an array of objects where each element has the attributes **optiontext** and **optionvalue**, which match the attributes in JSON file we're working with.

We next initialize a variable **drinks** and assign it a tag **<ul>** because we want to send the response to the web page in the form of an unordered list.

The information received in **data** contains two attributes: **optiontext** and **optionvalue,** and we want to return only the contents of the **optiontext** attribute to the web page, in the form of a list. We therefore make use of the **each()** method to parse each object stored in **data**. In the callback function of **each()** method, we use two parameters: **i** and **n** where **i** refers to the index location of the object in **data** and **n** refers to object containing information (in terms of attributes **optiontext** and **optionvalue**). We extract the information in attribute **optiontext** from the **n** object one by one, and nest it in between the **<li>** and **</li>** tags (to make them appear as list items) and concatenate them in the **drinks** variable.

Once that's done, we assign the contents to the **drinks** variable, so it contains the information stored in the **optionvalue** attribute of the objects in our JSON file). This is now in the form of list items and goes to the div element of **message** for display. Finally, we return **false** in the click event to suppress the default browser click behavior, because we want that click event to take action that is specified via our jQuery code rather than its default action. On execution, our web page will initially display the paragraph element and a submit button as shown in Figure 8-21.

For informaton from JSON file click the button given below :
[Submit Query]

Figure 8-21. Initial web page with text message and a Submit button

On clicking the submit button, the information stored in `optionvalue`, in the JSON file is displayed in the form of list items as shown in Figure 8-22:

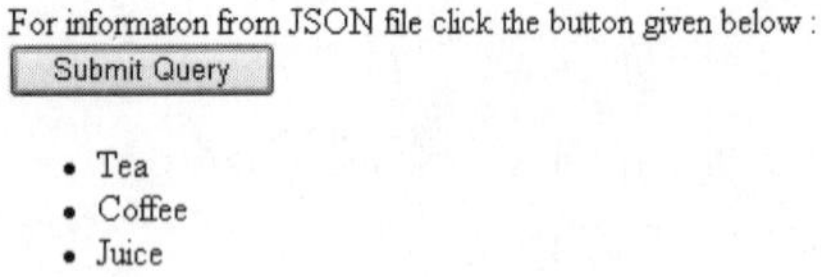

For informaton from JSON file click the button given below :
[Submit Query]

- Tea
- Coffee
- Juice

Figure 8-22. JSON data imported in the form of list items in the web page

We can also simplify the above jQuery code by making use of the `$.getJSON()` method, which is particularly designed for retrieving data from a JSON file. This method makes a `GET` request to the specified url address (on the server), along with its passed parameters, and returns information in the form of JSON encoded data. Its syntax looks like this:

`$.getJSON(url, parameters, callbackfuncton)`

And the parameters are:

- `url` is name of the file along with its address on the server

- `parameters` is a string containing information in the form of name and value pairs to be passed to the url

- `callbackfunction` is the response generated from the server , when the request succeeds

The jQuery code to use the `$.getJSON()` method is as shown here, and it works much the same way as our previous solution but as you can see, leads to some neater code:

```
$(document).ready(function() {
  $('#submit').click(function () {
    $.getJSON('drinkinfo.json', function (data){
      var drinks="<ul>";
      $.each(data, function(i,n){
        drinks+="<li>"+n["optiontext"]+"</li>";
      });
      drinks+="</ul>";
      $('#message').append(drinks);
    });
    return false;
  });
});
```

8-8. Getting XML data

Problem

You have an XML file that contains information about some students. You want to import that information from an XML file into the current web page asynchronously. The XML file contains some user defined tags to organize its information.

Solution

Let's first create an HTML file that contains a paragraph element, a submit button, and an empty div element. The HTML file should look like this:

```
<body>
<p>To see the Names of the students extracted from XML file click the button given below
:</p>
<input type="submit" id="submit"/>
<div id="message"></div>
</body>
```

The paragraph element just displays a message to our user in friendly fashion and, of course, we want the user to select the submit button when they are ready. We then want the information from the XML file to be imported and displayed in the div element message. Assuming the name of XML file be student.xml, its XML content can look like this:

```
<?xml version="1.0" encoding="utf-8" ?>
<school>
  <student>
    <roll>101</roll>
    <name>
      <first-name>Anil</first-name>
      <last-name>Sharma</last-name>
    </name>
    <address>
      <street>
        22/10 Sri Nagar Road
      </street>
      <city>
        Ajmer
      </city>
      <state>
        Rajasthan
      </state>
    </address>
    <marks>
      85
    </marks>
  </student>
```

```
    <student>
    <roll>102</roll>
    <name>
      <first-name>Manoj</first-name>
      <last-name>Arora</last-name>
    </name>
    <address>
      <street>
        H.No 11-B Alwar Gate
      </street>
      <city>
        Ajmer
      </city>
      <state>
        Rajasthan
      </state>
    </address>
    <marks>
      92
    </marks>
  </student>
</school>
```

The jQuery code to import the information stored in the XML tag `first-name` and display it in the form of list items, in the current web page, then looks like this:

```
$(document).ready(function() {
  $('#submit').click(function () {
    $.ajax({
      type:"GET",
      url:"student.xml",
      dataType:"xml",
      success: function (sturec) {
        var stud="<ul>";
        $(sturec).find('student').each(function(){
          var name = $(this).find('first-name').text()
          stud+="<li>"+name+"</li>";
        });
        stud+="</ul>";
        $('#message').append(stud);
      }
    });
    return false;
  });
});
```

Displaying roll, first name and marks from XML file

Before we look at how the code above works, it's worth noticing briefly that we can modify the above jQuery code to retrieve text from other tags very easily – here's some code that retrieves text from `<roll>`, `<first-name>`, `<last-name>` and `<marks>` tags:

```
$(document).ready(function() {
  $('#submit').click(function () {
    $.ajax({
      type:"GET",
      url:"student.xml",
      dataType:"xml",
      success: function (sturec) {
        var stud="<table border='1'>";
        $(sturec).find('student').each(function(){
          var roll = $(this).find('roll').text()
          var fname = $(this).find('first-name').text()
          var lname = $(this).find('last-name').text()
          var marks = $(this).find('marks').text()
          stud+="<tr><td>"+roll+"</td><td>"+fname+" "+lname+"</td><td>"+marks+"</td></tr>";
        });
        stud+="</table>";
        $('#message').append(stud);
      }
    });
    return false;
  });
});
```

How It Works

We start by attaching a click event to the submit button, and we then invoke the request through the `ajax()` method, where we specify that the method of request that we are going to use is GET and the url of the XML file on the server is `student.xml`.We also assert that the value of the `dataType` key is set to `xml` to signal that the url contains the data in XML form.

The information loaded from the XML file (which is assumed to be present on the server) is returned to the JavaScript file in the form of response generated from the server, and is received in the parameter `sturec` of the callback function. Here `sturec` is an array of objects, where each element contains following tags: `<school>`, `<student>`, `<roll>`, `<name>`, `<first-name>`, `<last-name>`, `<address>`, `<street>`, `<city>`, `<state>`, and `<marks>`. These correspond to the tags in XML file of course.

We initialize a variable `stud` and assign it a tag `<ul>` because we want to send the response (the first names of the students) to the web page in the form of unordered list. The information received in `sturec` contains several tags and we want to return only the contents in the `<first-name>` tag to the web page, in the form of list items. So, we first find the `<student>` tag in `sturec` and make use of an `each()` method to parse each student record in `sturec` one by one. In the `<student>` tag, we search for the `<first-name>` tag and its text is retrieved and stored in the `name` variable. The upshot of all this, is that the text in the `<first-name>` tag is extracted for each student, one by one, and that first name is nested inbetween the `<li>` and `</li>` tags , to make them appear as list items, having been concatenated in the `stud` variable. Finally, we assign the contents in the `stud` variable to the div element of `message` for display.

We do as usual return `false` in the click event to suppress the default browser click behavior, because we want that event to take action specified via our jQuery code and not by its default action On execution, our web page will initially display the paragraph element and a submit button as shown in Figure 8-23:

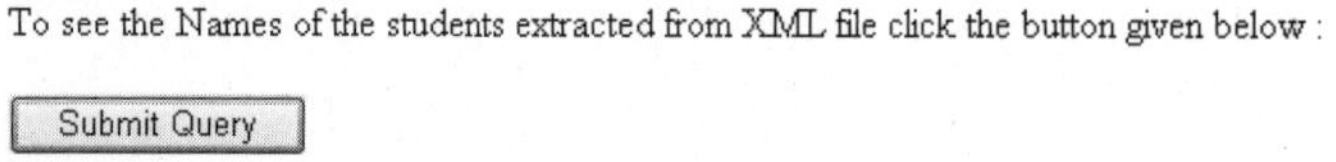

To see the Names of the students extracted from XML file click the button given below :

Figure 8-23. Initial web page with text message and a submit button to import XML contents

On selecting the submit button, the first names of all the students (in the XML file) will be displayed in the form of list items as shown in Figure 8-24:

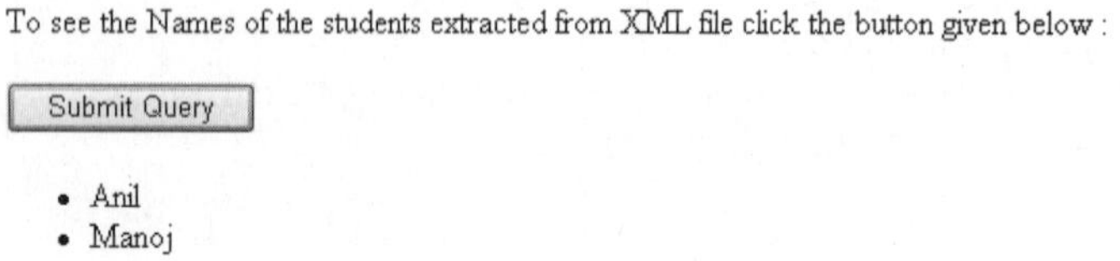

To see the Names of the students extracted from XML file click the button given below :

Submit Query

- Anil
- Manoj

Figure 8-24. The contents of first-name tag of XML file imported in the form of list items

When we modified the code, also, the content text from `<roll>`, `<first-name>`, `<last-name>` and `<marks>` tags is retrieved and nested inside `<tr>` and `<td>` tags so as to make them appear in the form of a table. On execution, we get the roll numbers, first and last names, and marks of all students in the form of table as shown in Figure 8-25:

To see the Names of the students extracted from XML file click the button given below :

| 101 | Anil Sharma | 85 |
| 102 | Manoj Arora | 92 |

Figure 8-25. The tags: roll, first-name, last-name and marks imported from XML file in the form of table

8-9. Paginating tables

Problem

You want to retrieve some student information from a table from a MySQL server, and you want to display them pagewise. You''ve been asked to display five records per page.

Solution

We'll begin by creating an HTML file that contains an empty div element message which will be used to display the table of student records pagewise. The IITML file should appear as shown below:

```
<body>
<div id="message"></div>
</body>
```

The jQuery code to divide the rows of the table in pages, with five rows per page, and to display the respective rows when a page number is clicked, is as shown right here:

```
$(document).ready(function() {
  $.ajax({
    type:"POST",
    url:"getstudrec.php",
    success:function(html) {
      $('#message').html(html);
      var rows=$('table').find('tbody tr').length;
      var no_rec_per_page=5;
      var no_pages=Math.ceil(rows/no_rec_per_page);
      var $pagenumbers=$('<div id="pages"></div>');
      for(i=0;i<no_pages;i++)
      {
        $('<span class="page">'+(i+1)+'</span>').appendTo($pagenumbers);
      }
      $pagenumbers.insertBefore('table');
      $('.page').hover(function(){
        $(this).addClass('hover');
      }, function(){
        $(this).removeClass('hover');
      });

      $('table').find('tbody tr').hide();
      var tr=$('table tbody tr');
      for(var i=0;i<=no_rec_per_page-1;i++)
      {
        $(tr[i]).show();
      }
```

```
        $('span').click(function(event){
          $('table').find('tbody tr').hide();
          for(i=($(this).text()-1)*no_rec_per_page;i<=$(this).text()*no_rec_per_page-1;i++)
          {
            $(tr[i]).show();
          }
        });
      }
    });
});
```

You can see that we are invoking the request through the `ajax()` method, in which we specify that the method of request is POST and the url of the server side script file is `getstudrec.php`. The response generated from that server side script file – all the records of students – is returned to the JavaScript file and received in the parameter `html` of the callback function. We then assign the server response (`html`) to the div element `message` for display. Here is the code four our `getstudrec.php` script file:

```php
<?php
$connect =
  mysql_connect("localhost", "root", "mce") or die("Please, check your server connection.");
mysql_select_db("college");
$query = "SELECT roll, name, marks from student";
$results = mysql_query($query) or die(mysql_error());
if($results)
{
  echo '<table border="1">';
  echo '<thead>';
  echo '<tr><th>Roll</th><th>Name</th><th>Marks</th></tr>';
  echo '</thead>';
  echo '<tbody>';
  while ($row = mysql_fetch_array($results)) {
    extract($row);
    echo '<tr><td>' . $roll . '</td><td>' . $name . '</td><td>' . $marks . '</td></tr>';
  }
  echo '</tbody>';
  echo '</table>';
}
?>
```

And to apply a hover effect to the page numbers, and assign spacing around those page numbers, you need to define two style rules in the style sheet file which may appear as shown below:

```
.hover { background-color: #00f; color: #fff; }
.page{ margin:5px; }
```

How It Works

In the server side script we begin by establishing a connection with the MySQL server and selecting the database college. We then write an SQL query to retrieve roll, name, and marks of all students from the student table. We then execute the SQL query and the rows returned by the table as outcome of the query are stored in the $results array.

The style rule hover contains the background-color and color property set to value '#00f' and '#fff' respectively to turn the background color of the hovered page number to blue, and its foreground color to white. The style rule page contains the margin property set to value 5px to create the space of 5px among page numbers.

In the jQuery code itself, we invoke the request through the ajax() method, where we specify that the method of request that we are going to use is POST and the url of the server side script is getstudrec.php. The response generated by the server side script file is returned to the JavaScript file, and received in the parameter html of the callback function. Note here of course that html is an array of student rows, so it is a table of student records (containing student data regarding their 'Roll', 'Name' and 'Marks').

The response generated by the server side script is assigned to the div element message for displaying the table of records on the screen. To do so, we count the number of rows (tr elements nested inside the tbody element) and store the count in variable rows. We assume that we want to see five rows per page, and we initialize the value of the variable no_rec_per_page equal to 5.

We find out the total count of the page numbers by dividing the total count of the rows by the number of records that we want to see per page. The count of the pages is assigned to variable no_pages and we define a div element pages and assign it to the variable $pagenumbers. Then with the help of a for loop, we create few span elements (equal to the number of pages) that contain the sequence of page numbers (so 1,2,3...) and the span element is assigned the class name page so that the style properties defined in the class selector page be automatically applied to all the page numbers. Finally, all the span elements containing the page numbers are appended to the div element of id pages.

Presentationally, we insert the div element pages that was stored in variable $pagenumbers before the table element, so that the page numbers will appear above the table

In the hover event to the page numbers (span element of class pages) you'll see that we highlight the page numbers when the mouse pointer moves over them by manipulating the properties defined in the style rule hover, which apply to the page numbers. We change their background and foreground color to 'blue' and 'white' respectively in that event – and when there is no hover, we remove those style properties and the associated visual effect.

We then hide all the rows (that is, tr elements nested inside tbody element) of the table, keeping only the column headings visible, and retrieve all the rows of the table and store them in variable tr. As you'll remember, tr is an array containing all the rows of the table, so we use the for loop to display the first five rows of the table.

We attach the click event to the span elements, so that all the page numbers and hidden rows of the table are displayed displayed, leaving only the column headings of course. Finally, we display the rows that actually fall within the page number that the user clicks, using the tr array. On execution, we get first five rows of the table and page numbers at the top as shown in Figure 8-26:

1 2 3

Roll	Name	Marks
101	John	87
102	Naman	90
103	Chirag	85
104	David	92
105	Kelly	81

Figure 8-26. A table displayed along with page numbers at the top

Summary

In this chapter, you saw how AJAX techniques can be applied to bring highly responsive web pages to your user experience. You saw how to display a welcome message, perform dynamic authentication, validate a user name and email address using AJAX techniques to create very responsive user experiences. Then you learned some recipe solutions for importing HTML, getting JSON data and XML data, and how to create table pagination presentations.

In the next chapter, we'll deal with several plugins that help us create recipes without writing jQuery code of our own, such as how to filter on any column of table, how to annotate an image with comments, plus dragging and dropping table rows. You will also discover how to get, serialize, and clear form controls, and how to find the exact position and dimension of elements using the Dimension plugin. You'll use the 3D Image Carousel plugin, a select date with Datepicker plugin, and sort a table with tablesorter plugin. So now you know the next chapter is about plugins, I'll see you there.

CHAPTER 9

■ ■ ■

Using Plugins

The jQuery library is rich enough to perform a wide variety of tasks, but additional functionality can also be added by using different plugins. There is an immense collection of jQuery plugins that we can see at plugins.jquery.com. It's impossible to try all the jQuery plugins in this book, so I have chosen few of them in the following recipes. In this chapter, we will be trying following recipes:

- Filtering on any column of a table with a limit on rows

- Annotating an image with comments

- Dragging and dropping table rows

- Getting, serializing and clearing form controls

- Submitting the form via Ajax

- Finding the exact position and dimension of an element

- Displaying images in a carousel

- Selecting a date with a datepicker

- Sorting tables

9-1. Filtering on any column of a table with a limit on rows

Problem

You have a text box followed by a table and you want to perform filtering on any column of the table to find instances of a specific character in that column. So, in the text box if you type in any character, only those entries that contain that character are shown. Similarly, if any numerical value is entered in the text box, only those entries that match with the value entered in the textbox are displayed. Also you want to limit the number of rows displayed in the table via a drop down list control. That is, you want to limit the number of rows of the tables to 10, 25, 50 or 100 depending on the value chosen from the drop down control.

Solution

I have used the 'DataTables' plugin for this recipe. Let's download its JavaScript file by name: `jquery.dataTables.js` from datatables.net. For this recipe, we need to create a HTML file that displays a `table` element displaying information about the students. The table will display Roll number, Name and Marks of 15 students. We will include the downloaded JavaScript file in the HTML file. The HTML file may appear as shown below:

```
<!DOCTYPE html PUBLIC "-//W3C//DTD XHTML 1.0 Transitional//EN"
        "http://www.w3.org/TR/xhtml1/DTD/xhtml1-transitional.dtd">

<html xmlns="http://www.w3.org/1999/xhtml" xml:lang="en" lang="en">
  <head>
        <meta http-equiv="Content-Type" content="text/html; charset=utf-8"/>
        <title>JQuery Examples</title>
        <script src="jquery-1[1].3.2.js" type="text/javascript"></script>
        <script src="jquery.dataTables.js" type="text/javascript"></script>
        <script src="d1.js" type="text/javascript"></script>

  </head>
</head>
<body>
<table border="1" class="studrec">
<thead>
<tr><th>Roll</th><th>Name</th><th>Marks</th></tr>
</thead>
<tbody>
<tr><td>101</td><td>John</td><td>87</td></tr>
<tr><td>102</td><td>Naman</td><td>90</td></tr>
<tr><td>103</td><td>Chirag</td><td>85</td></tr>
<tr><td>104</td><td>David</td><td>92</td></tr>
<tr><td>105</td><td>Kelly</td><td>81</td></tr>
<tr><td>106</td><td>Charles</td><td>77</td></tr>
<tr><td>107</td><td>Jerry</td><td>91</td></tr>
<tr><td>108</td><td>Beth</td><td>75</td></tr>
<tr><td>109</td><td>Caroline</td><td>82</td></tr>
<tr><td>110</td><td>Hanen</td><td>71</td></tr>
<tr><td>111</td><td>Douglas</td><td>57</td></tr>
<tr><td>112</td><td>Tim</td><td>86</td></tr>
<tr><td>113</td><td>Michael</td><td>68</td></tr>
<tr><td>114</td><td>Kimbley</td><td>88</td></tr>
<tr><td>115</td><td>Christina</td><td>72</td></tr>
</tbody>
</table>
</body>
</html>
```

To apply the filtering to the above table and limit the number of rows displayed, the jQuery code may appear as shown below:

```
$(document).ready(function() {
  $('.studrec').dataTable();
});
```

How It Works

We can see that the `dataTable()` method (from the JavaScript file `jquery.dataTables.js`) will be applied to the table element of class 'studrec'. The output may appear as shown in Figure 9-1.

Show [10 ▼] entries

Search: [   ]

Roll	Name	Marks
101	John	87
102	Naman	90
103	Chirag	85
104	David	92
105	Kelly	81
106	Charles	77
107	Jerry	91
108	Beth	75
109	Caroline	82
110	Hanen	71

Showing 1 to 10 of 15 entries

Figure 9-1. Displaying 10 rows of the table

We can see that a drop down list control and a text box appear before the table and a label appears after the table. The label represents the number of rows (of the table) being displayed. The drop down list control displays four options: 10, 25, 50 and 100 to decide the number of rows of the table to be displayed as shown in Figure 9-2.

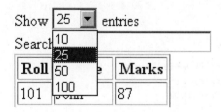

Figure 9-2. Options available in drop down list control

If we type character 'c' in the textbox, all the names of the students having the character 'C' or 'c' (anywhere – in the beginning or in middle) will be displayed as shown in Figure 9-3.

Show 10 ▼ entries

Search: c

Roll	Name	Marks
103	Chirag	85
106	Charles	77
109	Caroline	82
113	Michael	68
115	Christina	72

Showing 1 to 5 of 5 entries (filtered from 15 total entries)

Figure 9-3. Names having character 'c' are displayed

Similarly, we can enter any numerical value in the textbox to see the rows with the specified roll number or marks.

9-2. Annotating an image with comments

Problem

You start with a large image. The idea is that when you scroll the mouse pointer over different regions of the image, annotations appear automatically over the important regions of the image telling the user what that region of image irepresents.

Solution

I have used the 'jQuery Image Annotation' plugin for this recipe. Let's download its JavaScript file, `jquery.annotate.js` along with its CSS style sheet file named `annotation.css` from blog.flipbit.co.uk/2009/03/jquery-image-annotation-plugin.html. Let's make an HTML file that displays an image `shopcart.jpg` (any image). The HTML file includes the downloaded JavaScript file and links to the style sheet file. The HTML file may appear as shown below:

```
<head>
  <meta http-equiv="Content-Type" content="text/html; charset=utf-8"/>
  <title>JQuery Examples</title>
  <link rel="stylesheet" href="annotation.css" type="text/css" media="screen" />
  <script src="jquery-1[1].3.2.js" type="text/javascript"></script>
  <script src="jquery.annotate.js" type="text/javascript"></script>
  <script src="d1.js" type="text/javascript"></script>
  </head>
<body>
```

```
<img src="shopcart.jpg" class="shop"/>
</body>
```

Let's write the jQuery code to make the annotations appear at the specific places on the image along with text that represents what those places on the image are meant for. The jQuery code may appear as shown below:

d1.js
```
$(document).ready(function() {
  $('.shop').annotateImage({
    editable: true,
    useAjax: false,
    notes: [ { "top": 60,
               "left": 300,
               "width": 50,
               "height": 50,
               "text": "Header",
               "id": "h1",
               "editable": false },
             { "top": 200,
               "left": 600,
               "width": 50,
               "height": 50,
               "text": "Picture of Product",
               "id": "s1",
               "editable": false },
             { "top": 200,
               "left": 150,
               "width": 50,
               "height": 50,
               "text": "Menu",
               "id": "m1",
               "editable": false } ]
  });
});
```

How It Works

In the above code, we have created three annotations with width and height of 50px each at the specific places on the image dictated by the value entered in the 'top' and 'left' attributes. The three annotations are assigned text as "Header", "Picture of Product" and "Menu" respectively to define what the three places on the image represent. Also, these annotations are assigned unique id's as h1, s1and m1 respectively. The editable attribute is set to **false** as we don't want the user to edit the text. Initially, the **shopcart.jpg** file (without application of jQuery code) may appear as shown in Figure 9-4.

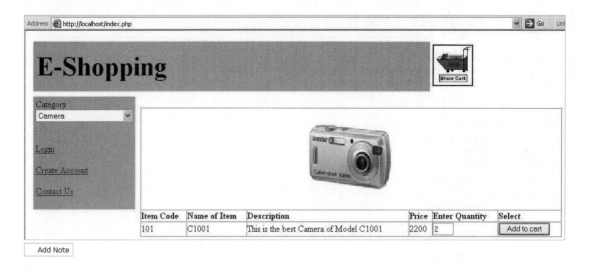

Figure 9-4. *Original image without annotations*

Upon application of the jQuery code, we find three regions marked with rectangles on the image as shown in Figure 9-5. These rectangles indicate that these regions of the image are annotated.

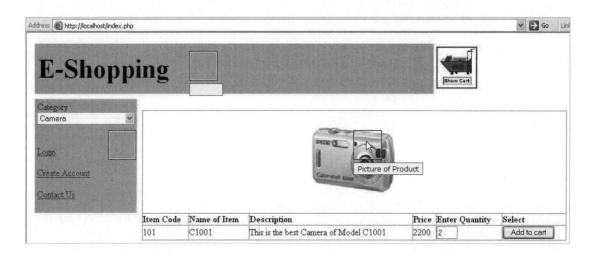

Figure 9-5. *Image with annotations applied*

We can see the text 'Picture of the Product' displayed when the mouse pointer is moved over the marked region.

9-3. Dragging and dropping table rows

Problem

You have a table that displays information and you want the user to be able to drag and drop any row (in any order).

Solution

I will use the 'Table Drag and Drop JQuery' plugin for this recipe. Let's download its JavaScript file `jquery.tablednd_0_5.js` from isocra.com/2008/02/table-drag-and-drop-jquery-plugin/. Let's create an HTML file that includes the downloaded JavaScript file and that contains a table element to display Roll number, Name and Marks of 15 students. The HTML file may appear as shown below:

```
<head>
  <meta http-equiv="Content-Type" content="text/html; charset=utf-8"/>
  <title>JQuery Examples</title>
  <script src="jquery-1[1].3.2.js" type="text/javascript"></script>
  <script src="jquery.tablednd_0_5.js" type="text/javascript"></script>
  <script src="d1.js" type="text/javascript"></script>
  </head>
<body>
<table border="1" class="studrec">
<thead>
<tr><th>Roll</th><th>Name</th><th>Marks</th></tr>
</thead>
<tbody>
<tr><td>101</td><td>John</td><td>87</td></tr>
<tr><td>102</td><td>Naman</td><td>90</td></tr>
<tr><td>103</td><td>Chirag</td><td>85</td></tr>
<tr><td>104</td><td>David</td><td>92</td></tr>
<tr><td>105</td><td>Kelly</td><td>81</td></tr>
<tr><td>106</td><td>Charles</td><td>77</td></tr>
<tr><td>107</td><td>Jerry</td><td>91</td></tr>
<tr><td>108</td><td>Beth</td><td>75</td></tr>
<tr><td>109</td><td>Caroline</td><td>82</td></tr>
<tr><td>110</td><td>Hanen</td><td>71</td></tr>
<tr><td>111</td><td>Douglas</td><td>57</td></tr>
<tr><td>112</td><td>Tim</td><td>86</td></tr>
<tr><td>113</td><td>Michael</td><td>68</td></tr>
<tr><td>114</td><td>Kimbley</td><td>88</td></tr>
<tr><td>115</td><td>Christina</td><td>72</td></tr>
</tbody>
</table>
</body>
</html>
```

The jQuery code to invoke the table drag and drop plugin is shown below:

```
$(document).ready(function() {
  $('.studrec').tableDnD();
});
```

How It Works

We can see that the method `tableDnD()` is invoked from the JavaScript file `jquery.tablednd_0_5.js` and is applied on the table element of class `studrec`. Initially, we get a table as shown in Figure 9-6.

Roll	Name	Marks
101	John	87
102	Naman	90
103	Chirag	85
104	David	92
105	Kelly	81
106	Charles	77
107	Jerry	91
108	Beth	75
109	Caroline	82
110	Hanen	71
111	Douglas	57
112	Tim	86
113	Michael	68
114	Kimbley	88
115	Christina	72

Figure 9-6. Table with original placement of rows

We can click on any row and drag it over any other row to shift it. The first row is clicked and dropped after fifth row in Figure 9-7.

Roll	Name	Marks
102	Naman	90
103	Chirag	85
104	David	92
105	Kelly	81
101	John	87
106	Charles	77
107	Jerry	91
108	Beth	75
109	Caroline	82
110	Hanen	71
111	Douglas	57
112	Tim	86
113	Michael	68
114	Kimbley	88
115	Christina	72

Figure 9-7. Table rows after dragging and dropping first row after fifth row

9-4. Getting, serializing and clearing form controls

Problem

You have a form with controls and you want to retrieve the values entered in those controls, serialize them and also want to clear the controls upon clicking the respective buttons.

Solution

I have used 'Form plugin' for this recipe. Let's download its JavaScript file `jquery.form.js` from jquery.com/plugins/project/form. Let's create an HTML file that contains a form with two controls to enter the userid and email address. The HTML file will include the downloaded JavaScript file and may appear as shown below:

```
<!DOCTYPE html PUBLIC "-//W3C//DTD XHTML 1.0 Transitional//EN"
"http://www.w3.org/TR/xhtml1/DTD/xhtml1-transitional.dtd">
<html xmlns="http://www.w3.org/1999/xhtml" xml:lang="en" lang="en">
  <head>
  <meta http-equiv="Content-Type" content="text/html; charset=utf-8"/>
  <title>JQuery Examples</title>
  <link rel="stylesheet" href="style.css" type="text/css" media="screen" />
  <script src="jquery-1[1].3.2.js" type="text/javascript"></script>
```

```
    <script src="jquery.form.js" type="text/javascript"></script>
    <script src="d1.js" type="text/javascript"></script>
    </head>
<body>
<form id="myForm">
<div><span class="label">User Id *</span><input type="text"  class="infobox" name="userid"
/><span class="error"> This field cannot be blank</span></div>
<div><span class="label">Email address *</span><input type="text" class="infobox"
name="emailid" /><span class="error"> Invalid Email address </span></div>
<input class="submit" type="submit" value="Submit"/>
<input class="clear" type="submit" value="Clear Form"/>
</form>
</body>
</html>
```

The form is assigned an id named 'myForm' so that it can be accessed via jQuery code. The label messages: User Id * and Email address * are enclosed in span elements that are assigned the class names label. The input text fields are assigned the class name infobox and the error messages 'This field cannot be blank' and 'Invalid Email address' respectively are stored as a span element of class error.

The reasons for assigning the classes to all three items: label, input text field and error message is to automatically apply the properties defined in the class selectors .label, .infobox, and .error (defined in the style sheet style.css). The two buttons with value 'Submit' and 'Clear Form' are assigned the class names submit; and clear to apply the properties defined in the class selectors .submit and .clear. The controls are nested inside a div element so as to apply some spacing among them. The style sheet with the respective class selectors may appear as shown below:

```
.label {float: left; width: 120px; }
.infobox {width: 200px; }
.error { color: red; padding-left: 10px; }
.submit { margin-left: 50px; margin-top: 10px;}
.clear { margin-left: 125px; margin-top: 10px;}
div{padding: 5px; }
```

The class selector .label contains the float property set to left so as to make the label appear on its left (creating space for the input text field to appear on its right) and the width property is set to 120px to define the width that the label can consume. The class selector .infobox contains the width property set to 200px to specify the width of the input text fields and the class selector .error is used to assign red color to the error messages and to make the error message appear at a distance of 10px from the element on its left. The class selectors .submit and .clear contain the margin-left and margin-top property set to different values to place the two buttons 'Submit' and 'Clear Form' at the proper distance from the left border of the browser window and the element above it. The type selector div has the padding property set to 5px to create some space among the two div elements where each div element contains a combination of label, input text field and error message.

The jQuery code to retrieve and serialize the data entered in the two controls of the form is as shown below:

```
$(document).ready(function() {
  $('.error').hide();
  $('.submit').click(function(event){
    alert( $('#myForm *').fieldValue());
    alert( $('#myForm *').fieldSerialize());
    event.preventDefault();
  });
  $('.clear').click(function(event){
    $('#myForm').clearForm();
    event.preventDefault();
  });
});
```

In the above jQuery code, we have used three methods: `fieldValue()`, `fieldSerialize()` and `clearForm()`. Let's understand what these methods do:

fieldValue()

The `fieldValue()` method collects the data entered in all of the controls and returns them as an array of strings. Only the contents of controls that are active (controls that have 'name' attributes and are not disabled) are retrieved by this method.

fieldSerialize()

The `fieldSerialize()` method retrieves the contents in the controls and returns them after encoding them in the form of a query string. The query string is encoded in the format:
`control1=value1&control2=value2.....`

clearForm()

The `clearForm()` method clears the values entered in any control of the form.

How It Works

In the above jQuery code, we initially hide all the errors. When the Submit button, is clicked, contents of all the controls are retrieved and displayed in the form of an array of strings (making use of `fieldValue()` method) as shown in Figure 9-8.

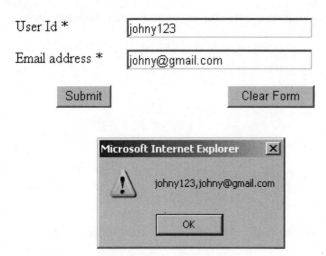

Figure 9-8. *The data entered in the controls displayed in the form of array of strings*

Also, the contents in the controls are serialized and displayed with the help of the `fieldSerialize()` method. We can see the data entered in the controls is encoded in the form of a query string and displayed as shown in Figure 9-9.

Figure 9-9. *The data entered in the controls displayed in serialized form.*

On selecting the 'Clear Form' button, the data entered in the controls will be erased.

9-5. Submitting the Form via Ajax

Problem

You have a form with controls and you want to submit the form as an AJAX request.

Solution

I have again used 'Form plugin' for this recipe. It can be downloaded under **jquery.form.js** from jquery.com/plugins/project/form. Let's make an HTML file that contains a form with two controls to enter the userid and email address. The HTML file will include the downloaded JavaScript file and may appear as shown below:

```
<!DOCTYPE html PUBLIC "-//W3C//DTD XHTML 1.0 Transitional//EN"
"http://www.w3.org/TR/xhtml1/DTD/xhtml1-transitional.dtd">
<html xmlns="http://www.w3.org/1999/xhtml" xml:lang="en" lang="en">
  <head>
  <meta http-equiv="Content-Type" content="text/html; charset=utf-8"/>
  <title>JQuery Examples</title>
  <link rel="stylesheet" href="style.css" type="text/css" media="screen" />
  <script src="jquery-1[1].3.2.js" type="text/javascript"></script>
  <script src="jquery.form.js" type="text/javascript"></script>
  <script src="d1.js" type="text/javascript"></script>
  </head>
<body>
<form id="myForm">
<div><span class="label">User Id *</span><input type="text"  class="infobox" name="userid"
/><span class="error"> This field cannot be blank</span></div>
<div><span class="label">Email address *</span><input type="text" class="infobox"
name="emailid" /><span class="error"> Invalid Email address </span></div>
<input class="submit" type="submit" value="Submit"/>
<input class="clear" type="submit" value="Clear Form"/>
</form>
</body>
</html>
```

The style sheet with the respective class selectors may appear as shown below:

```
.label {float: left; width: 120px; }
.infobox {width: 200px; }
.error { color: red; padding-left: 10px; }
.submit { margin-left: 50px; margin-top: 10px;}
.clear { margin-left: 125px; margin-top: 10px;}
div{padding: 5px; }
```

The jQuery code to submit the form as an AJAX request is as shown below:

```
$(document).ready(function() {
  $('.error').hide();
  $('#myForm').ajaxForm(function() {
    alert("Thank you for your comment!");
  });
});
```

339

Performing validation before submitting the form (in form of AJAX request)

Let's validate the two controls userid and email address in the above form before submitting the form. We must write the validation function that confirms that the userid control is not left blank and that email address contains the necessary '@' and '.' symbols. The HTML file is a bit modified as shown below:

```
<body>
<form id="myForm">
<div><span class="label">User Id *</span><input type="text"  class="usrinfo" name="userid"
/><span class="usrerror"> This field cannot be blank</span></div>
<div><span class="label">Email address *</span><input type="text" class="emailinfo"
name="emailid" /><span class="emailerror">Invalid Email address</span></div>
<input class="submit" type="submit" value="Submit"/>
</form>
</body>
```

The style sheet containing class selectors (to automatically apply the properties defined in them to different controls) may appear as shown below:

```
.label {float: left; width: 120px; }
.usrinfo {width: 200px; }
.emailinfo {width: 200px; }
.usrerror { color: red; padding-left: 10px; }
.emailerror { color: red; padding-left: 10px; }
.submit { margin-left: 125px; margin-top: 10px;}
div{padding: 5px; }
```

The jQuery code that validates the controls of the form and submits the form in AJAX is as shown below:

```
$(document).ready(function() {
  $('.usrerror').hide();
  $('.emailerror').hide();

  function validate_data()
  {
    var data=$('.usrinfo').val();
    var len=data.length;
    var pattern= new RegExp(/^[\w-]+(\.[\w-]+)*@([\w-]+\.)+[a-zA-Z]+$/);
    var flag=true;
    if(len<1)
    {
      $('.usrerror').show();
      flag=false;
    }
    else
    {
      $('.usrerror').hide();
    }
    var email=$('.emailinfo').val();
```

```
if(pattern.test(email))
{
  $('.emailerror').hide();
}
else
{
  $('.emailerror').show();
  flag=false;
}
if(flag==false)
{
  return false;
}
else
{
  $('.usrinfo').val("");
  $('.emailinfo').val("");
}
};

$('#myForm').ajaxForm({
  beforeSubmit: validate_data,
  success: function(){
    alert("Thank you for your comment!");
  }
});
});
```

How It Works

The form is assigned an id `myForm` sothat it may be accessed via jQuery code. The label messages `User Id` `*` and `Email address *` are enclosed in span elements that are assigned the class name `label`. The input text fields are assigned the class name `infobox` and the error messages 'This field cannot be blank' and 'Invalid Email address' respectively are stored as a span element of class `error`.

The reason for assigning the classes to all three items (label, input text field and error message) is to automatically apply the properties defined in the class selectors `.label`, `.infobox`, and `.error` (defined in the style `sheet style.css`). The two buttons 'Submit' and 'Clear Form' are assigned the class names: `submit;` and `clear` to apply the properties defined in the class selectors `.submit` and `.clear`. The controls are nested inside a div element so as to apply some spacing among them.

We can see that the `.ajaxForm()` method is used to submit the form in AJAX (without the need of refreshing the current page). With the help of its `beforeSubmit` option, the `validate_data` function is invoked to validate the contents in the two controls (userid and email address). The success option of the method will display a Thanks message via the `alert()` method if the form is successfully submitted.

This method submits the form as an AJAX request i.e. the form is submitted without having to refresh the page.

Here is the syntax:

```
.ajaxForm({
target:,
beforeSubmit:,
success:
});
```

where `target` refers to the element that we want to be updated by the server response. The `beforeSubmit` option performs the tasks before the form is submitted and the success option performs the tasks when the form is successfully submitted.

We are displaying an alert message saying: 'Thank you for your comment!' to the user on successful submission of the form (in the form of an AJAX request). After entering some data in the two controls, if we select the 'Submit' button, the alert message will be displayed as shown in Figure 9-10.

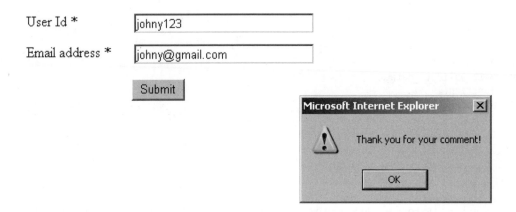

Figure 9-10. Alert message displayed on successful form submission

---

■ **Note** The Clear Form button was removed from the HTML form (above) as it was not required.

In the second solution, the form is assigned an id `myForm` sothat it may be accessedt via jQuery code. The label messages `User Id *` and `Email address *` are enclosed in span elements that are assigned the class name `label`. The input text fields are assigned the class names 'usrinfo' and `emailinfo` to access their contents individually for validation. The respective error messages 'This field cannot be blank' and 'Invalid Email address' are stored as a span element with class names `usrerror` and `emailerror` so that only the error message of the related control will be displayed. The controls are nested inside a div element so as to apply some spacing among them.

The `validate_data` method retrieves the userid entered in the input text field of class `usrinfo` and computes its length. If the length of the userid is less than 1 i.e. nothing is entered in the input text field, then the error message of class `usrerror` will be displayed and the value of the variable `flag` is set to `false` so that the form cannot be submitted. Similarly, the email address entered in the input text field of class `emailinfo` is retrieved and tested to see if it matches the regular expression `'/^[\w-]+(\.[\w-]+)*@([\w-]+\.)+[a-zA-Z]+$/'`. If the email address doesn't match with the regular expression supplied, the error message related to the email address of class `emailerror` is displayed and the variable `flag` is set to `false` so that the form cannot be submitted.

If the userid is not left blank and a valid email address is entered, then the `validate_data()` method will return true (by default) and the form will be submitted. We clear the fields to show that the data is accepted and submitted. When both of the fields, userid and email address, are left blank, we get the two respective error messages as shown in Figure 9-11.

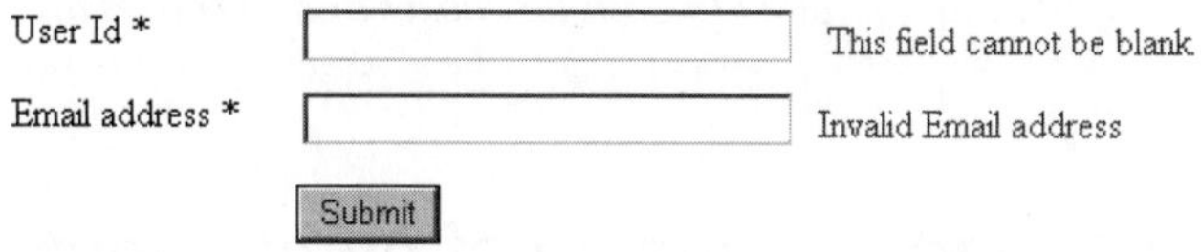

Figure 9-11. Error message if both text box left blank

If an invalid email address is entered, then the error message displaying 'Invalid Email address' will be displayed as shown in Figure 9-12.

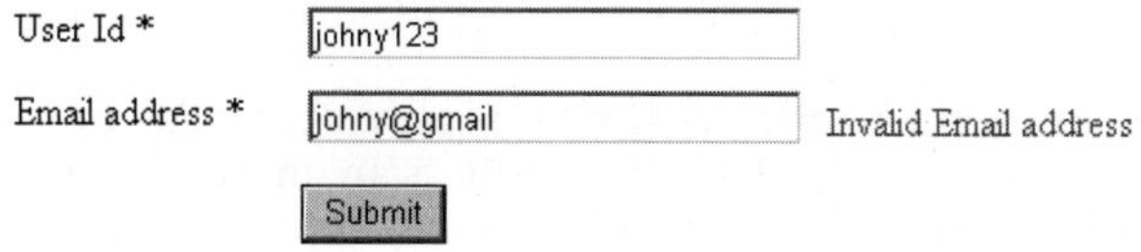

Figure 9-12. Error message: Invalid Email Address appears

If the data in both of the controls are valid, the form is successfully submitted in the form of an AJAX request and a message: 'Thank you for your comment!' will be displayed as shown in Figure 9-13.

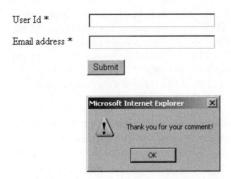

Figure 9-13. *Alert message displayed in case the valid data is entered in both text boxes and the boxes are cleared to show that the data is submitted*

9-6. Finding the exact position and dimension of an element

Problem

You have an image and you want to know its width, height, inner width, offsets etc.

Solution

I have used 'Dimension' plugin for this recipe. Let's download its JavaScript file `jquery.dimension.js` from plugins.jquery.com/project/dimensions. Let's make an HTML file that displays an image whose dimensions we want to find. The file includes the downloaded JavaScript file and may appear as shown below:

```
<!DOCTYPE html PUBLIC "-//W3C//DTD XHTML 1.0 Transitional//EN"
"http://www.w3.org/TR/xhtml1/DTD/xhtml1-transitional.dtd">
<html xmlns="http://www.w3.org/1999/xhtml" xml:lang="en" lang="en">
  <head>
  <meta http-equiv="Content-Type" content="text/html; charset=utf-8"/>
  <title>JQuery Examples</title>
  <link rel="stylesheet" href="style.css" type="text/css" media="screen" />
  <script src="jquery-1[1].3.2.js" type="text/javascript"></script>
  <script src="jquery.dimensions.js" type="text/javascript"></script>
  <script src="d1.js" type="text/javascript"></script>
  </head>
```

```
<body>
<div class="pic">
<img src="cell.jpg"/>
</div>
</body>
</html>
```

We can see that the image is nested inside the div element of class `pic` so that we can apply desired style properties to it via a class selector. The class selector defined in the style sheet file may appear as shown below:

```
.pic {
height: 150px;
width: 100px;
margin: 5px;
border: 5px solid #000000;
overflow: auto;
}
```

We can see that the class selector `.pic` contains the height, width and margin property set to the values 150px, 100px and 5 px respectively (to make the image appear within the given area while keeping some space from the boundary) and also the border property is set to display a solid black border of 5px thickness around the image. The overflow property is set to `auto` to make the scroll bars appear if the image is larger than the specified width and height.

The jQuery code to display the width, height and innerwidth of the image is as shown below:

```
$(document).ready(function() {
  alert("Width: " +$('.pic').width()+" Height :"+$('.pic').height()
    +" Inner Width :"+$('.pic').innerWidth());
});
```

Finding offset and position

Before we find out the offset and position of the image within its parent element (body element if none), let's take a brief look at the offset() and position() methods.

offset()

The `offset()` method helps in locating the top and left positions of an element anywhere in the page regardless of the value of its 'position' and 'overflow' property i.e. whether the position property is set to static, relative or absolute or the overflow property is set to `auto`.

position()

This method returns the position of the element in relation to its offset parent. It has two attributes, `top` and `left`, to return the top and left positions of the element. The offset parent means the first element in the wrapped set (closest ancestor).

In the following jQuery code, we will be also be scrolling the image. The two methods to scroll the element are: `scrollTop()` and `scrollLeft()` :

scrollTop() and scrollLeft()

These two methods scroll the element to the top and left with the specified value; they work for both visible and hidden elements.

The jQuery code to display the offset of the image (i.e. its position in relation to the window origin or body element) and its position in relation to its offset parent is as shown below:

```
$(document).ready(function() {
  alert("Offset top: " +$('.pic').offset().top+", Offset left : "
    +$('.pic').offset().left+", Position top: "+$('.pic').position().top+", Position left: "
    +$('.pic').position().left);
  $('.pic').scrollTop(50);
  $('.pic').scrollLeft(50);
});
```

How It Works

Let's have a look at the different methods for Dimension plugin:

- `width()` It returns the width of window, the document object or element.

- `height()` It returns the height of window, the document object or element.

- `innerWidth()` & `innerHeight()` It returns the width and height of the element including the padding space applied to it.

- `outerWidth()` & `outerHeight()` It returns the width and height of the element including the padding space as well as borders applied to it.

With the help of the alert message, we display the assigned width and height to the image along with its inner width (excluding the space consumed by scrollbars and border) as shown in Figure 9-14.

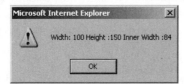

Figure 9-14. Width, Height and Inner width that is assigned to the image is displayed

When finding the offset and position, from the output shown in Figure 9-15, we can see that the image is located at a distance of 20px (from top) and 15 px (from left) from the window origin and at 0 px in relation to the offset parent.

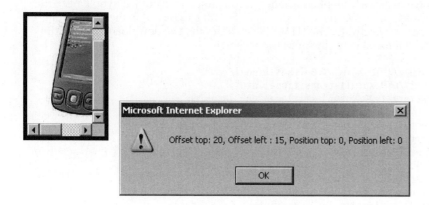

Figure 9-15. Offset and Position of the image is displayed

Also on selecting the OK button, the image will be scrolled to the top and left side by 50px respectively (with the help of the `scrollTop()` and `scrollLeft()` methods) as shown in Figure 9-16.

Figure 9-16. Image after being scrolled up and to the left

9-7. Displaying images in a carousel

Problem

You want some images to be arranged and displayed in a 3D circle along with left and right arrows. When the mouse is moved over the left arrow, you want the images to scroll in a counter-clockwise direction and when the mouse pointer is moved over the right arrow, the image should rotate in a clockwise direction. Also when any image is selected it should be zoomed.

Solution

I have used the '3D Image carousel' plugin for this recipe. Let's download its JavaScript files `jquery.carousel3d.js` and `Tween.js` along with its CSS style sheet file (from the documentation). All files comes in a single zip file downloadable from plugins.jquery.com/project/carousel3d (you'll need the images folder as well). Let's make an HTML file that displays a few images nested in the div elements of ids `carousel` and `holder_images` respectively. The HTML file includes the two downloaded JavaScript files and links to the style sheet file and may appear as shown below:

```
<!DOCTYPE html PUBLIC "-//W3C//DTD XHTML 1.0 Transitional//EN"
"http://www.w3.org/TR/xhtml1/DTD/xhtml1-transitional.dtd">
<html xmlns="http://www.w3.org/1999/xhtml" xml:lang="en" lang="en">
  <head>
  <meta http-equiv="Content-Type" content="text/html; charset=utf-8"/>
  <title>JQuery Examples</title>
  <link rel="stylesheet" href="style.css" type="text/css" media="screen" />
  <script src="jquery-1[1].3.2.js" type="text/javascript"></script>
  <script type="text/javascript" src="Tween.js"></script>
  <script src="jquery.carousel3d.js" type="text/javascript"></script>
  <script src="d1.js" type="text/javascript"></script>
  </head>
<body>
<div id="carousel"></div>
  <div id="holder_images">
    <img src="image5.jpg"  width="500" height="375"  />
    <img src="a1.jpg"  width="500" height="375" />
    <img src="a2.jpg"  width="500" height="375" />
    <img  src="a3.jpg"  width="500" height="375" />
    <img src="a4.jpg"  width="500" height="375" />
    <img  src="image1.jpg"  width="500" height="375" />
    <img src="image2.jpg" width="500" height="375" />
    <img src="image3.jpg"  width="500" height="375" />
    <img  src="image4.jpg"  width="500" height="375" />
  </div>
</body>
</html>
```

The style sheet contains the id selectors as shown below:

```
#buttonwrapper
{
width: 100px;
height: 50px;
position: relative;
}
```

```
#left
{
background: url(left.gif) bottom left no-repeat;
width: 39px;
height: 50px;
float: left;
}

#right
{
background: url(right.gif) bottom left no-repeat;
width: 39px;
height: 50px;
float: right;
}

#left:hover, #right:hover
{
cursor: pointer;
background-position: top left;
}

#holder_images { display: none; }
#carousel img { border: 2px solid #ddd; }
#carousel img.link:hover { border: 4px solid #0e0893; }
```

The jQuery code to invoke the carousel is shown below. The code makes the images scroll when hovering over the left and right arrow buttons and it also zooms in on the selected image.

```
$(document).ready(function() {
  $("#carousel").html($("#holder_images").html()).carousel3d(
    {control: 'buttons', centerX: $('#carousel').offset().left + $('#carousel').width()/2 }
  );
});
```

How It Works

Initially, the images appear in the form of a 3D circle along with left and right arrows at the top as shown in Figure 9-17. The images will rotate in clockwise and counter-clockwise directions when the mouse is moved over the right and left arrow buttons respectively.

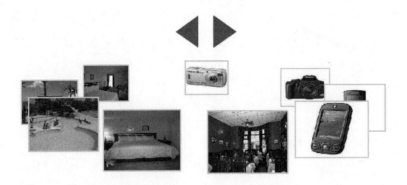

Figure 9-17. Images displayed in a 3D circle with left and right arrows

When any image is selected, it is zoomed as shown in Figure 9-18.

Figure 9-18. Selected image is zoomed

9-8. Selecting a Date with a Datepicker

Problem

You have an input text field where you want to enter a particular date. When you click on the input text field, you want the calendar of the current month be displayed with the facility to move forward and backward to see the calendar of the next and previous months. When any day is selected from the calendar, you want the selected date to be inserted in the input text field.

Solution

I have used the 'Datepicker' plugin for this recipe. Let's download its JavaScript file `ui.datepicker.js` and its CSS style sheet file `ui.datepicker.css` from jqueryui.com/demos/datepicker/. Let's create an HTML file that displays an input text field nested inside the `div` element class 'demo'. The input text field is assigned the id `datepicker`. The HTML file includes the downloaded JavaScript file and links the CSS style sheet file. The HTML file may appear as shown below:

```
<!DOCTYPE html PUBLIC "-//W3C//DTD XHTML 1.0 Transitional//EN"
"http://www.w3.org/TR/xhtml1/DTD/xhtml1-transitional.dtd">
<html xmlns="http://www.w3.org/1999/xhtml" xml:lang="en" lang="en">
  <head>
  <meta http-equiv="Content-Type" content="text/html; charset=utf-8"/>
  <title>JQuery Examples</title>
  <link rel="stylesheet" href="ui.datepicker.css" type="text/css" media="screen" />
  <script src="jquery-1[1].3.2.js" type="text/javascript"></script>
  <script src="ui.datepicker.js" type="text/javascript"></script>
  <script src="d1.js" type="text/javascript"></script>
  </head>
<body>
<div class=demo>
<p>Date: <input id="datepicker"/></p></div>
</body>
</html>
```

The jQuery code to invoke the `datepicker()` method of the Datepicker plugin is as shown below:

```
$(document).ready(function() {
  $("#datepicker").datepicker();
});
```

How It Works

On clicking inside the text box, the calendar of the current month will appear as shown in Figure 9-19. We can select the Next or Prev link to see the calendar of the next or previous month.

Date: [   ]

Prev		December 2009			Next	
Su	Mo	Tu	We	Th	Fr	Sa
		1	2	3	4	5
6	7	8	9	10	11	12
13	14	15	16	17	18	19
20	21	22	23	24	25	26
27	28	29	30	31		

Figure 9-19. Calendar of current month displayed

351

On selecting a date, it will be automatically entered in the input text field as shown in Figure 9-20. The date is entered in format: mm/dd/yyyy.

Date: 12/18/2009

Figure 9-20. Selected date appears in the text box

To get the date in the desired format, we make use of the `dateFormat` option. The jQuery code to get the date in the format 'yy-mm-dd' is as shown below:

```
$(document).ready(function() {
  $("#datepicker").datepicker({dateFormat: 'yy-mm-dd'});
});
```

Now, the selected date will appear in the specified format as shown in Figure 9-21.

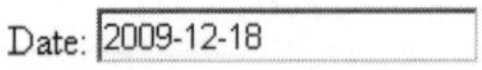

Date: 2009-12-18

Figure 9-21. Date in the selected format

9-9. Sorting tables

Problem

You have a table and you want the table be sorted on the basis of a selected column.

Solution

I have used 'Tablesorter' plugin for this recipe. Let's download its JavaScript file `jquery.tablesorter.js` from tablesorter.com. Let's create an HTML file that includes the downloaded JavaScript file and that contains a table element to display Roll number, Name and Marks of 15 students. The HTML file may appear as shown below:

```
<head>
  <meta http-equiv="Content-Type" content="text/html; charset=utf-8"/>
  <title>JQuery Examples</title>
  <script src="jquery-1[1].3.2.js" type="text/javascript"></script>
  <script src="jquery.tablesorter.js" type="text/javascript"></script>
  <script src="d1.js" type="text/javascript"></script>
</head>
</head>
<body>
```

```
<table border="1" class="studrec">
<thead>
<tr><th>Roll</th><th>Name</th><th>Marks</th></tr>
</thead>
<tbody>
<tr><td>101</td><td>John</td><td>87</td></tr>
<tr><td>102</td><td>Naman</td><td>90</td></tr>
<tr><td>103</td><td>Chirag</td><td>85</td></tr>
<tr><td>104</td><td>David</td><td>92</td></tr>
<tr><td>105</td><td>Kelly</td><td>81</td></tr>
<tr><td>106</td><td>Charles</td><td>77</td></tr>
<tr><td>107</td><td>Jerry</td><td>91</td></tr>
<tr><td>108</td><td>Beth</td><td>75</td></tr>
<tr><td>109</td><td>Caroline</td><td>82</td></tr>
<tr><td>110</td><td>Hanen</td><td>71</td></tr>
<tr><td>111</td><td>Douglas</td><td>57</td></tr>
<tr><td>112</td><td>Tim</td><td>86</td></tr>
<tr><td>113</td><td>Michael</td><td>68</td></tr>
<tr><td>114</td><td>Kimbley</td><td>88</td></tr>
<tr><td>115</td><td>Christina</td><td>72</td></tr>
</tbody>
</table>
</body>
</html>
```

We can see that the above HTML code includes the table element of class **studrec** that displays information concerning the fifteen students. The jQuery code invokes the **tablesorter()** method on the table element of id **studrec**:

```
$(document).ready(function() {
  $('.studrec').tablesorter();
});
```

How It Works

On execution of the above jQuery code, initially the table will be appear with rows in its original sequence as shown in Figure 9-22.

Roll	Name	Marks
101	John	87
102	Naman	90
103	Chirag	85
104	David	92
105	Kelly	81
106	Charles	77
107	Jerry	91
108	Beth	75
109	Caroline	82
110	Hanen	71
111	Douglas	57
112	Tim	86
113	Michael	68
114	Kimbley	88
115	Christina	72

Figure 9-22. Original table

On selecting a column heading, the table will be sorted on the basis of the selected column. If we select the 'Name' column heading, the table will be sorted in the alphabetical order of the names as shown in Figure 9-23.

Roll	Name	Marks
108	Beth	75
109	Caroline	82
106	Charles	77
103	Chirag	85
115	Christina	72
104	David	92
111	Douglas	57
110	Hanen	71
107	Jerry	91
101	John	87
105	Kelly	81
114	Kimbley	88
113	Michael	68
102	Naman	90
112	Tim	86

Figure 9-23. Table sorted on name

Summary

In this chapter we have seen different plugins that help in performing so many tasks without writing any code like filtering on any column of a table, annotating an image with comments, dragging and dropping table rows, getting, serializing and clearing form controls, submitting a form via Ajax, finding the exact position and dimension of an element, displaying images in a carousel, selecting a date with a datepicker and sorting tables. In the next chapter, we will see several recipes that rely heavily on CSS. We will learn about distinguishing HTML elements, applying styles to an element nested inside another element, indenting paragraphs, applying an initial cap to a paragraph, removing the gap between a heading and paragraph, applying styles to heading text and more.

CHAPTER 10

■ ■ ■

Using CSS

In this final chapter I provide a set of recipes that rely heavily on CSS. These recipes are a complement to the others in this book, as CSS is never far away from a JavaScript developer's work. These are some of the CSS techniques I use most often, so I've included them here for your quick reference while developing your own web applications.

In this chapter I provide the following recipes:

- Distinguishing HTML elements

- Applying styles to an element nested inside another element

- Indenting paragraphs

- Applying an initial cap to a paragraph

- Removing the gap between heading and paragraph

- Applying styles to heading text

- Indenting the first line of multiple paragraphs

- Creating paragraphs with hanging indents

- Creating a bordered pull quote

- Creating a pull quote with images

- Applying list properties to list items

- Applying styles to only selected list items

- Placing dividers between list items

- Applying image markers to the list

- Creating inline lists

- Applying styles to hyperlinks and mailto

- Assigning different dimensions to HTML elements

- Placing HTML elements

- Creating a multicolumn layout

- Wrapping text around images

- Placing a drop shadow behind an image

- Changing the cursor when the mouse moves over a link

- Displaying a long piece of text within a specific area

- Making a rounded corner column

- Applying text decorations

- Scaling images

- Setting a background image

- Centering a background image in the browser

- Making the background image stationary

10-1. Distinguishing HTML Elements

Problem

When you want to apply different styles to two different paragraphs or two different **h1** elements of an HTML file, you have to differentiate them by assigning different classes to them. Also, we need to write style rules that can be individually applied to these classes.

Solution

We will first write an HTML file consisting of two paragraph and two **h1** elements. To differentiate them, we assign them different classes. The paragraph elements are assigned the classes **feature1** and **feature2**, respectively, and the h1 elements are assigned the classes **feature2** and **feature3**, respectively.

```
<body>
<p class="feature1">Styles make the formatting job much easier and efficient.</p>
<p class="feature2">To give an attractive look to web sites, styles are heavily used.</p>
<h1 class="feature2">Using jQuery</h1>
<h1 class="feature3">Power of selectors</h1>
</body>
</html>
```

To apply styles to these HTML elements of different classes, we write the following style rules in the style sheet:

```
.greencolor{color:green;font-style:italic}
.highlight{background-color:aqua;color:blue;font-family:arial;}
.redandbold{color:red;font-family:arial;font-weight:bold}
```

To apply the style rules to the paragraphs and **h1** elements, the jQuery code is as follows:

```
$(document).ready(function() {
  $('p.feature1').addClass('greencolor');
  $('.feature2').addClass('highlight');
  $('h1.feature3').addClass('redandbold');
});
```

How It Works

The first statement applies the properties defined in the style rule **greencolor** to only the paragraph elements that also belong to the class **feature1**; that is, those that begin with the **<p class="feature1">** tag. The second statement applies the properties defined in the style rule **highlight** to any HTML element that belongs to the class **feature2**. In the HTML file, one paragraph element and one h1 element belong to the class **feature2** (represented by **<p class="feature2">** and **<h1 class="feature2">** tags), so the properties defined in this rule will be applied to both of them. The third statement applies the properties defined in the style rule **feature3** to only the h1 element(s) that belongs to the class **feature3**. The output is shown in Figure 10-1.

Styles make the formatting job much easier and efficient.

To give an attractive look to web sites, styles are heavily used.

Using jQuery

Power of selectors

Figure 10-1. Different classes applied to <p> and <h1> tags

10-2. Applying Styles to an Element Nested Inside another Element

Problem

Sometimes the **span** element is nested inside another HTML element of a specific ID or a class, and we need to apply styles to that nested **span** element.

Solution

In the following HTML file, we define a paragraph element of the class **feature**. In this paragraph element, we define a **span** element:

```
<body>
<p class="feature">Styles make the formatting job much easier and efficient. <span>To give
an attractive look to web sites,</span> styles are heavily used.</p>.
</body>
```

The style rules to be applied to the paragraph element of the class **feature** and to the **span** element nested inside it are written in the style sheet as shown here:

```
.greencolor{color:green;font-style:italic}
.highlight{background-color:aqua;color:blue;font-family:arial;}
```

To apply styles to the paragraph element of the class **feature1** and to the **span** element nested inside the paragraph element of the class **feature**, the jQuery code appears as shown here:

```
$(document).ready(function() {
  $('p.feature').addClass('greencolor');
  $('p.feature span').addClass('highlight');
});
```

How It Works

First, let's look at how we define CSS styles.

This defines a style that can be applied to any HTML elements with **class="feature"**:

```
.feature{property:value; property:value;...}
```

This defines a style that can be applied to the **span** element nested inside any HTML elements with **class="feature"**:

```
.feature span {property:value; property:value;...}
```

The following defines a style that can be applied to the **span** element nested inside the paragraph element with **class="feature"**:

```
p.feature span {property:value; property:value;...}
```

This defines a style that can be applied to the **span** element with **class="feature2"** nested inside the any HTML elements with **class="feature1"**:

```
feature1 span.feature2 {property:value; property:value;...}
```

The following defines a style that can be applied to the **span** element with **class="feature2"** nested inside the paragraph element with **class="feature1"**:

```
p.feature1 span.feature2 {property:value; property:value;...}
```

The first jQuery statement applies the style properties defined in the style rule **greencolor** to the paragraph element with **class="feature"**. The second statement applies the properties defined in the style rule **highlight** to the **span** element that is defined within the paragraph element with **class="feature"**. In other words, the styles will be applied to the region of text enclosed between the

<span> and </span> tags that are defined within the paragraph element with class="feature". The output after the application of styles is shown in Figure 10-2.

Styles make the formatting job much easier and efficient. To give an attractive look to web sites, *styles are heavily used.*

Figure 10-2. *Applying style to the span element nested in another HTML element*

10-2. Indenting Paragraphs

Problem

You have three paragraphs in an HTML file and you want to indent them at three different levels.

Solution

The HTML containing the three paragraphs is shown here:

```
<body>
<p class="feature1">Styles make the formatting job much easier and efficient. To give an
attractive look to web sites, styles are heavily used. Styles can be written within the HTML
document or can be attached externally. External styles are considered better</p>
<p class="feature2">jQuery is a powerful JavaScript library that allows us to add dynamic
elements to our web sites. Not only it is easy to learn, but it's easy to implement too.</p>
<p class="feature3"> jQuery Selectors are used for selecting the area of the document where
we want to apply styles. jQuery has the power of handling events also, meaning we can apply
styles when a particular action takes place</p>
</body>
```

We can see that the three paragraphs are assigned three different class names: feature1, feature2, and feature3, respectively. We will be using the margin property to indent these paragraphs. The style rules written in the external style sheet are as follows:

```
.indent1{
margin-left:10%;
}
.indent2{
margin-left:20%;
}
.indent3{
margin-left:30%;
}
```

To apply the style rules to the three paragraphs, we write the following jQuery code:

```
$(document).ready(function() {
  $('p.feature1').addClass('indent1');
  $('p.feature2').addClass('indent2');
  $('p.feature3').addClass('indent3');
});
```

How It Works

The first statement selects the paragraph element of the class `feature1` from the HTML file and applies the properties defined in the style rule `indent1` to it. Similarly, the second and third statements select the paragraph elements of the class `feature2` and `feature3` and apply the properties defined in the style rules `indent2` and `indent3`, respectively. The output appears as shown in Figure 10-3.

> Styles make the formatting job much easier and efficient. To give an attractive look to web sites, styles are heavily used. Styles can be written within the HTML document or can be attached externally. External styles are considered better
>
> > jQuery is a powerful JavaScript library that allows us to add dynamic elements to our web sites. Not only it is easy to learn, but it's easy to implement too.
> >
> > > jQuery Selectors are used for selecting the area of the document where we want to apply styles. jQuery has the power of handling events also, meaning we can apply styles when a particular action takes place

Figure 10-3. Three paragraphs indented at three different levels

10-3. Applying an Initial Cap to a Paragraph

Problem

You want to make the first character of a paragraph an initial cap. Initial caps could be in a different font or a different color, or you could even use images for the initial caps.

Solution

Let us consider the following HTML file with a single paragraph element:

```
<body>
<p><span class="cap">S</span>tyles make the formatting job much easier and efficient. To
give an attractive look to web sites, styles are heavily used. Styles can be written within
the HTML document or can be attached externally. External styles are considered better
</body>
```

The style rule that we will apply is written in the style sheet as follows:

```
.initialcap{
font-size: 2em;
}
```

The jQuery code to apply the style rule to the span element with the class name cap is as shown here:

```
$(document).ready(function() {
  $('span.cap').addClass('initialcap');
});
```

How It Works

We can see in the HTML that to distinguish the first character of the paragraph from the rest of the body of the paragraph, it is enclosed in a span tag and is assigned a class cap. To this cap class we apply the style rule via jQuery code. We can see that the font size of the first character is made double the size of the default font (of the rest of the paragraph), as is shown in Figure 10-4.

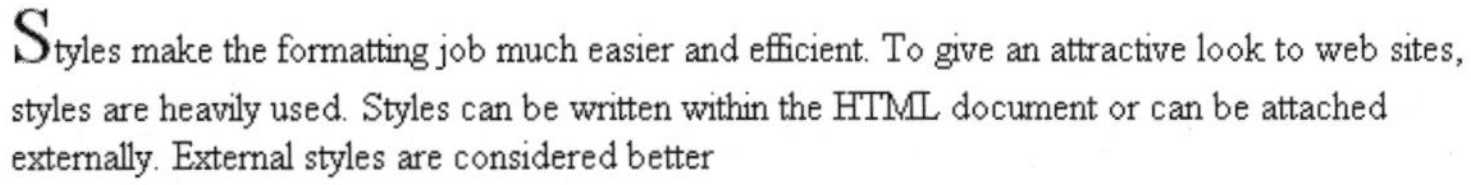

Styles make the formatting job much easier and efficient. To give an attractive look to web sites, styles are heavily used. Styles can be written within the HTML document or can be attached externally. External styles are considered better

Figure 10-4. The first character of the paragraph is set to be an initial cap.

We can also change the foreground and background colors of the first character, as shown in the following style rule:

```
.initialcap{
font-size:2em;
background-color:black;
color:white;
}
```

10-4. Removing the Gap between Heading and Paragraph

Problem

Whenever we apply a heading to any paragraph, there is a gap between the heading and the paragraph. You want to remove this gap.

Solution

The HTML of the heading and the paragraph are as follows:

```
<body>
<h3>Formatting Makes Attractive</h3>
<p>Styles make the formatting job much easier and efficient. To give an attractive look to
web sites, styles are heavily used. Styles can be written within the HTML document or can be
attached externally. External styles are considered better</p>
</body>
```

The style rule to remove the gap between the paragraph and the heading is shown here:

```
.heading{
margin:0;
padding:0;
}

p{
margin:0;
padding:0;
}
```

The jQuery code to apply the style to the h3 element is as follows:

```
$(document).ready(function() {
  $('h3').addClass('heading');
});
```

How It Works

The original output of the HTML without applying any jQuery code is as shown in Figure 10-5. We can see that there is a large gap between the heading and the paragraph.

Formatting Makes Attractive

Styles make the formatting job much easier and efficient. To give an attractive look to web sites, styles are heavily used. Styles can be written within the HTML document or can be attached externally. External styles are considered better

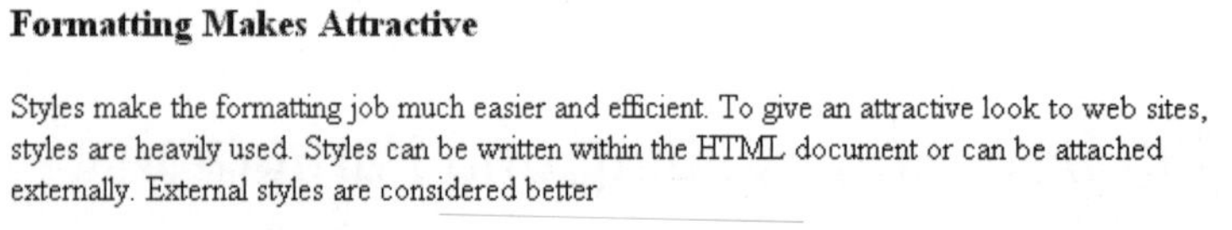

Figure 10-5. The paragraph and heading, along with the usual gap in between

In preceding style sheet, we have applied the class selector `.heading` to the h3 element, and the type selector p{} to the paragraph element.

On application of styles to the paragraph and heading, the gap between them is removed, as shown in Figure 10-6.

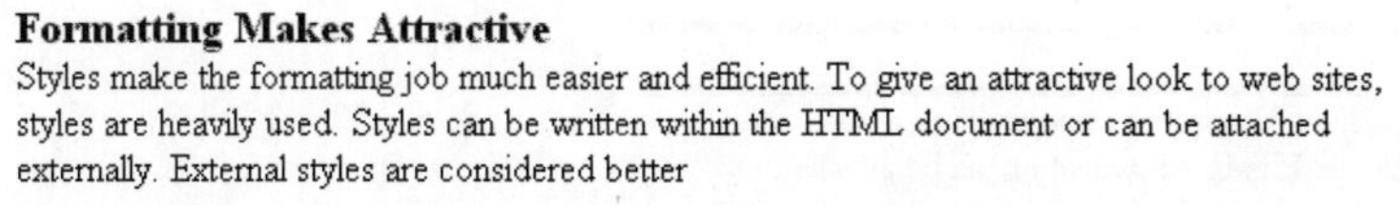

Formatting Makes Attractive

Styles make the formatting job much easier and efficient. To give an attractive look to web sites, styles are heavily used. Styles can be written within the HTML document or can be attached externally. External styles are considered better

Figure 10-6. The usual gap between the paragraph and heading is removed.

10-5. Applying Styles to Heading Text

Problem

You want to apply styles to a heading.

Solution

We will use the same HTML that we used in Recipe 10-5, which contains a paragraph and a heading. To highlight the heading, we first need to remove the usual gap between the heading and the paragraph. Then we make it italic and apply borders to it. We write the following style rules in the style sheet:

```
.heading{
margin:0;
padding:0;
font-style: italic;
border-top:5px solid black;
border-bottom:5px solid black;
}

p{
margin:0;
padding:0;
}
```

Let us apply the style to the h3 element with the following jQuery code:

```
$(document).ready(function() {
  $('h3').addClass('heading');
});
```

How It Works

The `margin` and `padding` properties in the preceding style rules remove the usual gap between the heading and paragraph, and the `font-style` makes the heading appear in italic. The `border` property attaches a top and a bottom border to the heading.

On application of the styles, the heading of the paragraph appears as in Figure 10-7.

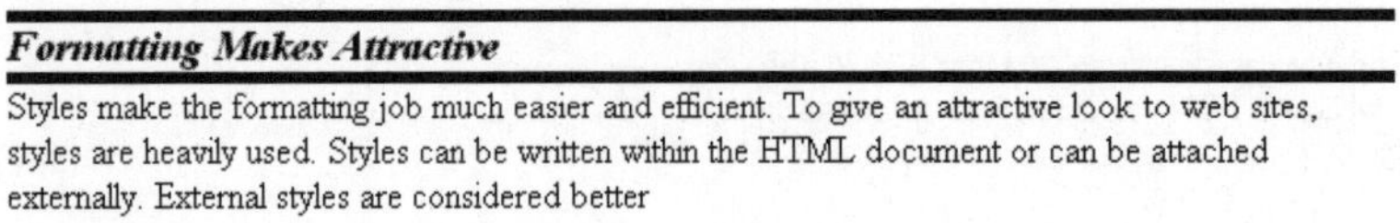

Formatting Makes Attractive

Styles make the formatting job much easier and efficient. To give an attractive look to web sites, styles are heavily used. Styles can be written within the HTML document or can be attached externally. External styles are considered better

Figure 10-7. The paragraph with a styled heading

10-6. Indenting the First Line of Multiple Paragraphs

Problem

You want to indent the first line of the paragraphs in your document.

Solution

Let us write some HTML with a few paragraphs in it, as shown here:

```
<body>
<p>Styles make the formatting job much easier and efficient. To give an attractive look to
web sites, styles are heavily used. Styles can be written within the HTML document or can be
attached externally. External styles are considered better</p>
<p>jQuery is a powerful JavaScript library that allows us to add dynamic elements to our web
sites. Not only it is easy to learn, but it's easy to implement too.</p>
<p> jQuery Selectors are used for selecting the area of the document where we want to apply
styles. jQuery has the power of handling events also, meaning we can apply styles when a
particular action takes place</p>
</body>
```

This HTML will display three paragraphs without any indentation. To apply the indentation in the first line of the paragraphs, we need to use the `text-indent` property. The style rule in the style sheet appears as follows:

```
.firstindent{
text-indent:10%;
}
```

The jQuery code to apply the style rule `firstindent` to all the paragraph elements of the HTML file is as follows:

```
$(document).ready(function() {
  $('p').addClass('firstindent');
});
```

How It Works

On application of the style, the paragraphs of the HTML file have the first line indented as shown in Figure 10-8.

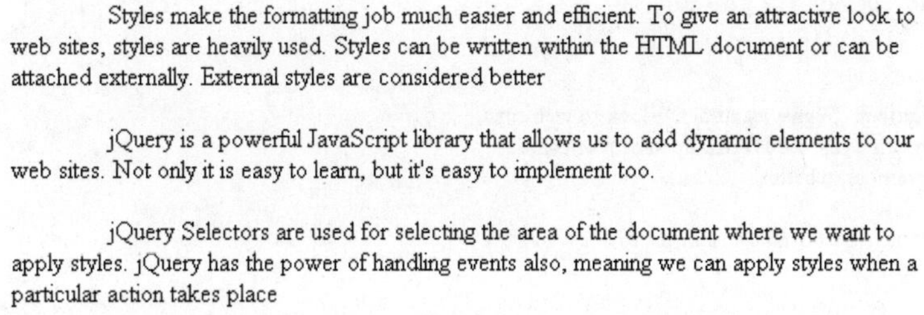

> Styles make the formatting job much easier and efficient. To give an attractive look to web sites, styles are heavily used. Styles can be written within the HTML document or can be attached externally. External styles are considered better
>
> jQuery is a powerful JavaScript library that allows us to add dynamic elements to our web sites. Not only it is easy to learn, but it's easy to implement too.
>
> jQuery Selectors are used for selecting the area of the document where we want to apply styles. jQuery has the power of handling events also, meaning we can apply styles when a particular action takes place

Figure 10-8. The paragraphs with the first line indented

10-7. Creating Paragraphs with Hanging Indents

Problem

You want to have hanging indents in the first line of the paragraphs in your document.

Solution

In this recipe, we will make use of the same HTML that we used in Recipe 10-6. The HTML has three paragraph elements.

We will make use of the `text-indent` and `margin-left` properties for creating hanging indents. The style rule is written as follows:

```
.hangingindent{
text-indent:-10%;
margin-left:10%;
}
```

The jQuery code to apply the `hangingindent` style rule to the paragraphs is as follows:

```
$(document).ready(function() {
  $('p').addClass('hangingindent');
});
```

How It Works

By setting the `margin-left` property to 10%, we set the paragraph to a distance of 10% of the browser window's width from the left side of the browser window; that is, the whole paragraph is shifted right by 10% of the browser window's width. By making the value of `text-indent` –10%, we make the first line of the paragraph shift toward the left by 10% of the width of the browser window, giving it a hanging indentation as shown in Figure 10-9.

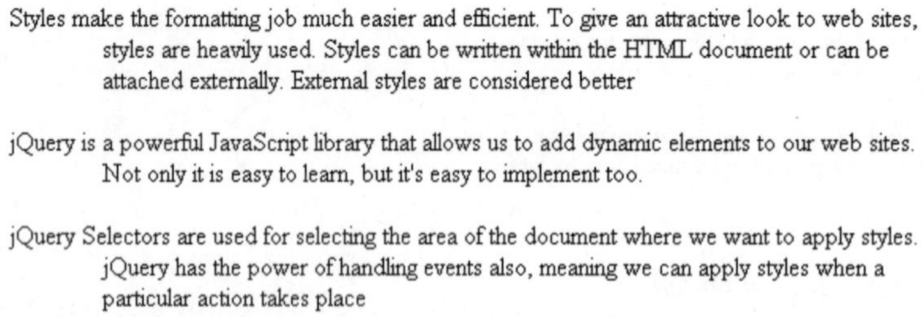

Styles make the formatting job much easier and efficient. To give an attractive look to web sites,
 styles are heavily used. Styles can be written within the HTML document or can be
 attached externally. External styles are considered better

jQuery is a powerful JavaScript library that allows us to add dynamic elements to our web sites.
 Not only it is easy to learn, but it's easy to implement too.

jQuery Selectors are used for selecting the area of the document where we want to apply styles.
 jQuery has the power of handling events also, meaning we can apply styles when a
 particular action takes place

Figure 10-9. The paragraphs with the hanging indent on the first line

10-8. Creating a Bordered Pull Quote

Problem

In the middle of a large piece of text, you want to highlight certain text to catch the reader's eye. You need to make a bordered pull quote.

Solution

Let us write some HTML with three paragraphs, and differentiate the paragraph that we want to highlight by assigning it a class name of `feature`. The HTML is shown here:

```
<body>
<p>Styles make the formatting job much easier and efficient. To give an attractive look to
web sites, styles are heavily used. Styles can be written within the HTML document or can be
attached externally. External styles are considered better</a>
<p class="feature">jQuery is a powerful JavaScript library that allows us to add dynamic
elements to our web sites. Not only it is easy to learn, but it's easy to implement too.</a>
<p> jQuery Selectors are used for selecting the area of the document where we want to apply
styles. jQuery has the power of handling events also meaning we can apply styles when a
particular action takes place</a>
</body>
```

We will make use of the `margin`, `color`, and `font-style` properties to highlight the text. The style rules that we will write in the external style sheet are as follows:

```
.quote{
margin:5%;
color:#00a;
font-style: italic;
border:5px solid black;
padding: .5em;
}
```

The jQuery code to apply the style rule **quote** to the paragraph with the class name **feature** is as follows:

```
$(document).ready(function() {
  $('p.feature').addClass('quote');
});
```

How It Works

The **margin** property indents the paragraph 5% from all four boundaries, the **color** property will make the color of the paragraph blue, and the **font-style** property will give it an italic appearance. To make a border around the pull quote, we add two more properties to the **quote** style rule: **border** creates a border of a specified width around the paragraph, and **padding** creates a gap between the border and the paragraph text.

On application of the style rule, the paragraph will appear as a bordered pull quote, as shown in Figure 10-10.

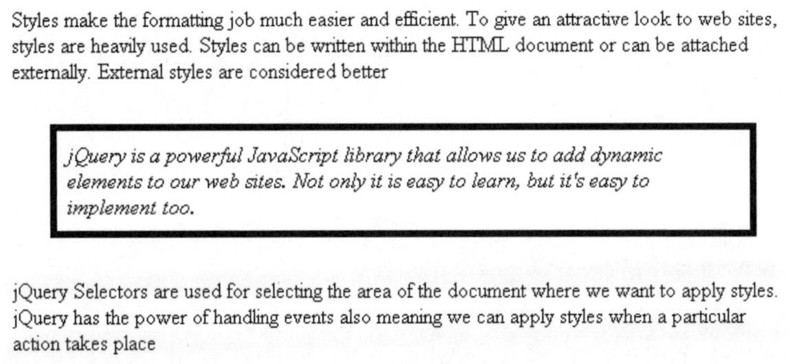

Styles make the formatting job much easier and efficient. To give an attractive look to web sites, styles are heavily used. Styles can be written within the HTML document or can be attached externally. External styles are considered better

jQuery is a powerful JavaScript library that allows us to add dynamic elements to our web sites. Not only it is easy to learn, but it's easy to implement too.

jQuery Selectors are used for selecting the area of the document where we want to apply styles. jQuery has the power of handling events also meaning we can apply styles when a particular action takes place

Figure 10-10. The paragraph distinguished as a bordered pull quote

10-9. Creating a Pull Quote with Images

Problem

In order to make text appear attractive and dynamic within a larger piece of text, you want to make a pull quote act like an image to give text-heavy documents something to focus on without needing full graphics.

Solution

For this recipe, we will make use of the same HTML that we used in Recipe 10-7. We know that in that HTML, the paragraph that we want to distinguish from the rest of the text is assigned a class name `feature`.

To apply images at the two opposite corners of the pull quote, we make two figures: `leftfig.jpg` and `rightfig.jpg`. The image to be placed at the bottom-right corner of the pull quote, `leftfig.jpg`, appears as shown in Figure 10-11.

Figure 10-11. leftfig.jpg

The image to be placed at the bottom-right corner of the pull quote appears as shown in Figure 10-12.

Figure 10-12. rightfig.jpg

We need to apply two images to the pull quote. We can apply only one style to an element, so to apply two images to the paragraph element, we will enclose it in a `div` element. Now we can apply one style to the paragraph element to add one image, and another style to the `div` element to add the other image. The HTML file after enclosing the paragraph of the class `feature` in the `div` element is shown here:

```
<body>
<p>Styles make the formatting job much easier and efficient. To give an attractive look to
web sites, styles are heavily used. Styles can be written within the HTML document or can be
attached externally. External styles are considered better</p>
<div>
```

```
<p class="feature">jQuery is a powerful JavaScript library that allows us to add dynamic
elements to our web sites. Not only it is easy to learn, but it's easy to implement too.</p>
</div>
<p> jQuery Selectors are used for selecting the area of the document where we want to apply
styles. jQuery has the power of handling events also, meaning we can apply styles when a
particular action takes place</p>
</body>
```

The style rules to apply two images to the pull quote are as follows:

```
.quote{
background-image:url(leftfig.jpg);
background-repeat: no-repeat;
margin:5%;
color:#00a;
font-style: italic;
padding:20px 5px 5px 20px;
}

.closing{
background-image:url(rightfig.jpg);
background-repeat: no-repeat;
background-position: bottom right;
}
```

The jQuery code to add the style rules `quote` and `closing` to the paragraph of the class name `feature` and to the `div` element is shown here:

```
$(document).ready(function() {
  $('p.feature').addClass('quote');
  $('div').addClass('closing');
});
```

How It Works

The style rule `quote` applies `leftfig.jpg` at the top-left corner of the paragraph. The value of `background-repeat` is set to `no-repeat` to display the image only once. The `margin` property makes the paragraph indented from all four sides at 5% of the browser window's width. The `font-style` property makes the paragraph appear in italic, and the `padding` property sets the distance between the paragraph text and the images. The style rule `closing` applies `rightfig.jpg` at the bottom-right corner of the paragraph. On application of styles, the pull quote is displayed as shown in Figure 10-13.

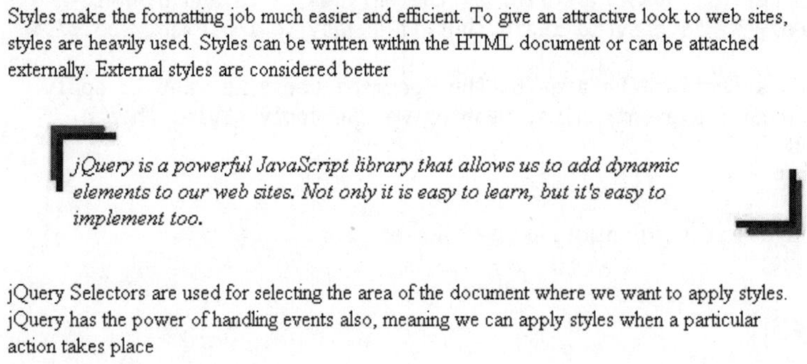

Styles make the formatting job much easier and efficient. To give an attractive look to web sites, styles are heavily used. Styles can be written within the HTML document or can be attached externally. External styles are considered better

jQuery is a powerful JavaScript library that allows us to add dynamic elements to our web sites. Not only it is easy to learn, but it's easy to implement too.

jQuery Selectors are used for selecting the area of the document where we want to apply styles. jQuery has the power of handling events also, meaning we can apply styles when a particular action takes place

Figure 10-13. The paragraph distinguished as a pull quote with images

10-10. Applying List Properties to List Items

Problem

List items are used heavily in displaying drop-down menus, displaying a hierarchy of items, and so on. You want to apply list properties to list items.

Solution

Let us make HTML that contains certain list items. The HTML file is shown here:

```
<body>
<ul>
  <li>Tea
    <ul>
      <li>Darjeeling</li>
      <li>Assam
        <ul>
          <li>Green Leaves</li>
          <li>Herbal</li>
        </ul>
      </li>
      <li>Kerala</li>
    </ul>
  </li>
```

```
  <li>Coffee
    <ul>
      <li>Cochin</li>
      <li>Kerala</li>
    </ul>
  </li>
</ul>
</body>
```

The list items appear as shown in Figure 10-14 before applying list properties to them.

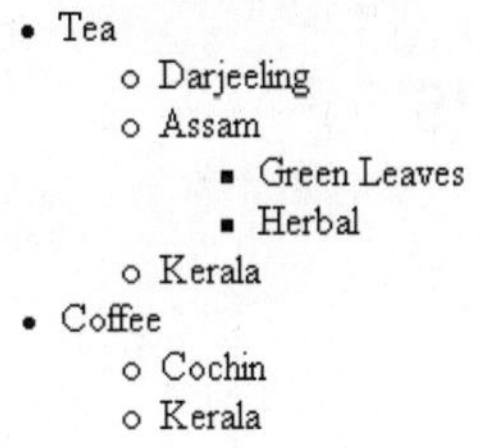

- Tea
  - Darjeeling
  - Assam
    - Green Leaves
    - Herbal
  - Kerala
- Coffee
  - Cochin
  - Kerala

Figure 10-14. Unordered list items before applying any style

Let us a define style rule as shown here:

```
.dispdisc{list-style-type:disc}
```

The style rule `dispdisc` will make a disc appear before list items. The jQuery code to apply the style rule `dispdisc` to the list items is shown here:

```
$(document).ready(function() {
  $('li').addClass('dispdisc');
});
```

How It Works

The list style type is set to `disc`, and we can see in Figure 10-15 that all list items are preceded with a disc shape.

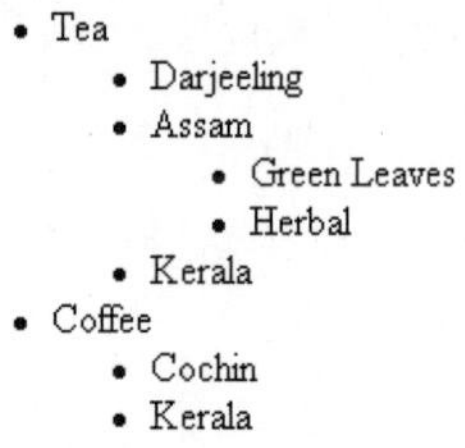

- Tea
  - Darjeeling
  - Assam
    - Green Leaves
    - Herbal
  - Kerala
- Coffee
  - Cochin
  - Kerala

Figure 10-15. Unordered list items after applying the list style

10-11. Applying Styles to Only Selected List Items

Problem

In order to highlight them, you want to apply styles to some of the list items.

Solution

To apply a style to only the selected list items, we need to distinguish them from the rest. For selecting a part of a list, we assign it a class name or an ID. In this solution, we assign the ID intro to the list item that we want to highlight:

```
<body>
<ul>
  <li>Tea
    <ul id="intro">
      <li>Darjeeling</li>
      <li>Assam
        <ul>
          <li>Green Leaves</li>
          <li>Herbal</li>
        </ul>
      </li>
      <li>Kerala</li>
    </ul>
  </li>
  <li>Coffee
    <ul>
      <li>Cochin</li>
      <li>Kerala</li>
    </ul>
  </li>
</ul>
</body>
```

Let us define a style rule to be applied to the list items with the ID intro in the style sheet file:

```
.dispdisc{color:green;font-style:italic}
```

To apply the properties defined in the style rule to the list items of ID intro, we write the jQuery code shown here:

```
$(document).ready(function() {
  $('#intro').addClass('dispdisc');
});
```

Applying Styles to the List Items Selected with a Child Selector

The symbol > is a child combinatory that finds each list item that is child of the element that has the specified ID (or class) and applies the given style rule to it. Let's assign the ID drink to an unordered list as shown here:

```
<body>
<ul>
  <li>Tea
    <ul id="drink">
      <li>Darjeeling</li>
      <li>Assam
        <ul>
          <li>Green Leaves</li>
          <li>Herbal</li>
        </ul>
      </li>
      <li>Kerala</li>
    </ul>
  </li>
  <li>Coffee
    <ul>
      <li>Cochin</li>
      <li>Kerala</li>
    </ul>
  </li>
</ul>
</body>
```

Let us assume that the style sheet contains a style rule highlight that applies a green color and makes the text appear in italic:

```
.highlight {
  font-style: italic;
  background-color: #0f0;
}
```

The jQuery code to apply the style rule `highlight` to the child of the unordered list with ID `drink` is shown here:

```
$(document).ready(function() {
  $('#drink >li').addClass('highlight');
});
```

Applying Styles to List Items to Which a CSS Class Is Not Applied

We can also apply styles to the elements to which a particular CSS class is not applied. Let us write the following jQuery code in the JavaScript file:

```
$(document).ready(function() {
  $('#drink >li').addClass('highlight');
  $('#drink li:not(.highlight)').addClass('redandbold');
});
```

The style sheet file is assumed to contain two style rules: `highlight` and `redandbold`, as shown here:

```
.highlight {
font-style: italic;
background-color: #0f0;
}
.redandbold{
color:red;
font-family:arial;
font-weight:bold
}
```

How It Works

The preceding style rule applies the `color` and `font-style` properties to the list items with ID `intro`. Figure 10-16 shows that only a part of the list is highlighted.

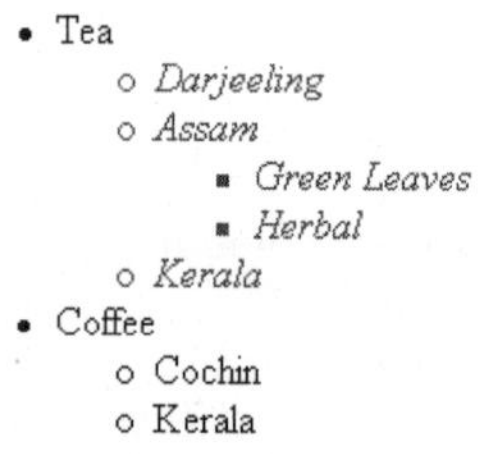

- Tea
  - Darjeeling
  - Assam
    - Green Leaves
    - Herbal
  - Kerala
- Coffee
  - Cochin
  - Kerala

Figure 10-16. Applying style properties to list items with ID intro

When we work with the child selector, it simply finds each list item that is a child of the element with ID `drink` and applies the `highlight` class to it.

Figure 10-17 illustrates finding all list items to which `highlight` is not applied, and applying to them the properties defined in the `redandbold` class.

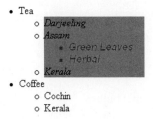

- Tea
  - *Darjeeling*
  - *Assam*
    - Green Leaves
    - Herbal
  - *Kerala*
- Coffee
  - Cochin
  - Kerala

Figure 10-17. *Applying two different styles*

10-12. Placing Dividers between List Items

Problem

You want list items to be displayed in a straight line (without indentation), and every list item to be separated by a line.

Solution

For this recipe, we will use the same HTML that we used in Recipe 10-10. The HTML displays certain list items, as shown in Figure 10-14.

The style rules are as shown here:

```
.applytopborders
{
border-top: 1px solid black;
}

.applybottomborder
{
border-bottom: 1px solid black;
}

.liststyle {
list-style-type:none;
margin: 0;
}
```

We apply one style rule to the unordered list, one to all list items except the last, and a third to the last item:

```
$(document).ready(function() {
  $('ul').addClass('liststyle');
  $('li').addClass('applytopborder');
  $('li:last').addClass('applybottomborder');
});
```

How It Works

We will use three style rules for this recipe:

- liststyle—We use this on the unordered list to remove the traditional bullets from the list items and to remove the hierarchical indentation.

- applytopborder—We apply this to all the list items except the last one to apply the top border to each of them.

- applybottomborder—Using this on the last list item lets us apply the bottom border to it.

The output that we get by applying the preceding styles is shown in Figure 10-18.

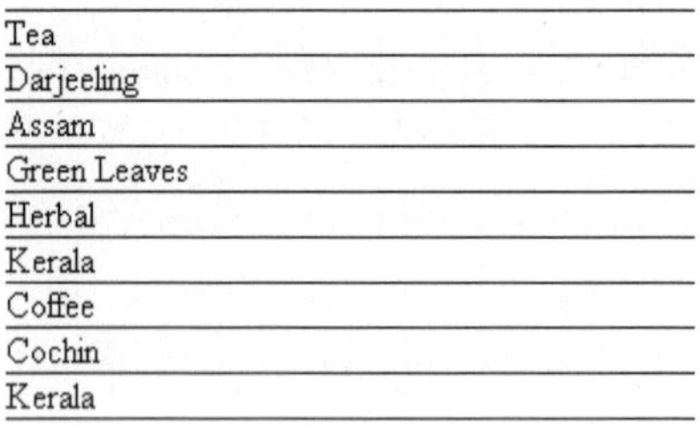

Tea
Darjeeling
Assam
Green Leaves
Herbal
Kerala
Coffee
Cochin
Kerala

Figure 10-18. List items in a straight line, with dividers in between

10-13. Applying Image Markers to the List

Problem

You want to use images to replace the traditional bullets in a list.

Solution

For this recipe, we will create HTML that displays certain list items, as shown here:

```
<body>
<ul>
  <li>Tea
    <ul>
      <li>Darjeeling</li>
      <li>Assam
        <ul>
          <li>Green Leaves</li>
          <li>Herbal</li>
        </ul>
      </li>
      <li>Kerala</li>
    </ul>
  </li>
  <li>Coffee
    <ul>
      <li>Cochin</li>
      <li>Kerala</li>
    </ul>
  </li>
</ul>
</body>
```

In this recipe, the style rule will make use of two properties: `list-style-type` and `list-style-image`. The former will be used for removing the traditional bullets from the list items, and the latter will apply the specified image instead of the bullets.

The image that we want to apply instead of bullets is `flower.jpg`. The style rule in the style sheet is as shown here:

```
.liststyle {
list-style-type: none;
list-style-image:url(flower.jpg);
}
```

The jQuery code to apply the style rule `liststyle` to the unordered list is shown here:

```
$(document).ready(function() {
  $('ul').addClass('liststyle');
});
```

How It Works

Assigning `none` to the `list-style-type` property makes the bullets disappear from the list items, and assigning `flower.jpg` to the `list-style-image` property applies the image stored in this file to the list items.

On application of the style rule, the traditional bullets from the list items will be replaced by the image stored in `flower.jpg` and we will get the output shown in Figure 10-19.

Figure 10-19. List items with images used in place of traditional bullets

10-14. Creating Inline Lists

Problem

You want list items to appear in a horizontal row without any hierarchical levels.

Solution

For this recipe, we will create HTML that displays certain list items, as shown here:

```
<body>
<ul>
  <li>Tea
    <ul>
      <li>Darjeeling</li>
      <li>Assam
        <ul>
          <li>Green Leaves</li>
          <li>Herbal</li>
        </ul>
      </li>
      <li>Kerala</li>
    </ul>
  </li>
  <li>Coffee
    <ul>
      <li>Cochin</li>
      <li>Kerala</li>
    </ul>
  </li>
</ul>
</body>
```

In this recipe, the style rule will make use of properties like `display`, `list-style`, `margin`, and `padding`, as shown in the style sheet:

```
.liststyle {
display: inline;
list-style:none;
margin:0;
padding:0;
}
```

The jQuery code to apply the style rule `liststyle` to the unordered list and its list items is as follows:

```
$(document).ready(function() {
  $('ul').addClass('liststyle');
  $('li').addClass('liststyle');
});
```

How It Works

The `inline` value of the `display` property will make the list items display in a row; that is, on the same line. Setting the value of `list-style` to `none` will remove the traditional bullets from the list items. Finally, the value `0` assigned to `margin` and `padding` will remove the hierarchical indentation in the list items.

On application of the style properties, the list items will be displayed in a row without any traditional bullets, as shown in Figure 10-20.

Tea Darjeeling Assam Green Leaves Herbal Kerala Coffee Cochin Kerala

Figure 10-20. List items displayed in a row

10-15. Applying Styles to Hyperlinks

Problem

Traditionally, hyperlinks carry an underline to distinguish them from static text. You want to remove that underline and apply a different style to these links.

Solution

To apply styles to the hyperlinks, let us make an HTML file that has a hyperlink, as is shown here:

```
<body>
<div>Styles make the formatting job much easier and efficient. To give an attractive look to
web sites, styles are heavily used. A person must have a good knowledge of HTML and CSS and
a bit of JavaScript.
jQuery is a powerful JavaScript library that allows us to add dynamic elements to our web
sites. Not only it is easy to learn, but it's easy to implement too.
```

```
jQuery is an open source project. <a href="abc.com">Click Here</a> for more information
</div>
</body>
```

We can see that the text *Click Here* is a hyperlink and will appear as underlined on the web page. When the visitor selects this link, he will be navigated to `www.abc.com`.

To remove the underline from the hyperlink and to apply other style properties to it, we write the following style rule in the external style sheet file:

```
.linkstyle{
font-weight:bold;
background-color: #00f;
color:#fff;
text-decoration:none;
}
```

To apply the style rule `linkstyle` to the hyperlink, the jQuery code is as follows:

```
$(document).ready(function() {
$('a[@href]').addClass('linkstyle');
});
```

Now let's see how to apply styles to a `mailto` hyperlink. Here is an HTML file that has a `mailto` hyperlink, which, when selected, opens an email client:

```
<body>
<div>Styles make the formatting job much easier and efficient. To give an attractive look to
web sites, styles are heavily used. A person must have a good knowledge of HTML and CSS and
a bit of JavaScript.
jQuery is a powerful JavaScript library that allows us to add dynamic elements to our web
sites. Not only it is easy to learn, but it's easy to implement too.
jQuery is an open source project. <a href="mailto:bmharwani@yahoo.com">Contact Us</a> for
more information </div>
</body>
```

The content of the JavaScript file containing jQuery code is as follows:

```
$(document).ready(function() {
  $('a[@href^="mailto:"]').addClass('linkstyle');
});
```

How It Works

Our CSS style rule uses the `font-weight` property to make the hyperlink appear in bold, the `background-color` property to set the background color of the hyperlink to blue, and the `color` property to make the text white. The value of the `text-decoration` property is set to `none` to remove the traditional underline from the hyperlink.

The following jQuery statement

```
$('a[@href]').addClass('linkstyle');
```

selects all the anchor elements (a) that have a href attribute in the document and applies the linkstyle class to them. The output is shown in Figure 10-21.

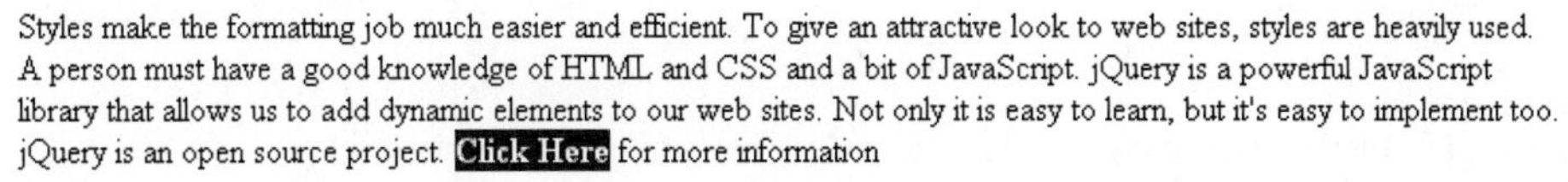

Styles make the formatting job much easier and efficient. To give an attractive look to web sites, styles are heavily used. A person must have a good knowledge of HTML and CSS and a bit of JavaScript. jQuery is a powerful JavaScript library that allows us to add dynamic elements to our web sites. Not only it is easy to learn, but it's easy to implement too. jQuery is an open source project. Click Here for more information

Figure 10-21. Removing the traditional underline from the hyperlink

The following statement selects all the anchor elements (a) that have the href attribute and begin with mailto, and applies the linkstyle class to them:

```
$('a[@href^="mailto:"]').addClass('linkstyle');
```

The output may is shown in Figure 10-22.

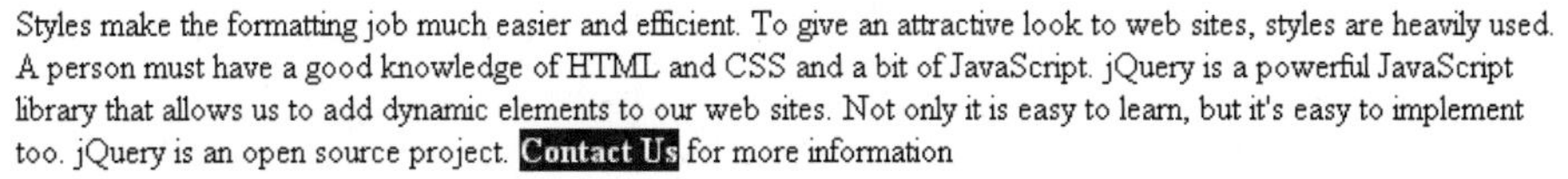

Styles make the formatting job much easier and efficient. To give an attractive look to web sites, styles are heavily used. A person must have a good knowledge of HTML and CSS and a bit of JavaScript. jQuery is a powerful JavaScript library that allows us to add dynamic elements to our web sites. Not only it is easy to learn, but it's easy to implement too. jQuery is an open source project. Contact Us for more information

Figure 10-22. Applying the linkstyle class to the mailto option

10-16. Assigning Different Dimensions to HTML Elements

Problem

You want to constrain the size of certain paragraph elements.

Solution

For this solution, we create an HTML file that contains two paragraph elements that are assigned class names feature1 and feature2, as shown here:

```
<body>
<p class="feature1">Styles make the formatting job much easier and efficient. To give an
attractive look to web sites, styles are heavily used. A person must have a good knowledge
of HTML and CSS and a bit of JavaScript.  </p>
```

```
<p class="feature2">jQuery is a powerful JavaScript library that allows us to add dynamic
elements to our web sites. Not only it is easy to learn, but it's easy to implement too.
jQuery is an open source project that provides a wide range of features with cross-platform
compatiblity. jQuery has hundreds of plug-ins to extend its features. jQuery helps in
increasing interactions with a web site </p>
</body>
```

To apply the `width` property to the paragraph elements with the class names `feature1` and `feature2`, we write the following jQuery code:

```
$(document).ready(function() {
  $('.feature1').css({'width':'50%', 'padding':'10px', 'border':'1px dashed'});
  $('.feature2').css({'padding':'30px', 'border':'2px solid'});
});
```

How It Works

In the preceding solution, we have made use of the `css()` method (described in Recipe 3-7, from Chapter 3). In the jQuery code, the first statement confines the first paragraph to 50% of the width of the browser window. The `border` property creates a border of dashes 1px thick, and the `padding` property creates a spacing of 10px between the paragraph text and the border. The second statement makes the paragraph text use up the whole width of the browser window. The `border` property creates a solid border of 2px thickness, and the `padding` property creates a spacing of 30px between the paragraph text and the border. The output appears as shown in Figure 10-23.

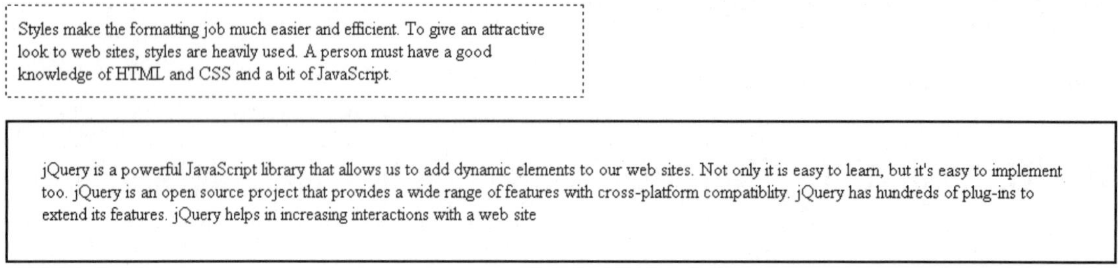

Styles make the formatting job much easier and efficient. To give an attractive
look to web sites, styles are heavily used. A person must have a good
knowledge of HTML and CSS and a bit of JavaScript.

jQuery is a powerful JavaScript library that allows us to add dynamic elements to our web sites. Not only it is easy to learn, but it's easy to implement
too. jQuery is an open source project that provides a wide range of features with cross-platform compatiblity. jQuery has hundreds of plug-ins to
extend its features. jQuery helps in increasing interactions with a web site

Figure 10-23. Specifying the width attribute as a percentage

We can also specify the width in terms of pixels, as shown in the following jQuery code:

```
$('.feature1').css({'width':'300px', 'padding':'10px', 'border':'1px dashed'});
$('.feature2').css({'padding':'30px', 'border':'2px solid'});
```

The width of the first paragraph will be limited to 300px, as shown in Figure 10-24.

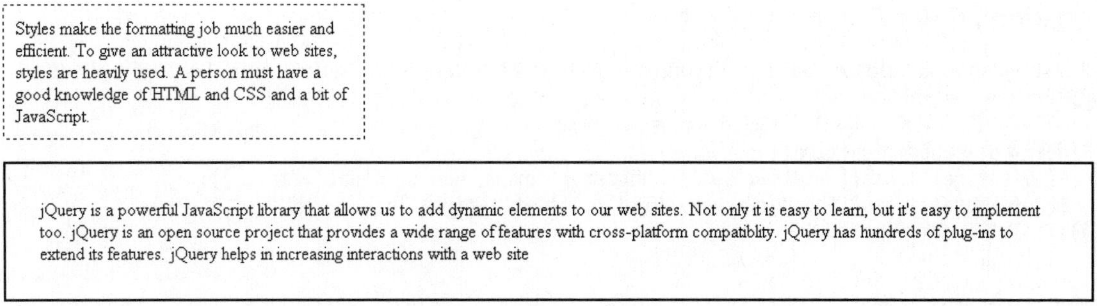

Styles make the formatting job much easier and
efficient. To give an attractive look to web sites,
styles are heavily used. A person must have a
good knowledge of HTML and CSS and a bit of
JavaScript.

jQuery is a powerful JavaScript library that allows us to add dynamic elements to our web sites. Not only it is easy to learn, but it's easy to implement
too. jQuery is an open source project that provides a wide range of features with cross-platform compatiblity. jQuery has hundreds of plug-ins to
extend its features. jQuery helps in increasing interactions with a web site

Figure 10-24. Specifying the width attribute in pixels

10-17. Placing HTML Elements

Problem

You want to make a paragraph element appear to the right or left of another paragraph element.

Solution

Let us create an HTML file that contains two paragraph elements that are assigned class names **feature1**
and **feature2**, as shown here:

```
<body>
<p class="feature1">Styles make the formatting job much easier and efficient. To give an
attractive look to web sites, styles are heavily used. A person must have a good knowledge
of HTML and CSS and a bit of JavaScript.  </p>
<p class="feature2">jQuery is a powerful JavaScript library that allows us to add dynamic
elements to our web sites. Not only it is easy to learn, but it's easy to implement too.
jQuery is an open source project that provides a wide range of features with cross-platform
compatiblity. jQuery has hundreds of plug-ins to extend its features. jQuery helps in
increasing interactions with a web site </p>
</body>
```

To apply the **float** property to the paragraph elements with the class names **feature1** and **feature2**,
we write the following jQuery code:

```
$(document).ready(function() {
  $('.feature1').css({'width':'50%', 'border':'1px dashed', 'float':'left'});
  $('.feature2').css({'border':'2px solid'});
});
```

Making a Two-Column Layout

We can also make the first paragraph float left and the second paragraph float right. Let us modify the jQuery code as shown here:

```
$(document).ready(function() {
    $('.feature1').css({'width':'50%', 'border':'1px dashed', 'float':'left'});
    $('.feature2').css({'border':'2px solid', 'float':'right'});
});
```

Reversing the Columns

We can also interchange the positions of the columns. That is, the first paragraph can be set to float right and the second paragraph to float left. The jQuery code for that purpose is as shown here:

```
$(document).ready(function() {
    $('.feature1').css({'width':'50%', 'border':'1px dashed', 'float':'right'});
    $('.feature2').css({'border':'2px solid', 'float':'left'});
});
```

How It Works

In the jQuery code, the first statement specifies the property `float:left` that makes the first paragraph appear on the left side of the browser window, creating a space of 50% on the right side, which will be then occupied by the second paragraph, as shown in Figure 10-25. The `border` property creates a border of dashes 1px thick around the first paragraph. The second statement creates a solid border 2px thick around the second paragraph.

Styles make the formatting job much easier and efficient. To give an attractive look to web sites, styles are heavily used. A person must have a good knowledge of HTML and CSS and a bit of JavaScript. cross-platform compatiblity. jQuery has hundreds of plug-ins to extend its features.	jQuery is a powerful JavaScript library that allows us to add dynamic elements to our web sites. Not only it is easy to learn, but it's easy to implement too. jQuery is an open source project that provides a wide range of features with jQuery helps in increasing interactions with a web site

Figure 10-25. Applying the float property

In the two-column layout, when the first paragraph is set to `float:left`, it creates a space on its right (which will be used by the second paragraph). Similarly, when the property `float:right` is applied in the second paragraph, it creates a space on the left of the browser window that can be used by the first paragraph. Figure 10-26 shows the output of these styles.

Styles make the formatting job much easier and efficient. To give an attractive look to web sites, styles are heavily used. A person must have a good knowledge of HTML and CSS and a bit of JavaScript.	jQuery is a powerful JavaScript library that allows us to add dynamic elements to our web sites. Not only it is easy to learn, but it's easy to implement too. jQuery is an open source project that provides a wide range of features with cross-platform compatiblity. jQuery has hundreds of plug-ins to extend its features. jQuery helps in increasing interactions with a web site

Figure 10-26. The output of the styles

The reversed layout is shown in Figure 10-27.

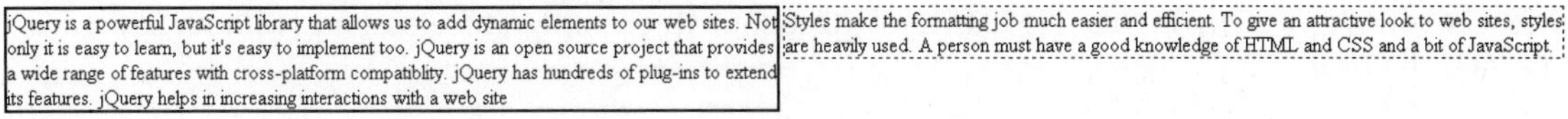

jQuery is a powerful JavaScript library that allows us to add dynamic elements to our web sites. Not only it is easy to learn, but it's easy to implement too. jQuery is an open source project that provides a wide range of features with cross-platform compatiblity. jQuery has hundreds of plug-ins to extend its features. jQuery helps in increasing interactions with a web site

Styles make the formatting job much easier and efficient. To give an attractive look to web sites, styles are heavily used. A person must have a good knowledge of HTML and CSS and a bit of JavaScript.

Figure 10-27. Interchanging the two columns

10-18. Creating a Multicolumn Layout

Problem

You want to create a three-column layout; that is, three paragraphs positioned at particular locations on the page.

Solution

We will create a three-column layout by positioning the columns at three different positions of the web page. Let us make an HTML file with three paragraph elements with the class names assigned as `leftalign`, `centeralign`, and `rightalign`. The HTML file appears as shown here:

```
<body>
<p class="leftalign">Styles make the formatting job much easier and efficient. To give an
attractive look to web sites, styles are heavily used. A person must have a good knowledge
of HTML and CSS and a bit of JavaScript.   </p>
<p class="centeralign">jQuery is a powerful JavaScript library that allows us to add dynamic
elements to our web sites. Not only it is easy to learn, but it's easy to implement too.
</p>
<p class="rightalign">jQuery is an open source project that provides a wide range of
features with cross-platform compatiblity. jQuery has hundreds of plug-ins to extend its
features. jQuery helps in increasing interactions with a web site. </p>
</body>
```

The jQuery code to place the three paragraph elements at the respective positions is as follows:

```
$(document).ready(function() {
  $('.leftalign').css({'position':'absolute', 'left':'50px', 'width':'300px'});
  $('.centeralign').css({'position':'absolute', 'left':'400px', 'width':'300px'});
  $('.rightalign').css({'position':'absolute', 'left':'750px', 'width':'300px'});
});
```

Applying Floats

We can have the same output (three-column layout) by applying the `float` property as is demonstrated in the following solution. In this HTML file, we just define three paragraph elements (without assigning any class names):

```
<body>
<p>Styles make the formatting job much easier and efficient. To give an attractive look to
web sites, styles are heavily used. A person must have a good knowledge of HTML and CSS and
a bit of JavaScript. </p>
<p>jQuery is a powerful JavaScript library that allows us to add dynamic elements to our web
sites. Not only it is easy to learn, but it's easy to implement too. </p>
<p>jQuery is an open source project that provides a wide range of features with cross-
platform compatiblity. jQuery has hundreds of plug-ins to extend its features. jQuery helps
in increasing interactions with a web site. </p>
</body>
```

We then write the following jQuery code:

```
$(document).ready(function() {
  $('p').css({'float':'left',  'width':'300px','margin':'5px'});
});
```

Increasing Gutter Size between Columns

Gutter means the spacing between the columns. By reducing the width of columns and increasing the size of the margin, we can increase the spacing (gutter size) between columns.

Let us reduce the `width` property and increase the `margin` value by a small amount, as shown in the following jQuery code:

```
$('p').css({'float':'left',  'width':'375px','margin':'15px'});
```

How It Works

In the first set of jQuery code under the "Solution" heading, we see that the first statement set the CSS properties of the HTML element of `class="leftalign"`. It displays the paragraph element with a width of 300px and positions it at a distance of 50px from the left in its containing element (the browser window in this case). Similarly, the second statement positions the HTML element of `class="centeralign"` at a distance of 400px from the left of the browser window, and the third statement positions the HTML element of `class="rightalign"` at a distance of 750px from the left of the browser window. The output is shown in Figure 10-28.

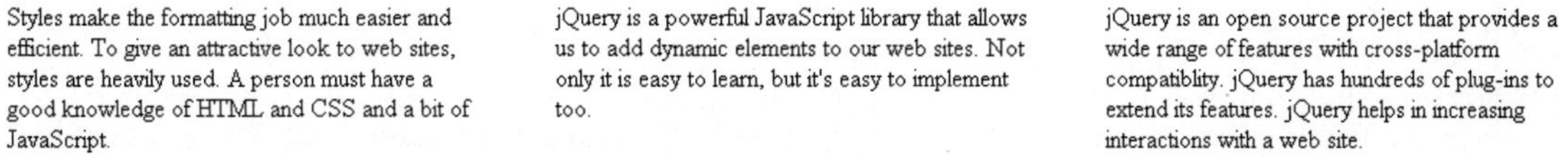

Styles make the formatting job much easier and efficient. To give an attractive look to web sites, styles are heavily used. A person must have a good knowledge of HTML and CSS and a bit of JavaScript.

jQuery is a powerful JavaScript library that allows us to add dynamic elements to our web sites. Not only it is easy to learn, but it's easy to implement too.

jQuery is an open source project that provides a wide range of features with cross-platform compatiblity. jQuery has hundreds of plug-ins to extend its features. jQuery helps in increasing interactions with a web site.

Figure 10-28. Three-column layout using the position property

In the `float` example, we give each paragraph element a width of 300px and make them float to the left of the browser window, one after the other. The first paragraph will appear first and have a width of 300px. After a margin of 5px, the second paragraph will appear; that is, after 305px from the left of the browser window. The second paragraph also has a width of 300px. Finally, the third paragraph will appear after keeping the margin of 5px for the second paragraph; that is, to the rightmost of the browser window, as shown in Figure 10-29.

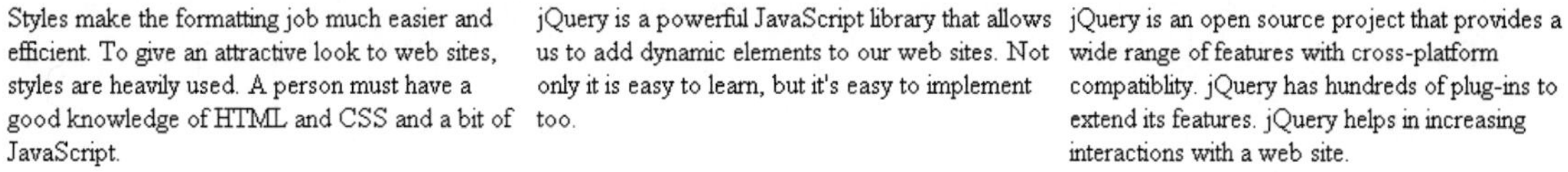

Styles make the formatting job much easier and efficient. To give an attractive look to web sites, styles are heavily used. A person must have a good knowledge of HTML and CSS and a bit of JavaScript.

jQuery is a powerful JavaScript library that allows us to add dynamic elements to our web sites. Not only it is easy to learn, but it's easy to implement too.

jQuery is an open source project that provides a wide range of features with cross-platform compatiblity. jQuery has hundreds of plug-ins to extend its features. jQuery helps in increasing interactions with a web site.

Figure 10-29. Three-column layout using the float property

Finally, Figure 10-30 shows the example after increasing the gutter size.

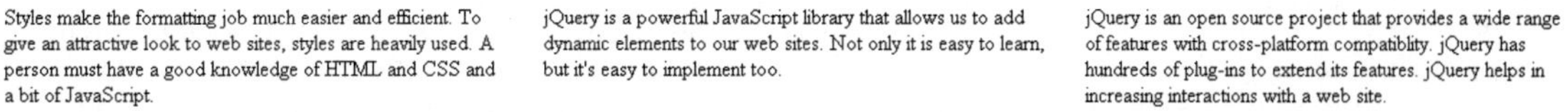

Styles make the formatting job much easier and efficient. To give an attractive look to web sites, styles are heavily used. A person must have a good knowledge of HTML and CSS and a bit of JavaScript.

jQuery is a powerful JavaScript library that allows us to add dynamic elements to our web sites. Not only it is easy to learn, but it's easy to implement too.

jQuery is an open source project that provides a wide range of features with cross-platform compatiblity. jQuery has hundreds of plug-ins to extend its features. jQuery helps in increasing interactions with a web site.

Figure 10-30. Three columns with increased gutter size

10-19. Wrapping Text around Images

Problem

Usually when we display an image and text on a web page, either image follows text or text follows image (depending upon their placement in the HTML file); the two don't appear adjacent to each other by default. Sometimes you want the image to have text wrapped all the way around it.

Solution

Let us place an image in an HTML file, as shown here:

```
<body>
<img src="cell.jpg"/>
</body>
```

We will now write jQuery code to wrap the `img` element within a `div` element and then append a paragraph element with some text to the `div` element. The jQuery code appears as shown here:

```
$(document).ready(function() {
  $('img').wrap('<div></div>');
  $('<p>Styles make the formatting job much easier and efficient. To give an attractive look
to web sites, styles are heavily used. A person must have a good knowledge of HTML and CSS
and a bit of JavaScript. jQuery is a powerful JavaScript library that allows us to add
dynamic elements to our web sites. Not only it is easy to learn, but it's easy to implement
too.  jQuery is an open source project that provides a wide range of features with cross-
platform compatiblity. jQuery has hundreds of plug-ins to extend its features. jQuery helps
in increasing interactions with a web site. </p>').appendTo('div');
  $('img').css({'float':'left',  'width':'200px','height':'200px'});
  $('p').css({'clear':'right'});
});
```

How It Works

The CSS properties applied to the image makes use of the `float` property to make the image float to the left in the browser window (allowing the text to appear on its right); the `width` property is used to confine the image to the size of 200px (any size less than the browser window's total width), so there's space for the text to wrap around the image. The `height` property is used to limit the image height to a particular size.

When `right` is assigned to the `clear` property, it will make the extra paragraph text move to the left. That is, it tries to make the space on the right side clear but fill the space on the left. Hence, the extra text of the paragraph that extends beyond the image height moves to the left side, wrapping text around the image.

When we apply the preceding CSS properties to the image and paragraph elements, we get the output shown in Figure 10-31.

 Styles make the formatting job much easier and efficient. To give an attractive look to web sites, styles are heavily used. A person must have a good knowledge of HTML and CSS and a bit of Javascript. jQuery is a powerful JavaScript library that allows us to add dynamic elements to our web sites. Not only it is easy to learn but easy to implement too. jQuery is an open source project that provides a wide range of features with cross platform compatiblity. jQuery has hundreds of plug-ins to extend its features. JQuery helps in increasing interactions with a web site.

Figure 10-31. Wrapping the text around the image

10-20. Placing a Drop Shadow behind an Image

Problem

You want to place a drop shadow behind an image.

Solution

In order to create a drop shadow, we need to make two images: one to server as a drop shadow on the right side of the image, and the other to create a shadow effect at the bottom of the image. Let us name the drop shadow on the right of the image shadowright.jpg , as shown in Figure 10-32.

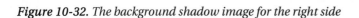

Figure 10-32. The background shadow image for the right side

391

Similarly, the drop shadow at the bottom of the image is named shadowbottom.jpg and appears as shown in Figure 10-33.

Figure 10-33. The background shadow image for the bottom

Assuming that an image file called image4.jpg exists, the HTML code to display the image is as shown here:

```
<body>
<span class="shadow"><img src="image4.jpg" /></span>
</body>
```

The style rules to be applied to the img element and the span element are applied via the css() method, as shown in the following jQuery code:

```
$(document).ready(function() {
  $('span').css({'background':'url(shadowright.jpg)', 'background-repeat':'no-
repeat','background-position':'bottom right', 'padding':'0 10px 0 0'});
  $('img').css({'width':'200px','height':'200px','background':'url(shadowbottom.jpg)',
'background-repeat':'no-repeat','background-position':'bottom', 'padding':'0 0 10px 0' });
});
```

How It Works

In the preceding HTML file, the img element is enclosed within a span element because we need to apply two style rules to the img element: one for the drop shadow on the right side of the image and the other for the drop shadow at the bottom of the image. But we cannot apply more than one style rule to an element. So, to apply two style rules to the img element, we'll enclose it with a span element so that one style rule can be applied to the span element (which will eventually be applied to the img element), and the other style rule can be applied to the img element itself.

The first css() call contains four properties:

- The background:url property is set to display the image stored in the file shadowright.jpg at the background of the image.

- The background-repeat property is set to no-repeat to display the shadow image only once.

- The background-position property is set to bottom right to display the shadow image at right side of the image, aligned with the bottom.

- The padding property is used to set the distance of the shadow image from the actual image. This helps in deciding the width of the shadow.

Similarly, the second css() call contains six properties:

- The **width** and **height** properties are set to **200px** to constrain the width and height of the actual image being displayed to 200 pixels.

- The **background:url** property is set to display the image stored in the file **shadowbottom.jpg** in the background of the image.

- The **background-repeat** property is set to **no-repeat** to display the shadow image only once.

- The **background-position** property is set to **bottom** to display the shadow image at the bottom of the actual image.

- The **padding** property is used to set the distance of the shadow image from the actual image.

On application of the preceding properties to the image in the HTML file, the image will appear with the drop shadows on the right and bottom, as in Figure 10-34.

Figure 10-34. An image casting a shadow

10-21. Changing the Cursor When the Mouse Moves over a Link

Problem

You want to change the style of the cursor when it moves over a link.

Solution

For this problem, we make an HTML file that contains some information in a **div** element, along with a hyperlink (Click Here), which, when selected, navigates us to **www.abc.com**. The HTML appears as shown here:

```
<body>
<div>Styles make the formatting job much easier and efficient. To give an attractive look to
web sites, styles are heavily used. A person must have a good knowledge of HTML and CSS and
a bit of JavaScript.
jQuery is a powerful JavaScript library that allows us to add dynamic elements to our web
sites. Not only it is easy to learn, but it's easy to implement too.
jQuery is an open source project. <a href="abc.com">Click Here</a> for more information
</div>
</body>
```

To apply different cursor property to the hyperlink, we write the following jQuery code:

```
$(document).ready(function() {
  $(a).hover(
    function(){
      $(this).css({'cursor': 'wait', 'color': 'blue' , 'background-color':'cyan'});
    },
    function(){
      $(this).css({'cursor': 'default', 'color': '#000000' , 'background-color':'#ffffff'});
    });
});
```

How It Works

The **hover()** method contains two functions: one is executed when the mouse pointer hovers over the selected element, and the other is executed when the mouse pointer is moved away from the selected element. Initially, the output will be as shown in Figure 10-35. We can see that the hyperlink is underlined and the typical arrow mouse pointer is the default pointer.

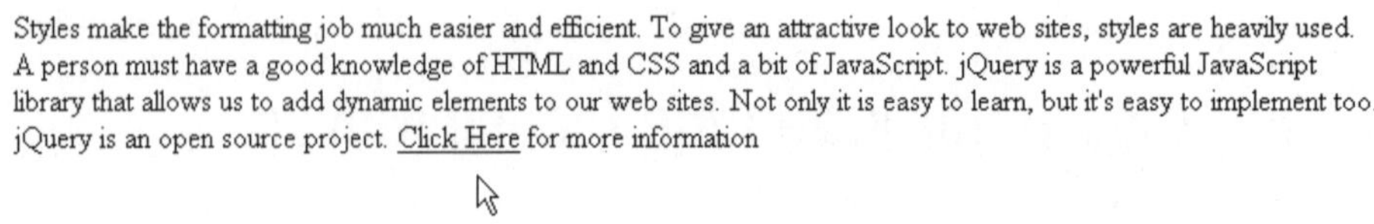

Styles make the formatting job much easier and efficient. To give an attractive look to web sites, styles are heavily used. A person must have a good knowledge of HTML and CSS and a bit of JavaScript. jQuery is a powerful JavaScript library that allows us to add dynamic elements to our web sites. Not only it is easy to learn, but it's easy to implement too. jQuery is an open source project. Click Here for more information

Figure 10-35. Default cursor when the link is not hovered over

On moving the mouse over the link, the CSS properties defined in **hover()** are applied to it, changing the shape of the mouse pointer to an hourglass, and changing the background color of the link to cyan and its foreground to blue, as shown in Figure 10-36.

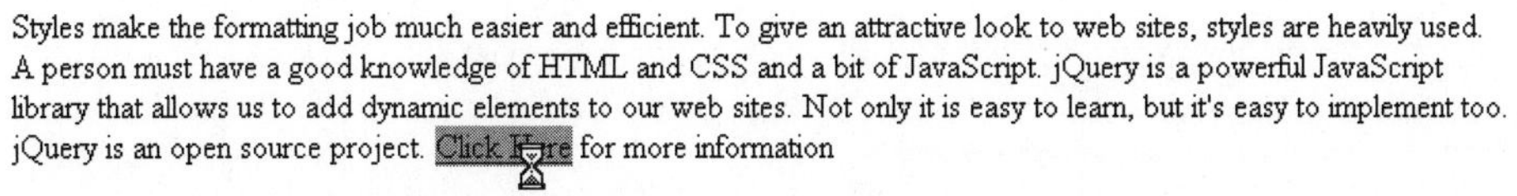

Styles make the formatting job much easier and efficient. To give an attractive look to web sites, styles are heavily used. A person must have a good knowledge of HTML and CSS and a bit of JavaScript. jQuery is a powerful JavaScript library that allows us to add dynamic elements to our web sites. Not only it is easy to learn, but it's easy to implement too. jQuery is an open source project. Click Here for more information

Figure 10-36. The cursor changes when the mouse hovers over the link.

10-22. Displaying a Long Piece of Text within a Specific Area

Problem

You want to display a long piece of text within a specific area.

Solution

In the HTML file shown here, we define a paragraph element that we want to confine to a certain area of the page:

```
<body>
<p>Styles make the formatting job much easier and efficient. To give an attractive look to
web sites, styles are heavily used. A person must have a good knowledge of HTML and CSS and
a bit of JavaScript.  <br/>
jQuery is a powerful JavaScript library that allows us to add dynamic elements to our web
sites. Not only it is easy to learn, but it's easy to implement too.  jQuery is an open
source project that provides a wide range of features with cross-platform compatiblity.
jQuery has hundreds of plug-ins to extend its features. jQuery helps in increasing
interactions with a web site </p>
</body>
```

To confine the text and apply the **overflow** property to the paragraph element, we use the following jQuery:

```
$('p').css({'width':'50%', 'height':'100px','overflow':'scroll'});
```

How It Works

We assign 50% of the browser window's size and a height of 100 pixels to the paragraph. By setting the value of **overflow** to **scroll**, we make scroll bars appear if the text of the paragraph element is not completely visible in the specified height and width. The output is as shown in Figure 10-37.

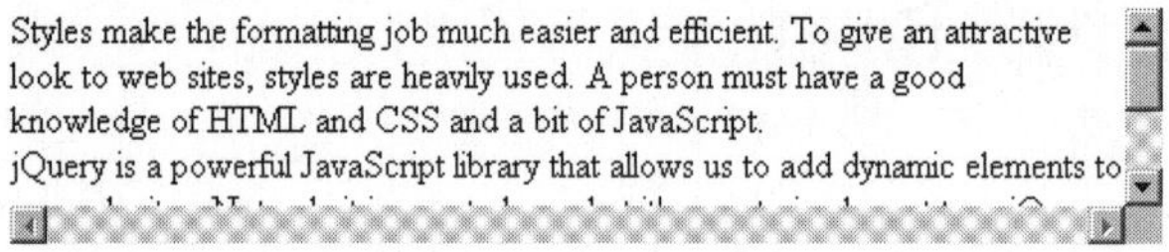

Styles make the formatting job much easier and efficient. To give an attractive
look to web sites, styles are heavily used. A person must have a good
knowledge of HTML and CSS and a bit of JavaScript.
jQuery is a powerful JavaScript library that allows us to add dynamic elements to

Figure 10-37. *Applying the overflow element with the scroll option*

Let us see what happens when we set the value of the **overflow** property to **hidden**. The paragraph text that does not fit within the assigned area becomes invisible, as shown in Figure 10-38.

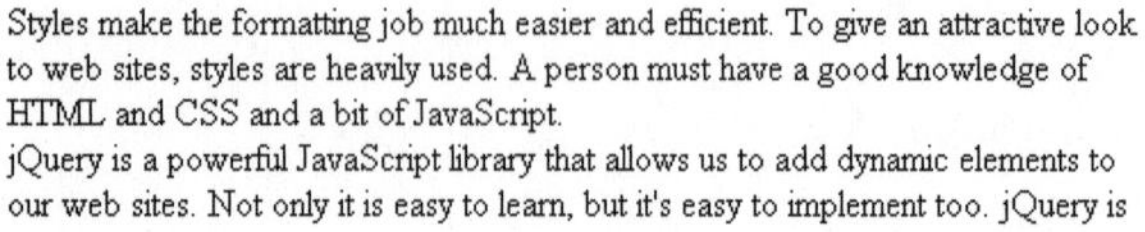

Styles make the formatting job much easier and efficient. To give an attractive look
to web sites, styles are heavily used. A person must have a good knowledge of
HTML and CSS and a bit of JavaScript.
jQuery is a powerful JavaScript library that allows us to add dynamic elements to
our web sites. Not only it is easy to learn, but it's easy to implement too. jQuery is

Figure 10-38. *Applying the overflow element with the hidden option*

Let us set the value of the **overflow** property to **auto**. The scroll bar will appear only for the height and not for the width (unlike with the value **scroll**); that is, the scroll bar will appears only where it is required. The output on application of this style is shown in Figure 10-39.

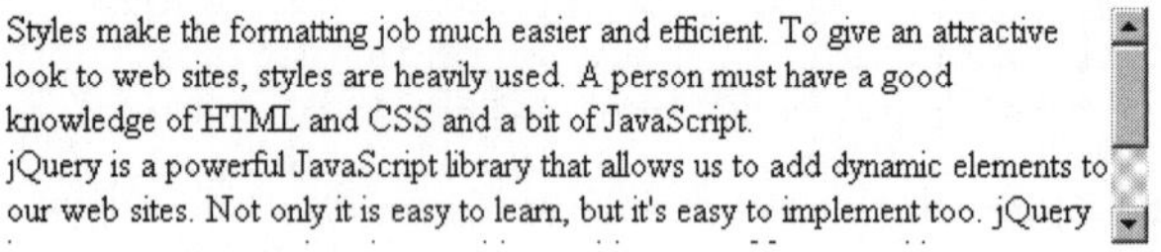

Styles make the formatting job much easier and efficient. To give an attractive
look to web sites, styles are heavily used. A person must have a good
knowledge of HTML and CSS and a bit of JavaScript.
jQuery is a powerful JavaScript library that allows us to add dynamic elements to
our web sites. Not only it is easy to learn, but it's easy to implement too. jQuery

Figure 10-39. *Applying the overflow element with the auto option*

Now let us set the value of the **overflow** property to **visible**. The text of the paragraph will be entirely visible; that is, it will not be confined to the region assigned to it (see Figure 10-40).

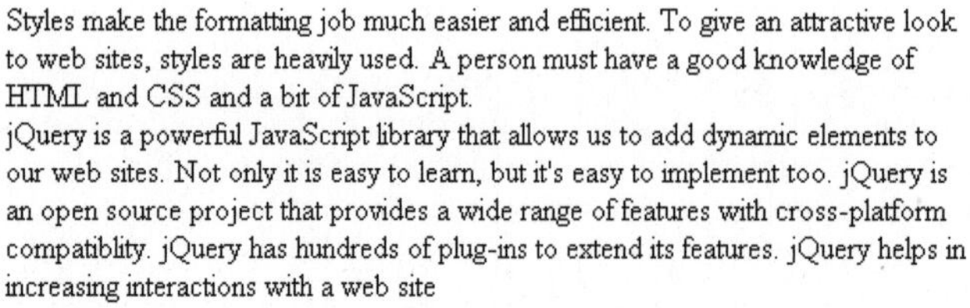

Styles make the formatting job much easier and efficient. To give an attractive look
to web sites, styles are heavily used. A person must have a good knowledge of
HTML and CSS and a bit of JavaScript.
jQuery is a powerful JavaScript library that allows us to add dynamic elements to
our web sites. Not only it is easy to learn, but it's easy to implement too. jQuery is
an open source project that provides a wide range of features with cross-platform
compatiblity. jQuery has hundreds of plug-ins to extend its features. jQuery helps in
increasing interactions with a web site

Figure 10-40. *Applying the overflow element with the visible option*

10-23. Making a Rounded-Corner Column

Problem

You want to make a single column with rounded corners.

Solution

To give a rounded-rectangle shape to the column, we need to make a rectangle with rounded corners and paste it as the background of the text. Let us make a rounded-corner rectangle like the one in Figure 10-41 and name it `columnfig.jpg`.

Figure 10-41. Rounded-corner rectangle

This image will be set as the background of the text. Let us make an HTML file with a paragraph element that has some text, as shown here:

```
<body>
<p>Styles make the formatting job much easier and efficient. To give an attractive look to
web sites, styles are heavily used. A person must have a good knowledge of HTML and CSS and
a bit of JavaScript.
jQuery is powerful JavaScript library used to make dynamic sites.</p>
</body>
```

In the style sheet, let us write a style rule to paste the rounded rectangle as the background of the paragraph element. The style rule will include the properties `width`, `padding`, `background`, and `background-repeat`, as shown here:

```
.backfig{
width:150px;
padding:10px;
background:url(columnfig.jpg);
background-repeat:no-repeat;
}
```

Let us write jQuery code to apply the `backfig` style rule to the paragraph element. The jQuery code appears as shown here:

```
$(document).ready(function() {
  $('p').addClass('backfig');
});
```

How It Works

The `backfig` style rule assigns a width to the paragraph text that is equal to the width of the rounded rectangle, so that the text of the paragraph remains confined within the boundaries of that rectangle. The `padding` property is used to keep some gap between the rectangle boundary and the paragraph text. The `background` property is for setting the rounded rectangle image stored in `columnfig.jpg` as the background of the paragraph text, and the value of `background-repeat` is set to `no-repeat` to make the rounded rectangle appear just once.

On application of the rounded rectangle image to its background, the paragraph text appears as shown in Figure 10-42.

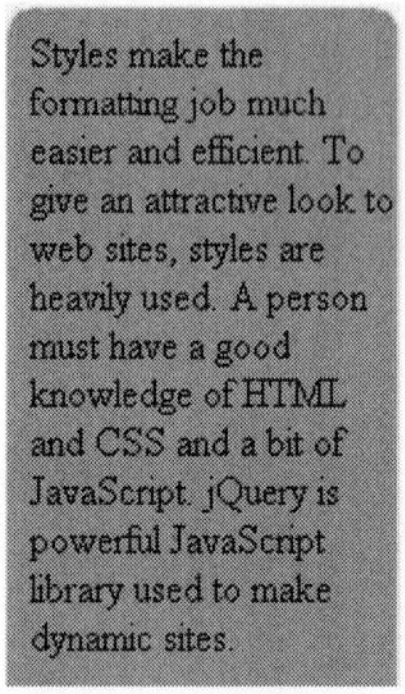

Figure 10-42. A single column with rounded corners

10-24. Applying Text Decorations

Problem

You want to apply text decorations, such as overline and underline styles, to certain text to draw attention to it. Additionally, you need to apply effects such as strike-through for comparison purposes—for example, to demonstrate the previous discount and the current discount on a certain item.

Solution

The following is HTML that contains three paragraph elements that are assigned three class names: feature1, feature2, and feature3.

```
<body>
<p class="feature1">jQuery is powerful</p>
<p class="feature2">Styles make the formatting job much easier and efficient. To give an
attractive look to web sites, styles are heavily used. A person must have a good knowledge
of HTML and CSS and a bit of JavaScript. jQuery is powerful JavaScript library used to make
dynamic sites.</p>
<p class="feature3">10% Discount on all products</p>
<p>20% Discount  on all products</p>
</body>
```

The jQuery to apply text decoration to the paragraph elements is as follows:

```
$(document).ready(function() {
  $('p.feature1').css({'text-decoration':'underline'});
  $('p.feature2').css({'text-decoration':'overline'});
  $('p.feature3').css({'text-decoration':'line-through'});
});
```

We can also apply both overline and underline values to the heading—that is, to the paragraph of the class feature1—to highlight it.

```
<div>
<p class="feature1">jQuery is powerful</p>
</div>
```

The style rules now change:

```
$(document).ready(function() {
  $('p.feature1').css({'text-decoration':'underline'});
  $('div').css({'text-decoration':'overline'});
  $('p.feature3').css({'text-decoration':'line-through'});
});
```

How It Works

The first call to `css()` displays the paragraph of `class="feature1"` as underlined text. The second call displays the paragraph of `class="feature2"` with a line over it. The third call displays the paragraph of `class="feature3"` with a line through it. The output is as shown in Figure 10-43.

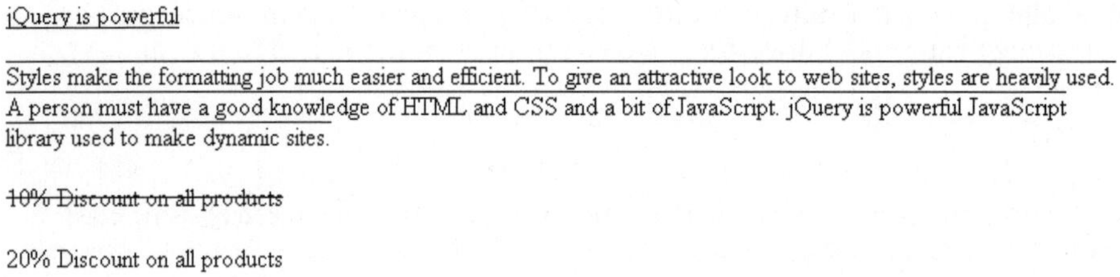

jQuery is powerful

Styles make the formatting job much easier and efficient. To give an attractive look to web sites, styles are heavily used. A person must have a good knowledge of HTML and CSS and a bit of JavaScript. jQuery is powerful JavaScript library used to make dynamic sites.

~~10% Discount on all products~~

20% Discount on all products

Figure 10-43. Applying different text-decoration options with the class

The advantage of using `line-through` is that the visitor can know what the earlier offers were and can compare with the current offers. Like the preceding solution shows, the earlier discount rate was 10%, but has now increased to 20%.

To highlight the heading, since we cannot apply two style rules to the same element, we enclose the paragraph of the class `feature1` inside a `div` element so that we can apply one style rule to the `div` and another style rule to the paragraph element. The first style rule makes the paragraph of the class `feature1` appear underlined. The second style rule makes an overline appear on the contents of the `div` element; that is, on the paragraph of the class `feature2`. The third style rule, as you have already seen, makes the paragraph of the class `feature2` appear crossed out. The output is shown in Figure 10-44.

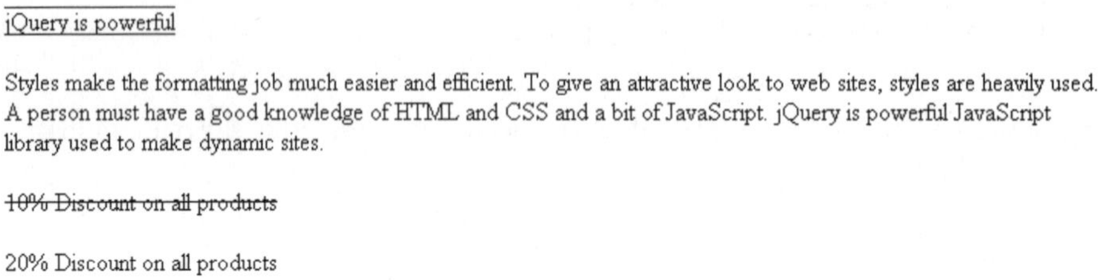

jQuery is powerful

Styles make the formatting job much easier and efficient. To give an attractive look to web sites, styles are heavily used. A person must have a good knowledge of HTML and CSS and a bit of JavaScript. jQuery is powerful JavaScript library used to make dynamic sites.

~~10% Discount on all products~~

20% Discount on all products

Figure 10-44. Applying overline and underline to the heading

10-25. Scaling Images

Problem

You want an image to be scalable; that is, if the size of the block in which the image is placed is reduced, the size of the image should also be reduced automatically. Similarly, if the size of the enclosing block is increased, you want the image size to increase automatically.

Solution

We'll use the same HTML that we used in Recipe 10-19 (refer to Figure 10-30 for the final results of that recipe). This time, we define the width of the image in terms of % (percentage) of the containing block element. Since the containing block of the image is the browser window, the width of the image will increase or decrease in response to the changes made to the size of the browser window. The modified style rules are shown here:

```
.moveleft
{
width:40%;
float:left;
}

.imagewrap {
clear:right;
}
```

The jQuery code to apply these style rules to the image and the paragraph element is as follows:

```
$(document).ready(function() {
  $('img').addClass('moveleft');
  $('p').addClass('imagewrap');
});
```

How It Works

If we increase the width of the browser window from Recipe 10-19, the image size remains the same, as is shown in Figure 10-45.

Styles make the formatting job much easier and efficient. To give an attractive look to web sites, styles are heavily used. A person must have a good knowledge of HTML and CSS and a bit of Javascript. jQuery is a powerful JavaScript library that allows us to add dynamic elements to our web sites. Not only it is easy to learn but easy to implement too. jQuery is an open source project that provides a wide range of features with cross platform compatiblity. jQuery has hundreds of plug-ins to extend its features. JQuery helps in increasing interactions with a web site.

Figure 10-45. The image is not scaled when we increase the width of the browser window.

The reason the image is not scaled lies in the original styles applied to it. The styles have been added to the following style rule for your reference:

```
.moveleft
{
width:200px;
height:200px;
float:left;
}
```

The width of the image is fixed to 200px, so the width of the image remains fixed despite any change in the browser window's size.

The new `moveleft` style rule contains two properties:

- The `width` property, which is set equal to 40% of the width of the browser window (that is, whenever the width of the browser window changes, the width of the image also changes to maintain the 40% ratio).

- The `float` property is set to `left` to keep the image on the left of the browser window, making space for the paragraph text to appear on its right side.

The style rule `imagewrap` will be applied to the paragraph text and contains a single property `clear` to make the extra paragraph text (the text that extends the size of the image) appear below the image so that the image is wrapped in text. The impact of this property is visible only when the size of the browser window is adjusted so that the paragraph text extends the full height of the image.

On application of the styles, the image becomes scalable with the size of the browser window, as shown in Figure 10-46.

Styles make the formatting job much easier and efficient. To give an attractive look to web sites, styles are heavily used. A person must have a good knowledge of HTML and CSS and a bit of Javascript. jQuery is a powerful JavaScript library that allows us to add dynamic elements to our web sites. Not only it is easy to learn but easy to implement too. jQuery is an open source project that provides a wide range of features with cross platform compatiblity. jQuery has hundreds of plug-ins to extend its features. JQuery helps in increasing interactions with a web site.

Figure 10-46. The image is scaled in conjunction with the width of the browser window.

10-26. Setting a Background Image

Problem

You want an image to appear as the background of your text.

Solution

Let us assume that we have the following HTML, which contains a paragraph element to display simple text:

```
<body>
<p>Styles make the formatting job much easier and efficient. To give an attractive look to
web sites, styles are heavily used. A person must have a good knowledge of HTML and CSS and
a bit of JavaScript.
jQuery is a powerful JavaScript library that allows us to add dynamic elements to our web
sites. Not only it is easy to learn, but it's easy to implement too.
jQuery is an open source project that provides a wide range of features with cross-platform
compatiblity. jQuery has hundreds of plug-ins to extend its features. jQuery helps in
increasing interactions with a web site. </p>
</body>
```

403

In order to apply an image as the background of this text, we need to write the style rule shown here:

```
.placeimage
{
background-image:url(cell.jpg);
background-repeat:no-repeat;
}
```

We now need to write the jQuery code to apply the style rule `placeimage` to the body tag. The jQuery code appears as shown here:

```
$(document).ready(function() {
  $('body').addClass('placeimage');
});
```

How It Works

We assume that the image file `cell.jpg` exists. In the style rule `placeimage`, we have used two properties: `background-image` and `background-repeat`. With the help of `background-image`, we make the image stored in `cell.jpg` appear as the background of the text. By default, the image is repeated several times to fill up the containing block. So, we set the value of the `background-repeat` property to `no-repeat` so that the image appears only once as the background.

On application of the `placeimage` style rule to the body of the HTML file, the image stored in `cell.jpg` appears as the background of the text, as shown in Figure 10-47.

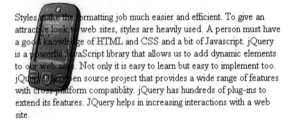

Figure 10-47. The image is set as the background of the text.

10-27. Centering a Background Image in the Browser

Problem

Usually when you set an image as the background, it is aligned to the left of the browser window. You want the background image to appear at the center of the browser window.

Solution

In this recipe, we will make use of the same HTML file that we used in Recipe 10-26, which displays an image as the background (which is left-aligned). To make the left-aligned background image appear at the center of the screen, we will use the `background-position` property. By setting the value of the `background-position` property to `center`, the background image will appear at the center of the browser screen.

So, let us add `background-position` to the style rule `placeimage` (from Recipe 10-26) as shown here:

```
.placeimage
{
background-image:url(cell.jpg);
background-repeat:no-repeat;
background-position:center;
}
```

The jQuery code to apply the `placeimage` style rule to the body of the HTML is shown here:

```
$(document).ready(function() {
  $('body').addClass('placeimage');
});
```

How It Works

Recall that the `background-image` property makes the image in `cell.jpg` appear as the background. To make the background image appear only once—that is, to stop it from repeating itself and filling up the block—we set the value of the `background-repeat` property to `no-repeat`. Finally, by assigning the value `center` to the `background-position` property, we make sure that the background image appears at the center of the browser window.

On application of the `placeimage` style rule to the body of the HTML file, the image stored in `cell.jpg` appears as the background at the center of the browser window, as shown in Figure 10-48.

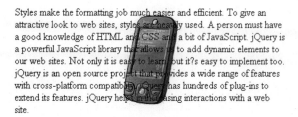

Styles make the formatting job much easier and efficient. To give an attractive look to web sites, styles are heavily used. A person must have a good knowledge of HTML and CSS and a bit of JavaScript. jQuery is a powerful JavaScript library that allows us to add dynamic elements to our web sites. Not only it is easy to learn but it?s easy to implement too. jQuery is an open source project that provides a wide range of features with cross-platform compatibility. jQuery has hundreds of plug-ins to extend its features. jQuery helps in increasing interactions with a web site.

Figure 10-48. *The background image is placed at the center of the browser window.*

10-28. Making the Background Image Stationary

Problem

When we browse any web page, the image and text scroll when we scroll down or up the page. You want the background image to remain stationary even when you scroll.

Solution

In this recipe, we make use of the same HTML file that we used in the Recipe 10-26. Here we will add some more text to the paragraph to make it large enough that we can apply scrolling to it. To keep the background image stationary while scrolling the web page, we use the `background-attachment` property. By setting the value `fixed` to the `background-attachment` property, we keep the background image stationary. So, let us add the `background-attachment` property to the style sheet that we used in the previous recipe:

```
.placeimage
{
background-image:url(cell.jpg);
background-repeat:no-repeat;
background-position:center;
background-attachment: fixed;
}
```

The jQuery code to apply the `placeimage` style rule to the body of the HTML file is shown here:

```
$(document).ready(function() {
  $('body').addClass('placeimage');
});
```

How It Works

The function of each of the properties used in the style rule `placeimage` is as follows:

- The `background-image` property makes the image in the file `cell.jpg` appear as the background.

- The background image is set to appear only once by assigning the value `no-repeat` to the `background-repeat` property.

- The `background-position` property is set to `center` to make the background image appear at the center of the browser window.

- The `background-attachment` property is set to `fixed` to make the background image remain stationary when we scroll the web page.

On application of the `placeimage` style rule to the body of the HTML file, the background image appears at the background, as shown in Figure 10-49.

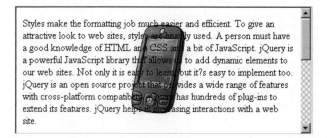

Figure 10-49. The scroll bar appears when the text is larger than the browser window.

Now, when we scroll the web page down (via the scroll bar on the right), the background image remains at the center of the browser screen, whereas the text scrolls (see Figure 10-50).

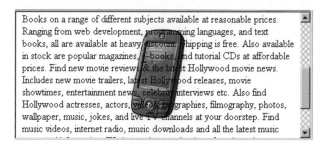

Figure 10-50. The background image remains stationary even when the text is scrolled.

Summary

In this chapter we saw recipes that explain different CSS techniques that are frequently applied to web pages like distinguishing HTML elements, applying styles to an element nested inside another element, indenting paragraphs, applying an initial cap to a paragraph, removing the gap between heading and paragraph, applying styles to heading text and indenting the first line of multiple paragraphs. Besides this, we have also seen the process for creating paragraphs with hanging indents, creating a bordered pull quote, creating a pull quote with images, applying list properties to list items, applying styles to only selected list items, placing dividers between list items, applying image markers to a list and creating inline lists. Finally, we also saw how to apply styles to hyperlinks and mailto, assign different dimensions to HTML elements, place HTML elements, create a multicolumn layout, wrap text around images, place a drop shadow behind an image, change the cursor when the mouse moves over a link, display a long piece of text within a specific area, make a rounded corner column, apply text decorations, scale images, set a background image, center a background image in the browser and make the background image stationary.

Index

■Symbols

* symbol, in regular expressions, 305

^ symbol, in regular expressions, 305

$ symbol, in regular expressions, 305

$() function, 3

− icon for collapsible items, 275

> selector, 282, 375

+ icon for expanding items, 275

+ symbol, in regular expressions, 301, 305

■A

accelerator keys for menu items, 175–79

accessing DOM nodes, 2, 5

accordion menus, 190–93

addClass() method, 4

after() method, 12

Ajax, 291–326

    auto-complete, 308–13

    displaying welcome message, 291–96

    importing HTML, 313–16

    paginating tables, 323–26

    performing authentication, 296–98

    to submit forms, 338–44

    validating email address, 302–8

    validating user name, 299–302

    XML data, getting, 319–22

ajax() method, 292

ajaxForm() method, 341

alert() method, 49, 281, 341

alphabetizing

    list items, 278–79

    string array elements, 31

    table rows, 280–86

anchor elements. *See* hyperlinks

animate() method, 95, 207, 211

animation effects with text, 82–83

    sliding (fading transition), 91–92

animator() method, 218, 221, 223

annotating images with comments, 330–32

append() method, 12

appendTo() method, 12

arranging images, 200–203

arrays

    counting length of, 19

    combining multiple, 35–36

    filtering to show desired data, 24–29

    manipulating elements of, 21–24

    of names, displaying in lists, 17–21

■F

password and confirm-password fields, 144–46

phone numbers, 114–16

radio buttons, 126–29

required fields, confirming not blank, 108–9

user IDs, 116–18

vertically arranging images, 200–203

vertically scrolling images, 217–21

visual effects, 199–251. *See also* images

arranging images, 200–203

changing cursor over hyperlinks, 393–95

displaying images in carousel, 347–50

dynamic visual menus, 193–98

enlarging image on mouse over, 231–37

horizontal image sliders, 204–6

with image enlargement, 235

news scrollers, 226–31

pendulum scrollers, 244–46

scrolling images

at center, 212–14

horizontally, 221–26

to invisibility when clicked, 206–12

using arrays, 247–51

vertically, 217–21

showing images pagewise, 238–40

showing multiple images on hover, 214–17

shuffling images in either direction, 240–44

■W

welcome message, displaying, 291–96

width() method (Dimension plugin), 346

word balloons, displaying, 79–82

wrapping text around images, 389–90

■X

XML data, getting, 319–22

XMLHttpRequest object, 292

Xpath selectors, 2

■Z

zero-based counting, 256, 257